Quality of Life and Pharmacoeconomics

An Introduction

OTHER BOOKS BY BERT SPILKER AND JOYCE CRAMER

Patient Compliance in Medical Practice and Clinical Trials—Cramer and Spilker
(Edited, Raven Press, 1991)
Patient Recruitment in Clinical Trials—Spilker and Cramer
(Raven Press, 1992)

OTHER BOOKS BY JOYCE CRAMER

Alcohol and Seizures: Basic Mechanisms and Clinical Concepts
(Edited, F.A. Davis, 1990)
Quantitative Assessment in Epilepsy Care
(Edited, Plenum Press, 1993)

OTHER BOOKS BY BERT SPILKER

Guide to Clinical Studies and Developing Protocols
(Raven Press, 1984)
Guide to Clinical Interpretation of Data
(Raven Press, 1986)
Guide to Planning and Managing Multiple Clinical Studies
(Raven Press, 1987)
Multinational Drug Companies: Issues in Drug Discovery and Development
(Raven Press, 1989)
Inside the Drug Industry
(with Pedro Cuatrecasas, Prous Science Publishers, 1990)
Quality of Life Assessments in Clinical Trials
(Edited, Raven Press, 1990)
Presentation of Clinical Data
(with John Schoenfelder, Raven Press, 1990)
Data Collection Forms in Clinical Trials
(with John Schoenfelder, Raven Press, 1991)
Guide to Clinical Trials
(Raven Press, 1991)
Multinational Pharmaceutical Companies: Principles and Practice (2nd edition)
(Raven Press, 1994)
Medical Dictionary in Six Languages
(compiled in collaboration with DTS Language Services, Inc., Raven Press, 1995)
Quality of Life and Pharmacoeconomics in Clinical Trials, 2nd edition
(Edited, Lippincott-Raven Publishers, 1996)
Spilker's Guide to Clinical Trials on CD-ROM
(Lippincott-Raven Publishers, 1996)

Quality of Life and Pharmacoeconomics

An Introduction

Joyce A. Cramer
Lecturer, Department of Psychiatry
Associate in Research, Department of Neurology
Yale University School of Medicine
New Haven, Connecticut
Project Director
Health Services Research
VA Connecticut Healthcare System
West Haven, Connecticut

Bert Spilker, Ph.D., M.D.
President
Orphan Medical, Inc.
Minnetonka, Minnesota
Adjunct Professor of Medicine
Clinical Professor of Pharmacy
University of North Carolina Schools of Medicine and Pharmacy
Chapel Hill, North Carolina
Clinical Professor of Pharmacy Practice
University of Minnesota School of Pharmacy
Minneapolis, Minnesota
Visiting Professor of Clinical Pharmacology
University of Illinois College of Medicine
Peoria, Illinois

Lippincott - Raven
P U B L I S H E R S

Philadelphia • New York

Acquisitions Editor: Elizabeth Greenspan
Developmental Editor: Rebecca Irwin Diehl
Manufacturing Manager: Dennis Teston
Production Manager: Cassie Moore
Cover Designer: David Levy
Indexer: Alexandra Nickerson
Compositor: Lippincott-Raven Electronic Production
Printer: Maple Press

Library of Congress Cataloging-in-Publication Data
Cramer, Joyce A.
   Quality of life and pharmacoeconomics : an introduction / Joyce A. Cramer, Bert Spilker.
       p.   cm.
   Includes bibliographical references and indexes.
   ISBN 0-397-51845-5
   1. Drugs—Cost effectiveness.   2. Quality of life.   I. Spilker, Bert.
II. Title.
   [DNLM: 1. Quality of life.   2. Economics, Pharmaceutical.   3. Treatment
Outcome.   WAS 30 C889q 1997]
RS100.C73   1997
338.4'36151—dc21
DNLM/DLC
For Library of Congress   97-37999
                                                                      CIP

Contents

Introduction

The second edition of *Quality of Life and Pharmacoeconomics in Clinical Trials* provides extensive material and thorough review of many issues. However, we believe that there is a large group of students, researchers, and clinicians who can utilize an introduction to quality of life and pharmacoeconomics with fewer details. To serve this audience, we have prepared an overview of these topics, based on abstracted material from the full-length volume.

Our goal in editing was to reduce the bulk, remove redundancies, eliminate most of the specific clinical examples, reduce details of instrument validation, and limit references. The basic structure of the Big Book is maintained, but segments that were duplicated in several chapters are integrated into one section. This volume is a broad overview that presents approaches to HRQOL assessment, evaluations of outcomes, and pharmacoeconomic methods. The integration of these three areas is one of the special features of this text.

The *Overview to Quality of Life and Pharmacoeconomics* is divided into seven chapters:

1. Introduction
2. Social and Psychological Assessment
3. Selected Instruments
4. Reported Methodology
5. Special Populations and Specific Diseases
6. Utilities and Outcomes
7. Pharmacoeconomics

Each section summarizes the pertinent issues and provides a number of references. As such, the overview can serve as a textbook for researchers and students in academia and industry who want to learn the basics or have a summary guide for reference and guidance.

Reducing the book from 127 chapters in 1,260 pages to the current size required deletion of many topics, examples, references, figures, and tables. Readers interested in more detail, particularly for specific clinical issues, should consult the full text in the Second Edition.

Joyce A. Cramer
Bert Spilker, PhD, MD

Acknowledgments

The material in this book is derived from the second edition of *Quality of Life and Pharmacoeconomics in Clinical Trials*, edited by Bert Spilker. Newell McElwee kindly provided comments on the pharmacoeconomic section.

We are grateful to the many authors who provided chapters for the original text. Following is a list of contributors:

Neil K. Aaronson
Linda N. Abetz
Catherine Acquadro
John P. Anderson
Roger T. Anderson
Andrew M. Baker
Ivan Barofsky
Judith T. Barr
Richard S. Beaser
C. Keith Beck
Thomas K. Beckett
Kathryn J. Bennett
Jurg Berbhard
Richard A. Berzon
Stefan Bjork
Amy E. Bonomi
Samuel A. Bozzette
Andrew L. Brickman
Dan Brock
Meryl Brod
Monika Bullinger
Gregory Burke
Barbara J. Burna
Kathleen A. Cagney
Barrie R. Cassileth
David F. Cella
Larry W. Chambers
Christopher C. Chapman

Paul D. Cleary
Jennifer J. Clinch
Alan Coates
Bernard F. Cole
John M. Conley
Carol E. Cornell
Joyce A. Cramer
Ann M. Cull
William E. Cunningham
Susan M. Czajkowski
Anne M. Damiano
Patricia M. Danzon
Richard F. Davis
Atara Kaplan De-Nour
Leonard R. Derogatis
Maureen F. Derogatis
Douglas A. Drossman
Michael F. Drummons
David M. Eddy
Jan M. Ellerhorst-Ryan
David Ellis
Robert S. Epstein
Pennifer Erikson
Margot K. Ettl
Diane L. Fairclough
Daivd H. Feeny
Betty R. Ferrell
Megan P. Fleming
Floyd J. Fowler

Michael A. Fraumeni
Marsha D. Fretwell
Michael A. Friedman
James F. Fries
Curt D. Furberg
William J. Furlong
Barbara L. Gandek
Sharon B. Barbus
Richard D. Gelber
Shari Gelber
Paul P. Glasziou
Christopher G. Goetz
Aron Goldhirsch
Michael D. E. Goodyear
Deborah R. Gordon
Carolyn Cook Gotay
Henry G. Grabowski
Marcia M. Grant
Edward Guadagnoli
Peter J. Guarnaccia
Harry A. Guess
Gordon H. Guyatt
Ronald W. Hansen
Ron D. Hays
Susan C. Hedrick
Alan L. Hillman
Pamela S. Hinds
Christoph D. T. Hurny
Janis F. Hutchinson

Alan M. Jacobson
Roman Jaeschke
Bernard Jambon
Magnus Johannesson
Deborah J. Johnson
Thomas M. Johnson
David A. Ones
Bengt G. Jonsson
Elizabeth F. Juniper
Stein Kaasa
Robert M. Kaplan
Elizabeth W. Karlson
Jeffrey N. Katz
Susan D. Keller
Paul Kind
Susan V. M. Kleinbeck
Richard A. Kreuger
Roberta labelle
Karen T. Labuhn
Jeanne M. Landgraf
Karen J. Lechter
Paul P. Lee
Victor C. Lee
Anthony F. Lehman
Alain P. Leplege
Joseph A. Leveque
Robert J. Levine
Matthew H. Liang
Stephen R. Lloyd
Brian Lovatt
Thomas M. Lumley
Eva G. Lydick
Carol M. Mangione
Patrick Marquis
Andrew J. Martin
Josephine A. Mauskopf
Mary S. McCabe
Newell E. McElwee
James McEwen

Mary S. McFarlane
William F. McGhan
Stephen P. Mckenna
Robin S. McLeod
A. John McSweeny
Joseph menzin
David S. Metzger
Andrew S. Mitchell
Vincent Mor
Louis A. Morris
Michelle J. Naughton
Susan G. Nayfield
Eugene C. Nelson
Paul Nordberg
Albert Oberman
Bernie J. O'Brien
Charles P. O'Brien
Charles L. M. Olweny
Flemming Ornskov
Gerry Oster
Eugenio Paci
Geraldine V. Padilla
A. David Paltiel
Donald L. Patrick
John E. Paul
Michael J. Power
Cary A. Presant
James M. Raczynski
Dena R. Ramey
Dennis A. Revicki
Brian E. Rittenhouse
Peter L. Rosenbaum
John C. Rowlingson
Lisa V. Rubenstein
Peter J. Rutigliano
Saroj Saigal
Harvey Schipper
John R. Schoenfelder

Stephen W. Schondelmeyer
Gerald E. Schumacher
Martin F. Shapiro
Cathy D. Sherbourne
Dale Shoemaker
Sally A. Shumaker
Geirge P. Simeon
R. John Simes
Gurkipal Singh
Carol E. Smith
William D. Spector
Bert Spilker
Mirjam A. G. Sprangers
Glenn T. Stebbins
Donald M. Steinwachs
Anita L. Stewart
Aaron A. Stinnett
David S. Sugano
Silvija Szabo
Richard C. Taeuber
Robert J. Temple
Hugh H. Tilson
George W. Torrance
Ralph R. Turner
Claudette G. Varricchio
John E. Ware
John H. Wasson
Milton C. Weinstein
Nanette K. Wenger
marie B. Whedon
Ingela K. Wiklund
David Wilkin
Alan H. Williams
T. Franklin Williams
Robert S. Wilson
Benjamin D. Wright
James G. Wright
Albert W. Wu

List of Figures and Tables

List of Selected Abbreviations

ADL   Activities of daily living
CBA   Cost/benefit analysis
CEA   Cost-effectiveness analysis
CES-D   Centers for Epidemiological Studies–Depression
CMA   Cost-minimization analysis
COOP   Dartmouth Function Charts
CUA   Cost/utility analysis
DABS   Derogatis Affects Balance Scale
EORTC   European Organization for Research and Treatment of Cancer
ESI-55   Epilepsy Surgery Inventory
EUROQOL European Quality of Life Index
FACT   Functional Assessment of Cancer Therapy
FLIC   Functional Living Index–Cancer
HAQ   Health Assessment Questionnaire
HRQOL   Health-related quality of life
HUI   Health Utilities Index
IQOLA   International Quality of Life Assessment
KPS   Karnofsky Performance Index
MACTAR   McMaster Toronto Arthritis Patient Function Preference
                    Questionnaire
MANOVA Multivariate analysis of variance
MHIQ   McMaster Health Index Questionnaire
MMSE   Mini-Mental State Exam
MOS   Medical Outcome Study
MOS SF-36 MOS 36-item Short-Form Health Survey
MPQ   McGill Pain Questionnaire
NHP   Nottingham Health Profile
NHRQOL   Nonhealth-related quality of life
PAIS   Psychosocial Adjustment to Illness Scale
PGWB   Psychological General Well-Being Index
POMS   Profile of Mood States
PORT   Patient Outcomes Research Team
QALY   Quality-adjusted life-year
QLI   Quality of life index

QOL	Quality of life
QOLIE	Quality of Life in Epilepsy
Q-TWiST	Quality-adjusted time without symptoms of disease and toxicity of treatment
QWB	Quality of Well-Being Scale
SCL-90	Hopkins Symptom Checklist
SF-36	Short Form 36 (of MOS Health Survey)
SG	Standard gamble
SIP	Sickness Impact Profile
TTO	Time trade-off
TWiST	Time without symptoms and toxicity
VAS	Visual–analog scale
WHO	World Health Organization

About the Authors

Joyce A. Cramer is Lecturer (Psychiatry), and Associate in Research (Neurology), at Yale University School of Medicine, New Haven, Connecticut, and Project Director for Health Services Research at the VA Connecticut Healthcare System, West Haven, Connecticut. Working in the areas of epilepsy and psychiatry clinical trials, she developed methods for the evaluation of drug efficacy and adverse effects, study design and management. These issues led to her interests in medication compliance, quality of life, and recruitment of patients for clinical trials. Currently, she is managing a multicenter health services clinical trial that includes cost-effectiveness and quality of life assessments, as well as clinical endpoints.

She has contributed more than 100 articles and book chapters to the medical literature, covering topics in medicine, epilepsy, psychiatry, pharmacology, research design, outcome assessment, quality of life assessment, and medication compliance. She collaborated in the development of epilepsy quality of life assessment instruments, and she lectures frequently on these topics. Her books are titled:

Patient Compliance in Medical Practice and Clinical Trials
Alcohol and Seizures
Quantitative Assessment in Epilepsy Care
Patient Recruitment in Clinical Trials.

She serves on the Board of Directors of the Society for Clinical Trials, chairs the Board of Trustees of the William G. Lennox Fund, is past Treasurer of the American Epilepsy Society, past member of the Editorial Board of the international journal *Epilepsia,* and the recipient of the Ambassador for Epilepsy award from the International League Against Epilepsy.

Mailing address:
Joyce A. Cramer
Yale-VA Connecticut Healthcare System
950 Campbell Avenue
West Haven, CT 06516
Telephone: 203-932-5711, ext 2610
FAX: 203-937-3468
E-mail: Joyce.Cramer@Yale.edu

Bert Spilker, PhD, MD, FCP, FFPM is the President of Orphan Medical, Inc. He holds faculty appointments as Adjunct Professor at the University of North Carolina in the Schools of Medicine (Department of Pharmacy Practice at the University of Minnesota). Dr. Spilker has more than 26 years experience in the pharmaceutical industry, having worked for Pfizer Ltd. (United Kingdom), Philips-Duphar B.V. (The Netherlands), Sterling Drug Inc. (Rensselaer, New York), and the Burroughs Wellcome Co. (Research Triangle Park, North Carolina). He has experience with a private consulting company in the Washington, DC area, and has worked in the private practice of general medicine.

Bert Spilker received his Ph.D. in pharmacology from the State University of New York, Downstate Medical Center, and did post-doctoral research at the University of California Medical School in San Francisco. He received his M.D. from the University of Miami Ph.D. to M.D. Program, and did a residency in internal medicine at Brown University Medical School. Bert Spilker is the author of more than 100 publications, plus 13 books in a wide area of pharmacology, clinical medicine, and medicine development. He is the recipient of numerous honors, including the FDA Commissioner's Special Citation for work on orphan medicines.

Dr. Spilker is married and has two grown children.

Mailing Address:
Bert Spilker, PhD, MD
President
Orphan Medical, Inc.
13911 Ridgedale Drive, Suite 475
Minnetonka, MN 55305
Telephone: 612-513-6900
FAX: 612-541-9209
E-mail: BSpilker@Orphan.com

1 / Introduction

DEFINITIONS AND TYPES OF QUALITY OF LIFE

Quality of life has become a relevant measure of efficacy in clinical trials. Its use is spreading, and its importance is growing as a valid indicator of whether or not a medical treatment is beneficial. Quality of life may be viewed in terms of an individual, group, or large population of patients.

While it is widely agreed that health-related quality of life is not the only type of quality of life, health-related quality of life (HRQOL) is the subject of this book within the broad definition of health proposed by the World Health Organization (WHO): "Health is a state of complete physical, mental and social well-being and not merely the absence of disease or infirmity." This broad definition, however, does not cover most nonhealth-type domains of quality of life. Personal life events often affect health through stress, anxiety, or other emotions. All domains should be assessed when health-related quality of life is measured. Therefore, descriptions of health-related quality of life domains include consideration of most personal issues.

The quality of life field is a rapidly changing and developing medical arena. It is premature to define golden rules for this field, although one of the most important is that only validated scales should be used in clinical trials. The question of disease-specific versus generic scales to evaluate quality of life had been widely debated, but there is now a general consensus to use generic measures supplemented with disease-specific measures for outcomes in quality of life trials. Some scales are function-specific (e.g., sexual or emotional function) or population-specific (e.g., geriatric) rather than disease-specific. Many disease-specific scales are fairly general in the type of information they elicit and, therefore, bridge the gap between general and disease-specific scales (e.g., Health Assessment Questionnaire for arthritis, Quality of Life Index for cancer).

It is hoped that this book will help advance the usefulness of quality of life assessments by (a) helping to standardize definitions and approaches to studying quality of life, (b) indicating which tests are validated for specific diseases and domains, (c) identifying state-of-the-art tools for measuring quality of life in many patient populations, (d) stimulating wider use of these measures in clinical trials, and (e) assisting the analysis and interpretation of quality of life data.

TAXONOMY

There are two main encompassing types of quality of life, health-related quality of life (HRQOL) and nonhealth-related quality of life (NHRQOL). HRQOL represents those parts of quality of life that directly relate to an individual's health (4,5). Many factors, both internal and external to an individual, may affect health perceptions, functioning, and well-being. For example, patient-specific characteristics such as motivation and personality may be important influences on HRQOL (9,10). Social networks, including friends and family, may be instrumental in helping a person cope and adapt to a serious chronic disease, resulting in improved psychological well-being compared to others who may have limited social resources. Factors in the natural environment may also have an impact on HRQOL, such as the impact of poor air quality on patients with asthma.

Conceptualization of NHRQOL includes four domains: (a) personal–internal, (b) personal–social, (c) external–natural environment, and (d) external–societal environment. Each of these domains consists of several components, and each component consists of individual factors. Thus, the organizational structure of NHRQOL is similar to that of HRQOL. A person's disease and treatment affect one's clinical signs, symptoms, adverse experiences, and clinical benefits in a rather complex way to be integrated by the person in terms of how it is deemed to influence his/her physical and psychological domains of HRQOL. These influences in turn then have an effect (i.e., an indirect effect) on the social and economic domains.

DOMAINS OF QUALITY OF LIFE

The four major domains of quality of life generally referred to by most authors include the following categories:

1. Physical status and functional abilities
2. Psychological status and well-being
3. Social interactions
4. Economic and/or vocational status and factors.

Some clinical studies claim to deal with quality of life issues when in fact they have studied only one or two of these broad domains. The most common argument for this plan is that not all domains are pertinent to study in every clinical trial. Nonetheless, excluding selected domains can be a pitfall in a study. In many cases, it is appropriate to evaluate a range of domains even when hypotheses are formulated for only some areas. The field of quality of life assessment is rarely well enough described in any specific population to assume that only one or two selected areas should be observed.

There is an important alternative to using tests to evaluate quality of life. One or more specific parameters or questions may be used in a clinical trial to evaluate a single or a few components of one or more domains. Those parameters or questions should be highly important measures of the particular component (e.g., evaluate only the impact of mobility in an arthritis population). Although these few questions do not represent a validated test of quality of life, their importance for assessing quality of life in a particular disease is often obvious. It may be appropriate to include pertinent quality of life questions in clinical trials rather than a standard (or new) test or scale, particularly in those diseases or conditions where a validated test does not exist.

QUALITY OF LIFE FOR INDIVIDUAL PATIENTS AND GROUPS OF PATIENTS

Quality of life must be viewed on a number of levels. Although the exact number and definition of levels is variable, the three-level model shown in Fig. 1.1 provides a generally accepted basic approach. The overall assessment of well-being is the top level and may be described as an individual's overall satisfaction with life and one's general sense of personal well-being. This overall assessment may be measured by summing the scores of an index test that evaluates each individual domain, or by simply asking patients, "On a scale of 1 to 10 (or 1 to 100, or by descriptive categories), how would you assess your overall well-

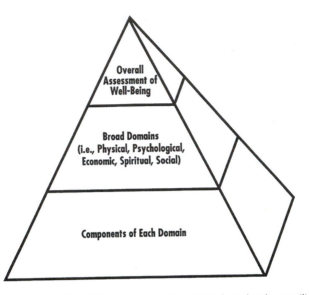

FIG. 1.1. Three levels of quality of life. In their totality, these three levels constitute the scope (and definition) of quality of life.

being?" In the clinical trial literature, this is referred to as a global quality of life assessment. It is also important to establish through careful wording whether the patient is to consider the present moment, the last 24 hours, the week or time since their previous clinic visit, or other time period in answering the question. Moreover, the question may ask the patient to compare the time period with their baseline state. This is particularly relevant in a trial. Given the highly personal way that patients judge their quality of life, it may readily be seen that this global quality of life assessment question is best answered by the patient and not by the physician. However, a global quality of life question that assesses disease severity is best answered by the physician because the assessment of disease severity involves clinical measures and clinical judgment and does not require an assessment of quality of life domains.

The middle level in Fig. 1.1 describes three to six broad domains. Both the number and general identity of these domains are defined similarly by different authors. Each cuts the overall pie (level 1) into different pieces of domains (level 2). The lower or third level of Fig. 1.1 includes all components of each domain that are specifically assessed by quality of life tests and scales. Among the components of the psychological domain are anxiety, depression, and cognition. A single index or an entire battery of tests may be used to evaluate the components of just one or all domains. When a single clinical index is created to evaluate a single disease, widely differing parameters may be included for assessment, and each one may be assigned a specific weight.

When people respond to the questions on a quality of life assessment, they use the same cognitive processes they would when responding to any type of question. For example, a person may be asked, "How are you?" This question is usually used as a greeting that also asks respondents to reflect about their status. It provides no direction on the content to include in a response and, in this sense, leaves the respondents free to select aspects of their life that they consider determinants of their current status.

In contrast, consider the self-assessed health status (SAHS) question, "In general, would you say your health is excellent, very good, good, fair, or poor?" This question is found in national health surveys and specific quality of life assessments (1–3). Here, too, respondents are to reflect on memories of past events, select those of importance to themselves, process this information, and use it to generate a response. What is different about the SAHS question compared with the previous question is that it refers to the more limited domain of a person's health status. Both questions, however, provide little insight into the elements actually used by a person to make a quality of life judgment. Multiattribute health status assessments, in contrast, provide a selected range of quality of life domains for the respondent to consider, such as physical performance, recreation, interpersonal relationships, and so on. In responding to items on a multiattribute questionnaire, the person would still select material from a broad array of experiences, but now experiences associated with a specific domain.

QUALITY OF LIFE FOR POPULATIONS OF PATIENTS

The purpose of studying quality of life of large populations of patients is to learn what treatments have the optimal effects on large groups of patients and to understand the burden of different diseases. This information may be used to help government and managed care decision makers allocate funds to those treatments shown to elicit the best quality of life outcomes. This assumes that all major efficacy and safety parameters are approximately equal among the treatments compared for the same disease. This is rarely the case in practice. Exceptions exist to virtually all generalizations and conclusions of population-based studies. Thus, every health care professional must be sensitive to the needs and responses of individual patients in the choice of treatment(s) as well as in the modification of those treatments.

The pyramidal hierarchy for overall assessment, domains, and components shown in Fig. 1.1 for individual patients also applies to a population of patients. On the other hand, the implications of these levels for patients and populations are quite different. The most specific and valuable data for determining optimal treatment for an individual patient arise from direct experience in the patient himself or herself; next comes the total experience gained by the health professional; followed by case reports from colleagues or the literature; and finally from population-based studies. In most instances, the population-based studies should have the greatest influence on the specific treatment an individual patient receives. But, in the real world, most physicians rely primarily on their own experience.

Some of the major issues addressed by decision makers regarding the implications of a quality of life trial or report for another patient population are listed below. The major questions are:

1. To what degree
   Are the patients similar in the test population and in the published report population?
   Are the conditions of use similar in the test population and in the published report population?
   May the results in the published report be extrapolated to the test population?
   Is the treatment appropriate for the test population?
2. What other products in the formulary are used for the same treatment and how do they compare with the test treatment?
3. Is the price for the new treatment reasonable or acceptable?
4. If there are issues about price, can creative answers be found to address them?

COMBINING QUALITY OF LIFE DATA FROM MULTIPLE DOMAINS OR TESTS

A table could be created that lists the major domains and the specific instruments or tests that are used to evaluate them. Quality of life tests measure either specific or general aspects of the various domains. If a single test that measures each of the domains (and is validated for each of these domains) is used in a clinical trial, then an aggregate overall assessment of quality of life can be obtained. In this case, it should be relatively straightforward to compare different medicines or treatments. One problem with obtaining a single overall score for quality of life, however, is that different domains may yield different results (e.g., treatment A was better than treatment B in two domains, but the opposite result was obtained in the other two domains). Even within a single domain it is common for a specific component to yield different results to different treatments.

If a battery of validated tests is used to evaluate a single domain (or all domains), it is impossible to combine all test results into a single number. Individual test results may be aggregated, however, by presenting them in a comparative manner. Investigators must establish the relative importance of each individual test used to measure one or more aspects of quality of life before conducting the trial. This practice ensures that data obtained from tests defined as minor are not later used to claim that a certain treatment is more or less effective than another. Different tests and scales may be required to measure specific aspects of each domain or component of a domain depending on the patients being evaluated and the interests of the investigators. Moreover, different weights may be assigned to each of the four broad domains, based on the patients' beliefs as influenced by the severity of the disease and other factors. Although, there is no a priori reason to state that each of these components must be measured and combined to understand changes in a patient's quality of life, failure to do so raises the question of whether important data were missed. Nonetheless, one domain or even a single component of a domain may reflect quality of life issues better than the combination of several or many separate measures.

Assessment of quality of life requires input from patients to ensure that the patients' perceptions are included and accurate. A study that compared physician and patient perceptions of quality of life using several different scales found that correlation between the two was poor (4). This supports the view that physicians cannot accurately assess a patient's quality of life in all, or perhaps most, situations. This may result from the fact that physicians usually judge patients' clinical responses rather than how clinical responses are filtered through a patient's values and beliefs.

Patient–Family Interrelationships and Perceptions

The effects of an illness or disability and its treatment often extend beyond the patient. Therefore, it is often advisable to address the impact of the condition on the family and/or close friends, in addition to the patient. Family members' reactions to the patient's condition, and the degree of emotional and tangible support they provide, have been shown to influence a patient's emotional well-being and compliance with medical therapy, as well as his/her morbidity and mortality. In addition, an ill family member may have differing impacts of the HRQOL of family members (e.g., fear of the patient dying or being disabled, caregiver strain), which may in turn have an effect on the patient.

The perceptions of the patients and their families regarding the condition will reflect their personal value systems and judgments regarding what constitutes well-being, life satisfaction, and health status. Often there is lack of congruence between the patients' and families' perceptions of the impact of the condition and its therapy. It is important to distinguish perceptions of health status from actual health. Individuals who are ill, and who perceive themselves as such, may after a period of adjustment reset their expectations and adapt to their life situation and, thus, possess a positive sense of well-being. Other persons with the same condition, however, may become gradually more dissatisfied with their life situation, and rate their overall quality of life as poor. In some area, perceived health ratings are strongly and independently associated with an increased risk of morbidity and mortality. In other words, individuals' health perceptions are important predictors of health outcomes, independent of their clinical health status.

Expectations (both the patient's and the family's) also constitute important determinants of satisfaction with the outcome of therapy. In many chronic and progressive illnesses, with time, as symptoms become increasingly severe and activities become more stringently restricted, patient expectations are likely to lessen as to the degree of improvement that can be obtained. As new therapies improve the outlook for both morbidity and mortality, it is important to assess patients' perceptions of their health status, as well as their expectations of treatment benefits. Figure 1.2 illustrates a model of the interrelationships among efficacy, safety, and other factors for integration into a patient's HRQOL domains. Although the arrows show flow only in one direction, flow can be bidirectional. Similar illustrations could be constructed for a broad population or health care sector.

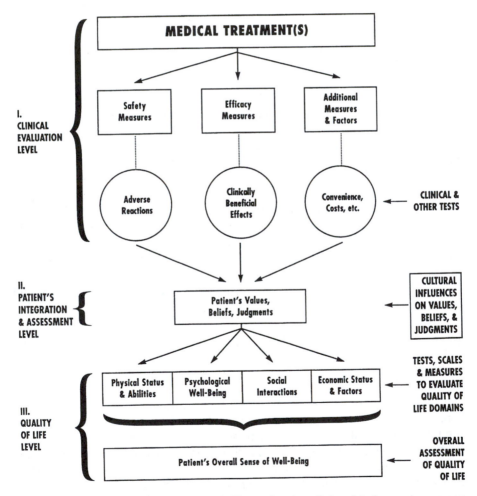

FIG. 1.2. Model of how clinical aspects of efficacy (i.e., benefits), safety (e.g., adverse reactions), or other factors are integrated and filter through the patient s values, beliefs, and judgments to influence his/her quality of life domains.

CATEGORIES OF INSTRUMENTS USED
TO MEASURE QUALITY OF LIFE

Of the many hundreds of instruments used to measure one or more aspects of quality of life, some focus on parameters universally agreed to be part of quality of life. In addition, some instruments are better validated than are others. The most frequently used and most well-validated instruments are referred to as core instruments. A more extensive discussion of this topic and prototype lists of specific core instruments plus name and address of a contact person is available (5–10). In addition, a CD-ROM is available containing 9,000 bibliographic references with abstracts related to the past 20 years of HRQOL research, more than 100 descriptions of instruments, and lists of Web pages and e-mail addresses of researchers in the field. [Contact Mario Di Floriano at http://www.glamm.com/ql or glam@glamm.com.]

Instruments used to measure quality of life can be broadly categorized as follows:

I. Instruments that focus on parameters or functions universally agreed to be part of health-related quality of life for all people.
II. Instruments that focus on parameters or functions that many believe to be part of health-related quality of life for all people and are primarily used to evaluate quality of life.
III. Instruments that focus on parameters or functions most believe to be part of health-related quality of life for patients with a specific disease or particular characteristic (e.g., elderly) and are primarily used to evaluate quality of life.
IV. Instruments that focus on parameters or functions that are sometimes part of quality of life but are usually viewed as clinical measures such as depression scales, pain scales, and tests of cognitive function.
V. Instruments that focus on tangential issues to quality of life but may be used, on occasion, to assess a component of quality of life (e.g., social functioning measure, personality test).

PHARMACOECONOMICS

The field of pharmacoeconomics is rapidly expanding for a variety of reasons (e.g., regulations, competition). The economics of medicines can be viewed at three levels:

Industry level: This level focuses on financial aspects of the many companies that make up the pharmaceutical industry. This level describes the financial forecasts, financial performances and related fiscal aspects of a company and is not discussed in this book. This area is not part of the field of pharmacoeconomics, but economics.

Specific medicine level: This level is the primary one referred to as pharmacoeconomics and includes studies to evaluate costs and benefits of specific medicines. The evaluation of these studies by a variety of decision makers on formulary committees, in government, and elsewhere is also discussed in this book. Studies usually compare a medicine with others or to other modalities but may evaluate a single treatment. The field of pharmacoeconomics identifies, measures, and compares the costs and outcomes of using treatments. Data at this level are used to make decisions on using medicines at all levels from international and national governments to specific patients.

Individual patient level: While assessments of individual patient costs and benefits are quantitatively evaluated as part of pharmacoeconomic studies at the medicine level, another economic aspect can be studied in clinical trials. This involves the attitudes of a person toward work and economic self-sufficiency as well as his/her abilities to perform work-related functions to be productive. An evaluation of how this changes as a result of treatment in a clinical trial is part of quality of life and is generally considered an independent domain. In addition to measuring patient attitudes, it is possible to assess actual parameters such as (a) Did the patient work? and (b) How many days did he/she work per month or year?

Many perspectives may be applied when viewing the pharmacoeconomic level. Some of the important perspectives include those of the patient, health provider, hospital administration, payer, formulary committee, regulatory authority, academic scientist, vendor organization, and the overall society. Many hospital charges to patients (and indirectly to the insurance companies) for products or services do not relate closely to the actual costs of those products or services. The procedures for determining charges and the amounts charged for identical products or services vary widely, even within the same geographic location. While there are many explanations for such differences, they may greatly influence results of a pharmacoeconomic study. The ramifications of pharmacoeconomics have become widespread in our society and will become even more so in the future. This occurs not only in establishing which pharmaceuticals enter formularies, but also in terms of prices, reimbursement, and promotional practices.

The actual economic methods used in pharmacoeconomics (e.g., cost/benefit, cost effectiveness, cost/utility, cost of illness, cost minimization) are well validated (as opposed to many instruments used in quality of life studies). But these pharmacoeconomic methods may be used in many ways, a number of which are not scientifically (or ethically) acceptable. Each method is desirable under specific conditions. Two of the most important principles in this field are to explain assumptions and to clarify what was done.

RELATIONSHIP OF PHARMACOECONOMICS AND QUALITY OF LIFE

The types of outcomes of a medical treatment for a specific patient include three broad areas:

1. **Clinical:** the changes in an individual patient's signs and symptoms of disease, as well as other directly measurable benefits. Health outcomes in medicine (as opposed to clinical trials) are assessed under the subject of outcomes research.
2. **Economic:** the costs of the patient's treatment, who is paying, and what limitations are being placed on the system because of economic factors. Health care costs are assessed under the subject of health economics.
3. **Personal:** the quality of life benefits the patient assesses himself/herself in terms of how treatment affects the broad domains and their components.

There is an overlap between pharmacoeconomic and quality of life assessments, depending on the specific situation. In the clinical area, certain measures are essential for assessing cost effectiveness. Although cost/benefit analyses express clinical benefits in monetary terms, the clinical parameters must be measured. Cost/utility analyses usually require patient judgments, although these may be estimated, based on clinician or investigator judgments. Although quality of life may change as a result of an individual's clinical changes, these changes are often an indirect result of the clinical effect. Economic parameters are clearly of paramount importance in pharmacoeconomics. Economics is also considered an independent domain in quality of life and usually focuses on vocational and work performance, although direct costs of treatment and its side effects are also critical in many cases for their impact on patients. Economics related to quality of life may overlap with, but generally differs greatly from, economic aspects of most pharmacoeconomic areas.

HEALTH POLICY AND OUTCOMES RESEARCH

Health policy, not pharmacoeconomics, wrestles with questions of whether the price for a particular treatment is appropriate or too high. To make this decision or to decide under which medical and social conditions an approved but expensive medicine should be used, it is essential to have meaningful clinical, economic, and quality of life data that are relatively complete and relatively free of bias. Paramount in this issue is the concept that the price of a new medicine may only represent the tip of the total treatment cost and may influence that substantially. It is imperative that the total clinical, economic, and quality of life value of the treatment be assessed in comparison with other alternative treatments. Health policy also deals with data obtained from outcomes research.

Health care costs are discussed in terms of health economics by trained economists, whereas health outcomes are discussed as outcomes research by epidemiologists, psychologists, and others trained in this area. The outcome of a medical intervention is the health state noticed by the patient. This includes satisfaction with care received, quality of life, morbidity, compliance measures, performance symptoms, patient performance, and other characteristics. If at least one treatment is a medicine, the outcomes may be viewed as pharmaceutical outcomes and may be measured in either efficacy or effectiveness studies. The latter incorporates the patient's perspective.

Outcome studies differ from traditional randomized trials in that outcomes research:

1. Presents outcomes from the patient's perspective and not the health care professionals
2. Extrapolates results more broadly than is done with randomized trials
3. Focuses on costs more than dose-randomized trials
4. Often assesses usual care of patients
5. Sometimes uses databases as their data source.

CONCEPTUAL ISSUES

From an operational perspective, health-related quality of life is a multifactorial construct, whose component parts remain consistent, but whose individual significance within the overall model may vary over time. The ability to ride a bicycle may be very important to a younger person, but with increasing age or a change in habitus or social circumstance, the ability to perform that skill may take on a very different meaning. Examination of individual components of patient function may play a valuable role in elucidating the impact of a disease and its treatment on overall quality of life. Figure 1.3 illustrates how a person's disease or treatment affects clinical signs, symptoms, adverse effects, and clinical benefit. The complex interrelationships are integrated by the person to formulate an individual HRQOL equation.

Psychologically and anthropologically speaking, quality of life reflects the patient-perceived illness side of the distinction between illness and disease (11). Physicians concentrate upon the disease process (the pathophysiology) and attempt to resolve it, often paying less attention to patients' perceptions of the disease, which are the experience of illness. An example is hypertension, which is usually detected by the physician when the patient is asymptomatic. The physician has diagnosed a "disease" while the patient is "well." The treatment may make the patient feel sick, known as a labeling phenomenon. Many variables contribute to the illness experience: the perception of symptoms, the way in which the patient labels them and communicates the distress they cause, the experience of being unable to function normally, and the methods of coping used by patients and families to gain some control over the disorder.

The psychological level is important as a disease category both in its own right and because it interacts with physical disease and response to treatment. It is clear that it affects, and is affected by, both. Psychological well-being is included with psychological distress, because most existing measures concentrate on the distress end of the continuum and are not sensitive to changes that occur at the well-being end. It may be that reduction in psychological well-being rather than overt distress is more likely to reflect the response to physical disease

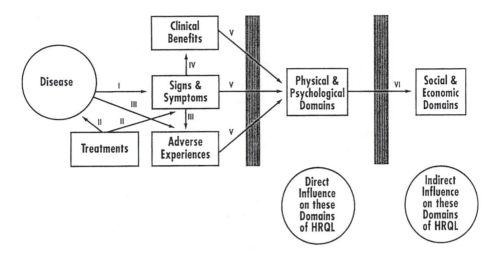

FIG. 1.3. The relationships among several factors influencing quality of life domains. I. Disease causes or leads to a constellation of clinical signs and symptoms. II. Medicine and other treatments are directed at the underlying disease and/or ameliorating adverse reactions. III. Treatments may elicit adverse experiences, either as a result of attempts to affect the underlying disease or the signs and symptoms resulting from the disease. IV. Treatments directed against clinical signs and symptoms may lead to clinical benefits. V. Signs and symptoms, benefits, and adverse experiments filter through the patient s beliefs, judgments, and values (see Chapter 1 for a description of this filtering phenomenon) to influence the physical and psychological domains. VI. Influences on the physical and/or psychological domain may, in turn, pass through the patient's beliefs, judgments, and values to influence the social and economic domain. For example, a patient who feels better physically or psychologically may then be able to interact socially or to work at his/her job. HRQL, health-related quality of life.

or its treatment. Psychological variables have been shown to be a factor in some disease states, e.g., the role of stress in the development of hypertension and the relative risk of developing heart disease in different personality types. Variables can be grouped in concentric domains starting with the physiological parameters of disease at the core and diffusing in turn to personal functioning, psychological distress/well-being, general health perceptions, and finally social/role functioning (12).

General health perception is felt to encompass the individual's evaluation of the three preceding concepts. However, the correspondence is far from perfect; there is clearly more involved in a general self-rating of health status, perhaps the personal values put upon each concept. The final circle is that of social/role functioning, which refers to an individual's capacity to perform activities associated with one's usual role, including employment, school, or homemaking. Ware (12) presents a concept that emphasizes a hierarchy by placing physical illness at the center of the circle. Thus, it opens the issue of weighting, apportioning relative values to the component parts of the quality of life construct.

Calman (13) defined quality of life as the gap between the patient's expectations and achievements. Thus, the smaller the gap, the higher the quality of life.

Conversely, the less the patient is able to realize his expectations, the poorer his quality of life. The gap between expectations and achievement may vary over time as the patient's health improves or regresses in relation to the effectiveness of treatment or progress of disease. Goals set by the patient must be realistic in order to thwart undue frustration. The professional may temper the patient's expectations and prepare him/her for the changes and limitations that will ensue as the disease progresses. The "impact of illness" may vary depending on the patient's perception of his quality of life when the diagnosis is given. Thus, a person who had been losing weight and becoming fatigued during the months prior to a serious diagnosis may have prepared himself psychologically and already reduced his expectations of returning to his normal state of wellness.

Another issue relates to baseline assessment. Unlike a disease, which often has a definable time of onset, quality of life is a lifelong continuous variable. Because it is multifactorial and encompassing, defining baseline norms can be difficult. Measurement tools are linear in their response properties, and usually evaluate the "change from time of intervention" rather than the time to "return to normal."

Return to Work as a Component of Quality of Life

Some studies have been characterized by an inordinate and probably disproportionate focus on return to work as a measure of HRQOL, so much so that in a number of reports, work appears to have been used almost as a surrogate for quality of life. Whereas return to work may be an important component of life quality for many patients, return to work measures only one aspect of HRQOL and does not, even for that dimension, address such components as job satisfaction, job performance, opportunities for advancement, and the adequacy of income.

In many populations, particularly the severely impaired, the elderly, and women who may have only been in the paid work force intermittently, return to remunerative work is not a reasonable goal of most interventions. Furthermore, there is abundant evidence that many other nonmedical (nonintervention-related) aspects predominantly influence return to work, including pre-illness employment history, patient and family preferences, the job category and skill level, the level of unemployment in the community, financial status, and the employer's and the patient's perceptions of limitations. Indeed, in a number of studies, the patient's pre-intervention expectation of the ability to return to work was the most important determinant of employment outcome. In many return-to-work studies, perception of health status, rather than actual health status, and perception of ability to work, rather than objective measures of functional capability, often proved the overwhelming determinant.

More recent studies assessing HRQOL have broadened the concept of work to include a range of productive activities, both paid and unpaid. Such measures include volunteer and community activities, household tasks and care giving activities, as well as paid employment. These instruments provide a more comprehensive view of the individual's functional status, with respect to productive activities, than focusing solely on return to work.

Physical and occupational function is the quality of life factor most nearly approximating the outcome measures physicians traditionally use. Questions about strength, energy, and the ability to carry on expected normal activities are typically asked. They correlate reasonably with physician estimates of patient well-being and function (14). Questions should elicit responses uninfluenced by age, sex, or geographical habitus. A question asking about difficulty climbing stairs is of little relevance in those parts of the world where there are no stairs. Likewise, questions in this domain must be answerable both by those who have traditional occupations, such as steelworkers and accountants, and by housewives who might interpret such questions as having something to do with employment.

One of the subtleties implicit in the design of instruments is that they be constructed so as to provide a scalar representation of the severity of impairment. Psychometricians use the term Guttman Scale when referring to a series of questions exploring gradations of difficulty, effort, or impact of a particular dimension. The goal is to establish either a linear or definably nonlinear response spectrum.

Of the many psychological parameters that have an impact on quality of life, the ones most studied are anxiety, depression, and fear. From a number of studies there seems to be an underlying natural evolution of emotions encompassing depression and anxiety at the time of diagnosis, anxiety with each approaching reassessment, and fear at moments of diagnostic or therapeutic uncertainty (15–17). The psychometric measures employed in quality of life studies may be simple questions inquiring directly as to mood, anxiety, or depression, or they may be more sophisticated borrowings from the psychometric testing literature.

Social interaction refers to a patient's ability to carry on the person-to-person interactions at the core of communal living. These interactions are traditionally thought of as forming a hierarchy: family, close friends, work and vocational associates, and the general community. The importance of this parameter has long been underestimated. Somatic sensation, or symptoms, encompasses unpleasant physical feelings that may detract from someone's quality of life. They include pain, nausea, and shortness of breath, among others. Attribution of discomfort has an impact on overall quality of life. Figure 1.4 summarizes the relationships between HRQOL and non-HRQOL (NHRQOL) with two levels of assessment.

Multifactoriality

It is apparent that the quality of life parameter measures more than one single aspect of a patient's overall function. Having operationally defined quality

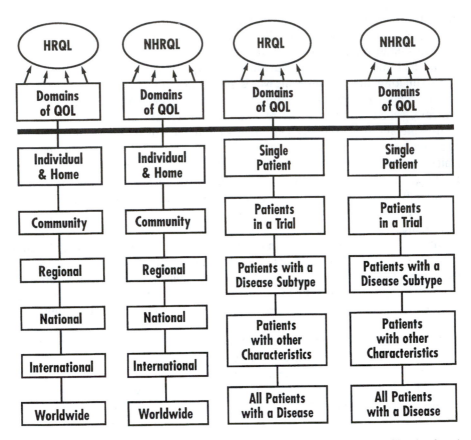

FIG. 1.4. A model of two types of quality of life, their domains, and two types of levels of quality of life.

of life as the synthesis of four domains (physical function, psychological function, social interaction, and economic factors), one needs to be satisfied that enough of a patient's overall daily living is encompassed by these measures for the score to be truly representative of the whole process. The next question to ask is whether the brief inquiries into each domain of quality of life reflect their target adequately. It is clear one cannot make a detailed psychosocial or occupational evaluation based on four or five questions. However, correlation studies comparing quality of life, on a factor by factor basis, with much more detailed measures representing each factor provide reassurance about their validity. The factor analysis process is a standard for instrument validation (18). This is a multistage technique whose intent is to reveal the constructs that underlie responses to batteries of questions, although the technique can be used in other settings. In interpreting factor analyses, it is important to distinguish between the factors, which are the underlying concepts, and the scales, which represent the sum of questions that load most highly on each factor. Put in other terms, the formal calculation of a factor score means taking the weighted sum of scores of each item multiplied by the factor weighting for that item. In contrast, a scalar score means summing the scores of those items loading most heavily on each factor. In general, the factor analysis process gives confidence that the questions point to specific factors rather than being vague probes of well-being.

The weighting problem is largely unresolved. How does one weigh the individual domain scores so as to arrive at a reasonable overall quality of life score? It may be that the relative weightings of quality of life domains are themselves time-variable. This means that before comparing quality of life outcomes of different trials, one is required to take into account differences in domain weightings between the quality of life measures used. The technique of judgment analysis has been applied to the development of the Schedule for the Evaluation of Individual Quality of Life (SEIQOL) (19,20). Judgment analysis is derived from social judgment theory and allows individual judgments to be modeled mathematically. The justification for applying this technique to quality of life assessments is that specific goals or behaviors important to individual quality of life are not represented adequately by broad questions about physical mobility or mental health; apparently similar behaviors do not have the same significance for all individuals; and they do not retain the same significance for a given individual with the passage of time or over the course of an illness.

The SEIQOL procedure allows the patient to select five areas of life considered most important in assessing overall quality of life, during a semistructured interview. Each cue is then rated on a vertical visual–analog scale between the upper and lower extremes of "As good as it could possibly be" and "As bad as it could possibly be." In the second stage, the relative contribution of each elicited cue to the overall judgment of quality of life is determined for each individual. Thirty different hypothetical profiles using the elicited cues unique to each patient are presented for visual–analog scale rating of overall quality of life, a procedure that takes 30 minutes. A computer program based on multiple regression analysis then uses these ratings to provide a weight for each cue. The final score is computed by multiplying each cue weight by the patient's current self-rating and summing across cues to obtain a total score. The same procedure can be used with provided cues representing standard quality of life dimensions. Allowing patients to choose and weight their quality of life domains in assessing overall quality of life may result in that greater sensitivity to treatment differences. There are two major drawbacks to the SEIQOL system: first, that the effect of treatment on a specific quality of life area can only be determined for the subset of patients that chose that area, and second, that the procedure is very time and resource intensive compared with other methods of quality of life assessment.

THE DIMENSIONS OF HEALTH OUTCOMES

Over the past several years, there has been a shift in emphasis in research studies from reliance on measures of medical process (e.g., erythrocyte sedimentation rate or joint count) to measures of outcomes of direct importance to patients. These elements have been identified by multiple surveys of both patients and the general population (21–23). Patients desire to be alive as long as possible, to function normally, to be free of pain and other physical, psychological, and social symptoms, to be free of iatrogenic problems from the treatment regimen, and to incur as few costs for medical care as possible. These five dimensions (death, disability, discomfort, drug side effects, and dollar costs), broadly construed, constitute a comprehensive set of domains of patient outcomes.

These primary outcome dimensions may be further separated into their natural subdimensions. Economic impact consists of direct medical costs and indirect medical costs due to effects on productivity. Iatrogenic effects may be due to medication(s) or to surgery. Discomfort may be physical, psychological, or social. Disability may involve fine movements of the upper extremities or locomotor activities of the lower extremities. Death can be broken down by specific cause and quantitated in terms of expected time to death. Each subdimension can, in turn, be subdivided into components comprised of specific individual questions or variables. Thus, a hierarchy of patient outcomes may be developed that is conceptually complete and provides a location in the framework for all possible measures.

HIERARCHY OF PATIENT OUTCOMES

The terms quality of life, health status, and patient outcome as generally used have overlapping meanings. As indicated, quality of life has a restricted meaning close to the WHO definition of health. Health status is a measure of that life quality at a particular point in time. Patient outcome usually refers to a final health status measurement after the passage of time and the application of treatment. In the future, patient life quality outcomes will be increasingly described by a cumulative series of health status measurements. It would be highly desirable to represent any of these terms by a single number. Thus, in clinical studies, one could conclude that the quality of life (or patient outcome) with treatment A was 86, whereas with treatment B it was 93; hence, treatment B was to be preferred. Unfortunately, there are major obstacles to calculation of a single index number that can serve as a primary dependent variable in clinical studies. Such an index would require, for example, face validity, reliability, and sensitivity in a clinical study situation.

There are two ways to develop a single index number. First, it can be obtained directly. For example, one could use an analog scale question with an appropriate stem that asks the subjects to make a mark that represents, broadly considered, their global health status at the moment. Such a simplistic approach can, in fact, be useful for validating more sophisticated approaches, but experience with such scales has shown them to be very insensitive and to fail to identify the specific positive and negative inputs that are included in the global judgment.

The second approach is to calculate a single index number indirectly, by combining numbers from different scales representing different facets of health status. Good measurement characteristics and sensitivity may be obtained by such an approach, but it involves an indefensible series of major value judgments by the investigator in the implicit or explicit weighting systems that must, of necessity, be employed. However, the value judgments that are required of individuals are known to vary substantially among individuals, in the same individual at different periods of life, and between patients with a particular illness and those without the illness (24,25). Figure 1.5 illustrates a conceptual hierarchy of

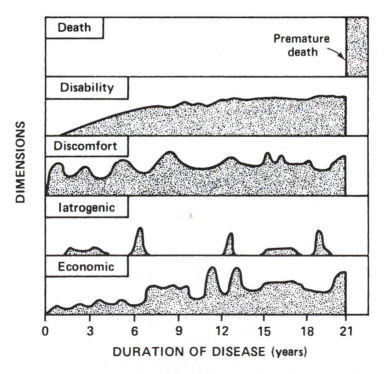

FIG. 1.5. The five primary dimensions of patient outcome. In this example, the health outcomes of a patient with rheumatoid arthritis are graphed over time. Over 21 years of illness, the patient suffers economic distress; iatrogenic difficulties; symptomatic physical, psychological, and social distress; becomes progressively disabled; and dies prematurely.

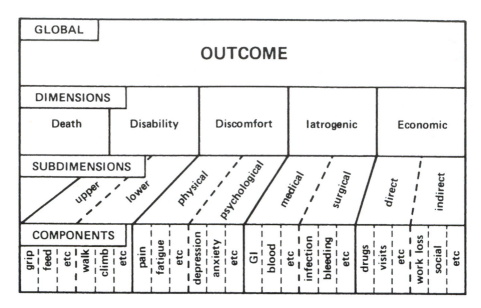

FIG. 1.6. The hierarchy of patient outcome.

patient outcomes. Figure 1.6 demonstrates an example of long-term outcome based on HRQOL dimensions.

Multiple surveys of patients or public, prompted or open-ended, have yielded similar outcome dimensions, although the rank order of importance of each dimension varies from survey to survey and situation to situation (26,27). Patients desire (a) to be alive as long as possible; (b) to function normally; (c) to be free of pain and other physical, psychological, or social symptoms; (d) to be free of iatrogenic problems from the treatment regimen; and (e) to remain in financial health after medical expenses. These five dimensions, called the 5 D's (death, disability, discomfort, drug side effects, and dollar cost), collectively define patient outcome and life quality (28).

Chronic illness must be measured chronically. As noted, health status generally refers to a patient's status at a particular point in the course of illness and outcome to the most recent (or end of study) health status measurement. A health status measurement represents an evaluation at a particular point in time. Conventional outcome assessment represents only the most recent of such measurements. Sequential health status measurements at regular intervals allow calculation of the approximate area under the curve. With this technique, the relevant dependent variables are measured in disability years, discomfort years, side-effect-index units recorded cumulatively, lifetime medical costs, and time to death as represented by life table determinations. The most sophisticated quality of life studies will utilize such measures.

MEASUREMENTS IN CLINICAL TRIALS:
CHOOSING THE RIGHT APPROACH

Following is a list of some general tactics for the conduct of quality of life trials.

1. Choose a trial in which you expect substantial differences in quality of life outcome. To conduct a trial in which you expect only subtle differences will likely prove frustrating and counterproductive.
2. The ideal trial measures quality of life and overall survival in addition to other clinical parameters, which may include disease-free survival as well as specific physiological data.
3. In calculating the number of patients required, a quality of life trial will not necessarily increase the sample size requirement. In fact, since each patient contributes repeated measures of the same variables over time, you will need fewer patients than are required for estimation of survival or disease-free survival. (Repeated measures designs have an increased power to detect between group differences) (29).
4. Use quality of life instruments that are both reliable and valid. Do not "reinvent the wheel." Understand the properties and limitations of the measurement tools selected.
5. Define precisely when the initial quality of life measurement is to be done and by whom. This serves as the key measurement against which subsequent results are compared.
6. Repeat the quality of life measurement at intervals frequent enough to track treatment and the natural history of the disease. Do not confound your trial by measuring some patients when they are sick and other patients when you expect them to be well. Where possible, it is best to measure quality of life with the same pattern of measurement in each treatment arm.
7. The period of accurate recall for a psychological variable reflecting feeling states is somewhere between 2 and 4 weeks (30). It reflects an average of the time in question with some emphasis on either major events or more recent experiences. To emphasize the effect of an intervention, do the test shortly after. To minimize that effect, and possibly better sample the overall progression of the disease, do the test before the next treatment event. Whatever your choice, be consistent across treatment arms.
8. Follow all patients until the natural endpoint of their disease is reached or until all influence of treatment is likely to have passed. Failure to do so may create biases related to "up-front" treatments.
9. Do not analyze your data solely by simple averaging. Techniques such as time series analysis and multivariate analysis of variance take into account the pattern of quality of life response and are much more revealing of the social and biological effects of therapy. These techniques are standard approaches to handling multivariate, time-variable data. Techniques are

being developed to alleviate problems such as missing data, nonlinearity, present versus future value, and loss of data due to patient death.

10. In addition to looking at overall quality of life outcome, it is reasonable to evaluate each of the component factors. However, one must be modest with extrapolations.

Discriminative, Predictive, and Evaluative Indexes

Before applying any HRQOL instrument in a clinical trial, one needs to address several issues. First, the purpose for which the instrument is being used must be clearly stated. Second, the instrument must have certain attributes, or measurement properties, that will determine its usefulness for a specific goal. Third, one needs to determine the general category of HRQOL instruments required, from which a suitable questionnaire can be chosen. Finally, if alternative formats of the questionnaire are available, one must select the appropriate format for one's trial. The potential applications of HRQOL measures can be divided into three broad categories: discrimination, prediction, and evaluation.

A discriminative index is used to distinguish between individuals or groups with respect to an underlying dimension when no external criterion or "gold standard" is available for validating these measures. Intelligence tests, for example, are used to distinguish between children's learning abilities. Use of an instrument from this category in a clinical trial can be illustrated by a following example: If one had a group of patients with a myocardial infarction and wanted to divide them into those with good and poor quality of life (with a view, for example, to intervening in the latter group), one would require a discriminative index.

A predictive index is used to classify individuals into a set of predefined measurement categories when a gold standard is available, either at the time of initial measurement or some time in the future. This gold standard is subsequently used to determine whether individuals have been classified correctly. Although there is no gold standard available for measurement of HRQOL, predictive instruments are still relevant. Let us assume that investigators had developed an HRQOL instrument that one believed was definitive, but took over an hour to administer. Since an hour represents rather a long interview, it would be desirable to have a shorter version. One might choose a subsample of questions from the original and examine the performance of the new, shorter instrument, using the original as a gold standard.

An evaluative index is used to measure the magnitude of longitudinal change in an individual or group. Such instruments are needed for quantitating the treatment benefit in clinical trials or investigating the impact of illness over time. Table 1.1 outlines the properties for useful discrimination of evaluative instruments.

TABLE 1.1 *What makes a good HRQOL measure?*

Instrument property	Evaluative instruments (measuring differences within subjects over time)	Discriminative instruments (measuring differences between subjects at a point in time)
High signal-to-noise ratio	Responsiveness	Reliability
Validity	Correlations of changes in measures over time consistent with theoretically derived predictions	Correlations between measures at a point in time consistent with theoretically derived predictions
Interpretability	Differences within subjects over time can be interpreted as trivial, small, moderate, or large	Differences between subjects at a point in time can be interpreted as trivial, small, moderate, or large

NECESSARY ATTRIBUTES OF AN HRQOL MEASUREMENT INSTRUMENT

Signal and Noise

HRQOL instruments must do two things: they must be able to detect differences in HRQOL (the signal) above the random error associated with any measurement (the noise), and they must really measure what they are intended to measure. For discriminative instruments the signal is the difference between patients at a point in time, and the noise is the differences observed in subjects whose HRQOL is stable. The way of quantitating the signal-to-noise ratio is called reliability. If the variability in scores between subjects (the signal) is much greater than the variability within subjects (the noise), an instrument will be deemed reliable. Reliable instruments will generally demonstrate that stable subjects show more or less the same results on repeated administration.

For evaluative instruments, those designed to measure changes within individuals over time, the way of determining the signal-to-noise ratio is called responsiveness. Responsiveness refers to an instrument's ability to detect change. If a treatment results in an important difference in HRQOL, investigators wish to be confident they will detect that difference, even if it is small. Responsiveness is directly related to the magnitude of the difference in score in patients who have improved or deteriorated (the signal) and the extent to which patients who have not changed obtain more or less the same scores (the noise).

The responsiveness of evaluative instruments may be compromised by ceiling effects, in which patients with the best score nevertheless have substantial HRQOL impairment, or floor effects, in which patients with the worst score may yet deteriorate further. For example, patients who already had the lowest possible score on a generic measure reported worsening health in the subsequent year that could not be detected by the instrument—a floor effect (31). Patients who all had the highest possible score (representing the best possible function) on a physical functioning scale, the Functional Status Index, varied considerably on their score on a generic utility measure, the Quality of Well-Being (32). This implies that some patients with the best possible Functional Status Index could still improve on their health status—a ceiling effect.

Validity When There Is a Gold Standard

Validity has to do with whether the instrument is measuring what it is intended to measure. For a predictive instrument, one determines whether an instrument is measuring what is intended using criterion validity, according to which an instrument is valid insofar as its results correspond to those of the criterion standard. Criterion validity is applicable not only when a shorter version of an instrument (the test) is used to predict the results of the full-length index (the gold standard) but when an HRQOL instrument is used to predict an outcome such as mortality. In this instance, to the extent that variability in survival between patients (the gold standard) is explained by the questionnaire results (the test), the instrument will be valid. Self-ratings of health, like more comprehensive and lengthy measures of general health perceptions, include an individual's evaluation of his/her physiological, physical, psychological, and social well-being.

Validity When There Is No Gold Standard

When there is no gold or criterion standard, HRQOL investigators have borrowed validation strategies from clinical and experimental psychologists, who have for many years been dealing with the problem of deciding whether questionnaires examining intelligence, attitudes, and emotional function are really measuring what they are supposed to measure. The types of validity that psychologists have introduced include content and construct validity. Face validity refers to whether an instrument appears to be measuring what it is intended to measure, and content validity refers to the extent to which the domain of interest is comprehensively sampled by the items, or questions, in the instrument. Quantitative testing of face and content validity are rarely attempted. Feinstein (33) has reformulated these aspects of validity by suggesting criteria for what he calls the sensibility, including the applicability of the questionnaire, its clarity and simplicity, likelihood of bias, comprehensiveness, and whether redundant items have been included. Because of their specificity, these criteria facilitate quantitative rating of an instrument's face and content validity (34).

The most rigorous approach to establishing validity is called construct validity. A construct is a theoretically derived notion of the domain(s) we wish to measure. An understanding of the construct will lead to expectations about how an instrument should behave if it is valid. Construct validity, therefore, involves comparisons between measures, and examination of the logical relationships that should exist between a measure and characteristics of patients and patient groups.

The first step in construct validation is to establish a "model" or theoretical framework, which represents an understanding of what investigators are trying to measure. That theoretical framework provides a basis for understanding how the system being studied behaves, and allows hypotheses or predictions about how the instrument being tested should relate to other measures. Investigators then administer a number of instruments to a population of interest and examine the data. Validity is strengthened or weakened according to the extent the hypotheses are confirmed or refuted.

For example, a discriminative HRQOL instrument may be validated by comparing two groups of patients: those who have undergone a very toxic chemotherapeutic regimen and those who have undergone a much less toxic chemotherapeutic regimen. An HRQOL instrument should distinguish between these two groups and, if it does not, it is very likely that something has gone wrong. Alternatively, correlations between symptoms and functional status can be examined, the expectation being that those with a greater number and severity of symptoms will have lower functional status scores on an HRQOL instrument. Another example is the validation of an instrument discriminating between people according to some aspect of emotional function. Results from such an instrument should show substantial correlations with existing measures of emotional function. The principles of validation are identical for evaluative instruments, but their validity is demonstrated by showing that changes in the instrument being investigated correlate with changes in other related measures in the theoretically derived predicted direction and magnitude. For instance, the validity of an evaluative measure of HRQOL may be supported by the finding of moderate correlations with changes in physical parameters (35).

Validation is not an all-or-nothing process. We may have varying degrees of confidence that an instrument is really measuring what it is supposed to measure. A priori predictions about the magnitude of correlations between the new instrument and other measures that one should find if the new instrument is really measuring what is intended strengthen the validation process. Without such predictions, it is too easy to rationalize whatever correlations between measures are observed. Validation does not end when the first trial with data concerning validity is published, but continues with repeated use of an instrument. The more frequently an instrument is used, and the wider the situations in which it performs as we would expect if it were really doing its job, the greater our confidence in its validity. Perhaps we should never conclude that a questionnaire has "been validated"; the best we can do is to suggest that strong evidence for validity has been obtained in a number of different settings and studies.

Interpretability

A final key property of an HRQOL measure is interpretability. For a discriminative instrument, we could ask whether a particular score signifies that a patient is functioning normally, or has mild, moderate, or severe impairment of HRQOL. For an evaluative instrument, we might ask whether a particular change in score represents a trivial, small but important, moderate, or large improvement or deterioration.

A number of strategies are available for trying to make HRQOL scores interpretable (36). For an evaluative instrument, one might classify patients into those who had important improvement and those who did not, and examine the changes in score in the two groups; interpret observed changes in HRQOL measures in terms of elements of those measures that will be familiar to readers (e.g., descriptions of changes in mobility); or determine how scores in HRQOL measures relate to marker states that are familiar and meaningful to clinicians. We now know that for instruments that present response options as seven-point scales, small, medium, and large effects correspond to average changes of approximately 0.5, 1.0, and greater than 1.0 per question (37,38). In a trial of patients with arthritis, interpretation was aided by the estimate that a change of 0.02 points in the Quality of Well-Being utility instrument was equivalent to all treated patients improving from moving their own wheelchair without help to walking with physical limitations (39).

CATEGORIES OF QUALITY OF LIFE MEASURES

Generic Instruments—Health Profiles

Two basic approaches characterize the measurement of HRQOL: generic instruments (including single indicators, health profiles, and utility measures) and specific instruments (Table 1.2) (40). Health profiles are instruments that attempt to measure all important aspects of HRQOL. The Sickness Impact Profile is an

TABLE 1.2 *Taxonomy of measures of HRQOL*

Approach	Strengths	Weaknesses
Generic instruments		

Health profile	Single instrument
	Detects differential effects on
	  different aspects of health status
	Comparison across interventions;
	  conditions possible
		May not focus adequately on area of
		  interest
		May not be responsive

Utility measurement	Single number representing net impact
	  on quantity and quality of life
	Cost-utility analysis possible
	Incorporates death
		Difficulty determining utility values
		Doesn't allow examination of effect on
		  different aspects of quality of life
		May not be responsive

Specific instruments
Disease specific
Population specific
Function specific
Condition or problem
  specific
	Clinically sensible
	May be more responsive
		Doesn't allow cross-condition
		  comparisons
		May be limited in terms of populations
		  and interventions
		Restricted to domains of relevance to
		  disease population, function, or
		  problem; other domains that are
		  important to overall HRQL not
		  measured

example of a health profile, and includes a physical dimension (with categories of ambulation, mobility, and body care and movement), a psychosocial dimension (with categories including social interaction, alertness behavior, communication, and emotional behavior), and five independent categories (eating, work, home management, sleep and rest, and recreations and pastimes). Major advantages of health profiles are that they deal with a wide variety of areas and can be used in virtually any population, irrespective of the underlying condition. Because generic instruments apply to a wide variety of populations, they allow for broad comparisons of the relative impact of various health care programs. Generic profiles may, however, be less responsive to changes in specific conditions.

Generic Instruments—Utility Measures

The other type of generic instrument, utility measures of quality of life, are derived from economic and decision theory, and reflect the preferences of patients for different health states. The key elements of utility measures are that they incorporate preference measurements and relate health states to death. This allows them to be used in cost/utility analyses that combine duration and quality of life. In utility measures HRQOL is summarized as a single number along a continuum that usually extends from death (0.0) to full health (1.0), although scores less than 0, representing states worse than death, are possible. Utility scores reflect both the health status and the value of that health status to the patient. The usefulness of utility measures in economic analysis is increasingly important in an era of cost constraints in which health care providers are being asked to justify the resources devoted to treatment.

Utility measures provide a single summary score of the net change in HRQOL—the HRQOL gains from the treatment effect minus the HRQOL burdens of side effects. Utility measures are, therefore, useful for determining if patients are, on the whole, better off as the result of therapy, but may fail to reveal the dimensions of HRQOL on which patients improved versus those on which they worsened. The simultaneous use of a health profile or specific instruments can complement the utility approach by providing this valuable information.

The preferences in utility measurements may come directly from individual patients who are asked to rate the value of their health state. Alternatively, patients can rate their health status using a multiattribute health status classification system (e.g., the Quality of Well-Being Scale, the Health Utilities Index). A previously estimated scoring function derived from results of preference measurements from groups of other patients, or from the community, is then used to convert health status to a utility score (41).

Specific Instruments

The second basic approach to quality of life measurement focuses on aspects of health status that are specific to the area of primary interest. The rationale for this approach lies in the potential for increased responsiveness that may result from including only important aspects of HRQOL that are relevant to the patients being studied. The instrument may be specific to the disease (e.g., heart failure, asthma), to a population of patients (e.g., the frail elderly), to a certain function (e.g., sleep, sexual function), or to a problem (e.g., pain). In addition to the likelihood of improved responsiveness, specific measures have the advantage of relating closely to areas routinely explored by clinicians.

CHOOSING THE RIGHT HRQOL MEASURE

The choice of an HRQOL measure depends very much on the purpose of the trial (42). Generic measures may be particularly useful for surveys that attempt to document the range of disability in a general population or a patient group. In one survey, for instance, investigators used the Sickness Impact Profile to examine the extent of disability in patients with chronic airflow limitation (4). Their striking finding was that the effect of chronic airflow limitation in patients' lives was not restricted to areas such as ambulation and mobility, but was manifested in virtually every aspect of HRQOL. This included social interaction, alertness behavior, emotional behavior, sleep and rest, and recreation and pastime activities. For surveys investigating the range of disability, specific measures are unlikely to be of much use and investigators will, therefore, rely on health profiles or the closely related multiattribute health status classification and utility function approaches.

Use of multiple types of measures in clinical trials yields additional information that may prove important. For instance, if a trial showed not only that patients receiving oral gold were better off in terms of disease-specific functional measures, but also that they had higher utility scores than patients receiving placebo, this demonstrates the impact of the treatment using measures of direct relevance to both patients and health workers and provides the information necessary for an economic cost/utility analysis. An argument can be made for inclusion of a specific measure, a health profile, and a utility measure in any clinical trial in which the major focus is patient benefit. Because disease-specific measures are of greatest interest to the patients themselves and to the clinicians who treat them, whereas generic measures, because they permit comparisons across conditions and populations may be of greatest interest to the policy or decision maker, use of both categories of measures will be most appropriate when the results could be of interest to both audiences. HRQOL measures may also find a place in clinical practice, providing clinicians with information they might not otherwise obtain. Forms that can be self-administered and immediately scored can provide rapid feedback of HRQOL data to clinicians.

Issues Associated with the Instruments Themselves

Some general questions that should be considered prior to using a quality of life measure in clinical trials include:

1. Has the instrument been validated? Is the instrument known to be linear over the range of measurement and is it sensitive to changes occurring in the patient? What is the clinical meaning of a given change in an instrument at each end of the scale? Does each instrument measure the same thing in patients with different disease subtypes and in the same patient at different stages of disease? If quality of life is to be used to support effectiveness, there must be a distinction made between disease-related and drug-related effects on the scores. Which statistical tests should be used to demonstrate significance?

2. Is improvement expected or is the best likelihood a change in rate of deterioration? When all the patients entered into a trial have good performance status or are asymptomatic, it may not be possible to demonstrate improvement. Instead, time to deterioration, probably using life table methods, may be the appropriate measure.

3. At what time points should assessment be made and how often should measurements be made? Should evaluations continue after the treatment is finished? If so, for how long? Should dropouts be censored?

4. Should results be adjusted using baseline scores on the instrument?

5. Should the observer and the patient be blinded as to treatment and whether or not there has been an objective response to treatment?

6. How much training of the patient and observer is necessary? What quality control measures of documentation should be used?

7. Should non-English-speaking patients be included? Is there a culturally relevant non-English questionnaire available?

MODES OF ADMINISTRATION

The strengths and weaknesses of the different modes of administration are summarized in Table 1.3. HRQOL questionnaires are either administered by trained interviewers or self-administered. The former method is resource intensive but ensures compliance and minimizes errors and missing items. The latter approach is much less expensive but increases the number of missing responses. A compromise between the two approaches is to have the instrument completed under supervision. Another compromise is the telephone interview, which minimizes errors and missing data but dictates a relatively simple questionnaire structure. Investigators have conducted initial experiments with computer administration of HRQOL measures, but this is not yet a common method of questionnaire administration.

TABLE 1.3 *Modes of administration of HRQOL measures*

Mode of administration	Strengths	Weaknesses
Interviewer-administered	Maximize response rate Few, if any, missing items Minimize errors of misunderstanding	Requires many resources, training of interviewers May reduce willingness to acknowledge problems
Telephone-administered	Few, if any, missing items Minimize errors of misunderstanding Less resource intensive than interviewer-administered	Limits format of instrument
Self-administered	Minimal resources required	Greater likelihood of low response rate, missing items, misunderstanding
Surrogate responders	Reduces stress for target group (very elderly or sick) Can include patients unable to respond for themselves (cognitively impaired, children, language barriers)	Perceptions of surrogate may differ from target group

Investigators may often consider using a surrogate respondent to predict results that one would get from the patient himself/herself. For instance, use of surrogate responses does not correspond to what patients would have said had they been capable of answering. In one trial of terminally ill patients and surrogates, large differences in responses demonstrated that surrogates cannot substitute for patients' responses (43). These results are consistent with other evaluations of ratings by patients and proxies. In general, the correspondence between respondent and proxy response to HRQOL measures varies, depending on the domain assessed and the choice of proxy. As might be expected, proxy reports of more observable domains, such as physical functioning and cognition, are more highly correlated with reports from the patients themselves. For functional limitations, proxy respondents tend to consider patients more impaired, i.e., overestimate patient dysfunction relative to the patients themselves (44). For other sorts of morbidity, patients tend to report the most problems, followed by close relatives, and clinicians the least. These findings have important clinical implications in that they suggest that clinicians should concentrate on careful ascertainment of the reported behaviors and perceptions of patients themselves, limiting the inferences they make on the basis of the perceptions of the caregivers.

Choosing the appropriate approach to the use of HRQOL measures will determine the accuracy of the conclusions obtained after clinical trial is completed. Defining the precise goal of the trial, and determining the relative merits of existing instruments should be done before a questionnaire is chosen. Investigators can access a large number of "proven" instruments, or refer to guidelines for construction of new, specific instruments.

Many of the problems associated with comparing people of different social, economic, and cultural milieus are circumvented when change in score within patients becomes the focus of the examination. Questionnaires can be designed to use patients as their own internal controls, without norms. With this approach, the critical quality of life value is not the score a patient provides, but rather the change in that patient's score over time. In other words, when making comparisons of groups of patients, the central issue is not whether the overall score in one group is better than the other, but rather whether the change in scores observed over time is different in each group. However, to employ this approach, timing of the initial quality of life assessment is critical. Insofar as it is possible, this first assessment must be done at the same time in the natural history of the investigation and treatment of the disease in every patient. Otherwise the baseline against which all comparisons are made will be inconsistent and the trial less evaluable. In clinical medicine, the ultimate observer of the experiment is not a dispassionate third party but a most intimately involved patient. There are real links between basic physiological function and the broader psychosocial issues that are encompassed in the quality of life paradigm. To a certain extent, what the psychosocial measure may lack in precision, it may compensate for in relevance.

Duration of the Follow-up Period

Although pharmacological effects might be distinguished almost immediately, it generally takes a much longer time before the patients themselves perceive the full benefits of treatment in terms of improved well-being and ability to enjoy day-to-day activities. Similarly, negative effects could occur during the first few weeks, whereas important differences may not appear until months later. A period of at least 3 months, and preferably 6 months, is recommended in clinical trials of chronic disease. Unless a sufficiently long follow-up period is allowed, the results may indicate no clear distinction between two different treatments, despite the fact that differences do exist.

Frequency of Assessments

In most cases, one assessment at randomization, and one at the end of the trial, are adequate, provided that all patients who discontinue the trial prematurely fill in a final set of the quality of life questionnaires at the time of discontinuation. Whether the quality of life assessments should be repeated during the course of the trial depends on whether there is need to explore how soon changes can be observed, and if they are transient or not. Repeated measurements could be used to clarify if, and when, patients become adapted to side effects. Typically, trial results seem to be reported in terms of changes from baseline to end of treatment, leaving the intermediate results unreported, even if quality of life has been measured as often as twice a month. It is desirable to report some information on the results of repeated measurements during a trial. Moreover, factors such as multiplicity problems and the risk of overburdening patients should be balanced against how often assessments should be repeated.

Sample Size Estimates

Many quality of life studies have lacked the sensitivity and power to identify treatment effects. Since it is part of the nature of well-being and subjective perceptions that they should vary considerably, the sample sizes required for quality of life data may be larger than for the clinical variables. Sample size calculations using data from previous quality of life studies should be performed prior to the start of the trial in the same way as is standard for all clinical efficacy outcomes. If the expected differences between treatments are small, even larger samples must be included. For example, in studies evaluating the effect of drug therapy on quality of life in hypertension, sample sizes exceeding 200 patients per treatment group are generally needed.

Is Standardized Measurement of Quality of Life Necessary?

Studies have shown that measurement of quality of life is necessary if clinicians are to be made aware of the effects of illness on patients' daily lives. Even experienced clinicians markedly underestimate or overestimate some aspects of function for many of their patients (45). Some patients mask or understate their disabilities or feel reticent about discussing them with physicians. Some patients who appear disabled can actually perform all important daily activities. Quality of life cannot be inferred from appearances; systematic screening seems to be required.

Who Should Be Evaluated for Quality of Life?

Because most medical interventions for improving quality of life involve treatment or palliation of impairments and disabilities, quality of life screening is particularly useful for evaluating individuals with poor functioning or who are at risk of functional deterioration. This includes elderly individuals, people with chronic diseases, and people who present with signs or symptoms of worsening disease or worsening functioning. Community-based screening of home-dwelling elderly individuals, followed by appropriate referrals, has reduced disability and mortality (46). Screening of hospitalized elderly patients for whom nursing home placement is contemplated, followed by geriatric assessment, has also reduced mortality (47). Screening of elderly individuals who have fallen has resulted in reduced hospitalization (48).

There is less evidence that quality of life screening of general medical populations is successful. Several studies have evaluated the effects of providing physicians in practice with information on the functional status of their ambulatory patients, and none of these has been successful in improving physical function (49–51). There is some evidence that mental health and social activities can be improved when feedback to physicians includes resource and management suggestions in addition to functional status results (52). In relatively healthy, younger clinic populations, typical of health maintenance organizations, symptoms of anxiety or depression are the most common quality of life deficits. There is little evidence that measuring quality of life, other than possibly measuring depressive symptoms, improves outcomes in low-risk populations, even when accompanied by resource and management suggestions.

Advantages and Disadvantages of Surveys, Performance-Based Measures and Direct Observation for Clinical Care

Surveys gather data by asking standardized questions and recording responses in a structured format. Performance-based measures gather data by asking people to perform structured tasks and judging their performance based on preset criteria. Direct observation of daily life uses timed sampling by trained observers or videotaping to document behaviors and activities. Each has advantages and disadvantages. For example, direct observation is impractical for most purposes, except perhaps for patients in nursing homes. Performance measures can be more precise than either surveys or direct observation in localizing and quantitating specific impairments and disabilities. For example, a survey may indicate that an individual has difficulty with household chores, but a performance-based measure may be necessary to establish that upper arm reach and hand grip are the key causes of this difficulty. Surveys can ask patients about the causes of their disabilities, but the information patients can provide reliably may not be specific enough to use for medical management purposes. On the other hand, compared with performance-based measures, surveys have the advantages of summarizing daily functioning outside the clinic rather than in an artificial situation, such as a doctor's or physical therapist's office; even if the performance test is carried out at home, test results may not reflect what the individual usually does on his/her own. Surveys generally require less data collector training than do performance-based tests, and cost less to administer. In addition, surveys can measure emotional and social aspects of quality of life, whereas performance-based measures are limited to measuring physical functions and impairments.

Rather than using one type of test, clinicians can benefit from becoming familiar with a variety of types of tests. Performance-based measures—in conjunction with surveys, clinical history, physical examination, and laboratory tests—may be very useful in identifying the causes of disabilities and impairments. For example, a normal result on performance-based evaluation of gait and balance in an individual who has difficulty walking one block might indicate that the problem is less likely to be neurological, muscular, or skeletal but more likely to be due to cardiovascular or pulmonary disease. Such suspicions can be confirmed using standard clinical diagnostic techniques. Although the ability to function better at home or in the community is a more definitive outcome of care than is the ability to perform better on a test, performance-based measures may have advantages as intermediate outcomes for interventions to improve physical functioning. For example, it may be useful to know that physical therapy succeeded in reducing the amount of time it took an individual to walk 50 feet (50-foot walk time), even though this reduction did not result in improved functioning at home. Finally, performance-based measures may be useful in confirming or identifying disability in high-risk populations. For example, hospitalized patients may have difficulty answering many survey questions, since standard quality of life surveys often refer to performance of activities that are not applicable to hospital life or to a time frame (e.g., one month) during which the individual has experienced major changes in functioning. Patients with language barriers or mental impairment may be unable to answer surveys, or may answer them inaccurately. Patients with severe disability may fall below the range within which survey instruments can distinguish levels of disability, yet they may be amenable to clinical intervention. Use of performance-based measures can ameliorate these detection problems.

ROUTINE EVALUATION OF QUALITY OF LIFE IN OFFICE PRACTICE

Table 1.4 depicts a strategy for incorporating routine and symptom-responsive or symptom-triggered screening into office practice: the types of patients to consider for screening, what types of measures might be most appropriate given the patient's characteristics, and examples of measurement tools to consider. The specific tools we suggest are only examples.

The first type of patient to consider for screening is the adult under age 65 years who does not have known chronic disease(s). In such individuals, an impaired sense of mental well-being, such as occurs with anxiety and depression, is a common cause of reduced quality of life (50). Very brief screens, such as a three-question lifetime depression measure (54), can indicate depression risk; individuals who are at risk can be further evaluated. The five-item Mental Health Index (55) is a complete component scale of two brief comprehensive health status measures [the Functional Status Questionnaire (56) and the RAND/Medical Outcome Study Short Form 36, or SF-36 (57)]. The General Health Questionnaire (53) is longer, but has been used extensively in primary care practices. Social and role function impairments are also relatively common. Social and role function scales are brief, complete component scales of the SF-36, and can be used to screen for these problems (57). An alternative strategy to screening for well-being and social and role function would be to use a brief, comprehensive health status measure like the SF-36 or COOP Charts (51,58), but this strategy would require more patient time for test taking (e.g., 10 minutes) and clinician time to interpret.

In adults under 65 years of age with chronic diseases, physical functioning deficits are more likely than among those without chronic diseases. The brief, comprehensive screens listed in Table 1.4 for this group of patients cover multiple domains of functioning, including physical functioning, and take 5 to 30 minutes to complete. Individuals with poor reading skills or less education may require assistance or encouragement to complete these screens.

Healthy adults 65 years of age or older can, in general, be screened similarly to the under 65 and chronically ill group. It should be remembered that mental status assessment and incontinence/toileting are omitted from the brief, comprehensive measures, and may need to be addressed separately. Addition of the Get Up and Go test (59,60) to the evaluation ensures that the clinician will pay particular attention to walking ability, since gait disorders are common in this group and may be detectable on clinical examination before they have marked effects on functioning in daily life.

Adults 65 years of age and older who have chronic diseases require a greater focus on physical functioning and need for assistance than do other groups. The approach of using brief, comprehensive measures could be considered, particularly among those with a lower burden of disease. Most geriatric groups, however, who work with a more disabled elderly group of patients, rely on measures such as the Katz Activities of Daily Living (ADLs) (61) and the Lawton-Brody Instrumental Activities of Daily Living (IADLs) (62). These instruments focus on the kinds of activities that are necessary for independent living (IADLs) or for living without 24-hour care (ADLs). Use of these measures alone, however, omits consideration of depression, mental status impairment, social or role functioning, and pain, all of which can be critical in this type of patient.

The final six categories in the table illustrate the use of quality of life measurement for evaluation of signs and symptoms. Technically, this kind of use of the measures is not screening at all, but rather part of the workup of identified problems. Individuals who are hospitalized, require more assistance at home, are admitted to a nursing home, fall, or have signs or symptoms of depression require immediate evaluation of quality of life, followed by assessment and management as depicted in Fig. 1.7. For many nursing home patients, the Minimum Data Set (MDS) (63) must be administered on admission and every 6 months as required by law. The information contained in the MDS includes data on functional status, mood, and other quality of life issues. Patients with chronic diseases who are facing therapeutic choices, such as arthritis patients scheduled to receive gold or patients whose diseases are rapidly evolving, may benefit from disease-specific screening using instruments such as those listed in the table for adults requiring close monitoring for chronic disease. Individuals who were screened routinely and were found to have disabilities such as depression, falls, or difficulty walking fall into the category of patients requiring evaluation for

TABLE 1.4 *Recommendations for incorporating routine and symptom-responsive quality of life screening into office practice*

Patient type and screening activity	Types of screening quality of life measures to use and examples of measurement tools					
	Brief, comprehensive health status measures	Depression, anxiety, well-being, and mental status	Physical functioning and independence measures	Social activities, social support, and role function measures	Disease or impairment specific measures
Outline screening					
1. Adult *under 65 years* and healthy: screen every 3 years	—	5-item Mental Health Index (55) Lifetime depression screen (54) General Health Questionnaire (53)	—	RAND/Medical Outcome Study Role Function (57)	— —
2. Adult *under 65 years* and chronically ill: screen every year	RAND/Medical Outcome Sickness Impact Profile Study Short Form Beth Israel/UCLA Functional Status Questionnaire (56) Nottingham Health Profile McMaster Health Index Quality of Well-Being COOP Charts (51,58)	—	—	—	—
3. Adult *65 years or over* and healthy: screen every year	Use *same* measurement tools as for adults 65 years or over and chronically ill	—	Get Up and Go (59,60)	—	—
4. Adult *65 years or over* and chronically ill: screen every year	—	CES-D Hamilton Yesavage Zung SDS Folstein Mini Mental State	Ktaz Basic Activities of Daily Living (61) Lawton/Brody Instrumental Activities of Daily Living (62) Barthel Index	Beth Israel/UCLA Social Activities (56) MOS Social Support and Role Functioning (57) Sarasan Social Support Questionnaire	McGill Pain Questionnaire (55) MOS Pain Measure (55)
Triggered screening					
5. Adult *65 years or over* and hospitalized: screen during admission and in 6 months	—	Use *same* measurement tools as for adults 65 years or over and chronically ill	Use *same* measurement tools as for adults 65 years or over and chronically ill	—	Use *same* measurement tools as for adults 65 years or over and chronically ill

TABLE 1.4 *Continued*

	Types of screening quality of life measures to use and examples of measurement tools				
Patient type and screening activity	Brief, comprehensive health status measures	Depression, anxiety, well-being, and mental status	Physical functioning and independence measures	Social activities, social support, and role function measures	Disease or impairment specific measures
6. *Adult* admitted to a nursing home: screen on admission and every 6 months thereafter	MDS(63)	—	—	—	—
7. *Adult* with increased need for assistance: screen urgently and in 6 months	—	Use *same* measurement tools as for adults 65 years or over and chronically ill	Use *same* measurement tools as for adults 65 years or over and chronically ill	—	Use *same* measurement tools as for adults 65 years or over and chronically ill
8. *Adult* requiring close monitoring for chronic disease: screen every 3–6 months with *either* disease—specific or brief, comprehensive measure	—	—	—	—	Arthritis Impact Measurement Scale (AIMS) Spitzer Quality of Life Index
9. *Adult*, falling or with difficulty walking: screen urgently	—	—	Use *same* measurement tools as for adults 65 years or over and chronically ill	—	Tinetti balance and gait evaluation
10. *Adult* with signs or symptoms of depression: screen urgently	If under 65 years use *same* measurement tools as for adults under 65 years and chronically ill	CES-D Beck Depression Inventory Hamilton A Hamilton D	If over 65 years use *same* measurement tools as for adults 65 years or over and chronically ill	—	—

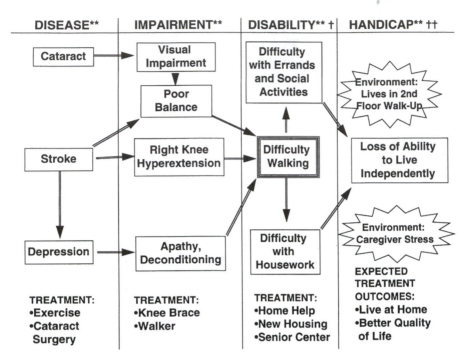

FIG. 1.7. A clinical assessment and management map of the results of a quality of life assessment. This map shows the results of assessment of quality of life impairments detected on screening of an elderly man. Assessment involved a physician interview and examination, as well as laboratory testing and examinations by a physical therapist, an occupational therapist, and a social worker. Assessment identifies the highest priority quality of life deficits and their clinical etiologies. The column headings indicate the type of information listed below them. For example, column 1 lists three diseases that are responsible for significant functional impairment in this patient—cataract, stroke, and depression. At the bottom of each column are listed the management plans that the physician and interdisciplinary team will implement to improve quality of life. Management is directed at diseases, impairment, disabilities, and handicaps.

—In this column, difficulty walking is indicated as the key disability from which the patient's other problems stem. The physician believes that if the patient s mobility can be improved, many of his other problems would be ameliorated.

—In this column, the result of the patient's disability that requires most attention is his ability to live independently (role functioning). Because of his social and environmental circumstances, the patient's difficulty walking is threatening to force him to move into a protected environment such as a nursing home. The physician thinks that nursing home placement is not necessary if treatment of the patient's disease, impairment, disability, and handicap are undertaken along with some later environmental modifiers (e.g., moving to the first floor). The remaining environmental stressor is his wife's level of caregiver stress, which can be expected to improve as the patient becomes more mobile. The expected outcome toward which management is directed is, therefore, maintaining independent living status.

specific signs and symptoms. Once basic screening is complete, patients found to have disabilities can be assessed using standard clinical methods. By using standard instruments as the basis for assessment, clinicians can take advantage of reliable and valid measures to identify problems, and focus on carrying out assessment and management activities that will maximize quality of life.

Barriers to Clinical Evaluation of Quality of Life

It is important to acknowledge that, although quality of life assessment is non-invasive and well accepted by patients, it is not without a price. Patients, families, and nonphysician medical personnel can administer questionnaires at relatively low cost. Expert time is required, however, to interpret the results and to use them to actually improve health. Most quality of life instruments require scoring either by hand or by computer. Physicians may need to spend extra, non-reimbursed cognitive time assessing quality of life deficits. Physicians may also lack the skills, particularly in terms of the musculoskeletal and neurological examinations, to assess impairments adequately. Finally, successful management of disabilities may depend upon the availability of an interdisciplinary team.

Recommendations

1. Clinicians should become more aware of the quality of life effects of diseases and their treatments through systematic quality of life screening.
2. Younger patients generally require routine screening for mental health and social or role functioning; older individuals (over 65 years of age) and those with chronic diseases require more comprehensive screening on a routine basis.
3. All patients consulting with clinicians for signs or symptoms of new or worsening disabilities, including patients considering nursing home placement, require comprehensive screening for quality of life deficits, followed by clinical assessment that identifies the key diseases, impairments, disabilities, and handicaps that are worsening the patient's quality of life.
4. Comprehensive clinical management plans for elderly patients with severe or worsening disability should be developed and implemented with input from all key members of the interdisciplinary team.

AN INDUSTRY PERSPECTIVE

Why Conduct Quality of Life Studies?

Five general reasons support the conduct of quality of life studies. Each of these reasons has important commercial implications for the company, and several reasons have important medical implications for physicians who prescribe medicines and for patients who take them.

First, improved quality of life benefits over traditional therapies may assist regulatory strategies. For example, the data may increase the pressure within regulatory agencies in some countries for a medicine to be approved more rapidly. In some cases, a new medicine or a new indication for a marketed medicine may be approved based primarily or secondarily on quality of life data. These data may enable medicines to be differentiated that are otherwise similar in terms of conventional efficacy and safety parameters. Quality of life studies may also be used to modify and improve the labeling of a marketed medicine.

Second, quality of life studies can assist in pricing products. If a company can demonstrate increased quality of life benefits to patients with a new medicine, they may charge patients more than for existing medicines and still maintain the same or better cost-to-benefit relationship. These data are, therefore, important in addition to pharmacoeconomic data.

Third, quality of life studies provide customers with complete product information. Advertising and other promotional vehicles as well as professional publications are important for disseminating information to customers. The degree to which these efforts are pursued depends on the company's culture and goals. Advances in life-prolonging technologies and increased public awareness of quality of life issues are focusing public attention on the risks as well as benefits of medicines. If an anticancer medicine prolongs the life of a patient who is severely ill but reduces his/her quality of life, what is the medical, economic, or societal wisdom for its use? This major ethical question is being discussed without adequate information about the effects of most medicine regimens on quality of life. This inadequacy must be addressed by the pharmaceutical industry to protect the future of its medicines.

Fourth, quality of life considerations help determine which types of information are most useful for specific audiences (e.g., to obtain formulary acceptance for a medicine). This information can be used to design appropriate pre- or post-marketing studies to evaluate the medicine.

Finally, in situations of therapeutic substitution, quality of life evaluations might show differences that help a company counter substitution practices. Differences might be as subtle as taste distinctions that lead to decreased patient compliance with the other medicine or as obvious as decreased medical benefits with other medicines. Quality of life trials should be used to evaluate possible differences.

As the economics of health care delivery have changed and cost-containment issues have become dominant, a more competitive marketplace has been created. Hospitals, health maintenance organizations, government programs, and some traditional insurance programs have established restricted formularies to control dispensing patterns. A restrictive formulary limits the number of medicines available for physicians to use for the same condition. Absence of a medicine from a formulary limits its sale. Placement on many formularies requires additional information beyond the usual efficacy and safety data available for a medicine. Quality of life information becomes an important marketing tool to help medicines achieve formulary approval and, thus, enhance sales. An improved product profile obtained through quality of life advantages provides the competitive advantage that marketing constantly seeks.

Information developed independently of a specific customer's needs may make it much more difficult to convince that customer to use the medicine. For example, marketing groups usually respond to specific needs of health marketing organizations, hospitals, and other providers, whose decisions may be influenced by quality of life data. Quality of life trials that include these provider groups as research sites will make the results of the trial more compelling to those groups.

How May Quality of Life Data Be Used in Marketing?

Quality of life trials can provide information to help a company determine a marketing strategy and establish the comparative advantage of one product over another. Information obtained in quality of life trials can help select the niche in which a medicine should compete. Data from such trials can help determine which attributes of a product to emphasize in positioning the product. Lastly, the data obtained can address the question of how to approach the different customers that marketing must reach.

Quality of life trials can provide information to enhance the medicine's efficacy and safety profile. These additional data allow a better comparison of a medicine's benefits (efficacy) to risks (adverse reactions) than using efficacy and safety data alone. These trials may demonstrate important advantages of one product over another in terms of benefits viewed by patients. Benefits might include aspects of psychological well-being (e.g., reduced worry, increased happiness), improved physical status (e.g., greater comfort), and increased social interactions.

How Will Data Obtained in Trials Be Used?

Among today's customers for the products of the pharmaceutical industry are those who make economic decisions affecting medical care. These groups include national, state or provincial, and local governments; managed care systems (including health maintenance and preferred provider organizations); buying groups; and insurance companies. These groups are using numerous mechanisms to control medical practice through controlling expenditures. The ability to demonstrate improved quality of life or cost savings versus another therapy increases the probability that these agencies will encourage the product's use.

Medical and marketing goals are not necessarily the same. To be successful, marketing must respond to the needs of its various audiences. Marketers would like information about a medicine that is individualized to specific customers (e.g., health maintenance organizations or state Medicaid programs). On the other hand, medical groups want to define the profile of a medicine that will be used by all of marketing's audiences.

A Marketing Perspective

Quality of life data are still relatively new to marketing, and how these data will be used to characterize products is still evolving. It is possible to describe three ways in which marketers have used, are currently using, or may use quality of life measurement in the future.

Category 1: A Better Product

The Food and Drug Administration (FDA) objects to the misuse of quality of life claims, especially claims that communicated therapeutic benefits that were not consistent with the therapeutic effects of the advertised products. Some manufacturers advertised that their drug "improved" quality of life when the data indicated that the drug merely had a less disruptive side effect profile. Those data would support claims that the drug "maintained" quality of life, but they would not support claims of improvement. Generally, the FDA has objected to vague and overly broad claims of quality of life. Drug marketers have responded by narrowing quality of life claims by adding qualifying language.

The usefulness of broad quality of life claims has decreased as competitors have made similar broad claims and as the FDA has begun to require greater substantiation. A once-differentiated product becomes undifferentiated as the competition begins to make identical or highly similar claims. The trend toward more specific quality of life claims has already begun, with claims being based on individual domains, such as mobility, cognitive processes, and dexterity. The trend is important because overuse of unqualified quality of life claims would likely lead to trivialization of the quality of life concept and would diminish its value in signifying unique product benefits. If these broad claims are reserved for marketers who have demonstrated real quality of life benefits, a quality of life claim can remain an important "signal" to prescribers about patient benefits of pharmaceutical products.

For institutional purchasing, the use of quality of life data integrated into cost-effectiveness analyses may serve as an indicator of the value of individual products. To the extent that institutions selecting therapies utilize measures of economic value over the long course of treatment, quality of life measures can help provide insight into the effects of therapy as moderated by patients' "utilities" for the general health states that result from treatment.

The use of quality of life data in pharmacoeconomic analyses is also important to the pharmaceutical industry. With the large increase in institutional purchasing and the increase in the power of formularies to control product selection, pharmaceutical companies are being increasingly asked by purchasing and approving boards to justify their product's selection. These institutional decision makers can determine whether large segments of the population will have access to particular drugs. Marketers are asked to demonstrate the superiority of their products or to justify charged prices. Quality of life research may be one way to help do this.

In clinical trials of pharmaceutical products, quality of life is being used increasingly as a therapeutic endpoint, particularly for diseases that are not associated with severe symptoms or disability. Quality of life studies may assist the industry in the regulatory approval process by supporting the primary efficacy outcome. Although the FDA does not currently require quality of life data to be provided during the drug approval process, data on drug effects on quality of life are included as a secondary endpoint in many new drug applications submitted to the FDA. In clinical practice, information on quality of life outcomes given to physicians and health care managers may facilitate decision making about alternative drug therapy. Similarly, the gains of treatment with regard to quality of life, in addition to the possibility of months or years of added survival, are particularly appealing to patients with asymptomatic disorders receiving preventive therapy, because treatment is typically initiated at an early age, is lifelong, and may induce side effects.

Quality of life outcomes are also being used in questions concerning the pricing of, and reimbursement for, new pharmaceutical entities. Quality of life data added to the efficacy and safety data may enhance the profile of one product by showing its advantages over another and may also help justify its market price. Quality of life advantages have long been used as an important marketing tool, for drugs which are in heavy competition. Among the many requirements of an ideal preventive therapy is that it is cost effective to the society by reducing morbidity and mortality in diseases. Quality of life measures can be used as independent indicators of health outcomes for cost-effectiveness analysis, or they can be combined with survival to produce quality-adjusted life-years (QALYs) for cost/utility analysis. Costs are also a key issue for many patients and may influence compliance, as suggested by the results of a study in which patients with uncontrolled blood pressure tended to have a lower income than that of subjects whose blood pressure was well controlled (64).

Category 2: A Different Product

As quality of life measurement becomes more psychometrically sophisticated, it is possible that marketers could utilize the information from quality of life studies to differentiate their products. The multidimensionality of psychometrically based quality of life measurement suggests the potential for new benefits to be discovered and new claims to be made. As long as promotional materials are truthful and fairly balanced, marketers could selectively emphasize certain quality of life scale outcomes where a particular product outperforms others. Thus, if a product performs better on a cognitive functioning scale than competing products but is no different on other scales, the marketer could use cognitive functioning as a major positioning variable. Promotional materials could be geared to emphasize cognitive functioning (e.g., a theme of "when alertness counts" might be used) and pictures of patients in tasks requiring alertness can be shown (e.g., an air traffic controller). A competitor whose product is outperformed on the cognitive functioning scale but which performs better on a physical functioning scale would logically emphasize this advantage when positioning the product. The promotional materials for this product might emphasize physical performance (e.g., when "endurance" counts) and display pictures of patients in tasks or roles requiring physical stamina (e.g., a firefighter). Not only would promotion be geared to reinforce this positioning, but the name of the product and any collateral materials developed (e.g., patient education materials, desktop media), public relations efforts, and associated activities could emphasize this theme.

When selecting drug therapy, the prescriber must decide which product is best for each patient. Given an equivalence of medical and diagnostic criteria, if plausible, the prescriber might attempt to match the quality of life theme emphasized for the drug to the prescriber's perception of the importance of the theme to the individual patient. The extent to which quality of life data are used as part of the prescriber's evaluation criteria when selecting drug products is unclear. Studies of physician prescribing indicate that efficacy, side effects, and cost are the most important criteria influencing selection of drug products (65,66). However, these studies may be dated, and the use of quality of life data in prescribers' decisions regarding drug product selection has not been adequately addressed in the scientific literature.

A more likely interpretation of the value of quality of life claims in advertising is that these claims do not represent wholly new claims for product performance. Nonetheless, as prescribers become more interested in satisfying their patients, they may perceive quality of life claims as indicative of the effects of drugs on patients' life style and performance. Thus, quality of life information may not be perceived as a unique contribution to drug effects assessment, but as a means of translating physiological effects to patient performance measures.

Category 3: A Basis for Patient Segmentation

Even if the prescriber is aware of the advantages of different therapies, how is the prescriber to know which therapy an individual patient would prefer? There are three possible ways for the prescriber to learn about a patient's preferences and use that information as a basis for decision making.

First, the prescriber could make a determination about patient preferences based on gross observations of the patient, background data in the chart, and as the result of simple questions posed to the patient about life style and preferred activities. Using this approach, the prescriber can make broad assumptions based on general characteristics of the patient. Thus, a prescriber may presume that cognitive functioning is important for a college professor, whereas physical performance is important for a laborer. Gross observation of the patient and simple, indirect questions may not provide enough information for the prescriber to reach a valid conclusion about patient preferences. In addition, there is no guarantee that the prescriber's perceptions are representative of the patient's. A laborer may value cognitive functioning (e.g., alertness) more than physical function (e.g., ambulation), whereas a college professor may hold the opposite set of values.

Formal quality of life assessment may provide a more objective and complete set of parameters on which to evaluate outcomes. Second, the prescriber could integrate the quality of life preferences of the patient into clinical decision making by questioning the patient in depth and soliciting feedback along a number of critical dimensions. This is the optimum solution to the problem of how to build patient utilities into the process. Unfortunately, the prospect of soliciting and obtaining such precise feedback is likely to require enormous time and patience by the prescriber (67). There may be a large number of quality of life variables measured, and the prescriber would have to discuss all potential quality of life outcomes, or at least those on which therapies differed significantly. The prescriber would have to guard against framing effects (68) and other sources of bias, to ensure that the patient's stated preferences were forthright and reflective of personal values.

Quality of life data have the potential for helping pharmaceutical marketers to describe their products along dimensions that are meaningful to the patient. In addition to justifying the benefits of different medication to institutional purchasers and decision makers, quality of life data could help makers of pharmaceutical products be more responsive to the needs of the ultimate users of their products. For quality of life to exert its most profound effects, however, data from quality of life studies need to be part of the decision making process underlying therapeutic choice. We are only beginning to learn how to incorporate quality of life data into these decisions and much theoretical and empirical work lies ahead.

USE OF QUALITY OF LIFE DATA BY REGULATORY AGENCIES

Quality of life measurements are potentially important endpoints for clinical trials with anticancer agents. The design of these measurements for use in pivotal trials is critically important. In 1985, Temple (69) proposed that more attention be paid to resolution of unequivocal cancer symptoms (pain over involved bone, extreme anorexia, decreased pulmonary function) as potential endpoints that might be used to demonstrate clinical benefit even when response rates are low. Wittes (70) further proposed that if such symptoms and signs (elements relevant to quality of life) could be shown to improve, then nonrandomized Phase II trials could be persuasive in determining the benefit of an investigational agent. These controlled Phase II trials would probably be larger and more complex than conventional Phase II trials. It would be particularly important to include patients with unequivocal disease-related symptoms or signs at the start of therapy and to specify exactly how changes in these would be measured at various intervals throughout the course of treatment.

Appropriate Utilization of HRQOL Assessments in Clinical Trials

When HRQOL evaluations are considered for clinical trials, they should be an integral component of the research question (i.e., objectives), and not an appended companion evaluation. There should be a trial hypothesis companion and an expectation that the HRQOL instrument will provide information that is additive to the traditional drug development objectives. The instruments chosen should be selected to answer a specific research question that cannot be answered with simple performance status or traditional toxicity ratings. Many other issues discussed in this book have regulatory implications. It is up to the regulators to judge the standards used and the quality of the data obtained for HRQOL in clinical trials.

REFERENCES

1. National Center for Health Statistics (1973–91). Current estimates from the National Health Interview Survey: United States. Vital and health statistics. Washington, DC: U.S. Government Printing Office.
2. Stewart AL, Ware JE. *Functioning and well-being: the Medical Outcome Study approach.* Durham, NC: Duke University Press, 1992.
3. Jacobson AM, Barofsky I, Cleary P, Rand L (DCCT Writing Committee). A diabetes quality of life measure: preliminary study of its reliability and validity. *Diabetes Care* 1988;11:725–732.
4. Slevin MR, Plant H, Lynch D, Drinkwater J, Gregory WM. Who should measure quality of life, the doctor or the patient? *Br J Cancer* 1988;57:109–112.
5. Spilker B, Molinek FR, Johnston KA, Simpson RL, Tilson HH. Quality of life bibliography and indexes. *Med Care* 1990;28(suppl 12):DS1–DS77.
6. Spilker B, Simpson RL, Tilson HH. Quality of life bibliography and indexes: 1990 update. *J Clin Res Pharmacoepidemiol* 1992;6:87–156.
7. Spilker B, Simpson RL Jr, Tilson HH. Quality of life bibliography and indexes: 1991 update. *J Clin Res Pharmacoepidemiol* 1992;6:205–266.
8. Berzon RA, Simeon GP, Simpson RL, Tilson HH. Quality of life bibliography and indexes: 1992 update. *J Clin Res Drug Devel* 1993;7:203–242.
9. Berzon RA, Simeon GP, Simpson RL, Donnelly MA. Quality of life bibliography and indexes: 1993 update. *Qual Life Res* 1994;4:53–74.
10. Berzon RA, Donnelley MA, Simpson RL, Simeon GP, Tilson HH. Quality of life bibliography and indexes: 1994 update. *Qual Life Res* 1995;4:547–569.
11. Kleinman A. Culture, the quality of life and cancer pain: anthropological and cross-cultural perspectives. In: Ventafridda V, ed. *Assessment of quality of life and cancer treatment.* Excerpt Medica International Congress Series 702. Amsterdam: Elsevier, 1986;43–50.
12. Ware JE Jr. Conceptualizing disease impact and treatment outcomes. *Cancer* 1984;53:2316–2323.

13. Calman KC. Quality of life in cancer patients—an hypothesis. *J Med Ethics* 1984;10:124–127.

14. Schipper H, Clinch J, McMurray A, Levitt M. Measuring the quality of life of cancer patients: the functional living index—cancer: development and validation. *J Clin Oncol* 1984;2:472–483.

15. Morris JN, Sherwood S. Quality of life of cancer patients at different stages in the disease trajectory. *J Chronic Dis* 1987;40:545–556.

16. Mor V. Cancer patients' quality of life over the disease course: lessons from the real world. *J Chronic Dis* 1987;40:535–544.

17. Lasry JM, Margolese RG, Poisson R. Depression and body image following mastectomy and lumpectomy. *J Chronic Dis* 1987;40:529–534.

18. Harman HH. *Modern factor analysis,* 3rd ed. Chicago: University of Chicago Press, 1976.

19. McGee HM, O'Boyle CA, Hickey A, O'Malley K, Joyce CR. Assessing the quality of life of the individual: the SEIQOL with a healthy and a gastroenterology unit population. *Psychol Med* 1991;21: 749–759.

20. Brown BP, O'Boyle CA, McGee H, et al. Individual quality of life in the healthy elderly. *Qual Life Res* 1994;4:235–244.

21. White KL. Improved medical care: statistics and the health service system. *Public Health Rep* 1967; 82:847–854.

22. McNeil BJ, Pauker SG, Sox HC, Tversky A. On the elicitation of preferences for alternative therapies. *N Engl J Med* 1982;306:1259–1262.

23. Lorig K, Cox T, Cuevas Y, et al. Converging and diverging beliefs about arthritis: Caucasian patients, Spanish-speaking patients and physicians. *J Rheumatol* 1984;11:76–79.

24. Sox HC, Blatt MA, Higgin MC, Marton KI. *Medical decision making.* London: Butterworths, 1988.

25. Moskowitz AJ, Kuipers B, Kassirer JP. Academia and clinic: dealing with uncertainty, risks, and tradeoffs in clinical decisions: a cognitive science approach. *Ann Intern Med* 1988;108:435–449.

26. Lorig K, Cox T, Cuevas Y, Kraines GH, Britton MC. Converging and diverging beliefs about arthritis: Caucasian patients, Spanish-speaking patients and physicians. *J Rheumatol* 1984;11:76–79.

27. Potts M, Mazzuca S, Brandt K. Views of patients and physicians regarding the importance of various aspects of arthritis treatment. Correlations with health status and patient satisfaction. *Patient Educ Couns* 1986;8:125–134.

28. Fries JF, Spitz PW, Kraines RG, Holman HR. Measurement of patient outcome in arthritis. *Arthritis Rheum* 1980;23:137–145.

29. Kirk RE. *Experimental design: procedures for the behavioral sciences.* Belmont, California: Brooks/Cole, 1968.

30. Nunnally JC. *Psychometric theory.* New York: McGraw-Hill, 1967.

31. Bindman AB, Keane D, Lurie N. Measuring health changes among severely ill patients. *Med Care* 1990;28:1142–1152.

32. Ganiats TG, Palinkas LA, Kaplan RM. Comparison of Well-Being Scale and Functional Status Index in patients with atrial fibrillation. *Med Care* 1992;30:958–964.

33. Feinstein AR. *Clinimetrics.* New Haven, CT: Yale University Press, 1987:141–166.

34. Oxman A, Guyatt GH. Validation of an index of the quality of review articles. *J Clin Epidemiol* 1991; 44:1271–1278.

35. Guyatt GH, Berman LB, Townsend M, Pugsley SO, Chambers LW. A measure of quality of life for clinical trials in chronic lung disease. *Thorax* 1987;42:773–778.

36. Guyatt GH, Feeny D, Patrick D. Proceedings of the International Conference on the Measurement of Quality of Life as an Outcome in Clinical Trials: Postscript. *Controlled Clin Trials* 1991;12: 266S–269S.

37. Jaeschke R, Guyatt G, Keller J, Singer J. Measurement of health status: ascertaining the meaning of a change in quality-of-life questionnaire score. *Controlled Clin Trials* 1989;10:407–415.

38. Juniper EF, Guyatt GH, Willan A, Griffith LE. Determining a minimal important change in a disease-specific quality of life instrument. *J Clin Epidemiol* 1994;47:81–87.

39. Thompson MS, Read JL, Hutchings HC, et al. The cost effectiveness of auranofin: results of a randomized clinical trial. *J Rheumatol* 1988;15:35–42.

40. Patrick DL, Deyo PA. Generic and disease-specific measures in assessing health status and quality of life. *Med Care* 1989;27:F217–F232.

41. Feeny D, Barr RD, Furlong W, et al. A comprehensive multiattribute system for classifying the health status of survivors of childhood cancer. *J Clin Oncol* 1992;10:923–928.

42. Patrick DL. Health-related quality of life in pharmaceutical evaluation. Forging progress and avoiding pitfalls. *Pharmacoeconomics* 1992;1:76–78.

43. McCusker J, Stoddart AM. Use of a surrogate for the Sickness Impact Profile. *Med Care* 1984;22: 789–795.
44. Rothman ML, Hedrick SC, Bulcroft KA, Hickam DH, Rubenstein LZ. The validity of proxy-generated scores as measure of patient health status. *Med Care* 1991;29:1151–1224.
45. Calkins DR, Rubenstein LV, Cleary PD, Davies AR, Jette AM, Fink AR, Kosecoff J, Yong RT, Brook RH, Delbanco TL. Failure of physicians to recognize functional disability in ambulatory patients. *Ann Intern Med* 1991;114:451–454.
46. Vetter NJ, Jones DA, Victor CR. Effects of health visitors working with elderly patients in general practice: a randomized controlled trial. *Br Med J* 1984;288:369–372.
47. Rubenstein LZ, Josephson KR, Wieland GD, English PA, Sayre JA, Kane RL. Effectiveness of a geriatric evaluation unit: a randomized clinical trial. *N Engl J Med* 1984;311:1664–1670.
48. Rubenstein LZ, Josephson KR, Robbins AS. Falls in the nursing home. *Ann Intern Med* 1994; 121(6):442–451.
49. Rubenstein LV, Calkins DR, Young RT, et al. Improving patient function: a randomized trial of functional disability screening. *Ann Intern Med* 1989;111(10):836–842.
50. Wasson J, Hays R, Rubenstein L, Nelson E, Leaning J, Johnson D, Keller A, Landgraf J, Rosenkrans C. The short-term effect of patient health status assessment in a health maintenance organization. *Qual Life Res* 1992;1:99–106.
51. Wasson J, Keller A, Rubenstein L, Hays R, Nelson E, Johnson D, The Dartmouth Primary Care COOP Project. Benefits and obstacles of health status assessment in ambulatory settings: the clinician's point of view. *Med Care* 1992;30(5 suppl):42–50.
52. Rubenstein LV, McCoy JM, Cope DW, Barrett PA, Hirsch SH, Messer KS, Young RT. Improving patient functional status: a randomized trial of computer-generated resource and management suggestions. *Clin Res* 1989;37(2):801A.
53. Goldberg DP. Identifying psychiatric illness among general medical patients. *Br Med J* 1985;29: 161–163.
54. Burnam MA, Wells KB, Leake B, et al. Development of a brief screening instrument for detecting depressive disorders. *Med Care* 1988;26:775–789.
55. Stewart AL, Hays RD, Ware JE. Communication: the MOS short-form general health survey: reliability and validity in a patient population. *Med Care* 1988;26(7):724–735.
56. Jette AM. The functional status questionnaire: reliability and validity when used in primary care. *J Gen Intern Med* 1986;1:143.
57. Sherbourne CD, Stewart AL. The MOS social support survey. *Soc Sci Med* 1991;32(6):701–714.
58. Nelson E, Wasson J, Kirk J, et al. Assessment of function in routine clinical practice: description of the COOP chart method and preliminary findings. *J Chronic Dis* 1987;40(1):55S.
59. Wasson JH, Gall V, McDonald R, et al . The prescription of assistive devices for the elderly: practical considerations. *Rev J Gen Intern Med* 1990;5:46–54.
60. Mathias S, Nayak USL, Isaacs B. Balance in elderly patients: the "get up and go" test. *Arch Phys Med Rehabil* 1986;67:387–389.
61. Katz S, Akpom CA. Index of ADL. *Med Care* 1976;14:116–118.
62. Lawton MP, Brody EM. Assessment of older people: self-maintaining and instrumental activities of daily living. *Gerontologist* 1969;9:179.
63. Morris J, Hawes C, Fries BE, et al. Designing the National Resident Assessment Instrument for nursing homes. *Gerontologist* 1990;30:293–307.
64. Shulman NB, Martinez B, Brogan D, Carr AA, Miles CG. Financial cost as an obstacle to hypertensive therapy. *Am J Public Health* 1986;76:1105–1108.
65. Lilja J. How physicians choose their drugs. *Soc Sci Med* 1976;10:363–365.
66. Miller RR. Prescribing habits of physicians (parts I–III). *Drug Intell Clin Pharm* 1973;7:492–500.
67. Earker SA, Sox HC. An assessment of patient preferences for therapeutic outcomes. *Med Decis Making* 1981;1:29–39.
68. McNeil BJ, Weichselboom R, Pauker SG. Fallacy of the five-year survival rate in lung cancer. *N Engl J Med* 1978;299:1397–1401.
69. Temple R. Transcript of the Oncologic Drugs Advisory Committee meeting, June 28, 1985.
70. Wittes RE. Antineoplastic agents and FDA regulations; square pegs for round holes? *Cancer Treat Rep* 1987;71:795–806.

2 / Social and Psychological Assessment

Social interaction scales as outcome measures
Psychological aspects of health-related quality of life measurement
Cognition and quality of life assessment: an overview
Cognitive interviewing methods and quality of life assessments
Functional disability scales
Defining disability and impairment

Although psychological assessment is a well-defined field, there is a difference between evaluation of cognitive function or mood and the impact of those domains on daily life. Of the domains selected to represent the concept of quality of life as defined in this book, social interaction or social participation is the least well conceptualized. The practical use of this concept as a measure of quality of life in clinical trials depends upon a definition that encompasses features of an individual's functioning that realistically can be influenced by the medical treatment or intervention under study. This section reviews approaches to both social and psychological issues, as possible functional disabilities. Figure 2.1 illustrates how relationships between changes in psychosocial variables and HRQOL measures follow a dose response function as disease severity increases.

Social Interaction

Social interaction is a component of the broader concept, social well-being. Donald and Ware (1) suggest that social well-being is made up of social contact (social interaction) and social resource dimensions. Social interaction encompasses the activities of an individual and his/her involvement with others; social resources relate to the resources or reserves available to an individual (1). Using this broad definition for social well-being, the concept is not appropriate for use in clinical trials designs since improved social resource availability is not likely to be an intended outcome of a medical intervention. An assessment of patients' activities with others and in social situations, however, is a potential outcome of interest. Few measures have been designed specifically to measure social inter-

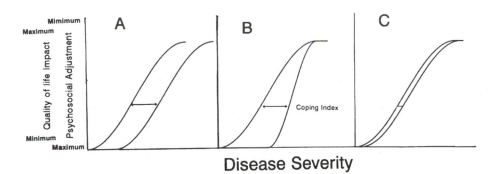

Disease Severity

FIG. 2.1. Plotted in this figure are three models of the relationship between psychological adjustment and quality of life impact. The basic relationship depicted is that as disease severity increases, the capacity of an individual to adapt psychosocially decreases, and the quality of life impact of the disease increases. Also implied in each panel is the fact that the quality of life impact (right-hand function) will be delayed relative to psychological change. (A) Parallel relationship with the distance between functions, at the midpoint of adjustment or impact, as reflecting the coping index. (B,C) Suffering—when the ability of a person to adjust psychologically provides no advantage to the person. (B) This occurs at the point of minimal psychological adjustment and maximum quality of life impact. (C) Situation in which there is minimal coping advantage, so that little of the person s life can be protected from the adverse consequences of increases in disease severity.

action. This construct is typically included as part of a more comprehensive health status battery [e.g., the Sickness Impact Profile (2)] or as a component of a social health or well-being scale [e.g., the Rand Social Health Battery (1)].

Social interactions occur within several domains: family, friends, community, and work. Social interaction scales that include independent measures of each of these domains are rare. In fact, expectations that social interaction items will cluster statistically by domain have not been met (1). Typically, a total interaction score made up of responses to items spanning each of these domains is calculated. A problem arises when this approach is used because all individuals may not be able to respond to all items that make up the overall scale (e.g., items dealing with employment).

Another potential problem in the measurement of social interaction is that individuals' preferences differ with respect to interactions with others. It is a safe assumption that maximum physical or emotional functioning is valued by all individuals. However, individuals' preferences with respect to the quantity and quality of social interactions is more variable. The solution typically has been to assess the quantity of social interactions and to operate under the assumption that more social interaction is better. Ware (3) argues that assessment of the quantity of social interactions should be a health outcome measure because society values social functioning.

Social interaction is sometimes confused with the concept of social support. Although social interaction can be conceived of as a component of social support, it is not synonymous with this construct. Social support is defined in a much broader manner and is used rarely, if ever, as an outcome measure in research designs. It is defined as "the emotional, instrumental, and financial aid that is obtained from one's social network" (4). The role of social support is postulated as either a buffer effect, providing protection from the negative influences of stress, or as a main effect, enhancing health or well-being without reference to level of stress (5). In research designs, social support measures are typically independent variables included as potential correlates of physical and mental health indicators.

SOCIAL INTERACTION SCALES AS OUTCOME MEASURES

Social interaction measures have been included in research designs that do not directly involve medical interventions. For example, investigators who conducted the Health Insurance Experiment (6) initially included social health as a component of their overall model of health, and therefore assessed social interaction as an outcome measure in their study of the influence of health care financing mechanisms on health status. Other "social experiments" such as the National Hospice Study (7) and the National Long-Term Care Channeling Demonstration (8) have included social interaction as an outcome measure with the assumption that improved community functioning will enhance individuals' physical capacity to deal with others.

The Health Insurance Experiment Social Battery

Following an extensive review of the literature (9), investigators at Rand generated an 11-item social well-being scale for use in the Health Insurance Experiment (HIE) (6). The battery was intended for use with the general population, although for the HIE, individuals aged 14 to 61 years made up the population of interest. As indicated above, Rand's social well-being model incorporates two dimensions: social interaction and social ties. The operational definition of social well-being included "interpersonal interactions (e.g., visits with friends) and activities indicative of social participation (e.g., memberships in clubs)". All but one of the 11 items deal with the behavioral aspects of social activity. The remaining item involves a subjective evaluation of one's ability to get along with others.

From the original 11-item scale, five items met internal and external consistency criteria established by the investigators for the construction of two multi-item scales. Both of these scales, Social Contacts and Group Participation, relate directly to the concept of social interaction. The Social Contacts scale is made up of three items documenting visits with friends or relatives, home visits by friends, and visits to homes of friends. Potential responses are not identical across items. Items are rated along several scales that involve six or seven categories. The Group Participation scale is made up of two items detailing number of voluntary group memberships and level of group activity. Based on item analyses, an item-response recoding scheme has been generated for each item. The battery, original item responses, and recoding scheme are presented in (1).

The very low correlation between these measures suggests that these scales measure different components of social well-being. Correlations with other health measures, positive well-being, emotional ties, and current health were low. This suggests that these measures are not redundant with other health dimensions. Correlations with functional or physical measures of health, however, were not reported. We would expect that correlations between functional status measures and social interaction scales would be higher than those reported for well-being, emotional ties, and current health. Finally, Donald and Ware (1) examined the influence of socially desirable response set (SDRS) on each of these scales. Adjusting for SDRS did not result in changes among relationships between the two social interaction scales and other measures of health.

The Medical Outcomes Study Health Measures

The concepts and measurements of the Medical Outcomes Study (MOS) health measures are derived from those associated with the Health Insurance Experiment. Because of the demands for efficiency in a study of more than 20,000 patients, standard and compact instruments were a matter of necessity and the definitions, survey items, and rating scales of the HIE were carefully culled and refined. There are four sets of MOS measures (10). The fullest, the 149-question MOS Functioning and Well-Being Profile, includes 35 scales and eight summary indices. A smaller subset, the 113-item Core Subset, includes 20 scales and four summary indices. The extremely brief 20-item MOS-20 includes a single question on social interaction. The Short-Form 36 (SF-36) includes a Social Functioning scale based on two questions.

The MOS investigators included social functioning as a component of their definition of health. "Social functioning is defined as the ability to develop, maintain, and nurture social relationships. We do not consider social functioning per se as health. Instead, we view social functioning measures as being indicative of physical and mental health status" (11). They studied three components of social functioning: changes due to health in social activities, quality of interaction in family functioning, and sexual function and dysfunction. Of these, emphasis has been on health-related limitations of the individual's normal social activities. The Social Activity Limitations Due to Health measure of the Functioning and Well-Being Profile has four questions that deal with limitations on social activities: frequency of interference, extent of interference, social activity compared to usual level, and social activity compared to others of similar age. The SF-36 includes a two-question Social Function scale made up of two (frequency of interference and extent of interference with social interaction) of the same four items (12). The Social Limitations scale was positively correlated, as predicted, with both physical and mental measures (13). These results demonstrate that Social Function is not independent of the physical and mental function aspects of health-related quality of life. As the evolution has progressed toward shorter forms of Medical Outcomes Study instruments, notable features have been the rejection of social function as a useful health measurement by itself and the focus on measurement of health-related change and departures from an individual's normal pattern of activity.

The Functional Status Questionnaire

The Functional Status Questionnaire (FSQ) is a 34-item self-administered survey assessing physical, psychological, social, and role function (14). The FSQ shares some concepts and items with the MOS instruments, reflecting common adaptations by the developers from existing instruments. The FSQ was specifically designed to measure functional disability and change in function in a clinical context (14).

The instrument includes two social scales, Social Activity (three items) and Quality of Interaction (five items), which the developers clearly differentiate from role function in work (14). Although reliability estimates were .65 for the Social Activity scale, and .64 for Quality of Interaction, these values are somewhat less than optimal for evaluation of individual patients. However, they are reasonable for group comparisons, especially given the relatively low number of items that make up the scales (14). The authors hypothesized that valid measures of social function would be inversely related to age, number of bed-disability days, and role limitations, and positively associated with health satisfaction, number of close friends, and frequency of social contact. In a validation study of primary care patients, all of the expected relationships were observed except for the association with patient reports of the number of close friends.

The Sickness Impact Profile (2)

The Sickness Impact Profile (SIP) is a behaviorally based measure of health status (2,15). Each item endorsed is assigned a standardized weight, and items are summed to create scale and total scales. In addition to individual category scores and a total score, Physical and Psychosocial dimension scores can be calculated. The latter scores are not independent of individual category scores (15,16). A 68-item abbreviated version of the SIP also is available (17).

The Psychosocial Adjustment to Illness Scale (18)

Seven dimensions of psychosocial adjustment underlie the construction of this 46-item instrument. The domains selected were deemed most germane to psychosocial adjustment to medical illness (18,19). Among the seven areas assessed are two that relate to social interaction: Extended Family Relationships (four items) and Social Environment (six items). Within the framework of typical family interactions, the Extended Family Relationships scale assesses "negative impact of the illness upon communication, quality of relationships, interest in interacting with family, and other variables reflective of this life domain" (18). Social environment "reflects the patient's current social and leisure time activities, as well as the degree to which the patient has suffered impairment or constriction of these activities as a result of the current illness and/or its sequelae" (18). Items in this category focus both on interest and behavior. Respondents rate Psychosocial Adjustment to Illness Scale (PAIS) items relative to "the past thirty days including today."

Compared to the Rand Social Health Battery and the SIP, the PAIS has undergone less instrument development work. The work performed thus far is impressive, however. The idea of establishing PAIS scale norms for separate illnesses should help researchers in the selection of social interaction scales. When selecting a potential scale for a clinical trials investigation, a researcher could review these norms to establish whether acceptable variability in scores has been observed for the particular illness of interest. In addition, scale scores would be available for comparison following data collection. The high correlations reported between Social Environment and Extended Family Relationship suggest that the use of both scales in a clinical trial design may not be necessary.

The Nottingham Health Profile (20)

The Nottingham Health Profile (NHP) is made up of two parts. Part I contains 38 items leading to six scales: Energy, Pain, Emotional Reactions, Sleep, Social Isolation, and Physical Mobility (20,21). Part II contains seven single-item statements relative to various aspects of life affected by health, including social life, family relations, sex life, and hobbies and interests. In addition, there is a single general question about present health. The developers intended to generate the social measurement concepts of the NHP through empirical study and screening of a large number of statements made by patients during interviews (the original set had 2,200 statements) rather than from a predetermined theoretical framework. The final set of Social Isolation questions of Part I has five yes-no items asking for respondents' subjective feelings about social relationships. Respondents receive a point for each yes response. The Item responses are summed and the score is converted to range from 0 (no problems) to 100 (all possible problems) (20,21).

The Duke-UNC Health Profile and Duke Health Profile (22)

The development of the Duke Health Profile (DUKE) and its longer forbearer, the Duke-UNC Health Profile (DUHP) spanned a period of at least a dozen years, beginning in the late 1970s. The 63-question DUHP was designed to be a comprehensive self-administered health status instrument suitable for use in both research and primary clinical care assessment (22). Rather than focusing on severe illness, the DUHP set as its goal to be "sensitive to small changes in health status" and "oriented toward health rather than disease" (22). The DUHP measures physical function, emotional function, social function, and symptom status. A decade's experience with the instrument identified important problems with it, including its longer than ideal length and "sequestration of all symptom items into a symptom status dimension separate from the three major World Health Organization (WHO) dimensions of physical, mental, and social health . . . and [a] definition of social function restricted to social role performance" (23).

Under the parent DUHP formulation, "Social function is measured in terms of a person's ability to perform his or her usual role in society (22)," a broadly inclusive definition. In the somewhat narrowed DUKE conceptualization, Social Health includes self-concepts about relationships with other people and frequency of social activities, but seems to remain more an empirical than a conceptual matter.

The McMaster Health Index Questionnaire (24)

The McMaster Health Index Questionnaire (MHIQ) contains 59 items producing three scales. The Physical Function scale has 24 items, the Social Function scale has 25 items, and the Emotional Function scale has 25 items. A number of items are common to both the social and emotional scales (24). The Social Function scale encompasses general well-being, work/social role performance/material welfare, family support/participation, and global social function. Some of the questions are broad self-assessments. Others probe the occurrence of particular social events within specified time frames, such as, "During the last year, have you had trouble getting along with friends/relatives?" and "Has a friend visited you in the last week?" Still others probe background issues such as church attendance or amount of television viewing.

Many items do not seem plausible as clinical outcomes, for instance, "Do you have a telephone?" For other items, the coding of the responses may produce an outcome measure inappropriate for particular contexts; e.g., in response to the question of occupational status, "retired" or no answer are scored as "poor" responses. The MHIQ may, however, provide a useful general assessment of Social Function complementing that of more specific clinical measures.

Social Engagement Scale (25)

In the most seriously impaired populations it is not always possible for the patient to describe his or her own state of being. This is particularly true of nursing home residents, over half of whom have varying levels of dementia (26). As in other fields of quality of life assessment, basic physical functioning dominates most measures of nursing home quality of life. Congress mandated the development of the Minimum Data Set (MDS) for resident assessment. The MDS includes other dimensions of quality of life more consistent with the premise that these facilities are homes to the residents (27). The six social well-being concepts addressed in these items focus on the extent to which the individual resident is engaged in the social life of the facility, including interacting with others, doing self-initiated activities or those initiated by others. Each item is scored dichotomously and staff are instructed to score a yes for any evidence of the behavior. Like the entire MDS, each of the six items is rooted in observable behaviors since the instrument is completed by staff members. Findings revealed that social engagement is strongly related to physical and cognitive functioning, and that the structure of the inter-item relations is comparable for the most and least severely physically and cognitively impaired (25). Furthermore, there was considerable variability in the measure in all but the most impaired residents, and this variance was partially explained by facility characteristics, including the types of services available.

PSYCHOLOGICAL ASPECTS OF HEALTH-RELATED QUALITY OF LIFE MEASUREMENT

The General Health Questionnaire (28)

The General Health Questionnaire (GHQ) was designed to measure current psychiatric/affective disorders (28). It was developed to be used in primary medical care settings, in general population or community surveys, and among general medical outpatients. It focuses on breaks in normal functioning rather than on lifelong traits. It is chiefly concerned with identifying an "inability to carry out one's normal, healthy" functions, and the appearance of new phenomena of a distressing nature" (29). The GHQ is not intended to detect serious illnesses, but is designed to identify individuals at risk who should then be examined using standard psychiatric interviews (28). The GHQ has been used extensively, however, to estimate the prevalence of affective disorders and to assess illness severity (30).

The items cover four main areas: depression, anxiety, social impairment, and hypochondriasis (as indicated by organic symptoms) (28). The original version of the GHQ contains 60 items and is generally recommended for use because of its superior validity. Shorter versions of the GHQ include 12- and 30-item scales, which exclude items most usually selected by physically ill individuals (28). A GHQ-28 was also developed using factor analysis, and contains four subscales: anxiety and insomnia, somatic symptoms, social dysfunction, and severe depression (29). There is only partial overlap between the GHQ-28 and GHQ-30, which share 14 items in common. A detailed guide on the different versions of the GHQ, and advice on their most appropriate uses in clinical practice and research, is available elsewhere (31).

Scores on the GHQ are interpreted to indicate the severity of psychological disturbance on a continuum, or as an initial screen in identifying cases applying cutoffs. There is no universally accepted cutoff point for each of the GHQ versions that identifies psychiatric cases. Instead, the cutoff points vary based on the purpose for which the GHQ is being used, and the characteristics of the population in which it is being applied.

Psychological General Well-Being Index (32)

The Psychological General Well-Being Index (PGWB) was designed to measure subjective feelings of psychological well-being and distress (32). The instrument has been used with a variety of sociodemographic groups to assess changes in subjective well-being due to mental health treatments. The 22-item instrument includes both positive and negative affective states, and covers six dimensions: anxiety, depression, general health, positive well-being, self-control, and vitality. The PGWB was designed to be self-administered, but it can be used in an interview format. It has been used as a proxy for HRQL in a number of studies within the United States and Europe. The PGWB has a high degree of reliability and validity in both population-based and mental health samples, although the validity of the PGWB has been ascertained primarily through its relationships with negative conditions instead of conditions that indicate more positive life events (32). The PGWB contains aspects of positive well-being, avoids references to physical symptoms of emotional distress, is not condition specific, and is not oriented solely toward discriminating psychiatric cases from healthy individuals.

The Profile of Mood States (33)

The Profile of Mood States (POMS) (33) was designed to assess mood states and transient changes in mood. Six identifiable moods or affective states are measured: tension–anxiety, depression–dejection, anger–hostility, vigor–activity, fatigue–inertia, and confusion–bewilderment. The POMS is self-administered and contains 65 adjectives relating to mood states during the past week, which are scored on a 5-point scale from 0 (not at all) to 4 (extremely). A score for each factor is produced by simply adding responses. A summary measure of total distress can also be obtained by summing all scores.

The evidence from large standardization samples suggests that the POMS is a valid and reliable descriptive tool for assessing mood states in both psychiatric and nonpsychiatric populations. Despite its being developed to address several specific moods, the moderate to high correlations among factor scores suggest that the POMS may be better suited to measuring general mood disturbance. Studies have shown that the strongest associations among the POMS's factor scores and extent of disease or prognostic factors have been for vigor and fatigue, and there is very little association with factors relevant to emotional distress. It is not clear to what extent disease affects emotional distress as measured by the POMS, but it is concluded that this instrument is a reasonably good measure of general mood disturbance in a wide range of populations, and may be a valuable test to include as the psychological component of an HRQL battery.

A battery approach to HRQL assessment of psychological well-being has the potential of providing rich data on this inherently multidimensional concept. Furthermore, a reliable measure of each dimension of HRQL recognizes the variable impact that any treatment has on various aspects of an individual's functioning and also allows for targeted interventions. Although there are instruments available to assess the various HRQL dimensions, a battery approach has its drawbacks. In most clinical trials, a separate instrument for each dimension of HRQL is impractical in terms of patient burden, staff time, and data analysis. Thus, a carefully selected subset of instruments is recommended for HRQL assessments of psychological well-being.

COGNITION AND QUALITY OF LIFE ASSESSMENT: AN OVERVIEW

There are four basic methods for collecting quality of life data; self reports, direct one-to-one interviewing, surrogate responders, and telephone interviews (34). Each method would be expected to involve different cognitive processes. To simplify the discussion, this section deals only with quality of life assessments based on self-reports. Self-reports, however, are complex behaviors involving the respondents' interpretation of the question, retrieval from their memory, and even their editing of their response for reasons of social pressure or to ensure privacy.

Liang et al. (35) suggest another approach to this task—the ability of different assessment instruments to monitor effect size. Thus, if instruments differ in their sensitivity to change then they are not providing the conditions necessary to generate the same level of information. Liang et al. compared the Functional Status Instrument (FSI) (36), the Health Assessment Questionnaire (HAQ) (37), the Arthritis Impact Measurement Scale (AIMS) (38), the Index of Well-Being (IWB) (39), and Sickness Impact Profile (SIP) (40). What they found for global indexes was that the FSI and the HAQ were relatively insensitive. They found that other measures of change (41,42) are available to compare assessment instruments. Thus, while the number of studies in this area is not large, it is clear that an adequate methodology exists to permit at least a first approximation of the comparative informational content among quality of life assessments.

What about comparing information about domains within an assessment? Liang et al. (35), using the same methodology described above, found that the HAQ and the IWB were least sensitive as measures of mobility, whereas the AIMS and IWB were least sensitive for measures of social functioning. All the measures had equal sensitivity to pain scales. Liang et al.'s study clearly indicates that not all quality of life assessments would be equally useful in providing information about specific quality of life domains. Parr et al. (43) compared the responses to a visual–analog measure of pain and the eight items on the Nottingham Health Profile (NHP) (44). They found that whereas the visual–analog measure of pain varied between drug treatments, the pain subscale of the NHP did not. This is just what would be expected if differences in question format and structure led to differences in cognitive processing, and therefore information generated by an assessment. Part of the problem here is that most quality of life assessments do not capture the complex nature of the phenomena being measured. For example, Salovey et al. (45) discuss the fact that the assessment of pain in surveys such as quality of life assessments can be expected to be a complex task involving several types of measures, including establishing a semantic space, scaling the intensity of the pain, defining pain in sensory, affective, and evaluative terms, distinguishing pain reports from pain behavior, and so on.

Explicit memory involves a direct test of memory, such as when subjects are asked to freely recall an event, use cues to recall, or recognize the event after being presented with some information about the event. Each of these methods differs in the degree that subjects are provided with information about what it is they are to recall. For example, when SF-36 item number seven lists pain intensity as possibly varying from none to very severe, the respondent is immediately told that pain can vary along this range. Thus, the item is an example of cued recall. In contrast, the items on the NHP would be an example of free recall; no information, other than presence or absence, is provided to help guide the person's response. Implicit memory refers to any memory task that is tested without direct or specific reference to the event. The notion that past adverse experiences can affect a person's current mentation is an old one, and frequently encountered in the psychologist's clinic (46).

COGNITIVE INTERVIEWING METHODS AND QUALITY OF LIFE ASSESSMENTS

Researchers at the National Center for Health Statistics, for example, have established a Questionnaire Design Research Laboratory (47), whose purpose is to design survey items whose meaning, and therefore, interpretation is clear. Willis (48) has provided a training manual that can be used to do cognitive interviewing when developing a questionnaire. He and his colleagues attempt to answer three questions as a result of their activities: First, do the respondents understand the question? Second, what cognitive processes are involved in their effort to retrieve memory or relevant information to answer the question? Third, how do the respondents use this information in making their response to the question?

A quality of life assessment is something that a person does as they answer questions about themselves, their health, their pain, and so on. Several distinct cognitive activities are associated with generating a quality of life assessment:

Recall from memory, scaling of the memories, valuating the importance of the memories, and aggregating the results of different memories into an index. Each of these activities reflects complex cognitive activities in which people engage.

FUNCTIONAL DISABILITY SCALES

The periodic assessment of disabilities has become an integral part of the standard medical evaluation of many patients, supplementing diagnosis, history, laboratory tests, and physical findings. Goals of treatment for chronic diseases include measures that go beyond notions of cure and survival, to more sensitive measures of progress that relate to overall functioning. Interventions for chronic diseases are applied at any point along the disease-impairment-disability-handicap continuum. Increasingly, clinicians and researchers need reliable and validated measures of functional disability in order to measure clinical progress, evaluate programs, and establish appropriate eligibility criteria for government and insurance programs. This section focuses mainly on four generic scales and variations of these scales: the Index of Activities of Daily Living (49), the Barthel Index (50), the Instrumental Activities of Daily Living Scale (IADL) (51), and the Functional Activities Questionnaire (FAQ) (52). Scales that combine IADL and ADL measures are also reviewed, mainly to discuss methodological issues.

DEFINING DISABILITY AND IMPAIRMENT

Terms are defined according to the World Health Organization's (WHO) International Classification of Impairments, Disabilities, and Handicaps. Using this approach impairments are defined as abnormalities of body structure and appearance and organ or system function, resulting from any cause. These include mental impairments and loss of limbs, and limitations in range of motion, for example. Disabilities are defined as "restrictions or lack of ability to perform an activity in a manner or within the range considered normal for a human being" (53). Impairments relate to performance of an organ or mechanism; disability relates to the performance of an activity by an individual. A person maybe mentally impaired, have restricted range of motion, or be missing an arm, but not show any disabilities by being able to carry out all basic activities independently. In another example, limitations in eye function, referred to as visual impairment, may result in an inability to dress or wash oneself, which are examples of disabilities.

Katz Scale of Activities of Daily Living Scale

The Katz Index of Activities of Daily Living (ADL) scale (49) is based on six functions: bathing, dressing, going to the toilet, transferring (bed to chair), continence, and feeding. The scale includes basic self-care activities. One of the items, transfer, may be classified as a measure of mobility; incontinence may be classified as an impairment. The items in the scale and their respective definitions are conceptually based to reflect the organized locomotor and neurologic aspects of basic activities necessary for survival independent of cultural and social forces. In studies of recovery from chronic disease, the order of recovery using the Katz scale is similar to the progression of functional development of a child (49).

Each activity is divided into three levels, but these levels can be combined so that each activity can be dichotomized to independence and dependence. Patients who are independent do the activity without human assistance, but they may use a prosthesis. Human assistance includes supervision as well as hands-on help. Using the dichotomies, an ordered unidimensional aggregate scale can be constructed. The levels of disability are as follows: independent in all six functions; dependent in one function; dependent in bathing plus one other; dependent in bathing and dressing plus one other; dependent in bathing, dressing, and toileting plus one other; dependent in bathing, dressing, toileting, and transferring plus one other; dependent in all six functions; and other, which includes all patterns that do not fit into the above categories. The scale was designed to be administered as an assessment completed by a professional, but experience by nonclinicians with knowledge of gerontology has been reported (49). Information is derived from direct observation of residents, discussion with primary caregiver, and from the medical record. For demented residents, information is derived from the primary caregiver and the medical record only. The final score is based on judgment of the assessor after reviewing information from all sources. The Katz scale is a measure of independence. Some scales, such as the Barthel Index, measure ability. The advantage of measuring independence is that it measures a real situation, whereas the second approach often assesses a hypothetical situation.

Barthel Index

The Barthel Index (50) includes 15 items: drinking, feeding, dressing upper body, dressing lower body, donning brace or prosthesis, grooming, washing and bathing, bladder control, bowel control, chair transfers, toilet transfers, tub/shower transfers, walking on level for 50 yards, climbing one flight of stairs, and maneuvering a wheelchair. The first nine activities may be classified as self-care items, whereas the next six items are measures of mobility (50). The Barthel Index includes a much more comprehensive assessment of mobility than the Katz scale. The Barthel Index has incontinence separated into bowel and bladder incontinence and provides more detail for dressing by distinguishing between upper body and lower body limitations. Each item is valued on three levels: can do by myself, can do with the help of someone else, and cannot do at all. In contrast to the Katz scale, these items are measures of ability ("can do") and not independence ("do"). Arbitrary weights ranging from 0 to 15 are used to create an aggregate score. A score of 0 represents complete inability and a score of 100 represents complete ability on all items.

REFERENCES

1. Donald CA, Ware JE. *The quantification of social contacts and resources.* Santa Monica, CA: RAND, 1982.
2. Bergner M, Bobbitt RA, Carter WB, Gilson BS. The sickness impact profile: development and final revision of a health status measure. *Med Care* 1981;19:787–805.
3. Ware JE. The assessment of health status. In: Aiken LH, Mechanic D, eds. *Applications of social science to clinical medicine and health policy.* New Brunswick, NJ: Rutgers University Press, 1986: 204–228.
4. Berkman L. Assessing the physical health effects of social networks and social support. *Annu Rev Public Health* 1984;5:412–432.
5. Cohen S, Syme SL. Issues in the study and application of social support. In: Cohen S, Syme SL, eds. *Social support and health.* Orlando, FL: Academic Press, 1985:3–22.
6. Brook RB, Ware JE, Rogers WH, et al. Does free care improve adults' health? Results from a randomized controlled trial. *N Engl J Med* 1983;309:1426–1434.
7. Mor V, Greer OS, Kastenbaum R, eds. *The hospice experiment.* Baltimore, MD: Johns Hopkins University Press, 1988.
8. Carcagno GJ, Kemper P. The evaluation of the national long term care demonstration: an overview of the channeling demonstration and its evaluation. *Health Serv Res* 1988;23:1–22.
9. Ware JE, Brook RH, Williams KN, Stewart AL, Davies-Avery A. *Conceptualization and measurement of health for adults in the health insurance study; Vol I, Model of health and methodology.* Santa Monica, CA: RAND, 1978.
10. Stewart AL, Sherbourne CD, et al. Summary and discussion of MOS measures. In: Stewart AL, Ware JE, eds. *Measuring functioning and well-being: the Medical Outcomes Study approach.* Durham, NC: Duke University Press, 1992.
11. Sherbourne CD. Social functioning: social activity limitations measure. In: Stewart AL, Ware JE, eds. *Measuring functioning and well-being: the Medical Outcomes Study approach.* Durham, NC: Duke University Press, 1992.
12. Ware JE, et al. *SF-36 Health Survey: manual and interpretation guide.* Boston: The Health Institute, New England Medical Center, 1993.
13. Hays RD, Stewart AL. Construct validity of MOS health measures. In: Stewart AL, Ware JE, eds. *Measuring functioning and well-being: the Medical Outcomes Study approach.* Durham, NC: Duke University Press, 1992.
14. Jette AM, Davies AR, Cleary PD, Calkins DR, Rubenstein LV, Fink A, et al. The Functional Status Questionnaire: reliability and validity when used in primary care. *J Gen Intern Med* 1986;1:143–149.
15. Bergner M, Bobbitt RA, Pollard WE, Martin DP, Gilson BS. The Sickness Impact Profile: validation of a health status measure. *Med Care* 1976:14:57–67.
16. Pollard WE, Bobbitt RA, Bergner M, Gilson BS. The sickness impact profile: reliability of a health status measure. *Med Care* 1976;14:146.
17. DeBruin AF, Buys M, DeWitte LP, Diederiks JP. The Sickness Impact Profile: SIP68, a short generic version. First evaluation and reproducibility. *J Clin Epidemiol* 1994;47:863–871.
18. Derogatis LR. The psychological adjustment to illness scale (PAIS). *J Psychosom Res* 1986;30:77–91.
19. Derogatis LR, Lopez M. *Psychological adjustment to illness scale(PAIS & PAIS-SR): scoring procedures & administration manual-I.* Baltimore, MD: Clinical Psychometric Research, 1983.
20. Hunt SM, McKenna SP, McEwen J, Backett EM, Williams J, Papp E. A quantitative approach to perceived health status: a validation study. *J Epidemiol Community Health* 1980;34:281–286.
21. McEwen J. The Nottingham Health Profile. In: Walker SR, Rosser RM, eds. *Quality of life assessment: key issues in the 1990's.* Lancaster, UK: Kluwer Academic, 1993.
22. Parkerson GR, Gehlbach SH, Wagner EH, et al. The Duke-UNC Health Profile: an adult health status instrument for primary care. *Med Care* 1981;19:806–828.
23. Parkerson GR Jr, Broadhead WE, Tse CK. The Duke Health Profile. A 17-item measure of health and dysfunction. *Med Care* 1990;28:1056–1072.

24. Chambers LW. The McMaster Health Index Questionnaire: an update. In: Walker SR, Rosser RD, eds. *Quality of life assessment: key issues in the 1990's.* Boston: Kluwer Academic, 1993;131–149.

25. Mor V, Branco K. Fleishman J, Hawes C, Phillips C, Morris J, Fries B. The structure of social engagement among nursing home residents. *J Gerontol Psychol Sci* 1995;50:P1–P8.

26. Sekscenski ES. Discharge from nursing homes: preliminary data from the 1985 National Nursing Home Survey. NCHS Advance data from Vital & Health Statistics of the National Center for Health Statistics, #142 September 1987 DHHS Publication Number (PHS) 87–1250. Hyattsville, MD: Public Health Service, 1987.

27. Hawes C, Morris JN, Phillips CD, Mor V, Fries BE, Nonemaker S. Reliability estimates for the minimum data set for nursing home resident assessment and care screening (MDS). *Gerontologist* 1995; 35:172–178.

28. Goldberg DP. *The detection of psychiatric illness by questionnaire.* Maudsley Monogram #21. London: Oxford University Press, 1972.

29. Goldberg DP, Hillier VF. A scaled version of the General Health Questionnaire. *Psychol Med* 1979; 9:139–145.

30. Wilkin D, Hallam L, Doggett M-A. *Measures of need and outcome for primary health care.* Oxford: Oxford University Press, 1992.

31. Goldberg DP, Williams P. *Users' guide to the general health questionnaire.* Windsor, England: NFER-Nelson, 1988.

32. Dupuy HJ. The Psychological General Well-Being (PGWB) Index. In: Wenger NK, Mattson ME, Furberg CD, Elinson J, eds. *Assessment of quality of life in clinical trials of cardiovascular therapies.* New York: Le Jacq, 1984:170–183.

33. McNair D, Lord M, Droppleman LF. *EITS manual for the Profile of Mood States.* San Diego, CA: Educational Testing Service, 1971.

34. Guyatt GH, Fenny DH, Patrick DL. Measuring health-related quality of life. *Ann Intern Med* 1993; 118:622–629.

35. Liang MH, Fossel AH, Larson MG. Comparison of five health-status instruments for orthopedic evaluation. *Med Care* 1990;28:632–642.

36. Jette AM, Deniston OL. Inter-observer reliability of a functional status assessment instrument. *J Chronic Dis* 1978;31:573–580.

37. Fries JR, Spitz P, Kraines RG, Holman HR. Measurement of patient outcome in arthritis. *Arthritis Rheum* 1980;23:137–145.

38. Meenan RF, Gertman PM, Mason JM. Measuring health status in arthritis: the Arthritis Impact Measurement Scale. *Arthritis Rheum* 1980;23:146–152.

39. Kaplan RM, Bush JW, Berry CC. Health status: types of validity of an index of well-being. *Health Serv Res* 1976;11:478–507.

40. Bergner M, Bobbitt RA, Carter WB, Gilson ES. Sickness Impact Profile: development and final revision of a health-status measure. *Med Care* 1981;19:787–805.

41. Guyatt G, Walter S, Norman G. Measuring change over time: assessing the usefulness of evaluative instruments. *J Chronic Dis* 1987;40:171–178.

42. Cohen J. *Statistical power analysis for the behavioral sciences.* New York: Academic Press, 1977.

43. Parr G, Darekar B, Fletcher A, Bulpitt C. Joint pain and quality of life: results of a randomized trial. *Br J Clin Pharmacol* 1989;27:235–242.

44. Hunt SM, McKenna SP, McEwen JA. A quantitative approach to perceived health status: a validation study. *J Epidemiol Community Health* 1980;34:281–285.

45. Salovey T, Phil FM, Smith AF, Turk BC, Jobe JB, Willis GB. Reporting chronic pain episodes on health surveys. *Vital and health statistics,* series 6, Cognition and Survey Measurement no. 6. Washington, DC: DHHS Publication #92–1081, 1992.

46. Parkin AJ. *Memory: phenomena, experiment, and theory.* Cambridge, England: Blackwell, 1993.

47. Jobe JB, Mingay DJ. Cognitive and survey measurement history and overview. *Appl Cognit Psych* 1991;5:175–192.

48. Willis GB. *Cognitive interviewing and questionnaire design: a training manual.* Cognitive working paper series #7. Office of Research and Methodology, National Center for Health Statistics, March 19, 1994.

49. Katz S, Ford AB, Moskowitz RW, Jackson BA, Jaffe MW. Studies of illness in the aged. The index of ADL: a standardized measure of biological and psychosocial function. *JAMA* 1963;185:914–919.

50. Mahoney FI, Barthel DW. Functional evaluation: the Barthel Index. *Maryland State Med J* 1965;14: 61–65.

51. Lawton MP, Brody EM. Assessment of older people: self-maintaining and instrumental activities of daily living. *Gerontologist* 1969;9:179–186.
52. Pfeffer RI, Kurosaki MS, Harrah CH, Chance JM, Filos S. Measurement of functional activities in older adults in the community. *J Gerontology* 1982;37:323–329.
53. World Health Organization. *International classification of impairments, disabilities, and handicaps.* Geneva: World Health Organization, 1980.

3 / Selected Instruments

Dartmouth COOP Functional Assessment Charts: brief measures for clinical practice
Derogatis Affect Balance Scale (DABS)
Modular Approach to HRQOL Assessment in Oncology
The EORTC QLQ-C30
The EuroQOL Instrument: an index of health-related quality of life
The Health Assessment Questionnaire (HAQ)
The McMaster Health Index Quesionnaire
Nottingham Health Profile (NHP)
Psychological Adjustment to Illness Scale (PAIS and PAIS-SR)
Quality of Life in Cancer (QOL-C)
Symptom Check List (SCL-90-R) and the Brief Symptom Inventory (BSI)
The Derogatis Psychiatric Rating Scale
The Medical Outcome Study Short Form (SF-36) Health Survey
The Sickness Impact Profile (SIP)
World Health Organization QOL Assessment (WHOQOL)

A number of scales that have become widely used to evaluate generic HRQOL and some of the more commonly problematic domains are described in this chapter. Selection of a scale can be determined by the content of the questionnaire, but should largely be based on the context of use. There is no single best instrument—just a "best fit" for the desired purpose.

DARTMOUTH COOP FUNCTIONAL HEALTH ASSESSMENT CHARTS: BRIEF MEASURES FOR CLINICAL PRACTICE

The Dartmouth Primary Care Cooperative Information Project (COOP) chart system has been developed and refined for over a decade for the purpose of making a brief, practical, and valid method to assess the functional status of adults and adolescents. The system was developed by the Dartmouth COOP Project, a network of community medical practices that cooperate on primary care research activities. The charts are similar to Snellen charts, which are used medically to measure visual acuity quickly in busy clinical practices. Each chart consists of a title, a question referring to the status of the patient over the past 2 to 4 weeks, and five response choices. Each response is illustrated by a drawing that depicts a level of functioning or well-being along a five-point ordinal scale (1,2). The illustration makes the charts appear "user-friendly" without seeming to bias the responses (3,4). Most clinicians and patients reported that the charts are easy to use and provide a valuable tool to measure overall function in a busy office practice (2,5).

The charts are a simple, easily administered, self-scoring system for screening, assessing, monitoring, and maintaining patient function. This system has been tested in many different practices, in both North America and elsewhere, to evaluate and establish its reliability, validity, and acceptability. One set of the charts—the WONCA version for adults (Fig. 3.1)—has been developed as the international standard for classifying the functional status of adult medical patients in primary care settings (6). The COOP/WONCA version of the charts differs somewhat from the original COOP charts by asking about function in the previous 2 weeks (rather than 4 weeks). The dimensions of health status measured by the health charts are Physical, Emotional, Daily Activities, Social Activities, Social Support, Pain, and Overall Health. The adult charts have been used widely (4). In accordance with clinical convention, high scores (i.e., patient ratings of 4 or 5) represent unfavorable levels of health (life quality or social support) on each chart. For example, Physical Chart responses range from 1 to 5 with a score of 5 representing major limitations.

The adolescent charts have been used in doctors' offices and school classrooms for both English-and Spanish-speaking youths (7,8). Six charts were determined to be the most effective in measuring mutually exclusive dimensions of health and social problems: Physical Fitness, Emotional Feelings, School Work, Social Support, Family Communication, and Health Habits. Compared with multi-item questionnaires, respondents found the charts easier to understand and less likely to induce dishonest replies. Adolescent girls generally score worse than boys on the Physical Fitness and Emotional Feelings charts but better on the (at-risk) Health Habits charts. The scores of teenagers known to have behavioral problems are worse on the Health Habits chart. Simplified versions of the adolescent charts suitable for administration to children, aged 8 to 12 years, have somewhat less reliability and validity.

Clinical Use of the COOP Charts

The clinical advantages of the charts are ease of administration and scoring. However, compared to longer multi-item instruments, single-item charts are likely to have less precision (9). Clinicians argue that this loss of precision is not critical (10) for medical decision making.

Practicing clinicians typically ask three questions about health status assessment:
Why do you measure functional status?
How do you fit functional measurement into a patient encounter of limited duration?
What do you do with the information from the assessment?

PHYSICAL FITNESS

During the past 4 weeks . . .
What was the hardest physical activity
you could do for at least 2 minutes ?

FEELINGS

During the past 4 weeks . . .
How much have you been bothered by
emotional problems such as feeling anxious,
depressed, irritable or downhearted and blue ?

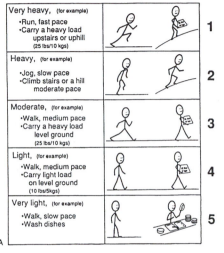

A

B

DAILY ACTIVITIES

During the past 4 weeks . . .
How much difficulty have you had doing your usual
activities or task, both inside and outside the house
because of your physical and emotional health ?

SOCIAL ACTIVITIES

During the past 4 weeks . . .
Has your physical and emotional health limited
your social activities with family, friends,
neighbors or groups ?

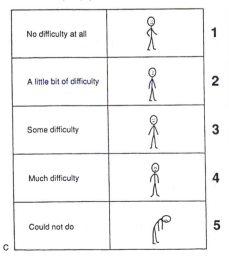

C

D

FIG. 3.1. COOP adult charts. (Trustees of Dartmouth College/COOP Project 1995. Permission to use the COOP charts specifically excludes the right to distribute, reproduce, or share the charts in any form for commercial purposes or sale.)

CHANGE IN HEALTH

How would you rate your overall health
now compared to 4 weeks ago ?

Much better	▲ ▲ ++	1
A little better	▲ +	2
About the same	◄► =	3
A little worse	▼ −	4
Much worse	▼ ▼ −−	5

E

OVERALL HEALTH

During the past 4 weeks . . .
How would you rate your health in general ?

Excellent	😊	1
Very good	🙂	2
Good	😐	3
Fair	🙁	4
Poor	☹️	5

F

SOCIAL SUPPORT

During the past 4 weeks . . .
Was someone available to help you if you
needed and wanted help? For example if you
— felt very nervous, lonely, or blue
— got sick and had to stay in bed
— needed someone to talk to
— needed help with daily chores
— needed help just taking care of yourself

QUALITY OF LIFE

How have things been going for you during
the past 4 weeks?

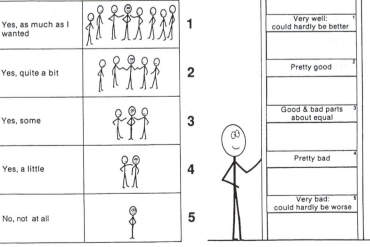

Yes, as much as I wanted		1
Yes, quite a bit		2
Yes, some		3
Yes, a little		4
No, not at all		5

Very well: could hardly be better	1
Pretty good	2
Good & bad parts about equal	3
Pretty bad	4
Very bad: could hardly be worse	5

G

H

FIG. 3.1. Continued

PAIN

During the past 4 weeks . . .
How much bodily pain have you
generally had ?

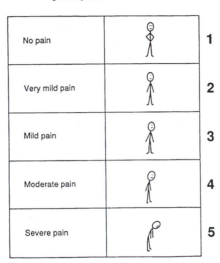

No pain		1
Very mild pain		2
Mild pain		3
Moderate pain		4
Severe pain		5

FIG. 3.1 Continued

For practical purposes, a chart score of 4 or 5 should always be considered abnormal. Once a clinician knows that a patient's score is "abnormal," the critical step is to verify the score and make a specific functional diagnosis. Once the specific cause for the dysfunction(s) is recognized, the clinician then has to determine the need for special resources to manage the problem.

The ease of administering the COOP charts has also made them helpful for efficiently evaluating care that patients have received, delivering patient education, and rapidly measuring patient opinion of care received to manage a functional problem (11). Patient-based information about the patients' health and their experiences with the health care system can be used to improve care in two ways: (a) to immediately improve patient care during the office visit, and (b) to feed back into the redesign of care for future patients.

The COOP chart-based questionnaire titled "Improve Your Medical Care" illustrates these two approaches. The questionnaire asks about function, clinical symptoms, and health risk. It also asks about the patient's perception of the doctor's awareness of problems, as well as perceptions of treatment benefit and doctor explanations about the problems. In short, the questionnaire allows the doctor to see through the patient's eyes. Many practices use bar-code scanning of the "Improve Your Medical Care" questionnaire to generate automatically a patient health report letter. Using computer-based algorithms, the letter immediately informs patients of health problems that could be addressed and, accordingly, tailors the prescription to treat the patient's problems. A computer-generated flow sheet is included in the medical record.

Individual patient feedback stimulates physicians and prompts them to discuss unmet needs and prescribe applicable and educational self-care "homework." When aggregated responses are examined, physicians are encouraged to focus on areas where improvements in the process of care will generate the greatest impact for future patients. Ongoing monitoring of patient-based information produces a constant stream of ideas for changing the delivery process to get better results. The cost of implementing these approaches is small. Patient and provider appreciation of the information is immediate.

DEROGATIS AFFECT BALANCE SCALE (DABS)

Extensive research in behavioral medicine and psychopathology has related affective or mood status to both psychological and physical health and well-being. For many years, such studies concentrated almost exclusively on the relationships between negative or dysphoric affects and mental and physical health. More recently, a discernible body of research has emerged concerned with *positive affect states* and their relationships to various indicators of health status, and with the importance of *affect balance* as a valid indicator of well-being. Although arising from disparate fields, research on the relationship between positive affects, affects balance, and health has suggested that positive mood states are a valid predictor of both physical and mental health status.

The DABS is a multidimensional mood and affects inventory composed of 40 adjective items that measures affectivity and affects balance via eight primary affect dimensions and five global scores (12). The positive affects dimensions are labeled *joy, contentment, vigor,* and *affection.* The negative affects dimensions are anxiety, depression, guilt, and hostility. The DABS global scores consist of the Positive Total score, Negative Total score, and the Affects Balance Index. Recently, two additional global measures, the Affects Expressiveness Index and the Positive Affects Ratio have been created for the DABS, and a brief form of the scale, the DABS-SF, has been normed and introduced.

The Positive Affects Total (PTOT) is defined as the sum of all scores on the four positive affects dimensions of joy, contentment, vigor, and affection, whereas the Negative Affects Total (NTOT) is represented as the sum of scores on the four negative dimensions of anxiety, depression, guilt, and hostility. The Affects Balance Index is defined as PTOT–NTOT/20. The Affects Expressiveness Index is defined as the sum total of affective expression, regardless of balance (i.e., regardless of positive or negative direction). It represents an attempt to measure the individual's affective "charge" or total affectivity. The Positive Affects Ratio illustrates a different approach to measuring global affectivity, in that it is designed to communicate the proportion of total affective expression that is positive. It is defined as the ratio of positive affectivity to total affectivity (i.e., positive plus negative affectivity) on the DABS and reflects the proportion of affective expression due to positive emotions. Three factors emerged that clearly reflected positive affects dimensions: a combined *joy/contentment* dimension, an *affection* dimension, and a *vigor* dimension. On the negative side, the largest factor represented a combined *depression/guilt* factor, with two additional components clearly reflecting *anxiety* and *hostility*.

Whichever posture one takes concerning the basic nature of the relationship between positive affectivity and health and well-being, affects balance has clearly been shown to have substantial associations with multiple health indicators. Just as certain personality constellations are believed to represent markers for the "disease-prone personality" (13), it is equally possible that positive affects balance represents a reliable marker for disease-resistance. The DABS is designed to be a brief, reliable, and valid measure of the primary constructs of affectivity and affects balance, and should help to address these questions in a valid and cost-effective manner. (The publisher of the DABS and DABS-SF is Clinical Psychometric Research of Towson, Maryland.)

MODULAR APPROACH TO HRQOL ASSESSMENT IN ONCOLOGY

Historically, the evaluation of new cancer therapies has focused on such biomedical outcomes as tumor response, disease-free and overall survival, and treatment-related toxicity. While these broad outcome parameters remain central in the evaluation process, there is increasing recognition of the need to assess more formally and systematically the impact of cancer and its treatment on the functional, psychological, and social health of the individual.

Such a culture-free research environment cannot be assumed, however, when one is interested in assessing more subjective outcomes such as symptoms, psychological well-being, and social functioning. On the contrary, the ways in which individuals define, recognize, and report their illness experience, whether expressed in terms of symptoms or levels of functioning, can be highly influenced by such factors as gender, culture, and socioeconomic status (14,15).

An important issue for the EORTC was to determine the optimal level of instrument specificity. Quality of life measures were placed on a continuum reflecting their intended spectrum of application: (a) generic instruments designed for both the general population and for a wide range of chronic disease populations; (b) disease-specific measures designed for use with cancer patients, in general; (c) diagnosis-specific measures (e.g., for use with breast cancer patients only); and (d) ad hoc, study-specific measures.

A major advantage associated with the most generic class of quality of life measures is that it allows for comparison of results across studies of different patient populations. This is particularly relevant if one is primarily interested in larger health policy and resource allocation issues. However, within the EORTC, the central research focus is on comparing treatments within well-defined, relatively homogeneous patient populations, rather than across populations. Serious concerns were raised about the ability of generic instruments to detect small, yet clinically meaningful group differences in quality of life, or in detecting changes in quality of life over time. At the opposite end of the spectrum, a measurement strategy based on study-specific quality of life instruments was viewed as both impractical and inefficient. Although such instruments can be designed to address very specific research questions, there is seldom time to assure that they meet even minimal standards of validity and reliability. Additionally, such measures rule out any possibility of cross-study comparisons, even within a single diagnostic group.

Rather than forcing a choice between the two remaining measurement strategies (disease-specific versus diagnostic-specific), a compromise was adopted that incorporated positive features of both. The intent was to generate a *core* questionnaire incorporating a range of physical, emotional, and social health issues relevant to a broad spectrum of cancer patients, irrespective of specific diagnosis. This core instrument could then be supplemented by diagnosis-specific (e.g., for lung cancer or breast cancer) and/or treatment-specific questionnaire modules. This *modular* approach was intended to reconcile two principal requirements of quality of life assessment in the EORTC clinical trials program: (a) a sufficient degree of generalizability to allow for cross-study comparisons; and (b) a level of specificity adequate for addressing those research questions of particular relevance in a given clinical trial (16).

General agreement was reached that the questionnaire should be (a) specific to cancer; (b) designed primarily for patient self-completion; (c) multidimensional in structure, covering at least four basic quality of life domains—physical symptoms, physical and role functioning, psychological functioning, and social functioning; (d) composed primarily of multi-item scales; and (e) relatively brief. Additionally, the instrument had to meet standards set for reliability, validity, and responsiveness to clinical changes in patients' health status over time. Finally, given the international context of EORTC clinical trials, the questionnaire had to be amenable for use across national and cultural boundaries (i.e., to exhibit cross-cultural as well as statistical validity).

Two Generations of Core Questionnaires: The EORTC QLQ-C36

The first-generation core questionnaire, the QLQ-C36 (17), consisted of 36 items organized into four functional scales (physical, role, emotional, and social functioning), two symptom scales (fatigue and nausea/vomiting), and a global perceived health status/quality of life scale. Additional single items assessed other common symptoms (e.g., pain, dyspnea, sleep problems), as well as the perceived financial impact of the disease and its treatment.

THE EORTC QLQ-C30

The second-generation core questionnaire, the QLQ-C30 (18), employs the same basic structure as the QLQ-C36. The QLQ-C30 includes five functional scales (physical, role, emotional, social, and cognitive functioning), three symptom scales (fatigue, pain, and nausea and vomiting), a global health status/quality of life scale, and a number of single items assessing additional symptoms (dyspnea, sleep disturbance, constipation, and diarrhea) and perceived financial impact. The principal changes in the QLQ-C30 from the QLQ-C36 include replacement of the eight-item emotional functioning scale with a shorter four-item scale, inclusion of an additional pain item (thus creating a two-item scale), and separating out memory and concentration problems, yielding a two-item cognitive functioning scale (see Appendix for the item content of the QLQ-C30).

For the majority of the QLQ-C30 items a four-point Likert-type response scale is used. Exceptions include the physical and role functioning scales (employing dichotomous response choices) and the global health status/quality of life scale (where a seven-point scale is used). For ease of presentation and interpretation, all subscale and individual item responses are linearly converted to a 0 to 100 scale. For the functional and global quality of life scales, a higher score represents a better level of functioning. For the symptom scales and items, a higher score reflects a greater degree of symptomatology. Results from the three studies that employed a longitudinal design (18–20) indicate that the reliability of the QLQ-C30 scales improves with repeated measurement. This may reflect the fact that the distribution of scores is often narrower at baseline assessment (i.e., prior to the start of treatment) than at later assessment points (i.e., during treatment).

The Development of Supplementary Questionnaire Modules

An essential component of the EORTC measurement strategy involves the use of supplementary questionnaire modules that, when employed in conjunction with the QLQ-C30, can provide more detailed information relevant to evaluating the quality of life of specific patient populations (21). A module may be developed to assess (a) disease symptoms related to a specific tumor site (e.g., urinary symptoms in prostate cancer); (b) side effects associated with a given treatment (e.g., chemotherapy-induced neuropathy); or (c) additional quality of life domains affected by the disease or treatment (e.g., sexuality, body image, fear of disease recurrence). In some cases, the content of a module is intended to expand on issues touched on only briefly within the core instrument (e.g., dyspnea or pain). In other cases, entirely new subject matter may be covered (e.g., alopecia, sexuality).

THE EUROQOL INSTRUMENT:
AN INDEX OF HEALTH-RELATED QUALITY OF LIFE

The EuroQOL was developed as a multidimensional measure of health-related quality of life, capable of being expressed as a single index value (22). The descriptive system is made up of five dimensions each of three levels, defining 243 health states, plus death and unconscious states, resulting in 245 states. A graphical rating system, based on a vertical 20-cm visual analog scale is used to capture valuations for health states. The end points of the scale are labeled "best imaginable health state" and "worst imaginable health state," and have numeric values of 100 and 0, respectively. A standardized questionnaire has been evolved for the collection of health state values. Descriptions of 16 health states, in two groups of eight, are presented over two consecutive pages. Each of these pages has a common format. Four states are printed on either side of the "thermometer" rating scale. Respondents are asked to draw a line from each state to the thermometer, indicating how good or bad that state is. The logically best health state (with no problem on any dimension), and the logically worst state (with extreme problems on all dimensions) are reproduced on both pages of the questionnaire. Although originally included as a test of consistency, this duplication has been maintained so as to provide a constant perceptual framework. As well as recording values for nonfatal health states, respondents are also requested to indicate a value for death by marking the visual analog scale accordingly.

One can distinguish between the classification of health states defined by the EuroQOL descriptive system and its associated set of health state valuations, and the method by which individuals describe and rate their current health status. Information generated by six items can be used in four distinct ways. First, for individual respondents or groups of respondents, a *profile* of health status can be formed, containing information on the level of reported problems. The second descriptive form in which these self-report data can be represented is achieved by converting the original responses for each respondent into one of the 243 unique EuroQOL states. For each EuroQOL state there exists a corresponding valuation. Hence, the third form in which these self-report data can be represented is an index, in which the appropriate valuation replaces the classified state. Repeated observation using this index form of the EuroQOL provides cardinal data on changes in health status, and thus on health outcomes. The second page of the EuroQOL instrument asks respondents to mark a point on the standard 20-cm thermometer, indicating their rating of their own health status on a scale bounded by 0 and 100. This generates a fourth form of self-reported health status.

THE HEALTH ASSESSMENT QUESTIONNAIRE (HAQ)

The Stanford Health Assessment Questionnaire (HAQ) has become one of the most widely used measures of functional status in studies of patients with rheumatic diseases and human immunodeficiency virus (HIV) as well as studies of the development of musculoskeletal disability with age (23). The full HAQ (as opposed to the HAQ disability index) was designed by first establishing a hierarchical model, then the specific items for each dimension were developed and validated. The HAQ was designed to be used in a variety of illnesses rather than only rheumatic disease and was designed to be supplemented with additional measures for particular studies for which detailed and specific assessment of particular dimensions is required.

This comprehensive instrument based on the differences in outcome hierarchy allows comparison of the impact of the different diseases across the full spectrum of patient outcomes. Most studies using the HAQ have involved patients with rheumatoid arthritis, but over the past 13 years there has been an increasing number of applications of the HAQ in other diseases. The HAQ disability scale has now been used in studies of osteoarthritis, juvenile rheumatoid arthritis, systemic lupus erythematosus, scleroderma, ankylosing spondylitis, fibromyalgia, and other rheumatic diseases, as well as HIV infection and normal aging. The HAQ disability scale was originally developed in U.S. English and was validated in United States and Canadian English-speaking populations.

The HAQ, a self-administered instrument, exists in two formats: a short form that requires 3 minutes to complete, and a longer version requiring 20 minutes. The short form is composed of 24 questions on activities of daily living and mobility. The answers to the short form yield a summated index between 0 and 3 on a continuous scale. The longer version adds additional questions relating to pain, global severity, income, job change, cost of medical care, and side effects of therapy. Various researchers have made adaptations to the content, format, and/or scoring of the HAQ to meet their needs. For example, there have been several studies of ankylosing spondylitis patients using two versions of the HAQ that have added additional items designed to assess disability specifically due to problems with the spine (e.g., 72). An abridged instrument, the modified Health Assessment Questionnaire (MHAQ measures patients' difficulty, satisfaction, and pain in activities of daily living using 8 of the 20 HAQ disability items (24).

The Childhood HAQ (CHAQ) developed by Singh and his colleagues (25) is a parent- and/or self-administered questionnaire designed to measure health status in children as young as 1 year of age. Singh et al. added several new questions and modified many existing ones so that for each functional area, there is at least one question that is relevant to children of all ages. The CHAQ has been validated in patients with juvenile rheumatoid arthritis and dermatomyositis; it has also been translated into several languages (Italian, Dutch, Norwegian, Swedish, Portuguese).

Over the past several years, the HAQ disability scale has increasingly been used in routine clinical practice in both private practices and in university clinic settings for patients with various rheumatic diseases. The physicians who have implemented the HAQ in their clinical practice have found that it can be easily completed by most patients without assistance in a few minutes before being seen by the physician. Scoring takes only a minute and the results can be displayed numerically in a flow chart or graphically to illustrate changes in disability over time. The HAQ correlates well with various clinical and laboratory parameters and provides useful current and predictive information regarding disease status, utilization of services, and mortality (26).

Several studies have shown the HAQ disability index to be sensitive to change over time and useful as a measure of functional status for clinical trials. It is recommended by the American College of Rheumatology Committee on Outcome Measures in Rheumatoid Arthritis Clinical Trials (27). The HAQ disability index has served as an outcome variable, predictor, stratifying variable, covariate, and standard of comparison for validation of other instruments in many studies. The disability index has been shown to be sensitive to change and changes in disability scores were consistent with, and often more sensitive than other outcome variables, particularly on a long-term basis.

The HAQ has been correlated with various health status, laboratory, physical, and psychosocial measures, including the Arthritis Impact Measurement Scales, visual analog pain scale, and measures of psychological functioning (anxiety, depression). The HAQ disability index has also often been used in conjunction with other, more traditional ways of evaluating both the short- and long-term impact of the rheumatic diseases. (For further information, or to obtain a copy of the HAQ, please write to Dr. James F. Fries, Division of Immunology and Rheumatology, 1000 Welch Road, Suite 203, Palo Alto, CA 94304.)

THE MCMASTER HEALTH INDEX QUESTIONNAIRE

The McMaster Health Index Questionnaire (MHIQ) was developed to serve as a measure of health-related quality of life and health status for the evaluation of interventions (28). The 59 items were identified by assessing their responsiveness to change in function (in before/after interviews of general hospital patients) and their ability to predict family physician global assessments of physical function, emotional function, and social function (29).

The three dimensions of health assessed by the MHIQ are physical, social, and emotional function. The 24 physical function items cover physical activities, mobility, self-care activities, communication (sight and hearing), and global physical function. The 25 social function items are concerned with general well-being, work/social role performance/material welfare, family support/participation, friends' support/participation, and global social function. The 25 emotional function items are concerned with feelings of self-esteem, attitudes toward personal relationships, thoughts about the future, critical life events, and global emotional function. In total, the MHIQ contains only 59 items, since some of the items address both social and emotional function.

All of the physical function items are designed to evaluate the patient's functional level on the day the MHIQ is administered. The social function items are explicitly concerned with a specific time period (usually the present). Agree–disagree emotional function items do not refer to a specific time period, but are phrased in the present tense. Other emotional function items refer to the recent past, as specifically defined (e.g., within the last year). None of the items asks the respondent to report changes in physical, social, or emotional function. The self-completed version of the MHIQ takes 20 minutes for administration.

Applications

The MHIQ adequately taps the magnitude of the task or performance, but it does not include items on the patient's effort or support in performance. Feinstein et al. (30) suggest that instruments such as the MHIQ should be supplemented with a single question about the availability of a person who is willing and ready to give support if needed, or, instead of trying to estimate patient's "motivation" in working at rehabilitative exercises, nurses or other therapists could be asked to rate the observed effort and cooperation. The MHIQ should also recognize certain nonhuman sources of support, such as including a question about the use of ramps or elevators for someone who is wheelchair bound, that can also make important distinctions in a patient's ability to function. Inclusion of one or more of these additions to the MHIQ would address this important issue of patient collaboration and result in an instrument that measures more than just the magnitude of the task alone. The MHIQ is a global measure of physical, emotional, and social function. Consequently, it should be supplemented with items that have a specific bearing on the study questions in order to improve the validity of the results in studies that evaluate health care interventions or describe or predict health status/quality of life.

The MHIQ physical function scores have been shown to reflect clinically important change, such as discharge from hospital (31). This responsiveness is presumably because the MHIQ physical function scores consist of items that cover a range of quality of life/health status categories, and few extraneous items contribute to the MHIQ physical function score.

NOTTINGHAM HEALTH PROFILE (NHP)

During the 1970s, there was considerable interest in the factors other than the disease process that contributed to health and ill health, and internationally there was considerable research commitment into the production of measures that would be more sensitive to such variations in states of health. Thus, although one of the prime aims of the Nottingham Health Profile (NHP) (32) was to produce an instrument that would be used in epidemiological studies of health and disease, it soon became evident that there was a demand for measures that could be used to evaluate different forms of intervention, either in prevention or treatment, and that would not only provide a more sensitive and detailed measure of health, but would reflect the views of the patient. NHP and its earlier version, the Nottingham Health Index (NHI), are intended to give a brief measure of perceived physical, social and emotional health. The NHP asks about feelings and emotional states directly, rather than by changes in behavior, and emphasizes the respondent's subjective assessment of his or her health. The NHP contains 38 items encompassing six dimensions: energy, pain, physical mobility, emotional reactions, sleep, and social isolation; and it takes under 10 minutes to complete (32,33).

When it was first published, the NHP was a two-part self-completion questionnaire providing a health profile on a number of different parameters. Part I of the profile consists of statements about how people feel or function, whereas part II inquires about the effect of ill health on seven areas of daily life. Part II, which was always considered to be less rigorous, is structurally different and is currently less frequently used. The goals of NHP development were to:

1. Provide some assessment of a person's need for care that was not based on purely medical criteria;
2. Enable the subsequent evaluation of care provided for persons in need;
3. Make a start on the development of an indicator that could be used for the survey of population health status.

Part I of the NHP consists of a total of 38 statements in six sections: energy level, emotional reactions, physical mobility, pain, social isolation, and sleep, with each section scored separately. Part II consists of seven questions, intended to reflect how perceived health problems were affecting a respondent's daily life. An item analysis of the original set of statements found that seven activities were most often reported to be affected by health problems: work, personal activities, social life, family life, sex, spare-time activities, and holidays and travel. It was not possible to devise and weight questions within each section, but only to identify by yes or no whether a particular area had been affected by the person's health.

Strengths

The NHP is the only generic health status measure derived entirely from lay people. As such, it reflects the values and concerns of the people who are required to complete the measure. Consequently, patients find the measure relevant and highly acceptable. Because the items are expressed in the words of ordinary people, biases associated with social class are minimized. The lack of artificial items aids translation into other languages.

The measure is easy to complete and score. It has a required reading age of 9 years and a simple response format—essential in countries where form-filling is uncommon. Respondents are asked to indicate whether or not each item applies to them. As a consequence of the simple items and response format, very few missing answers result. Where the measure is used in postal surveys, high response rates are achieved. The measure is available in a large number of languages. The adaptations that have been developed are of a high quality, allowing clinical trial data to be combined from different countries. Other language versions of the NHP are described below. The NHP is the most widely used measure of perceived health status in Europe. The measure is also becoming more common in North America and other English-speaking countries. As a consequence of this usage, many clinicians are familiar with the measure and interpretation of scores. NHP data are also acceptable to authorities evaluating clinical trial results (33). Manuals are available for each language version of the measure, as well as a Euroguide. Reference values are also available for some of the language versions, based on large-scale population studies using the NHP.

Like all the generic measures of health status, the NHP lacks sensitivity. The measure works best with chronic, disabling illnesses, and with elderly populations. The development of the Nottingham Health Profile was an unusually careful and thoughtful process, and its reliability and validity are highly satisfactory for its intended uses. As the instrument, developers have pointed out, "The NHP is clearly tapping only the extreme end of perceived health problems" (32). Because the measure is specific to the culture of the United Kingdom, it is not known whether it will perform well in other social contexts. The NHP was not designed to be used in clinical trials because of its simplicity. However, a profile (NHP, Sickness Impact Profile) such as the components of the SF-36 makes change more difficult to evaluate as improvements in some sections can be associated with worse scores in others. Furthermore, it is not possible to compare the importance of the different sections. It cannot be validly used with hospitalized patients. NHPs were developed for France, Spain, Italy, Sweden, and North America. More recently NHPs for Germany, the Netherlands, Denmark, Finland, and Norway have been produced. (Researchers wishing to use the NHP or purchase copies of the User's Manual or Euroguide should apply to Dr. McKenna, Galen Research, Southern Hey, 137 Barlow Moor Road, West Didsbury, Manchester, M20 2PW, England.)

PSYCHOLOGICAL ADJUSTMENT TO ILLNESS SCALE
(PAIS AND PAIS-SR)

The Psychosocial Adjustment to Illness Scale (PAIS) is a semistructured interview designed to assess the quality of a patient's psychosocial adjustment to a current medical illness or its residual effects (34). With minor alterations in format, the PAIS may also be used to measure the quality of spouses', parents', or other relatives' adjustment to a patient's illness, or their perceptions of the patient's adjustment. The PAIS is designed to be completed in conjunction with a personal interview with the respondent, conducted by a trained health professional or interviewer. The PAIS interview requires approximately 20 to 25 minutes to complete. When conducted within a broader interview, PAIS items should be presented consecutively without the interjection of external items or queries. The PAIS is typically made available in reusable booklets with separate answer and score/profile forms.

In addition to the PAIS interview, there also is a self-report version of the scale, the PAIS-SR. The PAIS-SR is designed to be completed directly by the respondent, with instructions printed in a consumable booklet. The PAIS-SR also requires from 20 to 25 minutes to complete, with separate answer and score/profile forms available. Interview questions are designed to assess the quality of adjustment in each of these primary adjustment areas. A total of 46 items are completed concerning the respondent in a PAIS interview, with each item being rated on a four-point (0–3) scale of adjustment. Higher ratings indicate poorer adjustment. There is an equivalent item for each of the 46 PAIS items on the PAIS-SR, rewritten or modified for a self-report format. A four-point scale of distress(0–3) is also used with the PAIS-SR but scale direction is alternated on every other item to reduce position response biases. The PAIS and PAIS-SR reflect psychosocial adjustment to illness via seven primary domains of adjustment:

  I. Health Care Orientation
       McMaster Health Index Questionnaire (MHIQ)
 II. Vocational Environment
III. Domestic Environment
IV. Sexual Relationships
 V. Extended Family Relationships
VI. Social Environment
VII. Psychological Distress

The PAIS and PAIS-SR are designed to be interpreted at three distinct but related levels: the *global* level, the *domain* level, and the *discrete* item level. Ideally, data from each of the three levels of interpretation should converge to deliver an integrated picture of the respondent's adjustment to the illness or condition of note. The PAIS Total Score, particularly when evaluated in terms of a relevant normative group, is a good indicator of the level of the patient's overall adjustment. Domain scores contribute a profile of areas of relative strength and vulnerability in the patient's adjustment.

The PAIS/PAIS-SR represents a multidimensional psychometric definition of the construct of adjustment to illness that ties the construct very closely to the functional efficiencies of primary social role behaviors. The guiding philosophy behind the development of the PAIS/PAIS-SR treats illnesses as distinct and specific entities, each of which calls for its own distinct norms. The PAIS/PAIS-SR system is designed to allow assessment based on either clinical judgment or self-report, and is sufficiently flexible to enable multiple respondents. Because of its design, not only can the nature of the index patient's adjustment be established from multiple perspectives, but the adjustment of significant others (e.g., spouses, children, caregivers) to the index patient's illness may also be assessed. (The publisher of the PAIS & PAIS-SR is Clinical Psychometric Research, 100 West Pennsylvania Avenue, Suite 302, Towson, MD 21204.)

QUALITY OF LIFE IN CANCER (QOL-C)

The generic version of the multidimensional HRQOL scale used to measure HRQL in persons with a variety of cancer diagnoses undergoing different types of treatments is called the Quality of Life Cancer Scale (HRQOL scale). This chapter describes the development of the basic 30-item HRQOL-CA instrument into its two current versions: the HRQOL and HRQOL-CA (35). Cancer patients adjust their quality of life expectations based on perceived health and function. For example, patients talk about making the best of life, refocusing life, planning one day at a time, and being active during good days. Patients readjust their definition of enjoying life to include those activities that still offer pleasure and happiness, such as being alive, appreciating surroundings, doing what one wants to do. Patients also tend to narrow their focus of concern to currently relevant attributes of quality of life. Controlling pain is critical to improving their quality of life (36). Although subjects use the whole 100-mm scale for most items, the majority of responses range between 25 mm and 75 mm for persons with cancer. This could indicate (a) a reluctance to use the lower and upper ends of the scale; (b) biased samples of patients whose quality of life was not poor enough or good enough to be scored in the extremes; (c) accidental exclusion of patients with the poorest quality of life who may have been too sick to participate in the studies, and those with the best quality of life who do not have cancer; and/or (d) a tendency for some patients to "save" the poor quality of life end of the scales for later use when they expect things will be worse.

SYMPTOM CHECK LIST (SCL-90-R) AND THE BRIEF SYMPTOM INVENTORY (BSI)

The SCL-90-R is a 90-item self-report symptom inventory designed to reflect the psychological symptom patterns of respondents in community, medical, and psychiatric settings (37,38). A prototype version of the scale (39) was amended and validated in the present revised form (40). The items of the SCL-90-R are rated on a five-point distress scale (0–4), ranging from "not-at-all" to "extremely." The inventory is scored and interpreted in terms of nine primary symptom dimensions and three global indices of distress. The primary symptom dimensions and globals are labeled as follows:

   I. Somatization
  II. Obsessive–compulsive
 III. Interpersonal sensitivity
  IV. Depression
   V. Anxiety
  VI. Hostility
 VII. Phobic Anxiety
VIII. Paranoid Ideation
  IX. Psychoticism
       Global Severity Index (GSI)
       Positive Symptom Distress Index (PSDI)
       Positive Symptom Total (PST)

The global indices have been developed to provide more flexibility in overall assessment of the patient's psychological distress status and to provide summary indices of levels of symptomatology and psychological distress. Previous research using analogs of these measures has confirmed that, although related, the three indicators reflect distinct aspects of psychological disorder (41).

Brief Symptom Inventory (BSI)

The BSI (42) is composed of 53 items and represents the brief form of the SCL-90-R, reflecting psychopathology and psychological distress in terms of the same nine symptom dimensions and three global indices as the SCL-90-R. It achieves reliable and valid measurement of the same symptom constructs as its longer companion through an item selection algorithm that retained items with the most "saturated" loadings on the nine primary symptom dimensions of the longer test. Correlations between the BSI and the SCL-90-R are very high (37,42), which has led some clinicians and investigators to employ the test even when time constraints are not an issue. Translations are available in Spanish, Portuguese, German, Italian, Dutch, French, Japanese, Korean, Chinese, Vietnamese, Swedish, Hebrew, Arabic, Danish, Norwegian, and other languages.

The SCL-90-R and the BSI are measures of current psychological symptom status and are not personality measures, except indirectly, in that certain personality types and Diagnostic and Statistical Manual (DSM) axis II disorders may tend to manifest characteristic profile on the primary symptom dimensions when distressed. The SCL-90-R and the BSI are designed to measure and quantify the psychological symptom status of patients with psychiatric disorders, medical patients, and community individuals who are not currently patients. They may be used appropriately with any respondents from these broad populations, since they represent the principal normative groups for both tests with norms (as young as 13 years of age) .

A unique feature of both the SCL-90-R and the BSI derives from the fact that two matching clinical observer's rating scales, measuring the same psychopathologic constructs as the self-report scales, are available to quantify clinician judgments concerning patient psychological distress levels. The Derogatis Psychiatric Rating Scale (DPRS) and the SCL-90 Analogue Scale, when used together, enable a broad range of clinical observers (e.g., psychiatrists, psychologists, physicians, nurses, social workers) to record systematic judgments concerning patient status.

THE DEROGATIS PSYCHIATRIC RATING SCALE

The DPRS is a multidimensional psychiatric rating scale designed to be a clinician's version of the SCL-90-R. The first nine symptom dimensions of the DPRS were constructed to match the nine primary symptom dimensions of the "90." The

DPRS also contains eight additional dimensions felt to be important to accurate clinical assessment, but not amenable to accurate patient self-report. The DPRS also contains a global rating scale termed the Global Pathology Index.

The SCL-90 Analogue Scale

The SCL-90 Analogue is a clinical observer's scale designed for the health professional without detailed psychiatric training or experience with psychopathology (e.g., physicians, nurses, clinical technicians). It is a graphic or analog scale in that each of the nine primary symptom dimensions of the SCL-90-R is represented on a 100-mm line, extending from "not-at-all" at one pole to "extremely" at the other.

A perennially important issue in psychological assessment concerns the reliable early identification of the suicidal patient. Four subscales (Somatization, Interpersonal Sensitivity, Paranoid Ideation, and Psychoticism) and the global scores significantly discriminated positive from negative suicide attempters (43). From their inception, the SCL-90-R and the BSI were designed for use in primary care and other medical populations. An early application of the SCL-90-R in a medical environment was reported by Snyder et al. (44). In a family practice setting, these investigators showed that those patients who revealed significant communication problems with their physicians also had significantly higher distress scores on the SCL-90-R. More recently, as part of the Family Heart Study, Weidner et al. (45) demonstrated significant reductions in SCL-90-R Depression and Hostility scores over a 5-year dietary intervention program designed to reduce plasma cholesterol. In a different chronic disease context, Irvine et al. (46) demonstrated that worry concerning hypoglycemia and behavior focused on avoiding this condition were clearly correlated with multiple SCL-90-R dimension scores among a cohort of insulin-dependent diabetics. (SCL-90-R and BSI are registered trademarks owned by Leonard R. Derogatis, Ph.D. The SCL-90-R and the BSI are available from their publisher, National Computer Systems (NCS) of Minneapolis, MN.)

THE MEDICAL OUTCOME STUDY SHORT FORM (SF-36) HEALTH SURVEY

The SF-36—a short-form with 36 items—is a multipurpose survey of general health status (47,48). It was constructed to fill the gap between much more lengthy surveys and relatively coarse single-item measures. The SF-36 multi-item scales yield a profile of eight concepts as well as summary physical and mental health measures. These summary measures are scored by aggregating the most highly related scales (49,50). The SF-36 has proven useful in comparisons of the relative burden of different diseases and preliminary results suggest that it may also be useful in estimating the relative benefits of different treatments.

The SF-36 was constructed to satisfy minimum psychometric standards necessary for group comparisons involving generic health concepts, i.e., concepts that are not specific to any age, disease, or treatment group. The eight health concepts were selected from 40 included in the Medical Outcomes Study (MOS) (51) to represent those hypothesized to be most frequently measured in widely used health surveys and those most affected by disease and treatment (48,52). They also represent multiple operational definitions of health, including function and dysfunction, distress and well-being, objective reports and subjective ratings, and both favorable and unfavorable self-evaluations of general health status (48). Most items have their roots in instruments that have been in use for more than 20 years (51), including the General Psychological Well-Being Inventory (53), various physical and role functioning measures (54–57), the Health Perceptions Questionnaire (58), and other measures that proved to be useful during the Health Insurance Experiment (HIE) (59). MOS researchers selected and adapted questionnaire items from these and other sources and developed new measures to construct the 149-item Functioning and Well-Being Profile (51), which was the source for SF-36 items. This model on which the instrument is based has three levels: (a) items, (b) eight scales that aggregate two to ten items each, and (c) two summary measures that aggregate scales. All but one of the 36 items (self-reported health transition) are used to score the eight SF-36 scales. Each item is used in scoring only one scale. Three scales (Physical Functioning, Role–Physical, Bodily Pain) contribute most to the scoring of the Physical Component Summary (PCS) measure (49). The Mental Health, Role–Emotional, and Social Functioning scales contribute most to the scoring of the Mental Component Summary (MCS) measure. Three of the scales (Vitality, General Health, and Social Functioning) have noteworthy correlations with both components. The SF-36 is suitable for self-administration, computerized administration, or administration by a trained interviewer in person or by telephone, to persons aged 14 years and older using standardized four-week recall (or an acute one-week recall version). The scoring algorithms aggregate items shown in Fig. 3.2 without score standardization or item weighting.

Norms for General and Specific Populations

The SF-36 has been normed in the general U.S. population and for representative samples from many countries using common translation and norming protocols developed by the International Quality of Life Assessment (IHRQOLA) Project (60–62). From the general U.S. population, norms for age and sex groups and for 14 chronic diseases have been published along with estimates of the effect of telephone-administered relative to self-administered versions (48,49,63). Because most SF-36 scales were constructed to reproduce longer scales, much attention has been given to how well the short-form versions perform in empirical tests relative to the full-length versions. Compared with the longer MOS measures they were constructed to reproduce, SF-36 scales have

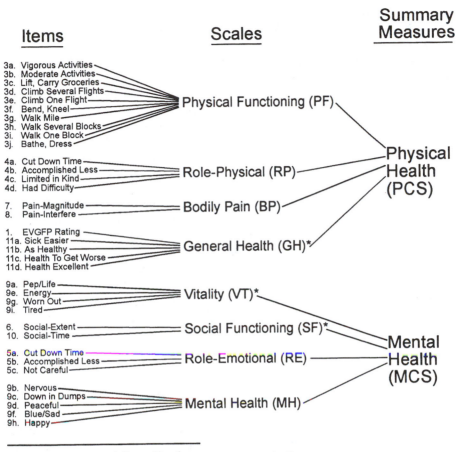

Items	Scales	Summary Measures

Items

3a. Vigorous Activities
3b. Moderate Activities
3c. Lift, Carry Groceries
3d. Climb Several Flights
3e. Climb One Flight
3f. Bend, Kneel
3g. Walk Mile
3h. Walk Several Blocks
3i. Walk One Block
3j. Bathe, Dress

4a. Cut Down Time
4b. Accomplished Less
4c. Limited in Kind
4d. Had Difficulty

7. Pain-Magnitude
8. Pain-Interfere

1. EVGFP Rating
11a. Sick Easier
11b. As Healthy
11c. Health To Get Worse
11d. Health Excellent

9a. Pep/Life
9e. Energy
9g. Worn Out
9i. Tired

6. Social-Extent
10. Social-Time

5a. Cut Down Time
5b. Accomplished Less
5c. Not Careful

9b. Nervous
9c. Down in Dumps
9d. Peaceful
9f. Blue/Sad
9h. Happy

Scales

Physical Functioning (PF)

Role-Physical (RP)

Bodily Pain (BP)

General Health (GH)*

Vitality (VT)*

Social Functioning (SF)*

Role-Emotional (RE)

Mental Health (MH)

Summary Measures

Physical Health (PCS)

Mental Health (MCS)

* Significant correlation with other summary measure.
Source: Ware et al. (1994)

FIG. 3.2. SF-36 measurement model.

been shown to perform with about 80% to 90% empirical validity in studies involving physical and mental health "criteria" (64).

The validity of each of the eight scales and the two summary measures has been shown to differ markedly as would be expected from factor analytic studies of construct validity (49,65,66). Specifically, the Mental Health, Role–Emotional, and Social Functioning scales and the MCS summary measure have been shown to be the most valid mental health measures in both cross-cultural and longitudinal tests using the method of known-groups validity. The Physical Functioning, Role–Physical, and Bodily Pain scales and the PCS have been shown to be the most valid physical health measures. Criteria used in the known-groups validation of the SF-36, which include accepted clinical indicators of diagnosis and severity of depression, heart disease, and other conditions, are well documented in peer-reviewed publications and in the two users' manuals (48–50,65,67).

Although many studies appear to rely on the SF-36 as the principal measure of health outcome, it may be best to rely upon it as a "generic core," pending further research. A generic core battery of measures serves the purpose of comparing results across studies and populations and greatly expands the interpretation guidelines that are essential to determining the clinical, economic, and human relevance of results. Because it is short, the SF-36 can be reproduced in a questionnaire with ample room for other more precise general and specific measures.

Some SF-36 scales have been shown to have 10% to 20% less precision than the long-form MOS measures they were constructed to reproduce (64). This disadvantage of the SF-36 should be weighed against the fact that some of these long-form measures require five to ten times greater respondent burden. Empirical studies of this tradeoff suggest that the SF-36 provides a practical alternative to longer measures and that the eight scales and two summary scales rarely miss a noteworthy difference in physical or mental health status in group-level comparisons (48,49,68). Regardless, the fact that the SF-36 represents a documented compromise in measurement precision (relative to longer MOS measures) leading to a reduction in the statistical power of hypothesis testing should be taken into account in planning clinical trials and other studies. The user's manuals include five tables of sample size estimates for differences in scores of various amounts for conventional statistical tests (48,49).

THE SICKNESS IMPACT PROFILE

The Sickness Impact Profile (SIP) is a behaviorally based health status measure. The developers of the SIP chose to measure sickness-related behavior for several reasons (69,70). First, behaviors can be directly reported by the individual or they can be observed and reported by another respondent referring to the individual. Second, medical treatment can affect behavior independent of effects on the disease itself. Third, behaviors can be measured whether or not the individual seeks medical care. Finally, the effects of sickness as manifested in behavioral changes is a concept that is familiar and accepted by both consumers and providers of health care. The 136 items in 12 categories describe activities associated with everyday living. Each item is written in the first person case and the present tense (Table 3.1). Respondents are asked to endorse (i.e., say "yes" to if interview-administered or place a check by if self-administered) those items that they are sure describe them on that day and that are related to their health.

The SIP is scored according to the number and type of items that are endorsed (Table 3.2). Each item has a numeric scale value that reflects its degree of dysfunction. Higher scale values indicate greater dysfunction. An individual's total SIP score is computed by summing the scale values for the items that he or she endorses, dividing by the total possible score (if all items were endorsed), and

TABLE 3.1 *Sample SIP Items*

Category	Sample Item
Sleep and Rest	I sit during much of the day
Emotional Behavior	I act nervous or restless
Body Care and Movement	I change position frequently
Home Management	I am not doing any of the clothes washing that I usually do
Mobility	I am not going into town
Social Interaction	I am going out less to visit people
Ambulation	I walk more slowly
Alertness Behavior	I do not keep my attention on any activity for long
Communication	I don't write except to sign my name
Work	I am not working at all
Recreation and Pastimes	I am doing fewer community activities
Eating	I am eating much less than usual

multiplying by 100. The score is expressed as a percentage and can range from 0 to 100, where 0 represents no dysfunction and 100 represents maximal dysfunction. Scoring is also possible at the level of categories and dimensions. The 136 items are aggregated into 12 categories that represent specific areas of activity. To score an individual category, the scale values for all endorsed items in that category are divided by the total possible score for the category and multiplied by 100. Four categories, Emotional Behavior, Social Interaction, Alertness Behavior, and Communication, can be further aggregated into a Psychosocial dimension. Three categories, Body Care and Movement, Mobility, and Ambulation, define a Physical dimension. Dimension scores are computed in the same manner as category and total scores.

Guidelines for Use

The SIP is designed to be either interview- or self-administered. For interview administration, all interviewers should receive standardized training outlined in

TABLE 3.2 *Categories and dimensions of the Sickness Impact Profile*

Dimension	Category
Physical	Ambulation
	Mobility
	Body Care and Movement
Psychosocial	Communication
	Alertness Behavior
	Emotional Behavior
	Social Interaction
Independent Categories	Sleep and Rest
	Eating
	Work
	Home Management
	Recreation and Pastimes

the "Administration Procedures and Interviewer Training for the Sickness Impact Profile" manual. Special attention should be paid to instructions for administration of the SIP by telephone, since telephone interviews lack the visual cues present during in-person interviews. Self-administration has been tested in two ways. The first method requires an interviewer to deliver the SIP, provide verbal instructions and answer questions, and then leave the SIP to be self-administered. The second method is a mail-delivered SIP with written instructions. Mail-delivered SIPs have demonstrated lower, although acceptable, levels of internal consistency, reliability, and validity than interviewer-delivered SIPs. Thus, it is recommended that self-administration be accompanied by verbal instructions whenever possible.

The length of an interview ranges from 20 to 30 minutes depending on the severity of illness of the patient. Although some researchers have been reluctant to use the SIP because of its length, patients rarely complain about the length and interviewers report that the instrument is feasible. Researchers sometimes ask if the SIP can be shortened by deleting items or categories that they believe are not relevant to the population under study. Items should not be deleted from the instrument because the reliability and validity of category, dimension, and overall scores would be unknown. Although individual categories are reliable and valid, selective administration of categories is strongly discouraged because the discriminative capacity of the SIP will be decreased and because categories have demonstrated differential importance in accounting for the variance in overall SIP score for different patient groups.

Examples of the Sickness Impact Profile in Clinical Trials

In prospective studies in a variety of clinical disorders, the SIP provided a profile of patient-reported, health-related dysfunction and contributed to the assessment of the effectiveness of various treatment and rehabilitation strategies. In some cases, SIP findings were unexpected and generated new hypotheses. Bergner et al. (71) showed that, contrary to earlier studies and beliefs, home care services do not improve functional outcomes for COPD patients. Sugarbaker et al. (72) found that, contrary to their a priori hypothesis, limb-sparing surgery with radiation and chemotherapy does not lead to better functioning than amputation for patients with lower extremity soft tissue sarcoma. In other cases, SIP findings confirmed previously hypothesized relationships, such as the physiological basis for behavioral dysfunction in patients with hyperthyroidism (73).

The SIP was instrumental in assessing the burden of illness of a population, such as the lower extremity fracture population (74). The burden of illness relative to other conditions or diseases is possible because of the wealth of published SIP scores for different populations. By virtue of its multidimensionality, the SIP identifies specific types of dysfunction experienced by a population. Knowledge of both level and type of dysfunction are critical for the development of effective treatment and rehabilitation strategies. The availability of published SIP scores for numerous samples representing healthy and various disease populations demonstrates its feasibility and utility in a variety of settings. (Copies of the SIP are available from the Johns Hopkins University, which holds the copyright for the instrument. Interested researchers should write to: The Health Services Research and Development Center, The Johns Hopkins University School of Hygiene and Public Health, 624 North Broadway, Baltimore, Maryland 21205, Attn: Elizabeth Ann Skinner, MSW.)

WORLD HEALTH ORGANIZATION QOL ASSESSMENT (WHOQOL)

The World Health Organization's (WHO) initiative to develop a quality of life assessment arises from a need for a genuinely international measure of quality of life. The WHOQOL is being developed, according to a standardized protocol (75), simultaneously in a wide range of languages and cultures. Field centers were selected to provide differences in level of industrialization, health service organization, and other culture-specific determinants affecting quality of life (e.g., role of family, perception of time, perception of self, dominant religion). Responses to questions in the WHOQOL are given on five-point Likert-type response scales. According to the differences in the content of questions, five different response scales were needed. The scales addressed (a) Intensity (not at all/extremely), (b) Capacity (not at all/completely), (c) Frequency (never/always), (d) Evaluation (very dissatisfied/very satisfied; very poor/very good), (e) Importance (not important/extremely important).

TABLE 3.3 *WHOQOL domains and facets*

Domain I—Physical domain	16 Work capacity
1 Pain and discomfort	Domain IV—Social relationships
2 Energy and fatigue	17 Personal relationships
3 Sexual activity	18 Practical social support
4 Sleep and rest	19 Activities as provider/supporter
5 Sensory functions	Domain V—Environment
Domain II—Psychological domain	20 Freedom, physical safety, and security
6 Positive feelings	21 Home environment
7 Thinking, learning, memory, and	22 Work satisfaction
concentration	23 Financial resources
8 Self-esteem	24 Health and social care: accessibility
9 Body image and appearance	and quality
10 Negative feelings	25 Opportunities for acquiring new
Domain III—Level of independence	information and skills
11 Mobility	26 Participation in and opportunities for
12 Activities of daily living	recreation/leisure activities
13 Dependence on medicinal substances	27 Physical environment:
and medical aids	(pollution/noise/traffic/climate)
14 Dependence on nonmedical	28 Transport
substances (alcohol, tobacco, drugs)	Domain VI—Spirituality/religion/personal
15 Communication capacity	beliefs

The present form of the WHOQOL (Table 3.3), which allows for a comprehensive inquiry into quality of life, is envisaged as having some 100 items. Therefore, a shorter version will be developed that might address only the primary facets of quality of life or may utilize only the highest loading item for each facet. The short form could be used for screening, in clinical trials, repeated measures research design, or for clinical purposes where only a few minutes are available for its administration. Interviewer-assisted and interviewer-administered forms of the instrument have been developed for respondents who cannot, for health or education reasons, read or write. Research using a multitrait, multimethod approach will be directed at establishing the correspondence between these different forms of the instrument. Different versions of the WHOQOL will ensure its high "application potential" (76).

Population-Specific Modules

Specific WHOQOL modules will be developed for groups of persons whose quality of life might not be sufficiently or appropriately assessed with the described form of the WHOQOL instrument (core instrument or core module). A module will be a special set of facets/subfacets/questions that complement the core instrument for a particular group. WHO has identified five priority areas for module development: (a) persons suffering from chronic diseases (e.g., epilepsy, arthritis, cancer, AIDS, diabetes), (b) caregivers of the ill or disabled (e.g., a person taking care of a terminally sick patient), (c) persons living in highly stressful situations (e.g., elderly people living in poorly run institutions, refugees in camps), (d) persons with difficulty communicating (e.g., persons with severe learning disabilities), and (e) children.

WHO's commitment to the development of an international quality of life assessment arises from the lack of any genuinely international instruments that can be meaningfully used in both developed and developing world countries to measure the individual's view of the impact of disease and impairment on his/her life. The WHOQOL has been designed as a generic instrument for the assessment of both positive and negative aspects of quality of life. It provides instruments in a broad range of languages, each of which is closely comparable and yet each of which can retain features that might be unique to a particular language and culture. It yields a multidimensional profile with quality of life scores in six domains, encompassing more than 20 facets of quality of life. (Further information can be obtained from the WHOQOL Group, Division of Mental Health, World Health Organization, CH-1211 Geneva 27, Switzerland.)

REFERENCES

1. Nelson EC, Wasson, J, Kirk J, et al. Assessment of function in routine clinical practice: description of the COOP chart method and preliminary findings. *J Chronic Dis* 1987;40(S1):55S–63S.
2. Nelson EC, Landgraf JM, Hays RD, et al. The functional status of patients: how can it be measured in physician's offices? *Med Care* 1990;28(12):1111–1126.

3. Larson CO, Hays RD, Nelson EC. Do the pictures influence scores on the Dartmouth COOP charts? *Qual Life Res* 1992;1:247–249.
4. Nelson EC, Landgraf JM, Hays RD, et al. The COOP function charts: a system to measure patient function in physicians' offices. In: Lipkin M Jr, ed. *Functional status measurement in primary care: frontiers of primary care.* New York: Springer-Verlag, 1990:97–131.
5. Ware JE, Nelson EC, Sherbourne CD, et al. Preliminary tests of a 6-item general health survey: a patient application. In: Stewart A, Ware JE, eds. *Measuring functioning and well-being: the Medical Outcomes Study Approach.* Durham, NC: Duke University Press, 1992: 291–303.
6. Scholten JHG, Van Weel C. *Functional status assessment in family practice: the Dartmouth COOP functional health assessment charts/WONCA.* Lelystad, Netherlands: MEDITekst, 1992.
7. Wasson JH, Kairys SW, Nelson EC, et al. A short survey for assessing health and social problems of adolescents. *J Fam Pract* 1994;38(5):489–494.
8. Wasson JH, Kairys SW, Nelson EC, et al. Adolescent health and social problems: a method for detection and early management. *Archives Fam Med* 1995;4:51–56.
9. McHorney CA, Ware JE, Rogers W, et al. The validity and relative precision of MOS short- and long-form Health Status Scales and Dartmouth COOP charts: results from the Medical Outcomes Study. *Med Care* 1992;30(5):MS253–MS265.
10. Wasson J, Keller A, Rubenstein L, Hays R, et al. Benefits and obstacles of health status assessment in ambulatory settings: the clinician's point of view. *Med Care* 1992;30(5):MS42–MS49.
11. Nelson EC, Wasson JH. Using patient-based information to rapidly redesign care. *Health Care Forum* 1994; July/August:2529.
12. Derogatis LR. The Affects Balance Scale. Baltimore: *Clinical Psychometric Research,* 1975.
13. Friedman HS, Booth-Kewley S. The disease-prone personality. *Am Psychol* 1987;42:539–558.
14. Kleinman A, Eisenberg L, Good B. Culture, illness and care: clinical lessons from anthropologic and cross-cultural research. *Ann Intern Med* 1978;88:251–258.
15. Bullinger M, Anderson R, Cella D, Aaronson NK. Developing and evaluating cross-cultural instruments: from minimum requirements to optimal models. *Qual Life Res* 1993;2:451–459.
16. Aaronson NK, Bullinger M, Ahmedzai S. A modular approach to quality of life assessment in cancer clinical trials. *Recent Results Cancer Res* 1988;111:231–249.
17. Aaronson NK, Ahmedzai S, Bullinger M, et al. The EORTC core quality of life questionnaire: interim results of an international field study. In: Osoba D, ed. *Effect of cancer on quality of life.* Boca Raton, FL: CRC Press, 1991:185–203.
18. Aaronson NK, Ahmedzai S, Bergman B, et al. The European Organization for Research and Treatment of Cancer QLQ-C30: a quality-of-life instrument for use in international clinical trials in oncology. *J Natl Cancer Inst* 1993;85:365–376.
19. de Boer JB, Sprangers MAG, Aaronson NK, Lange JMA, van Dam FSAM. The feasibility, reliability and validity of the EORTC QLQ-C30 in assessing the quality of life of patients with a symptomatic HIV infection or AIDS (CVC IV). *Psychol Health* 1994;9:65–77.
20. Ringdal GI, Ringdal K. Testing the EORTC quality of life questionnaire on cancer patients with heterogeneous diagnoses. *Qual Life Res* 1993;2:129–140.
21. Sprangers MAG, Cull A, Bjordal K, Groenvold M, Aaronson NK. The European Organization for Research and Treatment of Cancer approach to quality of life assessment: guidelines for developing questionnaire modules. *Qual Life Res* 1993;2:287–295.
22. EuroQOL Group. EuroQOL—a new facility for the measurement of health-related quality of life. *Health Policy* 1990;16:199–208.
23. Ramey DR, Raynauld JP, Fries JF. The Health Assessment Questionnaire 1992: status and review. *Arthritis Care Res* 1992;5:119–129.
24. Pincus T, Summey JA, Soraci SA Jr, Wallston KA, Hummon NP. Assessment of patient satisfaction in activities of daily living using a modified Stanford Health Assessment Questionnaire. *Arthritis Rheum* 1983;26:1346–1353.
25. Singh G, Athreya B, Fries J, Goldsmith D. Measurement of health status in children with juvenile rheumatoid arthritis. *Arthritis Rheum* 1994;37:1761–1769.
26. Wolfe F, Kleinheksel SM, Cathey MA, Hawley DJ, Spitz PW, Fries JF. The clinical value of the Stanford Health Assessment Questionnaire functional disability index in patients with rheumatoid arthritis. *J Rheumatol* 1988;15:1480–1488.
27. Felson DT, Anderson JJ, Boers M, et al. The American College of Rheumatology preliminary core set of disease activity measures for rheumatoid arthritis clinical trials. The Committee on Outcome Measures in Rheumatoid Arthritis Clinical Trials. *Arthritis Rheum* 1993;36:729–740.
28. Chambers LW. *The McMaster Health Index Questionnaire (MHIQ): methodologic documentation*

and report of the second generation of investigations. Department of Clinical Epidemiology and Bio-statistics. Hamilton, Ont.: McMaster University, 1982.

29. Chambers LW, Sackett DL, Goldsmith CH, et al. Development and application of an index of social function. *Health Serv Res* 1976;11:430–441.

30. Feinstein AR, Josephy BR, Wells CK. Scientific and clinical problems in indexes of functional disability. *Ann Intern Med* 1986;105:413–420.

31. Sackett DL, Chambers LW, Macpherson AS, et al. The development and application of indexes of public health: general methods and a summary of results. *Am J Public Health* 1977;67:423–428.

32. Hunt SM, McEwen J, McKenna SP. *Measuring health status.* London: Croom Helm, 1986.

33. McKenna SP. Commonly used measures of health status in European clinical trials. *Br J Med Econ* 1993;6C:3–159.

34. Derogatis LR, Derogatis MF. *The psychosocial adjustment to illness scale (PAIS) & (PAIS-SR): administration, scoring F-3 & procedures manual-II,* 2nd ed. Baltimore, MD: Clinical Psychometric Research, 1992.

35. Ferrell BR, Ferrell BA, Ahu C, Tran K. Pain management for elderly cancer patients at home. *Cancer* 194;74:2139–2146.

36. Padilla GV, Ferrell BR, Grant MM, Rhiner M. Defining the content domain of quality of life for cancer patients with pain. *Cancer Nurs* 1990;13:108–115.

37. Derogatis LR. *SCL-90-R: Administration, scoring and procedures manual, 3rd ed.* Minneapolis, MN: National Computer Systems, 1994.

38. Derogatis LR, Lipman RS, Rickels K, Uhlenhuth EH, Covi L. The Hopkins Symptom Checklist (HSCL): a self-report symptom inventory. *Behav Sci* 1974;19:115.

39. Derogatis LR, Lipman RS, Covi L. SCL-90: an outpatient psychiatric rating scale—preliminary report. *Psychopharmacol Bull* 1973;9(1):1327.

40. Derogatis LR. *The SCL-90-R.* Baltimore: Clinical Psychometric Research, 1975.

41. Derogatis LR, Yevzeroff H, Wittelsberger B. Social class, psychological disorder, and the nature of the psychopathologic indicator. *J Consult Clin* 1975;43:183–191.

42. Derogatis LR. *Brief Symptom Inventory (BSI): administration scoring and procedures manual,* 3rd ed. Minneapolis: National Computer Systems, 1993.

43. Bulik CM, Carpenter LL, Kupfer DJ, Frank E. Features associated with suicide attempts in recurrent major depression. *J Affect Dis* 1990;18:27–29.

44. Snyder D, Lynch J, Derogatis LR, Gruss L. Psychopathology and communication problems in a family practice. *Psychosomatics* 1980;21:661–670.

45. Weidner G, Connor SL, Hollis JF, Conor WE. Improvements in hostility and depression in relation to dietary change and cholesterol lowering. The Family Heart Study. *Ann Intern Med* 1992;117:820–823.

46. Irvine AA, Cox D, Gonder-Fredrick L. Fear of hypoglycemia: relation to physical and psychological symptoms in patients with insulin-dependent diabetes mellitus. *Health Psychol* 1992;11:135–138.

47. Ware JE, Sherbourne CD. The MOS 36-Item Short-Form Health Status Survey (SF-36): 1. Conceptual framework and item selection. *Med Care* 1992;30:473–483.

48. Ware JE, Snow KK, Kosinski M, Gandek B. *SF-36 Health Survey manual and interpretation guide.* Boston: New England Medical Center, The Health Institute, 1993.

49. Ware JE, Kosinski M, Keller SD. *SF-36 physical and mental component summary measures—a users' manual.* Boston: The Health Institute, 1994.

50. Ware JE, Kosinski M, Bayliss MS, et al. Comparison of methods for the scoring and statistical analysis of the SF-36 health profile and summary measures: results from the Medical Outcomes Study. *Med Care* 1995;33:A5264–A5279.

51. Stewart AL, Ware JE, eds. *Measuring functioning and well-being: the Medical Outcomes Study approach.* Durham, NC: Duke University Press, 1992.

52. Ware JE. The status of health assessment 1994. *Annu Rev Public Health* 1995;16:327–354.

53. Dupuy HJ. The Psychological General Well-Being (PGWB) Index. In: Wenger NK, Mattson ME, Furberg CD, Elinson J, eds. *Assessment of quality of life in clinical trials of cardiovascular therapies.* New York: Le Jacq, 1984.

54. Patrick DL, Bush JW, Chen MM. Toward an operational definition of health. *J Health Soc Behav* 1973;14:6–24.

55. Hulka BS, Cassell JC. The AAFP-UNC study of the organization, utilization, and assessment of primary medical care. *Am J Public Health* 1973;63:494–501.

56. Reynolds WJ, Rushing WA, Miles DL. The validation of a function status index. *J Health Social Behav* 1974;15:271–288.

57. Stewart AL, Ware JE, Brook RH. Advances in the measurement of functional status: construction of aggregate indexes. *Med Care* 1981;19:473–488.

58. Ware JE. Scales for measuring general health perceptions. *Health Serv Res* 1976;11:396–415.

59. Brook RH, Ware JE, Davies-Avery A, et al. Overview of adult health status measures fielded in RAND's Health Insurance Study. *Med Care* 1979;17(7 suppl).

60. Sullivan M, Karlsson J, Ware JE. The Swedish SF-36 Health Survey: I. Evaluation of data quality, scaling assumptions, reliability, and construct validity across several populations. *Soc Sci Med* 1995; 41:1349–1358.

61. Bullinger M. German translation and psychometric testing of the SF-36 health survey: preliminary results from the IHRQOLA project. *Soc Sci Med* 1995;41:1359–1366.

62. Ware JE, Gandek B. The IHRQOLA Project Group. The SF-36 health survey: development and use in mental health research and the IHRQOLA project. *Int J Mental Health* 1994;23:49–73.

63. McHorney CA, Kosinski M, Ware JE. Comparisons of the costs and quality of norms for the SF-36 survey collected by mail versus telephone interview: results from a national survey. *Med Care* 1994; 32:551–567.

64. McHorney CA, Ware JE, Rogers W, et al. The validity and relative precision of MOS short- and long-form health status scales and Dartmouth COOP Charts: results from the Medical Outcomes Study. *Med Care* 1992;30(5):MS253–MS265.

65. McHorney CA, Ware JE, Raczek AE. The MOS 36-Item Short-Form Health Status Survey (SF-36): II. Psychometric and clinical tests of validity in measuring physical and mental health constructs. *Med Care* 1993;31:247–263.

66. Ware JE, Keller SD, Gandek B, and the IHRQOLA Project team. Evaluating translations of health status surveys: lessons from the IHRQOLA project. *Int J Technol Assess Health Care,* 1995;11: 525–551.

67. Kravitz RL, Greenfield S, Rogers WH, et al. Differences in the mix of patients among medical specialties and systems of care: results from the Medical Outcomes Study. *JAMA* 1992;267:1617–1623.

68. Katz JN, Larson MG, Phillips CB, et al. Comparative measurement sensitivity of short and longer health status instruments. *Med Care* 1992;30(10):917–925.

69. Bergner M, Bobbit RA, Kressel S, Pollard WE, Gilson BS, Morris JR. The Sickness Impact Profile: conceptual formulation and methodology for the development of a health status measure. *Int J Health Services* 1976;6:393–415.

70. Bergner M, Bobbit RA, Carter WB, Gilson BS. The Sickness Impact Profile: development and final revision of a health status measure. *Med Care* 1981;19:787–805.

71. Bergner M, Hudson LD, Conrad DA, Patmont CM, McDonald GJ, Perrin EB, Gilson BS. The cost and efficacy of home care for patients with chronic lung disease. *Med Care* 1988;26:566–579.

72. Sugarbaker PH, Barofsky I, Rosenberg SA, Gianola FJ. Quality of life assessment of patients in extremity sarcoma clinical trials. *Surgery* 1982;91:17–23.

73. Rockey PH, Griep RJ. Behavioral dysfunction in hyperthyroidism. *Arch Intern Med* 1980;140: 1194–1197.

74. MacKenzie EJ, Burgess AR, McAndrew MP, et al. Patient-oriented functional outcome after unilateral lower extremity fracture. *J Orthop Trauma* 1993;7:393–401.

75. World Health Organization. *WHOQOL study protocol.* Geneva: WHO (MNH/PSF/93.9), 1993.

76. Bullinger M. Indices versus profiles—advantages and disadvantages. In: Walker SR, Rosser RM, eds. *Quality of life assessment: key issues in the 1990's.* Lancaster, UK: Kluwer Academic, 1993:209–220.

4 / Reported Methodology

Patient-reported assessments versus performance-based tests
Primary statistical issues
Design issues
Analysis from the time perspective
The Q-TWiST method
Interpreting general health measures
Sources of misinterpretation
Clinical significance of quality of life data
Clinical versus statistical significance
Methods for developing and testing new instruments
Instrument development
Instrument testing
Critical properties of research instruments
HRQOL assessment: modes of administration
Measuring reliability and responsiveness and assessing validity and
    interpretability
Testing the quality of the data collection instrument
Quality control of data collection
Language and translation issues
Cross-cultural measurement equivalence

After selection of an appropriate instrument for HRQOL assessment, researchers should then consider how to best use the instrument to acquire HRQOL information. This chapter reviews methods of administration, trial design and data analysis, and data interpretation. Understanding the clinical significance of changes in HRQOL scores remains a challenge.

PATIENT-REPORTED ASSESSMENTS
VERSUS PERFORMANCE-BASED TESTS

Information about the impact of treatment on a patient's ability to fulfill basic human functions (e.g., ambulation, communication, emotional stability) and carry out day-to-day activities (e.g., self-care, roles in the family, workplace, and community) is fundamental to evaluating the impact of clinical trials on quality of life. When it comes to assessing patient performance, the researcher or clinician has two basic choices: to ask the patient to provide subjective information, or to obtain performance ratings from another source. Each of these approaches is subject to different potential biases and sources of error.

Approaches to Obtaining Ratings from Patients

Interviews

Interviews can be structured, including a set list of questions, or unstructured. Unstructured interviews generally begin with a broad question (e.g., "How would you describe your quality of life?"), with subsequent queries based on patient responses. Specific questions can be closed-ended (in which respondents are provided with specified response options from which they may choose), or open-ended (where respondents reply in their own words). In practice, many interviews follow a semi-structured protocol, including a mixture of standard questions and free responses. There are not many tools designed explicitly to be interviewer-administered. One notable exception is the Quality of Well-Being (QWB) Scale (1). This measure uses a structured interview to obtain information about functional level, symptoms, and medical problems. The interviewer then classifies the respondents' answers within a preexisting matrix.

Questionnaires

Questionnaires are by far the most frequent patient-rated quality of life assessment technique. Respondents may indicate their answers by placing a mark on a line (e.g., linear analog scales), indicating a unit on a scale (e.g., Likert scales, semantic differentials), checking a response with a predetermined score (e.g., Guttman scales), among other formats. Questionnaires can be self-administered (in a research setting or via mail), interviewer-administered (in person or over the telephone), or computer-assisted. Many quality of life questionnaires can be administered in several modes (e.g., by interview or self-administered) with equivalent results (2).

Diaries

Diaries represent a form of self-monitoring, which has been used extensively by behavior therapists both to record data and to effect behavior change (3). In the context of quality of life assessment, diaries have been used by asking patients to describe aspects of their life, generally on an ongoing, prospective basis. For example, Fraser et al. (4,5) used the "Qualitator," a daily diary card, in a study of chemotherapy. With this tool, patients selected their five most important questions from four quality of life domains. They then recorded their own experience on five-point scales daily for up to 6 months. Diaries may be particularly useful for outcomes that may vary considerably from day to day and where charting patient experience over time is important, e.g., treatment-related symptoms and pain.

Personal Narratives

Personal narratives represent a qualitative approach to quality of life assessment. Personal narratives may be written or utilize other recording techniques, such as tape recorders. Patients describe significant aspects of quality of life in their own words. Transcripts of the data are prepared and meaningful "units" of information can be abstracted, summarized, and compared.

Strengths and Weaknesses of Different Self-Report Methods

The strengths of patient-reported assessments are well known. In some cases, the patient is the only source of data, or the source that may be easiest to tap. Patient questionnaires are a relatively low-cost and efficient way to collect information. Most patients are well acquainted with completing forms, and questionnaires following standard formats are likely to be well accepted. Diaries require careful training (both initially and on follow-up) to ensure complete and consistent recording. No staff is needed to administer self-administered questionnaires, personal narratives, or patient diaries, although as Cella and Tulsky (6) point out, the value of information from self-administered forms can be enhanced by the participation of an interviewer who can check the questionnaire for accuracy and completeness, follow up on particular responses, and provide clarification or answer questions. Even when interviewers are required to collect information, they generally can be trained for the study and need not have a particular educational background. Finally, the value of patient self-reports can be supported empirically.

Form-Based Response Biases

Response biases occur when respondents are affected not only by their true response to a question, but also by how the question is worded or by their own motivations. These biases can add error to findings and, at their worst, could render findings useless. Response biases in questionnaires or interviews may include *yea-saying* (the tendency to always agree with items), *end aversion* (the tendency to use middle values rather than the endpoints of a scale), *halo* (in which an overall evaluation affects ratings in different domains), and *framing* (in which the manner of describing a question, e.g., whether one's prognosis is described in terms of probability of living or dying, affects responses). Many response biases can be prevented through appropriate instrument design; e.g., yea-saying can be addressed by ensuring that the wording of items is balanced so that there are both negative and positive items in the questionnaire or interview. Another drawback to most questionnaires and interviews and many diaries is that the questions themselves may change the way the patients assess their quality of life, e.g., leading the patient.

Performance-Based Evaluations

Performance-based evaluations are based on observable, and potentially repeatable and verifiable, information, preferably with documentation of the context in which a given behavior occurs. Technologies such as tape or video recording can provide a performance record that can be analyzed by multiple raters. Although behavioral ratings may seem to have the most applicability for physical functioning, patient performance is relevant in many other areas as well (e.g., psychological and social functioning).

Participant Observer Ratings

A number of observer-based tools are available, most being "participant observer" approaches, since the individual making the observations is generally someone who is interacting with the patient. For the most part, such ratings are made in a hospital or physician's office. Ratings reflect clinical judgments based on interaction with the patient: information from verbal, nonverbal, and physical cues that may include direct questions. Participant observation includes most scales of activities of daily living and instrumental activities of daily living (which focus on independence in self-care and daily life), which are also a frequent aspect of quality of life assessment, especially for elderly or institutionalized populations (7).

The Karnofsky Performance Index (KPI) (8) is an example of an observer measure that is widely used in clinical trials research. In cancer research, it has been used as an eligibility criterion for trial participation, as a patient stratification factor, and as an outcome measure for both treatment efficacy and quality of life (9). The KPI assigns a rating from 0 (dead) to 100 (no evidence of disease, able to carry out normal activity and to work); as such, the rating reflects a combination of disease status, independence, and role functioning. Spitzer et al.'s (10) Quality of Life Index (QLI) is one of the few multidimensional observer scales. (A self-report version is also available.) Observers assign one of three ratings in five different areas: activity, daily living, health, support, and outlook. Both the KPS and QLI have been used among health care providers, research workers, and family members (and patients as well).

Tests of Performance

Standard physical, psychological, or neurological tests can be used to measure patient abilities that are important aspects of quality of life. Appropriate tests depend on the disease, treatment, patient population, and study question, and some tests may even be administered in the context of patient care (e.g., cognitive functioning). Precise measurements of activity can be made with electronic and mechanical methods.

Product-of-Behavior Measures

Product-of-behavior measures (11) are temporary or permanent records that reflect specific, targeted behaviors. A concrete example is weight: if appetite is an important aspect of quality of life in a particular trial, one could monitor weight gain or loss in addition to or instead of asking the patient, "How is your appetite?" Similarly, absenteeism from school or work could provide information about energy or role status. Such indicators have their weaknesses (e.g., behaviors such as weight change are determined in multiple ways and reflect other factors beyond appetite, such as concurrent medications). However, these kinds of data are frequently available and accessible at low cost to collect.

Psychophysiological Measures

A number of physical measures in addition to studying endpoints (e.g., heart rate, galvanic skin response, oxygen consumption) have the potential to add additional information about patient well-being. Numerous possible outcomes and assessment techniques are possible that complement findings from self-report health status measures.

Strengths

Behavior-based measures have a number of strengths. The various biases that affect self-reports are less likely to play a role, especially when behavior is observed or measured in a naturalistic context. Focusing on specific behaviors and their environmental contingencies may guide the way to intervention: if better quality of life is manifested under some conditions than others, one has potentially identified a confounder to interpreting findings, or a potential way to improve well-being. Observer responses offer a particularly efficient and economical way of collecting data; for some patients (e.g., those who are very ill), observer ratings may offer the only way to obtain information. Based on studies of the Karnofsky Performance Index, observers can be trained to achieve acceptable levels of inter-rater reliability (12). Conditions that can interfere with one's ability to complete questionnaires, such as problems with vision, literacy, or language, are to a large degree removed in performance measures. Behavioral measures reflect the current situation; as such, they are not subject to selective memory, recall failure, or rapid changes in outcomes, an issue in a number of self-report measures; e.g., the Nottingham Health Profile (13) self-report questionnaire asks patients to consider the preceding month in their responses, an interval that may pose difficulties for debilitated patients. However, by the same token, behavioral measures are limited in the scope reflected by any one assessment and must be conducted repeatedly to obtain a perspective on changes over time.

Weaknesses

Probably the biggest problem with behavioral measures of quality of life is that many such measures (observer ratings excepted) have not been included traditionally in quality of life assessments, particularly in the clinical trials context. As such, individuals skilled in collecting these measures are not available in many settings, and specialized training is needed to ensure reliable assessments. Training protocols may need to be tailored to the individual observer (e.g., physicians, researchers, significant others). While psychophysiological measures seem to offer precision in measurement, they are frequently nonspecific; e.g., an increased heart rate may signify more than one possible quality of life domain.

How Do Patient Self-Reports Compare with Performance-Based Ratings?

While additional head-to-head comparisons of many different approaches to quality of life assessment are needed, there is considerable information available comparing patient self-reports with observer ratings. Sprangers and Aaronson (14) reviewed 48 studies that compared patient quality of life ratings to those of health care providers and/or significant others. Their overall conclusions were as follows: (a) there is far-from-perfect concordance between patients and observers; (b) the more concrete and observable a phenomenon, the more agreement; (c) both providers and significant others give lower estimates of quality of life than do patients; (d) there is more agreement between patients and significant others who live in close proximity to one another.

PRIMARY STATISTICAL ISSUES

Multiple Comparisons

Analysis of HRQOL data differs from the analysis of other clinical endpoints for several reasons. First, there are often a large number of measures resulting from both multiple dimensions of HRQOL (multiple instruments and/or subscales) and repeated assessments over time (15). Univariate tests for each subscale and time point can seriously inflate the type I (false positive) error rate for the overall trial, such that the investigator is unable to distinguish between the true and false positive differences. Furthermore, it is often impossible to determine the number of tests performed at the end of analysis and adjust post hoc. Methods that allow summarization of multiple outcomes both simplify the interpretation of the results and often improve the statistical power to detect clinically relevant differences, especially when small but consistent differences in HRQOL occur over time or across multiple domains. On the other hand, significant differences at a particular time or within a particular domain may be blurred by aggregation.

Missing Data

Missing data refers to missing items in scales and missed and/or mistimed assessments. If the assessment is missing for reasons that are unrelated to the patient's HRQOL, the data are classified as "missing at random" (16). Examples might be staff forgetting to administer the assessment, a missed appointment due to inclement weather, or the patient moved out of the area. Data that are administratively missing because the patient has not been on-study long enough to reach the assessment time point (i.e., the data are censored or incomplete) are also considered missing at random. Assessments may be mistimed if they are actually given but the exact timing does not correspond to the planned schedule of assessments for reasons unrelated to the patient's HRQOL. Although these types of missing/mistimed data make analyses more complex and may reduce the power to detect differences, the estimates of HRQOL are unbiased even if they are based only on the observed HRQOL assessments.

Nonrandomly missing or informatively censored data present a much more difficult problem. One example of this type of missing data is that due to death, disease progression, or toxicity where the HRQOL would generally be poorer in the patients who were not observed than in those who were observed. In the chronic disease setting, this relationship between HRQOL and missing data might manifest itself as study dropout due to lack of relief, presence of side effects, or, conversely, improvement in the condition. The difficulty occurs because analyses that inappropriately assume the data are randomly missing will result in biased estimates of HRQOL reflecting only the more limited population of patients who were assessed rather than the entire sample or population under study. One possibility is to limit the analysis, and thereby the inference, to patients with complete data. In most cases, however, this strategy is not acceptable to achieve the goal of comparing HRQOL assessments for all patients. Unless careful prospective documentation of the reasons for missing assessments is available in a clinical trial, it is generally impossible to know definitively whether the reason for the missing assessment is related to the patient's condition and/or HRQOL.

Integration of HRQOL and Time

In clinical trials with significant disease-related mortality there is a need to integrate survival with HRQOL. In studies where both HRQOL (or toxicity) and clinical endpoints indicate the superiority of one treatment over another, the choice of the best treatment is clear. Similarly, if either HRQOL or the efficacy outcome demonstrate a benefit and there is no difference in the other, the choice of treatment is straightforward. The dilemma occurs when there is a conflict in the HRQOL and efficacy outcomes; this is often the case when there is significant toxicity associated with the more effective treatment.

DESIGN ISSUES

HRQOL Instruments

HRQOL assessments should be limited to the briefest and least complicated instrument or combination of instruments that adequately address the primary question. Adding scales/instruments to obtain data that are not necessary to the primary objective will increase both the multiple comparisons problem and the likelihood that data will be incomplete. This will potentially compromise the ability of the trial to achieve the primary objective. The length of an instrument does not necessarily enhance its psychometric properties in proportion to the number of questions (e.g., 30 versus 150 questions).

Timing of Assessments

The timing of the HRQOL assessments must also be specified to achieve the study goals. Baseline measures that precede therapy allow for assessment of treatment-related changes within an individual. Depending on the goals of the study, it also is important to have a sufficiently long period of follow-up after therapy to allow for assessment of the long-term treatment effect and potential late sequelae. In the phase III treatment comparison setting, it is critical that HRQOL should be assessed regardless of treatment and disease status. Patients who have changes in status or who have discontinued treatment should not stop their assessment of HRQOL, because the biggest differences in HRQOL may be in these patients. Without these measurements it will be difficult to derive summary measures and impossible to make unbiased comparisons of the effects of different therapeutic regimens on HRQOL. Procedures for obtaining assessments for patients who have changed status or discontinued therapy should be explicitly stated in protocols.

The timing of assessments should be chosen to minimize missing data. It is generally recommended that the frequency of assessments be minimized for patient and staff considerations. However, in some cases, more frequent administration linked to the clinical routine (e.g., at the beginning of every treatment cycle) may result in more complete data because the pattern of assessment is established as part of the clinical routine.

Sample Size and Power

The sample size and power to detect meaningful differences for primary HRQOL hypotheses is critical to any study in which HRQOL is an important endpoint. In addition to the usual estimates of variation and correlations, the sensitivity of the HRQOL instrument to detect clinically significant changes is the most useful information that can be provided during the validation of an HRQOL instrument. Specific estimates of the changes in subscales and global scales related to clinical status give the statistician and the clinician a clear and familiar reference point for defining differences that are clinically relevant. This is critical for ensuring an adequate sample size for the study. It should be noted that because endpoints may involve both repeated measurements at different times and/or combinations of subscales, both test–retest correlations and among-subscale correlations are useful and should be reported for validated instruments. If the sample size requirements for the HRQOL component are substantially less than for the entire study, an unbiased strategy for selection of a subset of patients in which HRQOL will be assessed should be identified. For example, the first 500 patients enrolled in the study might be included in the HRQOL sub-study. This may have an additional advantage in studies with a long duration of HRQOL follow-up.

Dealing with Missing Items in HRQOL Scales

In scales based on multiple items, missing information results in a serious missing data problem. If only 0.1% of items are randomly missing for a 50-item instrument, 18% ($[1- .999^{4 \times 50}] * 100\%$) of the subjects will have one or more items missing over four assessments. If the missing rate is 0.5% (1 in 200 items), then only 37% ($[.995^{4 \times 50}] * 100\%$) of subjects will have complete data. Deletion of the entire case when there are missing items results in loss of power and potential bias if subjects with poorer HRQOL are more or less likely to skip an item. Individuals with high levels of nonresponse (>50%) should be dealt with on a case-by-case basis. Careful selection of a method for imputing missing items for an individual who has answered most questions would, in general, be preferable to deletion of the entire case or observation. A simple method based solely on the patient's own data would use the mean of all nonmissing items for the entire scale or the specific subscale. Methods based on other patients would include the mean of that item in individuals who had responded. Another method utilizing data from other subjects is based on the high correlation of items within a scale or subscale and utilizes information about the individual's tendency to score correlated items high or low and the tendency of a particular item to be scored high or low relative to other items. The procedure is to regress the missing item on the nonmissing items using data from individuals with complete data, and to then predict the value of the missing item using the information from the completed items in the individual with the missing item (17).

Univariate Methods

One approach to the reporting of HRQOL data has been descriptive univariate statistics such as means and proportions at each specific point in time. These descriptive statistics may be accompanied by simple parametric or nonparametric tests such as t-tests or Wilcoxon tests. Although these methods are easy to implement and often used (18), they do not address any of the three previously identified issues. One recommended solution to the multiple comparisons problem is to limit the number of a priori endpoints in the design of the trial to three or less (19). The analyses of the remaining scales and/or time points can be presented descriptively or graphically (15). Although theoretically improving the overall type I error rate for the study, in practice, investigators are reluctant to ignore the remaining data and may receive requests from reviewers to provide results from secondary analyses with the corresponding significance levels.

An alternative method of addressing the multiple comparisons problem is to apply a Bonferroni correction, which adjusts the test statistics on k endpoints so that the overall type I error is preserved for the smallest p value. The procedure is to accept as statistically significant only those tests with p values that are less than α/k, where α is the overall type I error usually set equal to .05. However, this results in a focus on the smallest p value and may yield conclusions that are counterintuitive. An example would be an analysis of $K = 4$ endpoints (either four different time points or four HRQOL dimensions) all with test statistics corresponding to $p = 0.02$ and effects in the same direction. Using the Bonferroni adjustment, the differences would not be considered statistically significant because all p values are greater than .0125.

Multivariate Methods

Multivariate analysis techniques include approaches such as repeated measures of analysis of variance (ANOVA) or multivariate ANOVA (MANOVA) (20). These techniques require complete data, which limits their use to settings where there is a low risk of mortality and very high compliance with HRQOL assessment. If the data are not complete, the inferences are restricted to a very select and generally nonrepresentative group of patients. Multivariate statistics such as Hotelling's T are frequently used to control for type I error. These statistics, however, answer global questions such as "Are any of the dimensions of HRQOL different?" or "Are there differences in HRQOL at any point in time?" without regard to whether the differences are in consistent directions. In general, the multivariate test statistics are not sensitive to differences in the same direction across the multiple endpoints.

The requirement for complete data can be relaxed by using repeated measures or mixed effects model with structured covariance (21). These methods assume that the data are missing for reasons unrelated to the patients' HRQOL, such as staff forgetting to administer the assessment. If the missing assessments can reasonably be assumed to be missing at random, a likelihood-based analysis approach, such as a mixed-effects models or EM (Estimation–Maximization) algorithm for repeated measures models, enables incorporating all patients with at least one assessment in the analysis (21,22). This approach has the additional advantages of estimation of within- and between-subject variation, inclusion of time-varying covariates, and testing of changes over time. Software for these methods is available in some of the major packages (SAS, Proc Mixed; BMDP, 5V).

However, in most settings where HRQOL is of interest, the causes of missing assessments are likely to be related to the patients' illness and thus to their HRQOL. There are a number of suggested approaches for longitudinal studies that are interested in change over time and where the change is expected to be linear over time. The simplest approach is an unweighted average of individual least-squares slopes. Alternative approaches include modeling of the censoring process (23) or use of a conditional linear model (24). Both methods are based on a growth curve model approach with the individual slope parameter(s) related to censoring of later observations (right censoring) either through a linear random effects model with a probit model for the censoring process or a conditional linear model.

A nonparametric approach to nonrandom missing data would involve ranking the data at each time point, with the lowest ranks assigned for missing assessments due to death, disease progression, or severe toxicity. The assumption is that the HRQOL values for these nonrandomly missing observations are lower than the observed data. Group differences could be examined at each time point with nonparametric tests, such as the two-sample Wilcoxon rank sum test. These statistics can be combined across time points using a procedure for combining two-sample Wilcoxon tests (25).

Summary of Global Statistics

One limitation of the multivariate methods is that they do not directly provide a summary measure that would facilitate the interpretation of longitudinal data, such as when early toxicity may be balanced by later HRQOL advantages (relapse-free, survival). In settings where HRQOL is expected to improve or decline over time, it may be possible to summarize the data as the slope of HRQOL versus time. If the trend in HRQOL is expected to be linear over time, unweighted analysis of individual slopes is a commonly recommended method. This has several advantages. First, it provides a single, easy-to-interpret summary of multiple measurements obtained over time. Second, if there are at least two measurements, randomly missing and/or mistimed observations are not a problem. Finally, when the censoring is informative (e.g., patients who die earlier have more negative slopes than those who survive), unweighted analyses of the slopes are not biased as long as all subjects have at least two measurements. Change from baseline to the last HRQOL assessment is a form of last-observation-carried-forward (26). The drawback of this approach is that if HRQOL is declining over time, the rate of change will be underestimated for patients with earlier final measurements. Figure 4.1 illustrates two different approaches to the graphical presentation of multidimensional HRQOL data.

Pocock et al. (27) and O'Brien (28) suggest summary statistics that are sensitive to consistent trends in the same direction across multiple endpoints and control the type I error rate for multiple outcomes. O'Brien (28) proposes a weighted average of the individual t-statistics for the k endpoints. The weights are based on the correlations between the k endpoints, such that endpoints that are more highly correlated are down-weighted. If the multiple endpoints are subscales of an HRQOL instrument, this weighted average of the subscale scores would be an alternative to a total score generated by the sum of the item scores. Another application would be the combination of t-statistics generated at different points in time. Pocock et al. (27) suggest the potential extension of this strategy to the combination of any asymptotically normal test statistics, which would include t-statistics for HRQOL scores and log-rank statistics for survival. The advantage is that the weights do not have to be prespecified. The corresponding disadvantage is that the weights will vary from study to study, thus limiting the generalizability and making it difficult to interpret from a clinical standpoint (29). Cox et al. (29) suggest an approach that provides a summary measure of HRQOL over time and accounts for missing data resulting from death or censoring where follow-up is not complete at the time of analysis. The summary statistic is the area under the curve (AUC) of HRQOL scores (Y_i) plotted versus time (t_i).

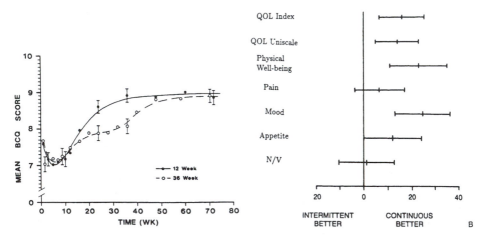

FIG. 4.1. Graphical displays of results from QOL studies. (A) Mean Breast Cancer Chemotherapy Questionnaire (BCQ) scores over time for two adjuvant chemotherapy programs of different duration. (From ref. 18, with permission.) (B) Comparison between continuous and intermittent chemotherapy program (after the programs diverged at 3 months but before disease progression) using a QOL-index questionnaire, a global uniscale, and LASA scales for individual domains. (From ref.19, with permission.)

Korn (30) suggests presenting these AUC values for groups of patients, as one would present survival data. This approach has the advantage of both displaying more information about the distribution of the AUC values and accommodating administrative censoring. Unfortunately, the administrative censoring is informative on the HRQOL scale (31,32) and the usual Kaplan-Meier estimate will be biased. Specifically, if the censoring mechanism due to staggered entry and incomplete follow-up is identical for two groups, the group with poorer HRQOL will have lower values of the AUC and will be censored earlier on the AUC scale. Korn (30) suggests a procedure to reduce the bias of the Kaplan-Meier estimator by assuming that the probability of administrative censoring in short intervals is independent of the HRQOL measures prior to that time. This assumption is probably not true. The violation, however, may be small enough that the estimator will not be badly biased, especially if HRQOL is measured frequently and the relationship of HRQOL AUC and censoring is weak.

ANALYSIS FROM THE TIME PERSPECTIVE

Time to a Prespecified HRQOL Endpoint

A simple univariate statistic incorporating time and HRQOL is the proportion of patients experiencing some HRQOL event. For example, the proportion of patients who drop more than ten points from baseline during 6 months of therapy or the proportion of patients improving to within five points of baseline after a particularly toxic therapy. In both cases, since the baseline measurement plays such a critical role in the endpoint, it would be advisable to obtain multiple assessments of baseline whenever feasible.

Time can be incorporated into this concept by graphically displaying the time to the HRQOL event in the form of a familiar Kaplan-Meier plot. This type of presentation was used by Rosenman and Choi (33) in which the HRQOL endpoint was the duration of time with Karnofsky Index > 60. Interesting differences between treatment groups may not be reflected by the time to reach a specific level of HRQOL; e.g., two patients might both decline to a Karnofsky score of 60 at 6 months (thus being considered equivalent in the analysis), while one maintained a consistent Karnofsky score of 70 and the other maintained a score of 90 for the entire 6 months prior to dropping to 60.

Quality-Adjusted Life-Years (QALY)

An intuitive method of incorporating HRQOL and time would be to adjust life-years by down-weighting time spent in periods of poor quality of life. However, what would seem to be a simple idea has many methodologic challenges. The first is the determination of weights. Torrance (34) describes several techniques for eliciting weights for states of health including direct ratings, time trade-offs, and standard gambles. In addition to the difficulties of administering some of these techniques in clinical trials, weights elicited by the different techniques or from different respondents may not result in equivalent measures (35). The choice of anchor points and content validity may mean that weights that are appropriate in one setting may be inappropriate in another. The other methodologic difficulty occurs in trials with censored data. Although it might seem appropriate to undertake a standard survival analysis of individual quality-adjusted survival times, the usual product limit estimator of the survival function is biased because censoring is related by the future outcome (31,32). For example, if two groups have the same censoring times due to death, the group with the poorer HRQOL will be censored earlier on the QALY scale. This latter problem can be addressed by estimating the average time spent in each health state and then computing a weighted average of the time as is done in the Q-TWiST approach.

Issues

Three characteristics of HRQOL studies present challenges for analysis and interpretation. The first is the occurrence of both randomly and nonrandomly missing data. The analysis of randomly missing data is generally well defined with enough experience to have addressed both practical and theoretical issues. In contrast, development of methods for the analysis of nonrandomly missing data is in its infancy, and we will need more experience to determine which methods are most practical and appropriate.

The second issue is the multivariate nature of HRQOL studies. Not only is HRQOL a multidimensional concept measured by multiple scales, but most studies are longitudinal. Separate analyses of each domain at multiple time points may make it difficult to communicate the results in a manner that is meaningful for clinicians and patients. Summary measures may reduce the multidimensionality of the problem but may not make the interpretation much easier. The issue of weights that vary by technique and study also adds to the complexity of interpretation. In general, it would be advisable to perform the analyses under various assumptions to verify that the results were not sensitive to small changes in the assumptions.

The third issue is the integration of survival data with HRQOL measures. This can be addressed from either the perspective of HRQOL or time. From a research perspective, both approaches can be informative; however, currently time is a dimension with which both clinicians and biostatisticians are most familiar. The existence of multiple HRQOL instruments with different relationships of scores with clinical impressions contributes to the difficulty of interpretation. Finally, interpretation of clinical trials may not always be helpful in guiding individual patient decisions. In theory, individual patients could utilize the threshold utility analysis of Q-TWiST, but this may require extensive patient education.

There are a number of statistical methodologies that can be employed in the analysis of HRQOL data, each of which is based on specific assumptions, yields a different summary measure, and thus emphasizes different aspects of HRQOL. When there are more than one analysis strategies that will answer the primary HRQOL questions, the strategy that best anticipates the above issues should be considered. Analyses should be clearly and concisely reportable so that the relevant differences can be readily understood by those who will use the results.

THE Q-TWiST METHOD

Efforts focused on the integration of both quality and quantity of life into a single analysis to be used for treatment comparisons led to the development of the TWiST method (36) and its extension into Q-TWiST, Quality-adjusted Time Without Symptoms of disease and Toxicity of treatment. The Q-TWiST method performs treatment comparisons in terms of quality and quantity of life by penalizing treatments that have negative HRQOL effects and rewarding those that increase survival and have other positive HRQOL effects. As in an ordinary survival analysis, the focus of the method is on time, but instead of using a single outcome such as overall survival or disease-free survival, multiple outcomes corresponding to changes in HRQOL are considered. The objective is to include both survival and HRQOL in an analysis highlighting specific trade-offs using defined clinical events of interest. Thus, Q-TWiST links aspects of HRQOL with the clinical outcomes (disease- and treatment-related) that are ordinarily used to separately evaluate the efficacy and toxicity of treatments. A Q-TWiST analysis can also be used to assist with treatment decision making when there is a trade-off between side effects and a possible future benefit. It can demonstrate to a patient what the benefit might be depending on his/her tolerance for the treatment toxicities; this might improve patient compliance.

The multiple outcomes partition the overall survival time into clinical health states that differ in HRQOL. These clinical health states are selected to be relevant to the clinicians and patients. Each clinical health state is assigned a weight that corresponds to its value in terms of HRQOL relative to a state of perfect health. A weight of 0 indicates that the health state is as bad as death, and a weight of 1 indicates perfect health. Weights between 0 and 1 indicate degrees between these extremes. These weights are called *utility scores*. The Q-TWiST outcome is obtained by summing the weighted clinical health state durations. Thus, the method highlights trade-offs that result from different weightings of the clinically relevant health states.

The main advantage of the Q-TWiST method is that it incorporates time into the analysis of HRQOL by using restricted survival means. This can be very important in clinical trials, because the HRQOL experienced depends on the amount of time spent with toxicity or adverse events and the time following disease recurrence or progression. Often these are directly affected by the treatment. Other HRQOL measures, which do not account for time, only indirectly reflect benefits of delayed disease recurrence or progression. Furthermore, Q-TWiST does not aggregate HRQOL results for an entire population; instead, it allows individual patients and physicians to determine the preferred treatment according to individual preferences. This advantage is derived from the threshold utility analysis, which gives the preferred treatment according to all combinations of the utility scores. Q-TWiST can also accommodate patient-derived utility scores. In addition, prognostic factors can be included in the analysis by proportional hazards regression, allowing the prediction of treatment effects according to different prognostic situations. Longer-term treatment effects can be approximated using parametric models. Finally, Q-TWiST can be incorporated into meta-analyses and, using Eco-TWiST, can evaluate cost considerations in treatment comparisons.

By defining the clinical health states to reflect specific trade-offs of concern to health professionals and patients, Q-TWiST provides a framework for treatment decision making. A Q-TWiST analysis of the efficacy of treatments designed to prolong event-free survival can highlight the influence of late sequelae by defining a clinical health state to capture the occurrence of late events. Thus, Q-TWiST can emphasize those aspects of a disease and its treatment that are the most relevant in making treatment decisions. By relying on the threshold utility analysis, Q-TWiST presents the implications that various choices for patient preference have on the treatment decision process. Q-TWiST provides a broad evaluation of treatment outcomes and costs considering the entire survival experience of patients.

Markov and Semi-Markov Models

Markov and Semi-Markov models have been used to compare treatments based on estimates of the time spent in different health states and the probabilities of transitions between these states. The relevant health states must be identified, and then each weighted to reflect the relative value of a health state compared to perfect health. The treatments are then compared in terms of the total quality-adjusted time, the weighted sum of the health state durations. In general, to calculate the transition probabilities an underlying model must be assumed. The most commonly used model is the Markov chain, which assumes that the transitions from one HRQOL state to another are independent and continuous and only depend upon the previous state (37). This requires that the assessments are made at time points independent of the patients' treatment schedule or health state.

INTERPRETING GENERAL HEALTH MEASURES

Among the questions most frequently asked about results from widely used health status surveys are: What do the numbers mean? What is a high score? What is a low score? Although a three-point difference on a health scale may be statistically significant, is it clinically relevant? Is it important to society? Can scores be used to determine the need for treatment? Can the same interpretation guidelines used in group-level analyses be applied to individual patients?

The Relationship Between Interpretation and Validation

Interpretation requires the assignment of meaning to health status scores, usually by studying their relationships to other variables. Interpretation guidelines include the results of validity analyses, but they also include other types of analyses and a different display of results than is typical of validity analyses. Validity is the extent to which a score measures what it is supposed to measure (38). Validity is supported when hypotheses about the relationship between scale scores and particular criteria are confirmed. Tests of these hypotheses usually include estimates of the statistical significance of results. By contrast, evidence useful in the interpretation of scale scores requires more than the establishment of statistical significance; namely, it requires demonstration of a clinically or socially relevant relationship between two variables. In addition, the display of results for validity and interpretation analyses differ. In validity analyses, the expression of relationships between scale scores and criteria are summarized in terms of statistical estimates of the strength of association. For example, the commonly used product moment correlation expresses the strength of a linear association in standard units (39). Yet, standard units are rarely as meaningful to people as are raw scores; moreover, the correlation coefficient does not express the fact that, as illustrated below, the relationship of scale scores to criteria is often nonlinear across a range of scores. Interpretation is facilitated most when differences in scale scores at a particular scale level are linked to units of the criteria in specific amounts that make sense.

Attributes of Scale Scores that Affect Interpretation

Although there are many attributes of scale scores that affect interpretation, the importance of three attributes—reliability, range of measurement, and the number of levels of measurement—is often not well understood. Reliability has to do with how confident we can be that a particular score is the true score (39). Scale score reliability is a precondition for interpretation. It would be an inefficient use of resources to try to understand the meaning of a number that did not represent a true value. Reliability is an issue of repeatability. We can be confident that a score is the true score if we would obtain the same score again and again upon repeated assessments of an unchanging respondent. There are several methods to estimate the repeatability of a scale score. The most common among them are (a) to treat the questions (items) in a scale as repeated measures of the same concept and estimate reliability from the relationships among them (internal consistency method) (39), (b) to determine the association between scores collected from a clinically stable sample at two points in time (test–retest correlation) (40), and (c) to assess the percentage of scores at time two that are statistically different from scores at time one (the confidence interval method) (41).

The range of measurement is important because it determines the levels of health for which the questionnaire is useful in describing differences in health status and changes in health over time. Health status measures cover health states ranging from very poor, including disability and dysfunction, to very good, including high levels of functioning and well-being. The range of measurement determines how many people are concentrated at the top (ceiling) and at the bottom (floor) of the scale score distribution, which, in turn, determines whether distinctions can be made among people and whether changes can be described over time. Because many health status measures focus on the lower levels of health, they often produce large "ceiling" effects in scale score distributions (41,42). This is similar to attempting to obtain the weight of adults with a scale that ends at 100 pounds. Everyone who steps on that scale who weighs 100 pounds or more is assigned the heaviest weight. Such a scale is not useful in describing differences in weight among those who weigh more than 100 pounds, nor is it useful in measuring an increase in weight among those people. Conversely, if a disabled population were given a health status measure designed for athletes, we would expect to find most respondents at the bottom of the scale score distribution ("floor" effect).

Content-Based Interpretation Characterization of Content of General Health Status Surveys

Table 4.1 summarizes the content of ten of the most commonly used "generic" health status measures (43). Most of these measures address the concepts of physical functioning, mental health, role functioning, pain, and general health perceptions. Other concepts not included in all measures are energy, cognitive functioning, and sleep. Measures that yield scores for a specific concept usually have a more direct interpretation in relation to criteria that are relevant to that

TABLE 1. *Summary of content of widely used general health surveys*

Concepts[a]	QWB	SIP	HIE	NHP	QLI	COOP	EUROQOL	DUKE	MOS FWBP	MOS SF-36
Physical functioning	•	•	•	•	•	•	•	•	•	•
Social functioning	•	•	•	•	•	•	•	•	•	•
Role functioning	•	•	•	•	•	•	•	•	•	•
Psychological distress		•	•	•	•	•	•	•	•	•
Health perceptions (general)			•	•	•	•	•	•	•	•
Pain (bodily)		•	•	•		•	•	•	•	•
Energy/fatigue	•		•	•				•	•	•
Psychological well-being				•				•	•	•
Sleep		•		•				•	•	
Cognitive functioning		•						•	•	
Quality of life				•		•			•	•
Reported health transition						•			•	•

[a]Rows are ordered in terms of how frequently concepts are represented; only concepts represented in two or more surveys are listed. Analyses of content were based on published definitions. Columns are roughly ordered in terms of date of first publication.

QWB, Quality of Well-Being Scale (1973); SIP, Sickness Impact Profile (1976); HIE, Health Insurance Experiment Surveys (1979); NHP, Nottingham Health Profile (1980); QLI, Quality of Life Index (1981); COOP, Dartmouth Function Charts (1987); EUROQOL, European Quality of Life Index (1990); DUKE, Duke Health Profile (1990); MOS FWBP, MOS Functioning and Well-Being Profile (1992); MOS SF-36, MOS 36-Item Short-Form Health Survey (1992).

concept. For example, role-functioning measures would have a more direct interpretation in terms of work behavior than would mental health measures.

Content-based interpretation should also consider the type of information sought about each health concept. For example, some scale items ask for reports of behavior, whereas others ask for a more subjective rating or evaluation. Another attribute of content is range of health states described, as discussed above. For the SIP, the Quality of Well-Being Scale (QWB), and the Nottingham Health Profile (NHP), the "best" or highest level of health measured is the absence of functional limitations and/or specific symptoms and problems. For example, four surveys [the Health Insurance Experiment battery, the Duke, the MOS Functioning and Well-Being Profile (FWBP), and the MOS SF-36] extend measurement of mental health well into the psychological well-being range, with proven advantages in interpretation and prediction (44). The range of health content sampled by a measure will determine the degree of floor and ceiling effects typically observed in "sick" and "well" populations.

Single-Item Scales

Content-based interpretation for a single-item scale, such as one of the COOP charts (45) is based on the content of the question and the response choices. That content determines what the respondent thinks about in replying to the question and, therefore, provides excellent clues as to what his/her answers mean. For example, a choice of "Heavy" defines the most strenuous activity that could be performed in the past week as jogging at a slow pace or climbing stairs at a moderate pace. Going from level 2 to level 1 is an improvement from being able to jog at a slow pace to being able to run at a fast pace.

Multi-Item Scales

While multi-item scales have the potential to provide a more comprehensive sample of the universe of content, more levels of measurement, and greater reliability relative to single-item scales (34), content-based interpretation of the scores they yield can be more complex. Scores for people who score at that top or bottom of the scale are easy to interpret by looking at the items and response choices necessary to earn those scores. For example, the top score of the SF-36 Physical Functioning scale (46) is earned only by being able to perform all physical activities measured, including vigorous activities, without limitations due to health. Conversely, the bottom score is assigned only to those limited a lot by their health in performing all physical activities, including bathing or dressing.

Weighting Questionnaire Content for Interpretation

Several widely used health status surveys weight items according to evaluations of item content (47). To form weights, item content is interpreted by judges either in terms of the degree of disability expressed [e.g., the Sickness Impact Profile (SIP), the Nottingham Health Profile] or in terms of the desirability of the health state expressed [e.g., the QWB, the European Quality of Life Index (EuroHRQOL)]. These weights are then averaged across the items endorsed by the respondent. The SIP (48) weights were formulated by asking 133 judges (including enrollees in a prepaid health plan, health professionals, and prepro-fessional students) to rate the degree of severity of dysfunction expressed by each item. These item weights are then summed and the total SIP score for a dimension is expressed as a percentage of the highest possible score (48). The SIP scores are, thus, directly interpretable as reflecting the subjective evaluations of the relative degree of disability as judged by patients and clinicians.

Weights for items in the QWB (49–51) and EuroHRQOL scales (52) were derived from judgments regarding the desirability of the different health states described in the items. For example, the QWB scale produces a single score that is "simply an average of the relative desirability scores assigned to a group of persons for a particular day or a defined interval of time" (50). Scale levels are the "weights, social preferences, or measures of relative importance that members of society associate with each of the Function Levels and Symptom/Problem Complexes" (50). The weights for these levels were obtained through a series of preference studies, wherein subjects rated case descriptions on a scale (50,51). In the development of the EuroHRQOL, weights for health states were identified by asking subjects to describe "how good or bad each of these states would be for a person like you" (52).

Construct-Based Interpretation

The meaning of scale scores can also be understood on the basis of how the scales relate to one another, to the dimensions of health they were designed to represent, and to other conceptually related measures. Constructs are unmeasured variables thought to be responsible for the relationship between measured variables. They are called constructs because they are "constructed" based on the relationships between measured variables (39). Construct-based interpretation answers questions such as: What do health scale scores reveal about underlying health concepts? Where do these scales fit into a general model of health? How are they likely to relate to other questionnaires in a battery? Will they provide new information or are they likely to be redundant?

The Relationships Among Health Status Scores from Different Questionnaires

Interpretation of health status scores can be accomplished by assessing the relationship of health status scores from one questionnaire to another. Scales that measure similar concepts will be highly related to one another and those that

TABLE 4.2 *Correlations between health status scales*

SF-20 Scales MOS Short-form	Duke Health Profile					
	Physical health[a]	Mental health[a]	Social health[a]	Perceived health[a]	Disability[b]	Pain[b]
Physical functioning[a]	.18	.08	−.03	.07	−.20	−.22
Mental health[a]	.27	.51	.22	.22	.05	.00
Social functioning[a]	.32	.13	.07	.18	−.38	−.27
Health perceptions[a]	.28	.49	.29	.42	−.12	−.28
Role functioning[a]	.10	.17	.10	.24	−.32	−.00
Pain[b]	−.40	−.20	−.10	−.09	.03	.60

Nottingham Health Profile	SF-36 scales				
	Physical functioning[a]	Social functioning[a]	Pain[a]	Mental health[a]	Vitality[a]
Physical morbidity[b]	−.52	−.35	−.45	−.19	−.36
Social isolation[b]	−.20	−.41	−.18	−.47	−.36
Pain[b]	−.47	−.35	−.55	−.21	−.33
Emotional reactions[b]	−.18	−.53	−.28	−.67	−.55
Energy[b]	−.37	−.51	−.37	−.47	−.68

[a]High scores = good health.
[b]High scores = poor health.
Shaded correlations are between the most similar scales from the two measures. The top table is adapted with permission from ref. 20. The bottom table is adapted with permission from ref. 6.

measure dissimilar concepts will have weaker relationships. A strong empirical relationship between scales indicates that they measure common concepts and therefore have overlapping interpretations. Table 4.2 shows correlations among MOS SF-20 and Duke Health Profile scales (53) and among NHP and SF-36 scales (41). These correlations demonstrate substantial relationships between scales that were designed to measure similar health constructs. The mental health scales from the MOS SF-20 and the Duke were highly correlated, as were the perceived health and pain scales. The correlations between the physical morbidity, pain, mental health, and vitality scales from the SF-36 and the NHP were also very high. These high correlations mean that these scales can be interpreted as measuring similar concepts. Although these correlational analyses tell us something about the meaning of the scale, they do not provide interpretations for specific scores on that scale. Correlational analyses do not calibrate scores on one scale to those of another. This type of calibration requires the use of other methods such as test equating procedures (54). It is also important to keep in mind that high correlations between measures, such as those illustrated above, can mask important differences in the range and coarseness of measures.

The Relationships Among Scales Within the Same Questionnaire

Examining the relationship among scales within a questionnaire is another way of interpreting the meaning of scales. For example, the SF-36 Physical

Functioning, Bodily Pain, and Role–Physical scales have high correlations with each other, as do the Mental Health, Role–Emotional, and Social Functioning scales; and the correlation between the Mental Health and Physical Functioning scales is low (55,56). We might hypothesize that the pattern of relationships among these scales is due to some scales targeting physical health, whereas others target mental health.

This hypothesis can be formally tested by performing a factor analysis of the matrix of correlations to identify a smaller set of dimensions that explain relationships among those scales (57,58). Such analyses have revealed that two components predict more than 80% of the reliable variance in the eight SF-36 scale scores (59–61) and that each scale has a very different interpretation in relation to these physical and mental health concepts. Those scales that have the largest relationship to the first component (Physical Functioning, Role–Physical, Bodily Pain) suggest that this component measures physical health, while those scales that have the largest relationship to the second component (Mental Health, Role–Emotional, Social Functioning) suggest that this component measures mental health. The two scales that measure physical and mental health about equally (Vitality and General Health Perceptions) may be interpreted as general health measures. These analyses also provide other information useful in interpretation, including the amount of unique reliable variance in each score.

Factor analysis has also been applied to SIP scores to identify summary health constructs (48). These findings were useful in scoring and interpreting summary measures and in interpreting each SIP scale (48). One study of hospitalized patients (62), for example, identified dimensions of psychosocial health (Social Interaction, Emotional Behavior, Alertness Behavior, and Communication) and physical health (Ambulation, Body Care, and Movement).

A practical advantage of interpreting scale scores based on relationships internal to the questionnaire is that such interpretations are not dependent on the definition or measurement of external variables. A theoretical advantage is that factor analytic results will predict how scale scores will be related to other measures. For example, research with the SF-36 has demonstrated that the three scales that best represent physical health, according to factor analytic evidence, tend to do best in detecting the impact of clinical changes in physical health (63). Similarly, those scales that best represent mental health do best in detecting the impact of clinical changes in mental health (60,61).

Criterion-Based Interpretation

Criterion-based analyses use information about how scale scores relate to external variables to determine their meaning or interpretation. Scale scores are studied in relation to criterion variables retrospectively, concurrently, or prospectively. These analyses answer questions such as: What is the clinical relevance of scores on a particular measure in relation to other measures (such as a concurrent measure of disease severity)? Can these scores predict socially relevant outcomes (such as work productivity or the cost of subsequent medical services)?

There are different ways of assessing the clinical and social relevance of scores. This can be done by looking at the relationship between scale scores and other life events (64), such as loss of a job (65,66), probability of clinical diagnoses (67,68), or death (69,70). Other types of criterion-related analyses include calculating the relationship between health status and role strain (71) or work behavior. These benchmarks address the social significance of scale scores. For example, Hunt et al. (72) found a significant association between scores on the NHP and absence from work. After controlling for the effects of chronic illness, sociodemographics (age, race/ethnicity, gender, and education), and psychosocial variables (social supports, life satisfaction), Lerner et al. (71) found a significant relationship between job strain and five SF-36 scales (Physical Functioning, Role–Physical, Vitality, Social Functioning, and Mental Health).

Norm-Based Interpretation

Norm-based comparisons are a popular method of interpreting scale scores (73–76). Scores are understood as departures from expected or typical scores; these expected or typical scores are called norms. Norms can be computed at the individual or group level. At the individual level, norms are the scores that are typical of the individual under stable conditions. At the group level, norms are the average values for the group and can be calculated based on a sample of the general population. Norm-based interpretation answers questions of whether or not an observed score is typical: Is this the score one would expect to see for this individual or group of individuals? Is there anything remarkable or out of the ordinary about this score?

SOURCES OF MISINTERPRETATION

Misinterpretation of health status scores can occur when there is a lack of standardization across comparisons made within groups over time or among groups at one point in time, with regard to types of respondents surveyed or methods used to collect the health status information. It is very important to standardize mode of data collection, questionnaire format (including instructions), and to take into account differences in sociodemographics of respondents. Research indicates that how data are collected, whether by face-to-face interview, telephone, or mail, will affect scale scores (77). Instructions, such as the recall period, also have been shown to influence scale scores (78). Every effort should be made to make questionnaire administration procedures, such as mode of administration and the format of the questionnaire, invariant across longitudinal and cross-sectional comparisons. The type of respondent also has an effect on scale scores. Proxy responses to health status surveys typically differ from personal responses (79). Thus, if proxy data are used, they should be used consistently throughout a study. Sociodemographic variables such as gender, age, education, income, and race/ethnicity (80–82) have been shown to be associated with health status, so comparisons should be restricted to groups that are equivalent in terms of these background variables or statistical controls for these variables should be implemented.

CLINICAL SIGNIFICANCE OF QUALITY OF LIFE DATA

Investigators must be prepared to describe how changes or differences seen with HRQOL instruments can be translated into clinically meaningful terms. The issue of clinical significance in non-HRQOL endpoints has received the most comprehensive attention from researchers involved in the design and analysis of clinical trials. Estimation of sample size is an essential element of the design of any clinical trial. For continuous measures, sample size estimates are based on the level of type I error, the acceptability of a type II error, the variance of the measurement, and the minimal difference considered clinically important. This clinical difference has often been chosen because of practical or economic concerns of accruing and following a large number of subjects. However, economic principles can be used to quantitatively derive the "clinically important" difference by balancing the cost of an increasingly large clinical trial capable of detecting increasingly small differences in risk reduction with the overall improvement in health status of the population that could occur as the result of adopting a truly effective therapy (83). More commonly, this difference is determined as (a) the amount of difference on a proxy that relates to a significant outcome difference; (b) previous experience, that is, a new intervention should be as good or better than the old; and (c) natural history and change in measures of the disease over time.

Thus, it would seem that a clinically important difference has traditionally been in the eye of the beholder. This is not to say that there is no commonly recognized threshold for a given test or result. Clinicians may "know" clinical significance when they see it and they may agree fairly well on what constitutes clinical significance (84), but they may not realize that their understanding of clinical significance of objective measures is based on their experience (or the experience of their teachers) with a large number of patients followed over time. Unfortunately, this experience is not available with HRQOL measures for most clinicians at this time.

Population Versus Individual Perspective

As is often the case, clinical relevance depends on the perspective taken. Results can be interpreted from the viewpoint of the patient under care, of the clinician treating the patient, of the patient's family or caregiver, of the political or economic body paying for the care, or of society as a whole evaluating the care in epidemiologic or public health terms (85). These different viewpoints can, in a rough sense, be divided into those that measure relevance to an individual (i.e., patient or someone else evaluating the patient's condition) and those that measure relevance to a population.

Reports of clinical significance for HRQOL, as with objective measures, include both those related to the individual and those related to population. For example, differences seen in a study can be applied to a much larger population (population attributable risk), as in this example from Testa (86): 20% of the patients receiving methyldopa and 15% of patients receiving propranolol would have remained stable or improved had they been treated with captopril. Given an average hypertensive clinical practice of size 500, this means that 100 individual patients receiving treatment with methyldopa could have maintained their quality of life on medication rather than experiencing a worsening. Of those 100, 45 could have been spared substantial worsening in their levels of positive well-being, vitality, depression, and anxiety. This model extended to a population of 1 million hypertensive patients translates into 90,000 individuals spared substantial decreases in their general well-being.

Another form of expressing population-level clinical significance may relate changes in HRQOL to other population-level measures such as resource utilization, thus employing the construct of medical care resources to benchmark the HRQOL change: Mental health status, as measured by the Medical Outcome Study—Mental Health Index (87), is a major predictor of the use of outpatient mental health services (87). The average patient scoring in the lowest tertile of the MHI score distribution spent over three times more per year for mental health care than the average person in the highest tertile (87). Contrast these population perspectives with that of an individual perspective such as reported by Brook et al. (88): A five-point difference on a standardized health perception scale = the effect of having been diagnosed as having hypertension. A 10-point difference on a standardized physical functioning scale equals the effect of having chronic, mild osteoarthritis.

The shifting perspective (from individual to population) when talking about clinical significance has added to the misunderstanding surrounding interpretation for both HRQOL and non-HRQOL measures alike. This confusion is exacerbated by the emphasis of reporting clinical trial results in terms of mean difference of the change from baseline between treated and control groups. Often the mean change is within the test variance for an individual patient. This mean difference has little relevance to an individual patient. For illustration, if the Scholastic Aptitude Test (SAT) score of a student seeking admission to Harvard improves by ten points on repeat examination, it is unlikely that this would warrant comment. If, however, a new statewide school program results in an improvement of ten points on mean SAT scores for all students in the state, it is likely that the teachers and developers of this new program would be congratulated and rewarded. Thus, a mean difference may have great relevance when assessing the impact of an intervention in a population and less relevance in understanding individual changes.

A useful way of presenting trial results for both HRQOL and non-HRQOL endpoints would be to describe the distribution of change; e.g., how many patients benefit, how many show no change, and how many worsen. Even on a population basis, the greatest impact of an intervention is often in the tails of the distribution. Statistics that describe the tails or a cumulative distribution function would more clearly indicate how many patients are likely to have a significant benefit than the mean or median. It would be easier to judge the likely significance of the therapy to an individual patient and the number of patients likely to benefit.

Defining Clinical Significance for an Objective Test

When faced with a completely new test and new units, interpretation of objective measures is no easier than interpretation of HRQOL results. Clinical trials of a new therapy for benign prostatic hyperplasia used urine flow as an outcome measure (89). Following one year of treatment, the urine flow in individuals who received the active treatment improved on average by 3 cc/sec over those who received placebo. Clinicians found it very difficult to judge whether an improvement of 3 cc/sec was clinically meaningful. A subsequently published epidemiologic study in untreated men aged 40 to 79 years found that urine flow rates decline by an average of approximately 0.2 to 0.3 cc/sec per year of life (90). A 3 cc/sec improvement in urine flow could be interpreted as roughly equivalent to restoring an individual's urinary status to what it was approximately 10 to 15 years earlier. Thus, the clinical trial results were not clear until put into context with the findings of the epidemiologic study.

CLINICAL VERSUS STATISTICAL SIGNIFICANCE

HRQOL results require some contextual relationship in order to understand their relevance. Jaeschke et al. (91) define "minimal clinically important difference" as the smallest difference in a score in a domain of interest that patients perceive as beneficial and that would mandate, in the absence of troublesome side effects and excessive cost, a change in the patient's management. This definition incorporates several important concepts. It focuses attention on the patient's perception of benefit from therapy. Also, it suggests that this benefit would prompt a change in management which emphasizes the clinical aspect. Finally, it incorporates the risk/benefit equation of costs and side effects. Although this is an excellent definition, it does not directly suggest an operational method for defining clinical meaningfulness. Based on a literature search and expert opinion on ways in which HRQOL researchers have operationally defined clinical meaningfulness, a taxonomy can be based on two broad categories that termed distribution-based and anchor-based interpretations (92).

Distribution-Based Interpretation

Distribution-based interpretations are those based on the statistical distributions of the results obtained from a given study. Most of these interpretations involve permutations of the means and standard deviations of changes seen in a particular study or comparisons of study results to the means or standard deviations of some reference population.

The most commonly cited of these measures is the effect size in which the importance of the change is scaled by comparing the magnitude of the change to the variability in stable subjects, for example on baseline or among untreated individuals (93). Guyatt et al. (94) believe that effect size is more a measure of responsiveness and, at best, an underestimate of the minimal clinically important difference. Nevertheless, this measure has been used in a number of publications as an estimate or as evidence of clinical significance (95). While the most common, effect size is certainly not the only measure of clinical significance built on distributions.

Clinically important difference is clearly related to magnitude of the difference. Burnand et al. (96) reviewed the levels at which investigators tended to view their results as quantitatively significant in evaluating (a) the ratio of two means, (b) odds ratios, (c) differences between two rates, and (d) correlation coefficients. In a survey of 142 published reports, they found that investigators do appear to use certain standards regularly for decisions of when to emphasize a clinical finding.

Anchor-Based Interpretation

Alternatively, HRQOL measures may be compared, or anchored, to other clinical changes or results. Thus, our second broad taxonomic grouping is that of anchor-based interpretations of clinical meaningfulness. Normative data, at first glance, appear to be a distribution-based measure of clinical significance, but it goes further than just restate a statistical change and "anchors" such changes to the population as a whole. For example, using population norms, Guess et al. (97) could conclude that treatment with finasteride for 36 months reduced symptoms (scores) from about the 86th population percentile to the 64th population percentile, whereas treatment for TURP (transurethral prostatectomy) at Mayo Clinic reduced symptoms from the 97th population percentile to the 49th population percentile. This comparison is likely to be more understandable to clinicians and patients than simply describing the finasteride results as having reduced mean symptoms scores by 3.5 points on a scale of 0 to 36.

Fortunately, population norms are becoming available for the more commonly used instruments (98,99). With the availability of normative data, comparisons can be made between treated and untreated patients, ill and well populations, and, in some instances, patients with different diseases.

The most commonly reported anchor-based interpretation is that suggested by Jaeschke et al. (91) and is based on a patient and/or clinician global rating question. To use these authors' example, they looked at changes in a global assessment question over time and compared changes seen on their disease-specific questionnaire between four groups of patients defined as (a) those having no change in their global health status, (b) those having small changes in function (absolute changes of one to three response items on the global question), (c) those having moderate changes in function (absolute changes of four or five response items), and (d) those having large changes in function (absolute changes of six or seven on the global question). Thus, the changes seen in a disease-specific questionnaire are "anchored" to reported changes in overall health status.

Other anchors may be time, as in the non-HRQOL example of urine flow or in this example from the HRQOL literature: Disability in rheumatoid arthritis appears to increase by approximately 0.1 units on Health Assessment Questionnaire each year for the first few years of disease and then rises more slowly, at a rate of approximately 0.02 units per year after that (100). An additional anchor may be changes with therapy; e.g., the heart failure score, as measured by Chronic Heart Failure Questionnaire, improved by a mean of 2.1 points, when patients received digoxin. In another study, the heart failure score improved 1.6 points when patients received digoxin (91). Thus, changes seen with other therapies can be tied to the clinician's understanding of the efficacy of digoxin.

In addition to the examples previously quoted from Brook et al. (88) correlating diagnosis or impact of living with a specific condition, there is also an example anchoring changes on an HRQOL questionnaire to observed life events: a three-point difference on standardized mental health scale equals the impact of being fired or laid off from a job. Being able to predict future outcomes is an obvious anchor that has not been as commonly used as one would expect. Marder et al. (101) describe levels at which changes on the Brief Psychiatric Rating Scale are shown to be predictive of a psychotic exacerbation within 4 weeks. Thus, a clinician may judge the level of change at which to institute a change in the patient's management. Deyo and Inui (102) correlated changes in the Sickness Impact Profile with changes in more traditional measures of functional status in patients with arthritis.

Ideally, an attempt should be made to describe HRQOL values or changes in a way that will convey meaning to a clinician. These anchor-based interpretations of clinical significance all relate the change in HRQOL not to the distribution of scores but to some outside measure that is more clearly understood or familiar to their audience than the HRQOL scores themselves. This strategy was put forth by Brook and Kamberg (103):

1. All clinical trials should include at least one readily understandable "nontraditional" measure of outcome that is of primary interest to clinicians. Work-loss days, days not confined to bed or chair, days out of hospital, and other similar measures are potential candidates.

2. Where possible, clinical trials should include one general health status measure, although it would not be used as the trial's primary outcome. At least at the beginning of this endeavor, we should be satisfied with learning more about the meaning and interpretation of these general health status measures.

Expressing changes in relation to an external anchor is of more value than the tautologic reference of clinical importance back to statistical significance. In time, as our audience becomes more familiar with HRQOL measures and their scores, anchoring to other conditions and results may no longer be necessary; however, the need to consider clinical significance along with statistical significance will not disappear.

The relevant anchor, or the amount of change judged clinically significant, may differ with different populations and one may need to estimate clinical significance in different patient groups, just as one needs to validate the same questionnaire in each different patient group. This is particularly true as many scales are not completely linear. Scales may contain both a floor and ceiling in their relationship to an anchor (104), or it may be that smaller differences in the extremes may be substantially more important than the same level of change in mid-range (105).

METHODS FOR DEVELOPING AND TESTING NEW INSTRUMENTS

A series of steps are taken in instrument development and testing (Table 4.3).

INSTRUMENT DEVELOPMENT

Specifying Measurement Goals

Before embarking on the development of any new instrument, the investigator should define exactly what the instrument is to measure. This initial definition will help the investigator design appropriate development and testing protocols and will enable other users of the instrument to recognize its applicability to their own patients and studies.

TABLE 4.3 *Major issues in instrument development and validation*

	Discriminative	Predictive	Evaluative
Item generation	Identify all items of impairment that might be important to patients	Identify all items of impairment that might be important to patients	Identify all items of impairment that might be important to patients
Item reduction	Delete items common to all patients	Delete items common to all patients	Select the most frequent and important items; delete nonresponsive items
Response options	Response options adequate to achieve fine or coarse discrimination, depending on goals	Response options adequate to predict criterion standard	Response options with sufficient gradations to register within-patient change
Reliability	Large and stable interpatient variation	Large and stable interpatient variation	Not relevant
Responsiveness	Not relevant	Not relevant	Able to detect small within-patient change over time
Validity	Cross-sectional construct validity	Cross-sectional criterion validity	Longitudinal construct validity

Patient Population

As in a clinical trial, there should be clear inclusion and exclusion criteria that identify the precise clinical diagnosis and basic patient characteristics. A detailed definition might include age, literacy level, language ability, and presence of other illnesses that might have impact on HRQOL. An investigator may be thinking of a particular trial in which the instrument is to be used, but constructing an instrument for too specific a population or function may limit its subsequent use. One can usually choose a patient population that is narrow enough to allow focus on important impairments in that disease or function but broad enough to be valid for use in other studies.

Primary Purpose

The investigator needs to decide whether the primary purpose of the instrument is going to be evaluative, discriminative, or predictive, as illustrated in a three-dimensional model (Fig. 4.2). Although some instruments may be capable of all three functions, it is difficult to achieve maximum efficiency in all three.

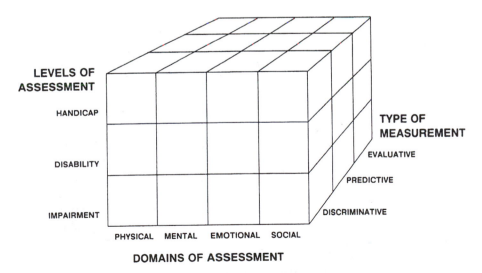

FIG. 4.2. A three-dimensional model for functional assessment.

Patient Function

In most disease-specific instruments, investigators want to include all areas of dysfunction associated with that disease (physical, emotional, social, occupational). However, there are some instruments that are designed to focus on a particular function (e.g., emotional function, pain, sexual function) within a broader patient population. The investigator should decide whether all or only specific functions are to be included.

Item Generation

The first task in instrument development is to generate a pool of all potentially relevant items. From this pool, the investigator will later select items for inclusion in the final questionnaire. The most frequently used methods of item generation include unstructured interviews with patients believed to have particular insight into their condition, patient focus group discussions, a review of the disease-specific literature, discussions with health care professionals who work closely with the patients, and a review of generic HRQOL instruments.

Item Reduction

Reducing Items on the Basis of Their Frequency and Importance

Having generated a large item pool, the investigator must select the items that will be most suitable for the final instrument. HRQOL instruments usually measure health status from the patients' perspective and so it is appropriate that patients themselves identify the items that are most important to them. Investigators should ensure that the patients selected represent the full spectrum of those identified in the patient population. If one is interested in checking that the final instrument is applicable to subgroups within that population (e.g., mild, moderate, and severe disease), then it is important to ensure that all of the subgroups are adequately represented.

One approach to item reduction is to ask patients to identify those items that they have experienced as a result of their illness. For each positively identified item, they rate the importance using a five-point Likert type scale ("extremely important" to "not important"). Results are expressed as *frequency* (the proportion of patients experiencing a particular item), *importance* (the mean importance score attached to each item), and the *impact*, which is the product of frequency and importance.

Very rarely, there are items that have absolutely no potential of changing over time, either as a result of an intervention or through the natural course of the disease. If one is developing an evaluative instrument, one may consider excluding such unresponsive items because they will only add to the measurement "noise" and the time taken to complete the questionnaire. However, if such an item is considered very important by patients and, therefore, potentially a future target for therapy, exclusion because of apparent unresponsiveness to current therapies may be unwise.

Let us assume one has decided that the final questionnaire will ask subjects whether they have, or have not, experienced a problem (i.e., a dichotomous response) rather than providing an opportunity to grade the severity of the problem. If virtually all subjects experience the problem, then it will not be useful to include such an item in a discriminative instrument. On the other hand, if the final instrument will grade the extent to which a problem affects the respondents, items that the entire population finds a problem may still prove very useful in discrimination.

A comprehensive set of items will inevitably include some redundancies. How does one decide whether to include, for instance, both fatigue and tiredness, if the two items have a high impact score? One approach is to test whether the items are highly correlated. If Spearman rank order correlations are high (i.e., patients who identify fatigue as a problem and rate its importance high are the same patients who identify tiredness as a high-impact item, and the same patients who rate one item low in impact also rate the other item low) one can consider omitting one of the items. This strategy is particularly appropriate for a discriminative instrument, for highly correlated items will add little to one another in distinguishing those with mild and severe quality of life impairment from one another. It is somewhat riskier for evaluative instruments; just because items correlate with one another at the item reduction phase does not guarantee that they will change in parallel when measured serially over time.

Investigators can select the sample size for the item reduction process by deciding how precise they want their estimates of the impact of an item on the population. The widest confidence interval around a proportion (the frequency with which patients identify items) occurs when the proportion is 50%; any other value will yield narrower confidence intervals. If one recruits 25 subjects, and an item is identified by 50% of the population, the true prevalence of that item is somewhere between approximately 30% and 70% (i.e., the 95% confidence interval around the proportion of .5 is approximately .3 to .7). If one recruits 50 subjects, the 95% confidence interval around a proportion of .5 will be approximately .14. For 100 subjects, the confidence interval will range from .04 to .06. We recommend recruitment of at least 100 subjects for this part of the questionnaire development process.

Individualized Items

Patients may identify that they experience limitation in their day-to-day activities and that these limitations are very important. However, because the types of activities undertaken by patients vary enormously, it is often difficult to find important activities that are common to all patients. A successful solution to this problem has been to include three to five "individualized" activity items (106).

At the beginning of any trial, each patient identifies activities that are limited by their condition, are important, and are done frequently. These are retained for the individual patient throughout the trial. This strategy is applicable to evaluative, but not to discriminative instruments.

Factor Analysis

Some investigators use mathematical modeling (factor analysis) to determine which items should be included in HRQOL instruments. In factor analysis, items that have high correlations with one another are grouped together. Items that are not strongly associated with one of the domains or factors that emerge from the factor analysis are excluded from the final questionnaire. The disadvantage of using factor analysis for item reduction is that the "orphan" items that are excluded from the factor analysis model may be important to patients. The issue is the relative importance one puts on the impact of an item and its relationship with other items.

Deciding on Instrument Domains

At the end of the reduction phase, the investigator has the required number of items for the final questionnaire and usually wants to group them into domains or dimensions (e.g., symptoms, emotional function, activity limitation). The easiest method is to review the items and use common sense, clinical experience, and domains described in established instruments to group the items. If one has defined in the initial criteria that certain functions are to be included in the final questionnaire, it is important to ensure that these criteria are met.

Intuition has its limitations in grouping items. First, different people may have a different intuitive sense as to where an item may fit. Second, an investigator may be uncertain where an item should be placed. Third, people's intuition may agree, but they may be wrong (i.e., not understand the underlying relation between items). Statistical strategies based on correlations between items offer an alternative approach to creating instrument domains, and factor analysis is the most popular of these strategies. The disadvantage of the factor analysis approach is that if one arrives at counter-intuitive groupings, how one should proceed is not self-evident. A compromise may be to place items in the domains that make intuitive sense and, if uncertainty remains about some items, examine the correlations of those items with items that clearly fall in particular domains.

Questionnaire Formatting

Selection of Response Options

Response options refer to the categories or scales that are available for responding to the questionnaire items. For example, one can ask whether the subject has difficulty climbing stairs; two response options, yes and no, are available. If the questionnaire asks about the degree of difficulty, a wide variety of response options are available.

An evaluative instrument must be responsive to important changes even if they are small. To ensure and enhance this measurement property, investigators usually choose scales with a number of options, such as a seven-point scale where responses may range from 1 = no impairment to 7 = total impairment or a continuous scale such as a 10-cm visual–analog scale (VAS). Although both yield similar data, the Likert scale has practical advantages over the VAS, being both easier to administer and easier to interpret (107).

Likert and VAS can be used for discriminative and predictive instruments, and are likely to yield optimal measurement properties (108). However, Likert and VAS are more complex than a simple yes/no response and they are very difficult to use for telephone interviews. In health surveys, investigators requiring only satisfactory discriminative or predictive measurement properties of their instrument may choose a simple response option format.

Time Specification

A second feature of presentation is time specification: patients should be asked how they have been feeling over a well-defined period of time. Two to four weeks is considered a time frame near the upper limit of what patients can accurately recall. Time specification can be modified according to the trial, and other investigators may have different impressions of the limits of their population's memory.

Questionnaire Administration

In the traditional approach to questionnaire administration, patients are not permitted to see the responses they gave on previous occasions. However, showing patients their previous responses improves the validity of the questionnaire without adversely affecting the responsiveness (109). Therefore, patients should see their previous responses when the questionnaires are being used for evaluative purposes.

Language Suitable for Translation

Very rarely will an instrument be used only in the country and culture in which it was developed. To make adaptation for use in a new country easier, it is wise to avoid jargon, idioms, or metaphors in a new instrument. Even within the English-speaking world, there are words and terms that are not common to all cultures and countries. For instance, *crook, down-in-the-dumps,* and *pooped* are used in some geographic areas and not in others. Therefore, it is best to use words that apply to the widest range of cultures and geographic areas.

INSTRUMENT TESTING

Pretesting

When a new questionnaire is first administered there are invariably some problems with patients not correctly understanding items and with the wording or format of the questionnaire. It is wise to pretest the instrument in a small number of patients to resolve these problems before embarking on a more costly and complex validation trial. Administer the new questionnaire to approximately five patients, selected to represent as wide a spectrum as possible in disease severity, educational background, age, and gender. After an uninterrupted administration of the questionnaire, ask patients to explain in their own words exactly how they understand each item. Note consistent problems in wording and understanding, make the necessary changes, and administer the revised instrument to another group of five patients. This process is repeated until no more changes are needed.

CRITICAL PROPERTIES OF RESEARCH INSTRUMENTS

Psychometric Properties

Whether an instrument has utility as a diagnostic or predictive indicator of behavior depends on the proper construction of the instrument, as well as on careful selection of a measure suitable to the behavior under consideration. Psychometric evaluation of an assessment instrument begins with questions regarding its reliability and validity. The responsiveness of the instruments to clinically significant changes over time is also important.

Reliability

Reliability refers to the consistency of a measurement, and is usually determined by the extent to which a score can be replicated in identical or equivalent testing situations. Conceptually, a test score contains a "true-score" component and an "error" component. To the extent that random error is large, a test score will be unstable and, therefore, unreliable. There are three basic ways to evaluate the reliability of a given instrument.

Internal consistency reliability is the most frequently used estimate of a measure's reliability. Multiple responses are obtained in most HRQOL assessments that are then summed or reduced to a single score. An implicit assumption in this approach is that the individual items measure the same thing, or that the items are consistent with each other. To the extent that this is true, a test can be held to measure the same attribute across subjects and time. Operationally, the higher the correlations of the items within the test, the higher is their multiple correlation with the single factor they measure in common. Thus, a measure of internal consistency is the average degree of association among the items on a test. Coefficient alphas are the basic formulas for determining the reliability of instruments based on internal consistency.

Test–retest reliability is the correlation between scores obtained by the same person on two separate occasions; the error variance corresponds to the random fluctuations of performance between the two observations. This interpretation is complicated by the fact that actual changes may have occurred in behavior or functional status during the time interval itself. Thus, low test–retest reliability does not necessarily reflect the psychometric properties of the test. For example, the stability coefficients for the State–Trait Anxiety Inventory range from .65 to .86, although its internal consistency has been reported to be in the .90s (110). Thus, test–retest is only useful when it appears that there are no changes in the person or the situation between test administrations.

Validity

Demonstrating reliability in measurement is essentially providing the existence of a stable or generalizable concept. However, reliability says nothing about the nature of that concept. Thus, a set of items may yield a repeatable score that may be an invalid indicator of the construct under study. Validity is defined as the extent to which an instrument measures what it was intended to measure. Establishing validity in instrumentation is achieved by the extent of agreement between the measure and a designated "gold standard" or "criterion." Some authors argue that validity is more important than reliability. However, both properties can seriously influence the correctness of inference and, therefore, should be viewed as equally important qualities. Both must be maximized in the selection or development of an instrument. Although it is true that validity in measurement is necessary to interpret what a test score means conceptually, it can be shown statistically that small decrements in reliability can result in large decrements in validity (111). The following kinds of evidence are generally used to infer validity of measurement.

Content validity is the extent to which an instrument measures a representative range of the attribute under study. In interpreting content validity, questions regarding item sufficiency for the proposed investigation and the nature of the patient sample should be addressed carefully. For example, the range of items needed to adequately assess physical functioning in arthritic patients would be too gross for application to many coronary heart disease samples. Similarly, some depression questionnaires cover mainly one or two aspects of depression, e.g., subjective and somatic complaints. A clear idea of what aspects of the behavioral or psychological attribute are of interest to the study is essential to judge the degree of content validity for a particular assessment instrument.

Construct validity refers to evidence that a measured construct behaves in a manner consistent with its referent theoretical or logical properties. Construct validity is established through a series of tests demonstrating that the variable, as measured (a) does not correlate positively with measures of related but different constructs (discriminant validity), (b) does correlate positively with related and similar constructs (convergent validity), (c) taps the measures of the construct intended, and (d) is not dominated by irrelevant factors. The process of assessing these aspects of validity is used to increase confidence that an observed effect pertains to the variable of interest. In HRQOL research, one of the largest problems in establishing construct validity is the lack of agreement regarding the operational definition of dimensions of HRQOL, as well as differences in population characteristics and the population-specific criteria used in many measures.

Criterion validity refers to the performance of the instrument against an external "gold standard" or actual outcome the test was developed to assess. Thus, one type of evidence of validity is prediction of future performance, events, or outcomes. Another type is agreement with clinical assessments or standards. Often a criterion will not exist for overall HRQOL measures but only for dimensions of HRQOL. All validation reports should describe the conditions under which the validation was conducted, including the demographic characteristics of the trial population, and the range of illness or symptoms experienced in the sample. As with known-groups validity, estimates should be provided regarding the sensitivity and specificity of the instrument in detecting the criterion. This can provide a basis for comparing results across clinical samples and populations.

Predictive validity is the degree to which a test can predict how well an individual will do in a future situation. Predictive validity is determined by the degree of correspondence between the assessment instrument and the specific criterion used for future performance. Again, all validation reports for assessment instruments should describe the conditions under which the validation was conducted. It is crucial that these be considered before employing an instrument. *No test is inherently "valid"; rather, a test is valid with regard to a specific purpose, range, and sample.*

Responsiveness

A final indicator of an instrument's validity, which is important in evaluation research such as in clinical trials, is the responsiveness of the instruments to clinically significant changes over time. Guyatt et al. (112) have suggested that responsiveness is a separate and distinct psychometric property, whereas Hays and Hadorn (113) purport that responsiveness is actually another type of validity that incorporates longitudinal information (change). Sensitivity to change should be reported for all HRQOL instruments developed for use in evaluation research; however, this is not done commonly. Evidence of responsiveness can include pre- and post-test comparisons, but is strengthened when correlations with other indicators of the HRQOL-related characteristics are included (e.g., clinically assessed change in status). Attention should be given to the phenomenon being measured and its expected responsiveness. Measures of psychological traits are less likely to change than psychological states in response to interventions.

MEASURING RELIABILITY AND RESPONSIVENESS AND ASSESSING VALIDITY AND INTERPRETABILITY

Under ideal circumstances, there is the time and the money to carry out a full "standalone" validation trial. Sometimes circumstances are not so kind and one is forced to build a validation study into an existing clinical trial. With a little ingenuity and a few additional questionnaires, this can be done quite satisfactorily. In distinct validation studies, patients are followed for a period of time with assessments at regular intervals. During this time, some patients will remain clinically stable, while others will change either spontaneously or as a result of some intervention. One can ensure that some patients will fall into the "change" category by offering an intervention of known therapeutic benefit to those patients who have the potential to improve. For each time interval between evaluations, each patient is categorized either as having "stayed stable" (group A) or "changed" (group B) using a global rating of change or clinical indices. When using the global ratings, patients scoring -1, 0, and -1 are considered to have remained stable and are placed in group A. Patients responding between -7 and -2 and between $+2$ and $+7$ are considered to have experienced a change in their health status and are categorized as part of group B.

Data from the clinically stable patients who fall into group A are used for estimating the reliability of the instrument. Data from both groups are used for the three methods of assessing responsiveness. First, data from group B are used to evaluate the change in HRQOL scores between consecutive assessments using a paired t-test. Second, change in HRQOL scores between consecutive visits for the two groups are compared using an unpaired t-test. Third, the responsiveness index is derived from the minimal important difference and the pooled standard deviation of patients in both group A and group B (114).

To assess construct validity, outcomes that are predicted to be related to the new instrument should be measured at follow-up visits. A group of investigators and clinical specialists should make predictions as to where they would expect to find correlations before the analysis of the validity study data. Investigators can assess both cross-sectional validity for discriminative instruments and longitudinal validity for evaluative instruments. This approach to instrument development and testing is robust and easily replicated. With care in choosing items that are important to patients, and careful structuring of the questionnaire, investigators can usually construct HRQOL instruments with satisfactory measurement properties.

Recently, attempts have been made to apply more sophisticated statistical methods to HRQOL data in order to better characterize the impact of interventions or specific conditions on HRQOL over time. One such technique has been to calibrate changes in HRQOL scores to determine their clinical significance. In a double-blind, randomized clinical trial of two antihypertensive medications, Testa et al. (115) constructed a calibration model that related longitudinal changes in HRQOL scores (e.g., overall quality of life, general perceived health, psychological well-being, and psychological distress) to longitudinal changes in scores for three objective indices: side effects and symptom distress, stress, and life events. Calibration with the life events index showed that drug-induced changes in HRQOL were substantial and that the different effects of these two medications on HRQOL had clinical meaning.

HRQOL ASSESSMENT: MODES OF ADMINISTRATION

HRQOL data can be collected in an interview format, either by telephone or in person, or from self-administered instruments, completed in person or through the mail. There is some debate regarding the relative merit of interviewer-administered versus self-administered instruments. Self-administered instruments are more cost effective from a staffing perspective, and may yield more disclosure on the part of the participant, particularly with the collection of sensitive information. However, self-administered instruments tend to yield more missing and incomplete data and do not allow for clarification. In the long run, and with some populations, they may actually prove to be more expensive than interviewer-administered instruments.

Interviewer-administered instruments usually provide more complete data and allow for probes and clarification. However, there may be a reluctance on the part of some participants to openly discuss some HRQOL issues (e.g., depression, sexuality), whereas they may be willing to respond to questions about these same issues in a self-administered format. Given the relatively high proportion of functional illiteracy in groups within the United States and elsewhere, in-person interviewer administration may be required, depending upon the particular population under study. Interviewer administration may also be the best way to obtain information for culturally diverse populations. Finally, interviewer-administered instruments are subject to interviewer bias and require intensive interviewer training, certification, and repeat training, especially within the context of studies of long duration; thus, they can be considerably more expensive than self-administered instruments. Serious thought must be given at the planning phases of a trial regarding the trade-offs between self-administered and interviewer-administered measures.

In practice, studies that include measures of HRQOL usually incorporate a combination of profiles augmented with either generic or population-specific measures of the dimensions most relevant to the trial population and intervention. In addition, most HRQOL measures are designed to be either interviewer- or self-administered, and both modes of administration can be used within single trials.

Telephone Versus In-Person Interviews

There are several advantages to telephone interviews. First, although the cost in interviewer time of interviewing people in the clinical setting will vary with the circumstances, it almost always is less expensive to interview people on the telephone than to send an interviewer to a subject's home. Second, telephone interviews can be conducted from a centralized setting, in which interviewer supervision can be maximized, possibly improving standardization and the quality of interviewing. Third, interviewers do not have to be proximate to the subjects. Widely scattered respondents can be interviewed by a small number of interviewers in a central place. Finally, providing computer assistance to telephone interviewers in a central location is particularly easy. A practical consideration is that there are some data collection activities that cannot be performed on the telephone. Those questions that require visual aids or involve lists of response alternatives are difficult to do on the telephone. In addition, if the protocol requires a patient to sign a consent form, a telephone data collection poses problems.

With respect to data quality, most comparisons suggest that data collected by telephone are very similar to those collected by personal interviewers (116,117). When differences in response have been detected, they often have been in the direction of suggesting people report fewer problems and less socially undesirable facts over the telephone than they do a personal interviewer. However, it should be emphasized that for most questions, the data collected in person and by telephone interviewers have been indistinguishable. Thus, telephone data collection is a realistic and appropriate option for many trial designs.

Computer-Assisted Data Collection

Having the data entered directly into a computer, researchers can ensure that interviewers do not enter any answer that was logically inconsistent or outside the field of legal answers. In addition, because the data were entered into a computer, data files are quickly created (118,119). Computers can be used for self-administered data collection as well. Questions can pop up on a screen, and respondents can enter their answers in a computer. The limit of this technology is that respondents vary in how comfortable they are in working with a computer. Self-administered data collection using computers has to be supervised. If technical assistance is available, people who are able to fill out self-administered questionnaires should be able to answer questions via computer. The task can be simplified, moreover, if respondents are not required to use a standard keyboard but can use some other kind of entry system that is easier and has fewer options.

Audio-Assisted Interviewing

Another way in which technology can be used to assist in the data collection process is audio-assisted interviewing. Questions are read out loud to respondents, who are asked to enter their answers either in a computer or on paper. Some computers have audio capabilities. Questions can also be recorded on tapes, which can be played with a portable tape player and a headset (120).

TESTING THE QUALITY OF
THE DATA COLLECTION INSTRUMENT

Survey questions have to meet at least two standards:

1. They have to be understood consistently.
2. They have to be questions people can answer.

Evaluating an Interview Schedule

Just because questions can be understood and answered in a laboratory setting does not mean that they will work in practice. If data collection is interviewer-administered, the data collection instrument is a script for the interviewer as well as a set of questions. If the instrument is to work well, the interview schedule must be one that interviewers can administer exactly as worded. Moreover, when interviewers read the question as written, respondents should be able to answer them readily. To find out how well the instrument works from that perspective, a field pretest under realistic conditions is necessary.

QUALITY CONTROL OF DATA COLLECTION

Self-Administration

The primary mechanism for quality control of self-administered data collection is to review completed questionnaires to make sure respondents are answering all the questions and they are following instructions. One common issue is whether or not respondents should be recontacted in the event that they fail to answer a question. If a question is factual in nature and it is critical to the trial, researchers may think it is worth the expense to do that. A more important strategy is to review early returns to make sure that there are no questions that are systemically being skipped because instructions are unclear. If such a problem is found, the most important thing to do is to change the data collection instrument to solve the problem.

Quality Control of Interviewers

If data are to be collected by an interviewer, it is critical that interviewers behave as standardized data collectors. Specifically, that means:

1. Asking questions exactly as worded.
2. Probing inadequate answers in nondirective ways.

3. Training respondents in their role in a consistent way.
4. Maintaining a neutral, nonbiasing relationship with respondents.

Particularly in clinical studies, it is tempting to use nurses, receptionists, or other staff in clinical settings as interviewers. Although that may be convenient, the risk is that people who are not primarily interviewers are being asked to do a very important job that they may not want to do or may not think is important. When possible, there probably are real advantages to using interviewers for whom interviewing is their main job. No matter who is the interviewer, interviewers must be properly trained and supervised. Simply explaining to a would-be interviewer how to behave is not enough. Studies have shown that training that includes a reasonable amount of supervised role-playing is essential to producing interviewers who can meet reasonable standards. In addition, interviewers must be supervised. If interviewers are working on telephones, one approach is to have a supervisor systematically monitor a sample of each interviewer's work. At a minimum, all of the early interviews should be monitored, until an interviewer has proven to be acceptable, and then monitor a sample of interviews. Continuing to monitor, even after interviewers have demonstrated that they can interview appropriately, is essential in order to maintain high-quality data collection.

If interviewers are doing interviews in person, or even if they are working on the telephone and a supervisor cannot be present at all times, tape recording interviews is an alternative way of monitoring the question-and-answer process. Again, early interviews plus a sample of subsequent interviews can be reviewed by a supervisor, systematically evaluated, and the results used to provide feedback and additional training as needed. It is very tempting to think that a professional, such as a nurse, would be well qualified to carry out an interview. However, unless a person is properly trained and supervised, he/she will not be a good interviewer, no matter what other kinds of training that person has received.

Proxy Administration of the Questionnaire

Patient self-report provides the best scientific and clinically relevant data for evaluating the impact of cancer treatments on the patient's quality of life. Substitution of proxy measures was generally not recommended. Neither physician nor family member measures have demonstrated good agreement with the patient report. There are, however, instances where proxy measures may be considered:

1. When the physician report provides a useful supplement to the patient report of quality of life, especially regarding physician-observed toxicities or performance status.
2. If the cognitive or physical function of the patient is expected to deteriorate significantly during the trial, it may be helpful for the investigator to include spouse or family members in the ratings.

3. It may be useful to include in the validation of new quality of life instruments an examination of the degree of differences and agreement in the patient and proxy reports.
4. When the purpose of the trial is to assess the impact of therapy on individuals other than the patient, it would be useful to document the degree of burden experienced by the family during the patient's treatment. A family member may contribute to the evaluation by assessing his/her own quality of life.

There are situations identified in which proxy measures of patient quality of life should not be used:

1. A proxy rating is not considered appropriate when the patient is non-English-speaking and there is no translation of the quality of life measure or culturally sensitive instrument that meets accepted standards for translated instruments.
2. A proxy should not provide a report on a patient's quality of life if the patient refuses to participate in the quality of life portion of the clinical trial.

There is no single right way to collect data. All of the strategies discussed in this chapter are appropriate for some projects, depending upon the constraints, the data requirements, and the design of the trial. However, regardless of strategies used for data collection, it is essential that all aspects of the protocol be carefully evaluated prior to the onset of full-scale data collection.

LANGUAGE AND TRANSLATION ISSUES

There is a specific need for cross-nationally and cross-culturally valid, reliable, and responsive HRQL instruments for use in multinational studies. The strategies required to develop HRQL questionnaires that can be used cross-nationally include three strategies:

1. Translation into one or several other languages of instruments that are developed essentially for and within one country only (121). This is the most frequently used method, although certain authors (122,123) criticize the lack of intercultural appropriateness of these questionnaires and the risk of producing texts translated without conceptual equivalence.
2. Translation of instruments of which conception and development in a source language have been the subject of a consensus among several international teams in order to ensure their intercultural relevance and their conceptual equivalence (124).
3. The World Health Organization (WHO) Quality of Life (HRQOL) Group approach aims to create an instrument applicable to a large variety of cultures, with equivalent versions developed simultaneously in several languages. The questions developed in each dimension or domain may be different from one country to another (125). Such is not the case with the other two strategies.

Indirect translation processes are defined as transposition, modulation, equivalence, and adaptation.

Transposition operates on grammatical elements, substituting one part of speech for another without changing anything in the global meaning. Examples abound and this process operates not only between languages but also within a given language (126).

Modulation operates on thought and not grammatical categories (e.g., modulation from the concrete to the abstract or from popular to learned terms: thus, "on bare skin" can be rendered "à même la peau" in French and "handwritten" can be translated as "manuscrit"). In simple terms, modulation is a change in the point of view of the author and can operate at the word, phrase, or sentence level. It is applied in many of the cliches or fixed expressions of everyday language translated from one language to another. Modulation encompasses the whole world of metaphor and metonymy.

Equivalence allows one to describe a given situation using different structural and stylistic means. Once more, this process can operate at all levels of the language and involves the total message. "You're welcome" becomes *"De rien"* in French or, by translation in British English, "Don't mention it."

In contrast to equivalence, adaptation seeks a recognizable correspondence between two situations. The process often has to be applied if the situation described in the original message is not common or does not exist in the language of translation. And this process is what most concerns us here as it falls into the sociocultural domain.

Cross-Cultural Equivalence

Comparable observations can be obtained only if the original instrument and the translation are equivalent (127,128). Several authors have proposed a taxonomy of equivalence in cross-cultural measurement (127,129). Hui and Triandis (127) postulate four levels of equivalence, each level being the prerequisite of the next: (a) conceptual/functional equivalence, (b) equivalence in construct operationalization, (c) item equivalence, (d) scalar (or metric) equivalence. As a result of this postulate, they propose several strategies (among which, performing an adequate translation is quoted), allowing these four levels of equivalence to be checked in the measure concerned. From their work, it can be concluded that the cultural adaptation of an instrument in a target language involves two stages: translation, followed by evaluation of the instrument (i.e., psychometric tests).

Translation Process

The translation of an HRQL questionnaire into one or more target languages may be accomplished by a combination of techniques, i.e., four interrelated headings or steps that may be iterative:

1. Forward step
2. Quality control
3. Pretest
4. International harmonization.

The aim of each step is to add quality to the preceding one in terms of conceptual equivalence between source and target versions, in order to produce a relevant final translated version. The communication triad of author, translator, and user intervenes at different points throughout the four steps. Consequently, the translation process is the result of a multidisciplinary team effort and, in order to ensure some consistency, has to be headed by one team leader taking responsibility for the project throughout its realization.

Forward translation is the translation of a questionnaire (originally developed in a source language) into one or more target languages. This step, which is crucial to the whole process, is not simple and is not merely the production of a single target version. It is in fact the creation of a commonly agreed-on version built up through various stages:

As soon as an HRQL questionnaire has been chosen for inclusion in a multinational clinical trial and before any translation work is undertaken, it essential to respect the following rule: make contact with the author(s). There are two reasons for this:

1. To secure authorization for use and translation of the questionnaire (rules of copyright, fees, etc.)
2. To define carefully the underlying concepts for each item and dimension in the questionnaire.

This step of conceptual clarification allows one to (a) respect the intentions of the author and avoid misinterpretations, (b) avoid a lack of conceptual equivalence in the target versions, (c) find acceptable equivalents, and (d) save time wasted in idle and unnecessary discussions.

Instructions are often neglected but they must be carefully translated to respect the replicability of the questionnaire (130). Benefiting from the data provided by the author, the panel examines the conceptual equivalence of each forward version (produced at the previous stage) with the original, the purpose being to obtain for each item a commonly agreed-on forward version that is satisfactory on the linguistic and conceptual levels. However, the translation of certain items often remains problematic and, in this case, it is advisable to propose alternatives (121,131) that will be checked and tested later.

To evaluate the measurement equivalence between the source and target questionnaires, it is advisable (125,132) to examine the ordinality (Are answer choices in the same rank order in each country?) and interval score properties (Are the distances between answer choices identical between countries?) of the Likert-type answer choice scales, using a Thurstone scaling exercise (133). If the answer choices of each Likert-type scale of the source questionnaire are equidistant, the target answer choices should respect this equidistance, in order for the source and target questionnaires to be equivalent.

Quality Control

A target version is required that is equivalent to the source version both conceptually and linguistically. However, despite their competence and due to the subjective nature of their task, a panel of experts cannot, on their own, guarantee this equivalence (134). This is why quality controls have to be carried out. Generally they are of two types: (a) quality ratings and (b) back-translation.

Pretest

Having checked the quality of the agreed-on forward version (i.e., having evaluated its degree of conceptual and semantic equivalence with the source questionnaire), testing of the translated questionnaire on a sample of the population is generally recommended (134,135). Therefore, it is at this stage that the third partner of the communication triad mentioned previously, i.e., the user of the translation, intervenes. This test has several aims:

1. To measure the comprehensibility level of the translation (i.e., Is the questionnaire correctly understood?) and, therefore, correct any overcomplicated or sophisticated wording
2. To test the translation alternatives and, therefore, the choice of the most suitable wording (when the translators have been unable to agree on a wording and have suggested several translation alternatives for the same item)
3. To highlight any unexpected translation errors and difficulties
4. To reveal items that may be inappropriate on the conceptual level.

International Harmonization Meeting

Generally speaking, the pretest marks the end of the translation process: forward step, quality control, pretest. But when a questionnaire has to be translated simultaneously into several languages, an international harmonization meeting is valuable. During this meeting, the various translations of the questionnaire developed during the pretest are compared with each other as well as with the original. The meeting brings together at least as many professional translators as there are target languages, each of them being a native speaker of one of the target languages and bilingual in English. The aim is to detect any remaining errors that may not have been identified during the preceding steps. It is also an appropriate method for highlighting the differences in expressions and sometimes in concepts between the countries concerned. Finally, it is a further safety measure that ensures the quality of the final target versions.

The Need to Document the Translation Process

To ensure the best results and correct analysis in the later stages of the cultural adaptation process (e.g., weighting and psychometric evaluation), the entire translation process must be documented, i.e., a series of validation reports need to be kept. These reports should record, step by step and item by item, the solutions adopted as well as all the intermediary translations. Among other things the following will be noted:

what items are difficult to translate and why
what items are easy to translate and why
what items need cultural modification
what are the idiomatic items that have been translated in an unidiomatic way and why.

The linguistic validation (or cultural adaptation) of an HRQL questionnaire is only achieved when the psychometric properties of the translated questionnaire are documented. In some cases, the psychometric evaluation may lead to the retranslation of certain items. In other words, translation and conceptual equivalence are finally validated (or not) through psychometric testing. Criteria for decision making in psychometric testing should include the control of

the adequacy of the translated version with respect to the measurement model elaborated by the author, through the study of its factorial structure and scaling assumption
its reliability (i.e., reproducibility, internal consistency and interrater reliability, if needed)
its validity (focusing on clinical validating, i.e., known-groups comparison)
its responsiveness over time.

The translation of an HRQL questionnaire is not a simple operation, because it is subject to one overriding requirement—equivalence between the source and target version(s); and it is subject to two constraints—time and cost. All of the techniques described in this chapter have one essential aim: to enable one to obtain equivalent source and target questionnaires. Choice of technique will be partly guided and limited by the constraints mentioned. However, it must be remembered that the translation conditions the results of future clinical trials. If certain items are badly worded or not understood correctly, the execution of the study and the interpretation of results will be adversely affected and distorted. For this reason, it is essential to respect a minimum number of basic rules:

1. Produce a meaningful forward version while following these guidelines: contact the author, produce several preliminary forward versions, work with local teams and in committee

2. Check the quality of this forward version
3. test the forward version
4. If several target translations are developed simultaneously, check their relative appropriateness by international harmonization.

CROSS-CULTURAL MEASUREMENT EQUIVALENCE

Evaluations of whether a measure can be used cross-culturally are qualified by specific issues involving the intended use of the measure, the population or sample, country, study design, and goals of the project. This includes an assessment of the level of measurement equivalence that has been achieved supporting cross-cultural use, and the types of information needed for a more definitive assessment of comparability. A distinction must be made between evidence collected on an instrument's conceptual and psychometric properties within various cultures, versus between cultures where data has been aggregated in a multinational (or cultural) study and analyzed. Although the ability to replicate an instrument's conceptual and psychometric properties within different countries is essential for conducting cross-cultural research, it does not of itself demonstrate validity for cross-cultural comparisons. A taxonomy of dimensions of equivalence is listed in Table 4.4.

Four types of equivalence that may be evaluated across research settings are (a) conceptual equivalence, (b) operational equivalence, (c) scale equivalence, and (d) metric equivalence (5). These are the major sources that affect reliability and validity across culturally adapted or language-adapted versions of an instrument.

Conceptual equivalence has to do with whether the items in the target language version of a scale are similar in meaning to the source version. This form of equivalence goes beyond mere literal equivalence of how items are worded or described.

Operational equivalence refers to the adapted instrument's relative performance using various modes of questionnaire administration supported by the

TABLE 4.4 *Types of cross-cultural equivalence of instruments*

Type of equivalence	Definition
Content	The *content* of each item is *relevant* to the phenomenon of each culture
Semantic	The *meaning* of each item is the same in each culture after translation into the language and idiom of each culture
Technical	The *method* of assessment (e.g., paper-and-pencil, interview) is comparable in each culture with respect to the data that it yields
Criterion	The *interpretation* of the measurement of the variable remains the same when compared with the norm for each culture studied
Conceptual	The instrument is measuring the same *theoretical construct* in each culture

Adapted from reference 136, with permission.

instrument (e.g., self-administered, telephone, and postal versions). This property can be evaluated by comparisons of psychometric performance (reliability and validity) and response distributions of items, as well as the quality of data obtained (e.g., missing data) for the different methods supported.

Scale or *construct equivalence* concerns how similarly the culturally adapted or translated versions perform psychometrically across versions. Key attributes on which the various language versions of the instrument are tested include reliability, validity, and responsiveness to change.

Finally, *metric equivalence* is the extent to which the adapted measures place individuals who are similar with regard to the HRQL states being measured on the same point in the continuum of scores. Investigating this property is difficult because an obvious "gold standard" is lacking. Calibrating scores using patient groups, clinical status outcomes, or population norms are some of the approaches taken to evaluating metric equivalence.

REFERENCES

1. Kaplan RM, Bush JW, Berry CC. Health status: types of validity and the Index of Well-Being. *Health Serv Res* 1976;11:478–507.
2. Kornblith AB, Anderson J, Cella DF, et al. Quality-of-life assessment of Hodgkin's disease survivors: a model for cooperative clinical trials. *Oncology* 1990;4:93–101.
3. Bornstein PH, Hamilton SB, Bornstein MT. Self-monitoring procedures. In: Ciminero AR, Calhoun KS, Adams HE, eds. *Handbook of behavioral assessment.* New York: John Wiley, 1986:176–222.
4. Fraser SCA, Ramirez AJ, Ebbs SR, et al. A daily diary for quality of life measurement in advanced breast cancer trials. *Br J Cancer* 1993;67:340–346.
5. Fraser SCA, Dobbs H, Ebbs SR, Fallowfield LJ, Bates T, Baum M. Combination of mild single agent chemotherapy for advanced breast cancer? CMF vs epirubicin measuring quality of life. *Br J Cancer* 1993;67:402–406.
6. Cella DR, Tulsky DS. Quality of life in cancer: definition, purpose, and method of measurement. *Cancer Invest* 1993;11:327–336.
7. Kane RA, Kane RL. *Assessing the elderly: a practical guide to measurement.* Lexington, MA: Lexington Books, 1981.
8. Karnofsky DA, Burchenal JH. The clinical evaluation of chemotherapeutic agents in cancer. In: Macleod CM, ed. *Evaluation of chemotherapeutic agents in cancer.* New York: Columbia University Press, 1949:191–205.
9. Orr ST, Aisner J. Performance status assessment among oncology patients: a review. *Cancer Treat Rep* 1986;70:1423–1429.
10. Spitzer WO, Dobson AJ, Hall J, et al. Measuring the quality of life of cancer patients: a concise QL-index for use by physicians. *J Chronic Dis* 1981;34:585–597.
11. Haynes SN. Behavioral assessment of adults. In: Goldstein G, Hersen M, eds. *Handbook of psychological assessment.* Elmsford, NY: Pergamon Press, 1990:423–463.
12. Schag CC, Heinrich RL, Ganz PA. Karnofsky Performance Status revisited: reliability, validity, and guidelines. *J Clin Oncol* 1984;2:187–193.
13. Hunt S, McKenna SP, McEwan J, Williams J, Papp E. The Nottingham Health Profile: subjective health status and medical consultations. *Soc Sci Med* 1981;15A:221–229.
14. Sprangers MAG, Aaronson NK. The role of health care providers and significant others in evaluating the quality of life of patients with chronic disease: a review. *J Clin Epidemiol* 1992;45:743–760.
15. Korn EL, O'Fallon J. Statistical considerations, statistics working group. *Quality of life assessment in cancer clinical trials, report on Workshop on Quality of Life Research in Cancer Clinical Trials, Division of Cancer Prevention and Control.* Bethesda, MD: National Cancer Institute, 1990.
16. Little RJ, Rubin DB. *Statistical analysis with missing data.* New York: John Wiley, 1987:14–17.
17. Buck SF. A method of estimation of missing values in multivariate data suitable for use with electronic computer. *J R Stat Soc B* 1960;22:303–306.

18. Schumacher M, Olschewski M, Schulgen G. Assessment of quality of life in clinical trials. *Stat Med* 1991;10:1915–1930.
19. Gotay CC, Korn EL, McCabe MS, Moore TD, Cheson BD. Building quality of life assessment into cancer treatment studies. *Oncology* 1992;6:25–28.
20. Zee B, Pater J. Statistical analysis of trials assessing quality of life. In: Osoba D, ed. *Effect of cancer on quality of life.* Boston: CRC Press, 1991:113–124.
21. Jennrich R, Schluchter M. Unbalanced repeated-measures models with structured covariance matrices. *Biometrics* 1986;42:805–820.
22. Dempster AP, Laird NM, Rubin DB. Maximum likelihood from incomplete data via the EM algorithm (with discussion). *J R Stat Soc B* 1972;39:1–38.
23. Wu MC, Carroll RJ. Estimation and comparison of changes in the presence of informative right censoring by modeling the censoring process. *Biometrics* 1988;44:175–188.
24. Wu MC, Bailey KR. Estimation and comparison of changes in the presence of informative right censoring: conditional linear model. *Biometrics* 1989;45:939–955.
25. Wei LJ, Johnson WE. Combining dependent tests with incomplete repeated measurements. *Biometrika* 1985;72:359–364.
26. Tandon PK. Application of global statistics in analyzing quality of life data. *Stat Med* 1990;9:819–827.
27. Pocock SJ, Geller NL, Tsiatis AA. The analysis of multiple endpoints in clinical trials. *Biometrics* 1987;43:487–498.
28. O'Brien PC. Procedures for comparing samples with multiple endpoints. *Biometrics* 1984;40:1079–1087.
29. Cox DR, Fitzpatrick R, Fletcher AI, Gore SM, Spiegelhalter DJ, Jones DR. Quality-of-life assessment: can we keep it simple? (with discussion). *J R Stat Soc A* 1992;155:353–393.
30. Korn EL. On estimating the distribution function for quality of life in cancer clinical trials. *Biometrika* 1993;80:535–542.
31. Gelber RD, Gelman RS, Goldhirsh A. A quality of life oriented endpoint for comparing therapies. *Biometrics* 1989;45:781–795.
32. Glasziou PP, Simes RJ, Gelber RD. Quality adjusted survival analysis. *Stat Med* 1990;9:1259–1276.
33. Rosenman J, Choi NC. Improved quality of life of patients with small-cell carcinoma of the lung by elective irradiation of the brain. *Int J Radiat Oncol Biol Phys* 1982;8:1041–1043.
34. Torrance GW. Measurement of health state utilities for economic appraisal: a review. *J Health Econ* 1986;5:1–30.
35. Froberg D, Kane R. Methodology for measuring health-state preferences: II. Scaling methods. *J Clin Epidemiol* 1989;42:459–471.
36. Gelber RD, Goldhirsh A. A new endpoint for the assessment of adjuvant therapy in postmenopausal women with operable breast cancer. *J Clin Oncol* 1986;4:1772–1779.
37. Gore S. Integrated reporting of quality and length of life—a statistician's perspective. *Eur Heart J* 1988;9:228–234.
38. Anatasi A. *Psychological testing.* New York: Macmillan, 1976.
39. Nunnally JC, Bernstein IR. *Psychometric theory,* 3rd ed. New York: McGraw-Hill, 1994.
40. Ghiselli EE, Campbell JP, Zedeck S. *Measurement theory for the behavioral sciences.* San Francisco: Freeman, 1981.
41. Brazier JE, Harper R, Jones NMB, O'Cathain A, Thomas KJ, Usherwood T, Westlake L. Validating the SF-36 health survey questionnaire: new outcome measure for primary care. *Br Med J* 1992;305:160–164.
42. Anderson RT, Aaronson NK, Wilkin D. Critical review of the international assessments of health-related quality of life. *Qual Life Res* 1993;2:369–395.
43. Ware JE. The status of health assessment. *Annu Rev Public Health* 1995;16:327–354.
44. Ware JE, Manning WG, Duan N, Wells KB, Newhouse JP. Health status and the use of outpatient mental health services. *Am Psychol* 1984;39(10):1090–1100.
45. Nelson EC, Landgraf JM, Hays RD, et al. The COOP function charts: a system to measure patient function in physicians' offices. In: Lipkin M, ed. *Functional status measurement in primary care.* New York: Springer-Verlag, 1990.
46. Ware JE, Sherbourne CD. The MOS 36-item short-form health survey (S-36): I. Conceptual framework and item selection. *Med Care* 1992;30:473–483.
47. Patrick DL, Erickson P. *Health status and health policy: allocating resources to health care.* New York: Oxford University Press, 1993.
48. Bergner M. Development, testing, and use of the Sickness Impact Profile. In: Walker SR, Rosser RM, eds. *Quality of life: assessment and application.* Lancaster: MTP Press, 1988:79–94.

49. Patrick DL, Bush JW, Chen MM. Methods for measuring levels of well-being for a health status index. *Health Serv Res* 1973;8:224–229.
50. Kaplan RM, Bush JW, Berry CC. *The reliability, stability, and generalizability of a health status index. Proceedings of the American Statistical Association, Social Statistics Section.* Washington, DC: ASA, 1978:704–709.
51. Kaplan RM, Anderson JP. A general health policy model: update and applications. *Health Serv Res* 1988;23:203–235.
52. EuroHRQOL Group. EuroHRQOL—a new facility for the measurement of health-related quality of life. *Health Policy* 1990;16:199–208.
53. Parkerson GR, Broadhead WE, Tse CJ. Comparison of the Duke Health Profile and the MOS short-form in healthy young adults. *Med Care* 1991;29:679–683.
54. Crocker L, Algina J. *Introduction to classical and modern test theory.* New York: Harcourt Brace Jovanovich, 1986.
55. Ware JE, Snow KK, Kosinski M, Gandek B. *SF-363 Health Survey manual and interpretation guide.* Boston: New England Medical Center, The Health Institute, 1993.
56. Ware JE, Keller SD, Gandek B, and the IHRQOLA Project Group. Evaluating translations of health status questionnaires: methods from the IHRQOLA Project. *Int J Technol Assess Health Care* 1995; 11(3).
57. Kim J, Mueller CW. *Factor analysis: statistical methods and practical issues.* Beverly Hills, CA: Sage, 1978.
58. Stevens J. *Applied multivariate statistics for the social sciences,* 2nd ed. Hillsdale, NJ: Lawrence Erlbaum, 1992.
59. Ware JE, Kosinski M, Keller SD. *SF-36 physical and mental component summary measures—a user's manual.* Boston: The Health Institute, 1994.
60. Ware JE, Kosinski M, Bayliss MS, McHorney CA, Rogers WH, Raczek A. Comparison of methods for scoring and statistical analysis of SF-36 health profile and summary measures: summary of results from the Medical Outcomes Study. *Med Care* 1994;33(suppl 4):AS264–AS279.
61. McHorney CA, Ware JE, Raczek AE. The MOS 36-Item Short-Form Health Survey (SF-36): II. Psychometric and clinical tests of validity in measuring physical and mental health constructs. *Med Care* 1993;31:247–263.
62. Brooks WB, Jordan JS, Divine GW, Smith KS, Neelon FA. The impact of psychologic factors on measurement of functional status: assessment of the Sickness Impact Profile. *Med Care* 1990;28:793–804.
63. Katz JN, Larson MG, Phillips CB, Fossel AH, Liang MH. Comparative measurement sensitivity of short and longer health status instruments. *Med Care* 1992;30:917–925.
64. Williams AW, Ware JE, Donald CA. A model of mental health, life events, and social supports applicable to general populations. *J Health Soc Behav* 1981;22:324–336.
65. Brook RH, Ware JE, Rogers WH, et al. Does free care improve adults' health? Results from a randomized controlled trial. *N Engl J Med* 1983;309:1426–1434.
66. Ware JE, Brook RH, Rogers WH, et al. Comparison of health outcomes at a health maintenance organization with those of fee-for-service care. *Lancet* 1986;1:1017–1022.
67. Berwick DM, Murphy JM, Goldman PA, Ware JE, Barsky AJ, Weinstein MC. Performance of a five-item mental health screening test. *Med Care* 1991;29:169–176.
68. Weinstein MC, Berwick DM, Goldman PA, Murphy JM, Barsky A. A comparison of three psychiatric screening tests using Receiver Operating Characteristic (ROC) analysis. *Med Care* 1989;27:593–607.
69. Idler EL, Kasl S. Health perceptions and survival: do global evaluations of health status really predict mortality? *J Gerontol* 1990;46:S55–S65.
70. Kazis LE, Anderson JJ, Meenan RF. Health status as a predictor of mortality in rheumatoid arthritis: a five-year study. *J Rheumatol* 1990:17.
71. Lerner DJ, Levine S, Malspeis S, D'Agostino RB. Job strain and health-related quality of life in a national sample. *Am J Public Health* 1994;84:1580–1585.
72. Hunt SM, McKenna SP, McEwen J, Williams J, Papp E. The Nottingham Health Profile: subjective health status and medical consultations. *Soc Sci Med* 1981;15a:221–229.
73. Stewart AL, Greenfield S, Hays RD, et al. Functional status and well-being of patients with chronic conditions: results from the Medical Outcomes Study. *JAMA* 1989;262:907–913.
74. Follick MJ, Smith TW, Ahern DK. The Sickness Impact Profile: a global measure of disability in chronic low back pain. *Pain* 1985;21:67–76.
75. Wells KB, Stewart A, Hays RD, et al. The functioning and well-being of depressed patients: results from the Medical Outcomes Study. *JAMA* 1989;262:914–919.

76. Deyo RA, Inui TS, Leininger J, Overman, S. Physical and psychosocial function in rheumatoid arthritis: clinical use of a self-administered health status instrument. *Arch Intern Med* 1982;142:879–882.
77. McHorney CA, Kosinski M, Ware JE. Comparisons of the costs and quality of norms for the SF-36 Health Survey collected by mail versus telephone interview: results from a national survey. *Med Care* 1994;32:551–567.
78. Keller SD, Bayliss MB, Ware JE, Hsu MA, Damiano A, Goss T. Comparison of responses to SF-36 health survey questions with one-week and four-week recall periods. *Health Serv Res* 1997;32: 367–384.
79. Sprangers MAG, Aaronson NK. The role of health care providers and significant others in evaluating the quality of life of patients with chronic disease: a review. *J Clin Epidemiol* 1992;45:743–760.
80. Mossey JM, Shapiro E. Self-rated health: a predictor of mortality among the elderly. *Am J Public Health* 1982;72:800–808.
81. Ren XS, Amick BC. Racial and self-assessed health status: the role of socioeconomic factors in the USA. *J Epidemiol Community Health* 1996;50:369–373.
82. Singer E, Garfinkel R, Cohen SM, Srole L. Mortality and mental health: evidence from the midtown Manhattan study. *Soc Sci Med* 1976;10:517–525.
83. Detsky AS. Using economic analysis to determine the resource consequences of choices made in planning clinical trials. *J Chronic Dis* 1985;38:753–765.
84. Bellamy N, Buchanan WW, Esdaile JM, Fam AG, Kean WF, Thompson JM, Wells GA, Campbell J. Ankylosing spondylitis antirheumatic drug trials. III. Setting the delta for clinical trials of antirheumatic drugs—results of a consensus development (Delphi) exercise. *J Rheumatol* 1991;18:1716–1722.
85. Spilker B. *Guide to clinical trials*. New York: Raven Press, 1991.
86. Testa MA. Interpreting quality-of-life clinical trial data for use in the clinical practice of antihypertensive therapy. *J Hypertens* 1987;5(suppl 1):S9–S13.
87. Ware JE Jr, Manning WG Jr, Duan N, Wells KB, Newhouse JP. Health status and the use of outpatient mental health services. *Am Psychol* 1984;39:1090–1100.
88. Brook RH, Ware JE Jr, Rogers WH, Keeler EB, Davies AR, Donald CA, Goldberg GA, Lohr KN, Masthay PC, Newhouse JP. Does free care improve adults' health? Results from a randomized controlled trial. *N Engl J Med* 1983;309:1426–1434.
89. Gormley GJ, Stoner E, Bruskewitz RC, et al. The effect of finasteride in men with benign prostatic hyperplasia. *N Engl J Med* 1992;327:1185–1191.
90. Girman CJ, Panser LA, Chute CG, Osterling JE, Barrett DM, Chen CC, Arrighi HM, Guess HA, Lieber MM. Natural history of prostatism: urinary flow rates in a community-based study. *J Urol* 1993;150:887–892.
91. Jaeschke R, Singer J, Guyatt GH. Measurement of health status: ascertaining the minimal clinically important difference. *Controlled Clin Trials* 1989;10:407–415.
92. Lydick E, Epstein RS. Interpretation of quality of life changes. *Qual Life Res* 1993;2:221–226.
93. Kazis LE, Anderson JJ, Meenan RF. Effect sizes for interpreting changes in health status. *Med Care* 1989;27:S178–S189.
94. Guyatt G, Walter S, Norman G. Measuring change over time: assessing the usefulness of evaluative instruments. *J Chronic Dis* 1987;40:171–178.
95. Fletcher A, Gore S, Jones D, Fitzpatrick R, Spiegelhalter D, Cox D. Quality of life measures in health care. II. Design, analysis, and interpretation. *Br Med J* 1992;305:1145–1148.
96. Burnand B, Kernan WN, Feinstein AR. Indexes and boundaries for "quantitative significance" in statistical decisions. *J Clin Epidemiol* 1990;66:1273–1284.
97. Guess HA, Jacobsen SJ, Girman CJ, Osterling JE, Chute CG, Panser LA, Lieber MM. The role of community-based longitudinal studies in evaluating treatment effects—example: benign prostatic hyperplasia. *Med Care* 1995;33:AS26–AS35.
98. Ware JE, Snow KK, Kosinski M, Gandek B. *SF-36 health survey manual and interpretation guide*. Boston: Health Institute, New England Medical Center, 1993.
99. Fryback DG, Dasbach EJ, Klein R, Klein BED, Dorn N, Peterson K, Martin PA. The Beaver Dam Health Outcomes Study: initial catalog of health-state quality factors. *Med Decis Making* 1993;13: 89–102.
100. Spitz PW, Fries JF. The present and future comprehensive outcome measures for rheumatic diseases. *Clin Rheumatol* 1987;6(suppl 2):105–111.
101. Marder SR, Mintz J, Van Putten R, Lebell M, Wirshing WC, Johnston-Cronk K. Early prediction of relapse in schizophrenia: an application of receiver operating characteristics (ROC) methods. *Psychopharmacol Bull* 1991;27:79–82.

102. Deyo RA, Inui TS. Toward clinical applications of health status measures: sensitivity of scales to clinical important changes. *Health Serv Res* 1984;19:275–289.
103. Brook RH, Kamberg CJ. General health status measures and outcome measurement: a commentary on measuring functional status. *J Chronic Dis* 1987;40(suppl 1):131S–136S.
104. Ware JE Jr. Content-based interpretation of health status scores. *Med Outcomes Trust Bull* 1994;2:3.
105. Gold D. Statistical tests and substantive significance. *Am Sociol* 1969;4:42–46.
106. Juniper EF, Guyatt GH. Development and testing of a new measure of health status for clinical trials in rhinoconjunctivitis. *Clin Exp Allergy* 1991;21:77–83.
107. Jaeschke R, Singer J, Guyatt GH. A comparison of seven-point and visual analogue scales: data from a randomized trial. *Controlled Clin Trials* 1990;11:43–51.
108. Juniper EF, Guyatt GH, Ferrie PJ, Griffith LE. Measuring quality of life in asthma. *Am Rev Respir Dis* 1993;147:832–838.
109. Guyatt GH, Townsend M, Keller JL, Singer J. Should study subjects see their previous responses: data from a randomized control trial. *J Clin Epidemiol* 1989;42:913–920.
110. Spielberger CD. *Manual for the State-Trait Anxiety Inventory (Form Y).* Palo Alto, CA: Consulting Psychologists, 1983.
111. Heitzmann CA, Kaplan RM. Assessment of methods for measuring social support. *Health Psychol* 1988;7(1):75–109.
112. Guyatt G, Walter S, Norman G. Measuring change over time: assessing the usefulness of evaluative instruments. *J Chronic Dis* 1987;40:171–178.
113. Hays R, Hadorn D. Responsiveness to change: an aspect of validity, not a separate dimension. *Qual Life Res* 1992;1:73–75.
114. Jaeschke R, Singer J, Guyatt GH. Measurement of health status: ascertaining the minimal clinically important difference. *Controlled Clin Trials* 1989;10:407–415.
115. Testa MA, Anderson RB, Nackley FN, Hollenberg NK, et al. Quality of life and antihypertensive therapy in men: A comparison of captopril and enalapril. *N Engl J Med* 1993;328(13):907–913.
116. Groves RM, Kahn RL. *Surveys by telephone.* New York: Academic Press, 1979.
117. Cannell C, Groves R, Magilary L, Mathiowetz N, Miller P. An experimental comparison of telephone and personal health interview surveys. In: *Vital and Health Statistics,* Series 2, 106. Washington, DC: Government Printing Office, 1987.
118. Saris W. *Computer-assisted interviewing.* Newbury Park, CA: Sage, 1991.
119. Weeks MF. Computer-assisted survey information collection: a review of CASIC methods and their implications for survey operation. *J Official Stat* 1992;8(4):445–465.
120. O'Reily JM, Hubbard M, Lessler J, Biemer P, Turner C. Audio and video computer assisted self-interviewing: preliminary tests of new technologies for data collection. *J Official Stat* 1994;10(2):197–214.
121. Aaronson NK, Acquadro C, Alonso J, et al. International quality of life assessment (IHRQOLA) project. *Qual Life Res* 1992;1(5):349–351.
122. Hunt SM. Cross cultural comparability of quality of life measures. *Drug Info J* 1993;27:395–400.
123. Guyatt GH. The philosophy of health-related quality of life translation. *Qual Life Res* 1993;2:461–465.
124. Aaronson NK, Ahmedzai S, Bergman B, et al. The European Organization for Research and Treatment of Cancer QLQ-C30: a quality of life instrument for use in international clinical trials in oncology. *J Natl Cancer Inst* 1993;85(5):365–376.
125. Sartorius N. A WHO method for the assessment of health-related quality of life (WHOHRQOL). In: Walker SR, Rosser RM, eds. *Quality of life assessment: key issues in the 1990's.* Dordrecht: Kluwer Academic, 1993:201–207.
126. Chuquet H, Paillard M. *Approche linguistique des problèmes de traduction,* revised ed. Paris: Ophrys, 1989.
127. Hui C, Triandis HC. Measurement in cross-cultural psychology: a review and comparison of strategies. *J Cross-Cultural Psychol* 1985;16(2):131–152.
128. Alonso J, Antó JM, Prieto L. El Perfil de Salud de Nottingham—Spanish version. In: The European group for quality of life and health measurement, eds. *European guide to the Nottingham Health Profile.* Manchester, UK: Galen Research and Consultancy, 1992:225–303.
129. Werner O, Campbell DT. Translating, working through interpreters and the problem of decentering. In: Narrol R, Cohen R, eds. *A handbook of method in cultural anthropology.* New York: American Museum of Natural History, 1970:398–420.
130. Feinstein AR. The theory and evaluation of sensibility. In: Feinstein AR, ed. *Clinimetrics.* New Haven, CT: Yale University Press, 1987:141–166.

131. Bucquet D, Condon S. L'Indicateur de Santé Perceptuelle de Nottingham—French version. In: The European group for quality of life and health measurement, eds. *European guide to the Nottingham Health Profile*. Manchester, UK: Galen Research and Consultancy, 1992:105–182.
132. Ware JE, Gandek B, the IQOLA project group. The SF-36 health survey: development and use in mental health research and the IQOLA project. *Int J Mental Health* 1994;23(2):49–73.
133. Thurstone LL, Chave EJ. *The measurement of attitude*. Chicago: Chicago University Press, 1928.
134. Brislin RW. Questionnaire wording and translation. In: Lonner WJ, Thorndike RM, eds. *Cultural research methods*. New York: John Wiley, 1973:32–58.
135. Guillemin F, Bombardier C, Beaton D. Cross-cultural adaptation of health-related quality of life measures: literature review and proposed guidelines. *J Clin Epidemiol* 1993;46(12):1417–1432.
136. Flaherty JA, et al. Developing instruments for cross-cultural psychiatry research. *J Nerv Ment Dis* 1988;176:257–263.

5 / Special Populations and Specific Diseases

Pediatric populations
Geriatric populations
Specific diseases
HRQOL assessment in cancer and AIDS
Cardiovascular disorders
Neurologic illness
Severe mental illness
Renal replacement therapies
Asthma and allergy
Chronic obstructive pulmonary disease
Diabetes mellitus
Chronic rheumatic disorders

Assessment of HRQOL differs among age groups and specific disease groups. This chapter describes the special problems to be considered when evaluating pediatric and geriatric populations, as well as a variety of medical disorders.

PEDIATRIC POPULATIONS

What Dimensions of Function Should Be Assessed?

The major limitation of most of the available measures of health status, well-being, and utility-based quality of life for the general population of children is that they are all largely based on the conceptualizations of their investigator. Recognizing the lack of explicit social value-based scales, Cadman et al. (1) generated an adult and child social value, preference, and utility-based definition of quality of life for children. Starting with 16 attributes of health and function measured in the Ontario Child Health Study (2), these investigators measured the relative importance of each of these attributes to children's overall quality of life as judged by a general population sample of parents and their children in grades 6 through 8 (ages 11 to 13 years), using previously developed preference and utility measurement scaling methods (3). Six attributes met criteria for inclusion in the multiattribute definition of children's quality of life: sensory and communication ability, happiness, self-care ability, freedom from moderate to severe chronic pain or discomfort, learning and school ability, and physical ability (1). These dimensions were subsequently incorporated by Feeny et al. (4) into a multiattribute health status classification measure called the Health Utilities Index-Mark II (HUI-Mark II).

Despite the face validity of the HUI-Mark II, it is obvious that allowances must be made "for age" in several attributes when classifying a child's multiattribute health status. Furthermore, there may be a lower age limit for the applicability of this system. There may be difficulty translating the system as written (for school-age children and youth) to the cognitive, behavioral and functional characteristics of preschool children.

Applying the HUI-Mark II multiattribute system to a small population of child survivors of brain tumors, Barr et al. found differences among physicians, nurses, and parents in their judgments of children's multiattribute health status (5). The general tendency was for both nurses and parents to report more morbidity than was reported by physicians. Comparisons between nurses and parents showed that parents perceived greater morbidity in their children than did nurses. Similarly, Churchill et al. (6), who examined visual–analog scale value scores for actual health status of 123 adults with end-stage renal disease. In general, patients tended to value their own health condition more highly than did nurses or physicians. In addition to the problem of parent–professional differences in judgments of children's HRQOL, it is important to remember that parental reports represent a proxy response about their children's function. Although parents are clearly the most knowledgeable source of information about their children, some attributes in a multiattribute health status measure are more difficult to observe than others; and although parents know directly whether a child needs glasses to see well or requires help with mobility, their judgments about emotion or pain are based on their interpretation of their child's behavior, and thus provide indirect accounts of HRQOL. Furthermore, because children's behavior may vary according to the setting (e.g., home or school) (7), parents' reports may be valid but incomplete accounts of children's status.

In studies of children as adolescents, measurement of health status by direct personal interviews independently with the children and their parents (8), used two preference measurement instruments (feeling thermometer and chance board) (9). Preferences were elicited for their "own" or "own child's" health state, as well as for four hypothetical health states common to preterm children. Comparison of the multiattribute health status of teens as reported by teen and parent dyads showed remarkable consistency between teens and parents. Differences were observed mainly in cognition, where teens tended to describe themselves at a higher level of function than did their parents; and in sensation, where teens identified more problems compared with parent reports. However, comparison of the HRQOL scores assigned by teens and parents revealed interesting results (10). Both groups of teens tended to rate themselves and the hypothetical health states lower than parental ratings. It appears that teens' HRQOL ratings were more consistent with each other than with their parents, suggesting a "developmental" influence on how adolescents evaluate their health status. These data have implications when parents act as proxy respondents for rating their children's quality of life.

When should children's self-reports be sought, and how should they be interpreted? The answer to these questions is unclear, and the issues require further study. In part, the answer reflects both developmental considerations about the capacity of children to comprehend the cognitive tasks involved in the assessment of HRQOL, and the purpose of the inquiry. Standardized, scientifically credible generic multiattribute health status measures can provide useful descriptive and discriminative information about populations of children with various health and developmental problems. These observations in turn can be used to compute a standardized cardinal utility [ranging from 0.0 (death) to 1.0 (perfect health)] that provides a summary of the "value" of that particular aggregation of functional attributes. Observer perspective remains an important variable regarding exactly what is reported and how it is valued.

Measuring Health Outcomes in Pediatric Populations: Issues in Psychometrics and Application

To meet the growing demand for child health assessment tools, practitioners often construct their own questionnaires or adapt adult forms without basing their instrument development on sound principles of measurement science. Questionnaire development is an iterative process, however, that demands scientific rigor beyond a single application. Evidence suggests that children's understanding of health is determined in part by their cognitive and emotional development, thereby affecting the overall reliability of self-reported health outcomes (11–13). Evaluating the validity of a child instrument is an ongoing process as new information about the meaning and interpretation of the data it yields in previously unexplored conditions, settings, and populations become known. In addition to establishing the validity of individual health concepts, the overall theoretical model or framework of a pediatric health assessment questionnaire should be empirically supported.

Application Issues

To be truly well grounded, a child development perspective needs to be incorporated into the construction, validation, and adoption of pediatric health assessment tools. Developmentalists appreciate that childhood is culturally distinct from adulthood. Adapting standardized adult tools for use with pediatric populations is a strategy that fails to recognize the importance and implication of this fundamental premise. Pediatric health assessment tools must reflect the full extent of the cultural uniqueness of childhood across its different developmental thresholds. Thus, central to issues concerning an instrument's application and use are important questions about its relevance or applicability. To be applicable, an outcomes instrument must apply to children at both the macro level (i.e., in the concepts to be measured) and at the micro level (i.e., in the items used to operationalize a given health concept).

It is commonly accepted that boys and girls develop and mature physically and psychosocially along different time trajectories. Given this fundamental premise, evaluating the applicability of individual items and sets of items to each gender seems warranted. Whenever possible, gender-neutral examples should be used. As children mature from infancy through middle childhood, adolescence, and late adolescence, there are conceptual and methodologic challenges to HRQOL assessment. For example, in addition to attending school and engaging in activities with friends, the "role" of mid-adolescent children (aged 14 to 16 years) often includes having a paying job. Appropriately, queries about limitations in activities need to capture the full multidimensionality of "role" expectations. However, items about work would not apply to children just a few years younger (e.g., early adolescent children—11 to 13 years of age). (Although one could effectively argue that babysitting and having a paper route represent "work" roles.) Thus, applicability at both the item level and concept level needs to be demonstrated empirically across developmentally appropriate age groups. Given the current state of the art for pediatric instruments, routine, empirical testing to determine the applicability of instruments to both boys and girls of different ages and cultural backgrounds is strongly recommended. This strategy will ultimately lead to more objective, robust, and universally applicable methods for assessing health outcomes in children.

Instrument Development

Once it has been determined that concepts and corresponding items are appropriate across gender, age, ethnicity, and socioeconomic status of the target child population, a cadre of related application issues needs to be considered. Given the absence of well-validated measurement strategies and tools for pediatric populations, achieving an appropriate balance between science and application is important. Lessons learned from real-life application experiences could greatly advance our understanding of fundamental measurement issues regarding trade-offs in using proxy-respondents versus children to report on pediatric health status.

Who Is the Most Appropriate Respondent?

Children as young as 5 years of age can provide empirically reliable reports on concrete concepts such as pain and over-the-counter medication use (14,15).

A more conservative estimate of 9 or 10 years of age is recommended for subjective concepts such as behavior (16,17) or self-esteem (18). According to previous literature, children's self-assessments of psychosocial health will differ from those of their parents. However, relatively high agreement can be obtained between maternal reporters and their children for some concepts, although not identical (19). The real question remains, "Is valuable information lost by focusing exclusively on the use of proxy-reporters to obtain standardized information about the health and well-being of the pediatric population?"

Will the Respondent Be Able to Comprehend and/or Read the Instrument?

Although readability generally refers to paper-and-pencil instruments, it is an equally salient issue for interview-administered questionnaires. The overall readability of an instrument is determined by assessing the difficulty of several factors, including the use of active or passive voice, syntactical complexity, the number of words per sentence, the number of syllables per sentence, and paragraph length (20,21). Currently, word processing software programs will calculate the reading and comprehension level of a questionnaire. However, as suggested, providing detailed information about the readability of instruments across groups differing in culture, ethnicity, and sociodemographic status is not currently a standardized practice. Readability of a pediatric questionnaire may also be influenced by factors such as print size, clarity of instructions, and layout. Feasibility tests of self-administered and interview-administered questionnaires for children and caregivers should be performed to identify problems with difficult items, phrases, or general layout of the instrument. Most importantly, there are insufficient data to truly understand the relative impact of score differences for acute and chronic disorders in pediatric populations.

Generic Pediatric Health Assessment Instruments

Useful questionnaires that are comprehensive (i.e., capture both physical and psychosocial health) and generic (applicable to children irrespective of age, gender, ethnicity, or medical condition) and for which published psychometric information is available include the Child Health and Illness Profile (22), Dartmouth COOP Charts for Children and Adolescents (23,24), Functional Status II (25,26), The Health Institute's Child Health Assessment Project (27–29), Health Insurance Experiment/RAND (30,31), National Health Interview Survey (32,33), Ontario Child Health Study (34), and the Quality of Well-Being Scale (35) (adaptable to children). The current length of most questionnaires is prohibitive; short forms are needed to reduce respondent burden and to make patient-based health assessment instruments more attractive to providers, payers, and consumers. Comprehensive instruments that measure health-related outcomes of infants and toddlers are also needed. Relatively few instruments were designed for parallel reporting between caregivers and children themselves, thereby compromising our potential to understand the trade-offs in this area. Finally, most caregiver completed instruments do not provide for a self-report of their own health (in addition to that of the target child), further circumscribing our appreciation of the relationship between self-perceived health and proxy-reported health.

GERIATRIC POPULATIONS

The later years of people's lives bring into sharper focus essential features of quality of life (HRQOL) and their interrelations with quality of care, which are actually important throughout life. Gerontology and geriatrics have much to contribute to understanding the entire life span. Factors that in earlier years of life at first seem to be optional become critical in old age for the maintenance of a person's integrity, independence, and autonomy; they become life-or-death matters, both figuratively and literally. As background for considering elements of quality of life and care, an accurate picture of what old age is really like is needed. This picture may be summarized as follows, with regard to older, and especially very old, people, who:

1. show great individual differences, greater than any other age; and
2. may maintain extraordinarily stable physical, mental, personality, and social characteristics; but
3. are likely to acquire disabilities in any or all of these realms, which may or may not be remediable;
4. may continue to contribute to the life and well-being of themselves, their families, and society;
5. are likely at times to need some or much care by others; and
6. such needs typically occur in clusters of events.

There are immense individual differences among older people, more than at any earlier age, in virtually all types of characteristics—physical, mental, psychological, health, and socioeconomic. Thus, consideration of what quality of life means to an older person and what features of quality of care may contribute to that quality of life, results in highly individualized conclusions. This principle is recommended for all ages, but it may not be so essential in some aspects of earlier life as it is in the lives of older people, as noted below.

Second, many older persons may continue to be remarkably healthy and functional in all or most ways into very late years. Contrary to pervasive earlier views of inevitable decline in physical and mental functions, changes in personality, and losses of social involvement, much recent research has established the stability of all these aspects for many persons into their 80s or beyond—for at least some, even beyond 100 years. Third, chronic disabling conditions become progressively more common as persons age, and impinge on reserves and threaten loss of functional independence (36,37). It is also clear that we can do more to restore or compensate for much of this functional loss, through rehabilitative measures (including physical and occupational therapy).

Disabling conditions, physical or mental, in older persons are clearly common threats to maintenance of the independence that is a key to their quality of life. Not only are affected persons at risk of losing some control over their own lives but they also face the depressing sense of being a "burden" to family members or others, as well as upsetting financial costs. Measures of physical and mental functioning in general, and in certain disease conditions in particular, are addressed. The most common disabling conditions for older, and especially very old (age 85+), persons may be noted: dementia, loss of mobility (due to arthritis, stroke, peripheral vascular disease, and hip fractures—usually associated with osteoporosis, loss of vision, loss of hearing, depression, and urinary incontinence. Assessment measures for all these features exist but could also use further refinement.

The older person's highest priority will usually be to regain as much independence as possible; thus the emphasis in the approach to care should be fundamentally *rehabilitative*. A comprehensive rehabilitation philosophy and approach should infuse virtually all care for disabled older persons, in acute as well as in chronic care settings, using the skills of a variety of professionals. A *comprehensive, multidisciplinary assessment* and development of a comprehensive care plan are essential first steps in achieving high-quality care.

Frail Older Patients: Creating Standards of Care

Personal preferences and individualized care plans are intrinsic to the definition of HRQOL and care in frail older patients. This requirement of individualized clinical therapies and care is then related to the research methodology used in the creation of standards of care and the evaluation of the effectiveness and efficiency of our medical and social interventions. The role of an individual's physical, cognitive, and emotional functions as pivotal outcomes in the evaluation of both quality of life and care is highlighted.

Care and Resource Evaluation Tool

The CARE Tool is organized into 11 standard domains or areas of concern: Diagnoses, Pain, Shortness of Breath, Medications, Nutrition, Urination, Defecation, Cognition, Emotion, Mobility, and Self-Care. These same domains or areas of concern also form the framework of the individualized care plan. These domains we redeveloped from a need to standardize the patient care plans and subsequent interventions in a randomized controlled trial designed to test the effectiveness of interdisciplinary geriatric assessment in acute care (38). In this study, the standardized care plan format was applied to 200 patients over the age of 75 years who were entering the hospital for the treatment of acute medical and surgical diseases. The standardized care plan format made it possible to categorize every diagnosis and patient problem and the subsequent recommendations of the treatment team into one of the 11 domains or areas of concern.

Functional Measures: Issues Relating to Standards of Care

Measures of appropriate care include the benefits, risks, and costs of care. Benefits usually include increased life expectancy, pain relief, reduced anxiety, and improved functional outcomes. Risks include morbidity, decline in functional outcomes, mortality, and psychological distress. As our population under care ages, the gold standard of care—survival at all costs—is slowly being replaced by relevant measures of physical, cognitive, and emotional function.

Basic functional measures, such as the Katz Index of Activities of Daily Living (39), have been used to predict outcomes, measure effectiveness of restorative interventions, and to orient the care of frail, older individuals toward issues related to their independence and dignity. Other indexes of functional disability, such as Barthel's Index (40), and the Older Americans Research and Service instrument (41), may also be helpful for higher levels of function. Spizter's Quality of Life Scale (42) includes both basic and higher levels of function. Evaluation of the impact of therapies, quality of life and care scales must focus on the expected changes in functional activities for adequate sensitivity.

The Katz Index, developed for neurological and structural impairments, has been applied to measure changes in function in a variety of populations of older individuals. The activities of daily living score is an integrated summary of the multiple physical and cognitive etiologic variables, serving as a concise source of information for evaluating progress.

Measuring Health-Related Quality of Life
in Older and Demented Populations

Because older persons on average have more sensory deficits, memory and attention difficulties, and physical limitations, and may be less educated than younger persons, it is more likely that data quality problems will occur in older age groups. However, the important point is that it is not age per se that accounts for data quality problems, but the presence of these other factors. Greater attention to reliability of measurement in older adult studies is needed. Virtually nothing is known about the reliability of different kinds of measures in cognitively impaired persons when data are collected directly from them by self-report. Some studies suggest that proxy ratings of observable behaviors (e.g., wandering, agitation, incontinence, memory loss) can be collected reliably.

One validity issue that may be especially relevant in quality of life studies of older adults is that of socially desirable or "rosy" response bias (43). These are tendencies of respondents to provide responses either to appear favorably (e.g., active, functional, nondepressed) or well-satisfied even if they are not. The latter is more likely to occur when questions are asked in general ways (e.g., overall life satisfaction) as opposed to being more specific (e.g., satisfaction with level of energy). Thus, care should be taken to develop instruments for older adults that minimize the possibility of socially desirable responding. One method is to vary the direction of item wording so that high scores do not always have the same meaning (e.g., use balanced scales).

When quality of life measures are to be used to monitor change over time, it is essential to know whether the measure selected is responsive to clinically important changes (44–46). The responsiveness (or sensitivity) of measures to change may be especially important in studies of older populations because of the tendency to use short-form or single-item measures to reduce respondent burden. These short-form measures may have less precision to detect change.

Each of the different methods of data collection has advantages for different populations. Self-administration is the least expensive and offers respondents the most privacy. However, it can be problematic for those with vision, reading, language, or cognitive problems as evidenced by the increased missing data when self-administration is used (47,48). Thus, use of self-administration may require extensive follow-up of missing and inconsistent responses. Personal and telephone interviews may be a viable alternative. Although they are more time consuming than self-administration, both in terms of staff and respondent burden, the savings of time needed to follow up on missing data and nonreturned self-administered forms may somewhat offset these costs. Although hearing impairments are prevalent in the elderly, only 5% of persons over age 65 reported having difficulty using a telephone (49). However, telephone interviews may be more stressful for those with hearing problems (50) and may take longer and thus be more taxing. When personal interviews are used, the use of response cards with response choices written out have proven helpful (51).

For measures of physical functioning, cognitive functioning, and self-care and self-maintenance activities, performance-based measures allow assessment of those who are moderately or severely cognitively impaired as well as those who have other problems (e.g., vision, hearing) precluding self-report. Advantages of performance-based assessments are that they can be used to test persons with language or communication problems and they are less influenced by culture and education than self-report measures (52). Disadvantages include their cost and time, the need for special equipment, special training of examiners, and the fact that they tend to assess individuals outside their own familiar environment which may result in atypical scores (53,54). One approach that is used in many studies is to use mixed modes of data collection, combining the advantages of different modes to obtain the highest response rate and the best data quality (55). In studies of dementia patients, especially when focusing on more affective dimensions of quality of life, the use of multiple modes of data collection may be useful, in order to converge on a valid score for a demented person (56). For example, Teresi et al. (56) suggest that one could obtain data on emotional well-being from a nurse, from direct observation, and from the demented person directly (in the case of mild or moderate dementia).

Proxies Versus Self-Report by Patients with Dementia: When to Use Proxies

For dementia patients and for older persons with functional disabilities, proxies must often be used to obtain reliable and valid data. However, it is important to determine at what point a proxy report is essential to obtain adequate data quality. Can self-report ever be used for persons with dementia? It is widely assumed that self-reports are not valid in patients with dementia. Although proxy reports may be necessary for those in advanced stages of dementia, it is probable that those in early and possibly middle stages could answer a limited set of questions for themselves. For example, although individuals with severe dementia self-reported few memory problems, those with mild and moderate dementia reported memory complaints corresponding to the severity of the dementia (57). In developing a caregiver-rated quality of life instrument, DeJong et al. (58) interviewed caregivers but reported that the dementia patients themselves often contributed their perceptions during the interviews. Others have also shown that early-stage dementia patients can participate in support groups, report feelings, and express concerns regarding their disease (59–61). Additionally, an early-stage dementia patient has written of her experiences with the disease (62). Several factors affect the ability of proxies to provide accurate reports, including the relationship of the proxy to the person being evaluated, the nature of the questions (objective versus subjective), the affective status of the proxy, and the cognitive and affective status of the person being evaluated (63,64). Despite this, the nature of the bias when using proxies appears to be reasonably consistent across studies. In one study, proxies overestimated patient disability in the area of instrumental activities relative to patients but were somewhat similar to the patients in ratings of self-care activities (69). Agreement was greater when proxies lived with the patient.

Kiyak et al. (63) found that the discrepancies between self-report and reports by a family member were large for those with Alzheimer's disease but not different for a normal comparison group on measures of activities of daily living and instrumental activities of daily living. Patients with Alzheimer's disease reported consistently higher scores (more functional) on all measures than did their family member. The investigators interpreted this as either a lack of insight among demented patients, or that caregivers are overestimating limitations due to the burden they themselves are experiencing. This is an important distinction to evaluate. However, the Alzheimer's patients did report declines in functioning over time, suggesting that they were aware of some decline. Winogrond and Fisk (65) note that families may exaggerate a patient's dysfunction because they are comparing the person to his/her previously high level of functioning.

Choosing Specific Instruments and Approaches

Several key multidimensional instruments are available that are appropriate for use in older populations, each providing a set of multi-item measures of a variety of quality of life domains. Multidimensional measures (described elsewhere) that would be useful in older adult populations include the MOS Functioning and Well-Being Profile (66), the Functional Status Questionnaire (67), the Duke UNC Health Profile (68), the Older Americans Resources and Services (OARS) Multidimensional Functional Assessment Questionnaire (MFAQ) (69), the Multilevel Assessment Instrument (70), and the Rand Health Insurance Experiment measures (71). Multidimensional overall quality of life indexes designed for older adults are also available such as the Life Satisfaction Index (72) and the Philadelphia Geriatric Center Morale Scale (73,74).

Because many depressive symptoms scales include a number of somatic items (appetite loss, sleep problems), there is concern that use of these scales to measure depressive symptoms in older adults (who have more of these somatic symptoms) may be less valid (75). Thus, the use of measures that do not contain the somatic symptoms may be more appropriate for older adults. For example, the Geriatric Depression Scale (GDS) (76) was developed to be applicable to those with physical health problems by not including somatic items, and was designed to provide a simple yes/no format to be easy for older persons to complete.

When selecting standard instruments that contain a profile of health-related quality of life measures such as the Sickness Impact Profile, the SF-36, or the Functional Status Index that have been developed for chronically ill persons in general, it is possible to select out those subscales that are not appropriate for certain older populations. For example, Krenz et al. (77) omitted the work subscale from the SIP when administering the SIP to patients referred for possible dementia. However, there are probably only a few settings in which this decision might be appropriate since many older adults continue to work well into their seventh decade.

Respondent burden may be a considerable problem for the oldest-old and those with multiple health problems. Because many older adults are not accustomed to elaborate paper and pencil tests, a long self-administered survey may seem tedious. If questionnaires must be long, respondents should be encouraged to complete them a little at a time (e.g., early and late in the day). Similarly, telephone interviews can be conducted in more than one phase (43), although this is likely to result in increased rates of noncompletion of the second part (55). No more than 1 to 2 weeks should elapse between the two evaluations. Use of pretesting in the population being studied can help determine the acceptable burden. Older individuals seem to be less tolerant of being asked a series of similar items, a belief confirmed by Wallace et al. (78), who report that redundant questions are considered demeaning and irritating by older adults. They suggest that efforts be made to develop abbreviated forms of some of the more commonly used scales. They further note that high internal consistency of multi-item scales is to an extent due to consistency bias—a tendency to respond to similar items in consistent ways, regardless of actual content, suggesting that many scales could be shortened without compromising their validity.

The formatting of the questions and the questionnaires both need to take into account the special needs of less advantaged segments of the older adult population. Guidelines for formatting are available (79,80). Questionnaires need to be readable by those who have vision problems. Allowing sufficient space on the page helps prevent confusion due to crowding of questions, reducing the chance that questions will be missed. Selection of background colors that are light so that the highest possible contrast is obtained facilitates this, as does use of a large print size (a font size of 14 points is preferred by many older adults). For interviews and surveys of older adults who may have numerous health problems to report, it is helpful to organize the questions to enable respondents to respond positively at the end (79).

Persons with Dementia

Although it is not clear at what stage a patient with dementia can answer for themselves regarding their quality of life, that is a possibility for at least some patients. Because patients with dementia have a shortened attention span, and because they may tire easily and be susceptible to anxiety during assessments (65), direct assessments may need to be truncated (e.g., 10 to 15 minutes at most). Face-to-face interviews should be used exclusively, to facilitate their motivation to complete the interview. If self-administration is used, patients may forget the instructions or get stuck and may need to be remotivated to complete the survey. The use of questions that are short and clear and that use very simple response scales may be necessary, such as yes/no scales. If more complex scales are needed, response trees can be used in which further discrimination is made after each yes/no response. For example, if the person answers "yes" to feeling happy, one can then ask if they feel a little bit happy or very happy. The use of visual cues might facilitate their response, although this remains to be tested. That is, if the person finds it difficult to answer questions, they might be able to point to the appropriate response on a chart. It is possible that the COOP charts with their added pictures might be helpful (81,82). Similarly, the faces scale published by Andrews and Withey (83) to assess overall life satisfaction includes a series of simple faces with different expressions.

The use of recognition rather than recall memory may facilitate assessment. That is, providing patients with a few response choices from which to choose rather than asking them to recall an answer should yield better quality data. Questions that contain a time frame may need to be modified to a very short time frame. Because patients lose their memory for the recent past, questions framed in the present or distant past may be more accurately answered.

SPECIFIC DISEASES

The goal of therapy for a chronic illness is generally not to cure the disease, but rather to alleviate its symptoms, improve the patient's functional capabilities, and retard the progression of the underlying disease. Thus, an evaluative component that addresses the way in which a patient's life is affected by the illness and its care, in addition to the traditional measures of morbidity and mortality is important. In the following sections, the issues important for patients with specific diseases are outlined with suggestions for types of assessments. The rationale for HRQOL studies varies with different subsets of patients with chronic disease. For example, in patients with advanced congestive cardiac failure, morbidity and mortality are insensitive measures for comparing outcomes because this is a highly symptomatic disorder with a generally poor prognosis. The goals of therapy, the relief of symptoms with a resultant comfort of the patient for the remaining duration of life, and the maintenance of a limited functional capacity are more likely to be influenced by treatment and can be ascertained by the assessment of HRQOL attributes. Determine of the appropriate role for interventions in serious, sometimes life-threatening medical conditions, it is necessary to compare the patient's quality of life under standard care and the potential for urgent intermittent hospitalizations for life-threatening problems with the possibly reduced mortality, but likely toxicity associated with an otherwise effective control of the disorder. Different considerations apply when preventive therapies are used for asymptomatic individuals. However, because most therapies may produce symptoms in an otherwise symptomless individual, it is important to address those features that may adversely alter the individual's functional status and sense of well-being.

Different dimensions of HRQOL might be important to people at different stages of an illness, making broad generalizations based on HRQOL data difficult. The difficulty in assessing particular health conditions further reflects the complex relationships among the HRQOL dimensions. For example, increasing severity of physical symptoms and resultant decrease in physical capacities may cause depression or other emotional dysfunction. On the other hand, depression or emotional dysfunction may lead to limitations of physical function. Although specific aspects related to the illness are addressed in greater detail when condition-specific measures are used, the total scope of HRQOL attributes must be assessed as well. These include general well-being; physical, cognitive, emotional functioning; social participation; and the like. This is why many investigators also use generic HRQOL instruments or subscales in the same study to supplement the information obtained from a condition-specific measure.

HRQOL ASSESSMENT IN CANCER AND AIDS

The Functional Assessment of Cancer Therapy (FACT) and Functional Assessment of HIV

The Functional Assessment of Cancer Therapy (FACT) and the Functional Assessment of HIV Infection (FAHI) measurement systems are collections of self-report scales of quality of life for people with cancer and HIV infection. The general version of the instrument (FACT-G) has been validated in English (84–88) and is being used extensively in North America. Because item wording avoids specific terms such as *cancer* and *HIV infection,* they have also been used for people with other chronic medical conditions, such as kidney failure, liver disease, benign urinary incontinence, and multiple sclerosis. Specific modifications in the FACT are under way for these and other conditions. All of the subscales of the FACT measurement system were first developed in the English language, and have subsequently been translated into Spanish, primarily for use among Spanish-speaking people in the United States health care system. More recently, the FACT has been translated into six other languages in preparation for its use in European clinical trials. Nearly all patients with a sixth grade reading level can easily complete the FACT without assistance. There are currently 14 scales available in English, 10 of which are disease-specific extensions of the 29-item general version (FACT-G) and include items relevant to a particular form of cancer. Nine of the 14 scales have been translated into Spanish. (Dutch, French, German, Italian, Norwegian, and Swedish versions are available.) Currently available versions of the FACT are listed below [an asterisk (*) indicates versions that are available in *English only*]:

FACT-G	A general version of the scale, which can be used with patients of any tumor type and constitutes the core of the following disease, treatment, or symptom-specific subscales
*FAACT	For patients with anorexia/cachexia related to cancer or HIV infection
FACT-A/F	For patients with cancer-related anemia or fatigue
FACT-B	For patients with breast cancer
*FACT-Bl	For patients with bladder cancer
FACT-BMT	For patients undergoing bone marrow transplant
*FACT-Br	For patients with primary brain tumors
FACT-C	For patients with colorectal cancer
*FACT-Cx	For patients with cervix cancer
FACT-H&N	For patients with head and neck cancer
FACT-L	For patients with lung cancer
FACT-O	For patients with ovarian cancer
FACT-P	For patients with prostate cancer
FAHI	For patients with HIV infection

The General Version (FACT-G)

There are 29 Likert-type items that make up five general subscales common across all 14 scales. The number of scored items specific to the disease, treatment, or symptom making up the sixth subscale varies from 9 to 21. For every instrument, the five general (FACT-G) subscales are (a) Physical Well-Being, (b) Social/Family Well-Being, (c) Relationship with Doctor, (d) Emotional Well-Being, and (e) Functional Well-Being. A total score can also be obtained by summing each of the subscales. Although the FACT-G (version 3) is composed of 29 items, only 28 are scored in version 3.

The FACT scales are designed for patient self-administration, but can also be administered in an interview. For self-administration, patients should be instructed to read the brief directions at the top of the page. After the patient's correct understanding has been confirmed, he/she should be encouraged to complete every item in order without skipping any, except where directed (e.g., item 15). For interview administration, it is helpful to have the patient hold a card on which the response options have been printed.

The FACT-G is the core of the FAHI scale. The HIV-specific items were developed using the same methodology as the FACT site-specific items, including interviews with five HIV specialists and 15 patients. The FAHI was rated as very relevant and easy to complete by these respondents. It has been selected by the ECOG as its measure to evaluate quality of life in all HIV-related malignancy trials.

The Functional Living Index–Cancer

The Functional Living Index–Cancer (FLIC) (89) was developed to cover all areas of life that might be affected by the symptoms and treatment of cancer. There were many questionnaires that covered separate aspects of physical, emotional, and social well-being. However, combining several questionnaires into one would have resulted in a battery that would have been burdensome to patients, especially to those who were very debilitated. The characteristic that differentiates this instrument from other available instruments is the emphasis on the extent to which patients' normal function is affected by cancer and its treatment. Questions regarding symptoms such as pain and nausea concern not only the extent of such symptoms but also the extent to which these symptoms interfere with normal life. This is in contrast to many instruments that focus on the extent of symptoms without asking if they are disturbing.

Ideally, the index should always be completed by the patient, but in the advanced disease setting patients may become too debilitated to complete the questionnaire as they approach death. Consequently, a caregiver version of the index was developed. Caregivers are instructed to complete the questionnaire to reflect how they perceive the patient to be feeling. The questions were reworded so that the word *you* was replaced by the patient.

Quality of life as measured by the CARES, EORTC-QLQ-C30, FACT, or FLIC is slightly different for each instrument. The results obtained from different instruments when used to determine group differences, changes over time, and prognosis will be slightly different. This will depend on what groups of patients are being assessed and the relative representation of the domains of interest. The FLIC provides a useful definition of quality of life in that it has shown the anticipated effects of time and treatment.

CARDIOVASCULAR DISORDERS

Condition-specific measures for cardiovascular disorders, such as the New York Heart Association functional classification (90) and the Specific Activity Scale (91) can be used to assess limitations of a person's ability to perform physical activity. The Rose chest pain questionnaire (92) and the Canadian Cardiovascular Society measure of severity (93) assess chest pain. Different dimensions of HRQOL may be of interest to the coronary patient with stable angina pectoris as compared with one who has acute myocardial infarction or who is undergoing coronary angioplasty or coronary bypass surgery.

Coronary Atherosclerotic Heart Disease— Angina Pectoris and Myocardial Infarction

The major concerns for patients with stable angina pectoris relate to physical functioning, symptoms, emotional well-being, personal productivity/occupation, social roles and activities, with attention to the requirements for follow-up medical care. The Rose Questionnaire (92) and the Canadian Cardiovascular Society classification (93) are frequently used instruments. The impact on function can be measured by the New York Heart Association classification. Generic HRQOL instruments are also used to assess the range of life domains affected by angina pectoris. The Sickness Impact Profile and the Nottingham Health Profile have been able to detect treatment effects in patients with angina (94), and the Psychological General Well-Being Index has been used to measure general positive and negative affective states (95).

The setting of acute myocardial infarction poses far different HRQOL issues; these differ in the intensive care setting and during the remainder of the hospital stay, as well as postdischarge from the hospital. The primary HRQOL areas include effects on mobility, symptoms, emotional well-being, cognitive and intellectual function, and interactions with family and friends. After discharge from the hospital, the additional concerns of performance of usual activities and social roles, personal productivity/work, sleep dysfunction and sexual functioning become important, as well as medication effects. The impact of the illness on HRQOL may vary by the age and gender of the patient (96).

Hypertension

The primary rationale for monitoring quality of life during antihypertensive therapy is to ensure that potential side effects do not interfere with the quality of life, as this leads to poor compliance. Even though hypertension is usually considered an asymptomatic condition, high blood pressure in itself may be associated with a number of symptoms, such as headache on waking, blurred vision, nocturia and unsteadiness, dizziness, sexual problems, and cognitive impairment. A further confounding factor in relation to symptom reporting and high blood pressure is "the labeling effect," i.e., being given a diagnosis of hypertension may actually give rise to symptoms and decrease the general well-being because the patient becomes more involved with personal health, including an increased awareness of bodily symptoms.

Several specific measures have been developed for use in antihypertensive drug trials. One of the earliest was the Symptom Complaint Rate, which has 30 symptoms and side effects (97), later modified to contain two additional symptoms, and with five graded response options instead of the yes/no alternatives of the original version (98). The Minor Symptom Evaluation (MSE) Profile has 24 items and uses bipolar analogue scales to assess primarily CNS-related side-effect symptoms (99). Some of the symptoms combine into three dimensions, i.e., vitality, sleep, and contentment. The Subjective Symptom Assessment (SSA) Profile includes 42 of the most frequently reported side-effect symptoms in conjunction with antihypertensive drug therapy, and has six dimensions depicting cardiac symptoms, dizziness, gastrointestinal symptoms, peripheral/circulatory symptoms, sex life, and emotional distress (100). The response format is based on visual–analog scales. Visual–analog scales also form the basis of the Aspect scale, which apart from 34 side-effect symptoms covers mood in terms of hedonic tone, relaxation and activity (101). Another scale assesses sleep disturbances, sexual dysfunction, and depression (102).

Comparatively few studies have employed generic health profiles to address quality of life in antihypertensive drug trials, most likely because they carry redundant questions and are likely to be subjected to typical floor effects, and are less responsive to the small changes involved in antihypertensive drug trials (103). For the assessment of positive well-being as well as of negative affects, mood scales are available. The Psychological General Well-Being (PGWB) index assesses anxiety, depression, vitality, self-control, health and well-being. The Profile of Mood States addresses aspects of mood using 65 positive and negative adjectives on a five-point scale, combined into dimensions such as anxiety, depression, anger, confusion, vitality, and fatigue (104). Psychiatric rating scales such as the General Health Questionnaire (105) or the Symptom Rating Test (106), which tap psychiatric morbidity in terms of anxiety, depression, somatic complaints, cognitive problems, and hostility, focus exclusively on negative symptoms and distress. The Health Status Index (HSI) is a measure of activity and perceived well-being derived from responses to questions on work, absence due to sickness, and interference with life style caused by treatment (107).

NEUROLOGIC ILLNESS

Quality of life studies have particular relevance in neurology. The brain, spinal cord, and peripheral nerves control neurologic function for the entire body, and damage to these organs can have highly specific or widespread consequences. Neurologic measures must accommodate implicitly the gamut of possible anatomic involvements, sensory and motor dysfunction, and cognitive impairment of both mild and severe intensity. For example, some neurologic conditions will produce highly focal abnormalities, such as a weak hand, involuntary eye closure, or isolated facial pain. Other degenerative conditions affect function throughout the body and may involve all neurologic spheres. By contrast, diffuse encephalopathies may cause few motor or sensory problems but cause cognitive and emotional abnormalities that devastate quality of life. Pharmacologic treatment of some disorders may succeed in alleviating signs and symptoms of neurologic illness, but at the cost of side effects that adversely affect quality of life. In short, the diverse manifestations of neurologic disorders and the agents used to treat these disorders underscore the importance of quality of life to any consideration of neurologic disorders or their treatment The heterogeneous manifestations of neurologic illnesses have made it difficult to apply a simple or single set of quality of life measures to all disorders. Age and level of cognitive dysfunction, in particular, are critical considerations in the selection, adaptation, or construction of various scales. However, in some domains of quality of life, such as physical function, the behaviors of interest are relatively finite, hence, the feasibility of the use of more general and psychometrically established scales.

Quality of Life Measures: Physical Function

The impact of illness on the ability to perform activities of daily living has long been recognized as an important and practical matter in the management of neurologic patients. Assessment of Parkinson's disease can be done with the Unified Parkinson's Disease Rating Scale (108), the Hoehn and Yahr stage (109), and the Schwab and England Scale (110). The Unified Parkinson's Disease Rating Scale includes objective measurements of Parkinsonian motor problems and subjective complaints by the patient and activities of daily living. The Hoehn and Yahr rating provides a global measure of parkinsonism and the Schwab and England Scale provides a global measure of functional independence. The Schwab and England Scale (110) and the Shoulson-Fahn Scale (111), used in Huntington's disease, are unidimensional scales that utilize an examiner's evaluation of multiple sources of physical and nonphysical disability to arrive at a single measure of functional capacity. The Northwestern University Disability Scale measures activities of daily living function in Parkinson's disease (112), rating six functional domains—walking, dressing, feeding, hygiene, speech, and eating. The most widely used other-report measures of activities of daily living in neurology are those developed by Lawton and Brody (113), Katz et al. (114), and Mahoney and Barthel (115). Lawton and Brody's Physical Self-Maintenance Scale, for example, identifies six areas of rudimentary physical activity: eating, dressing, bathing, toileting, walking, and hygiene. Each function is scored on a five-point behaviorally anchored interval scale. The scale was originally developed to evaluate disability among the elderly, hence is particularly appropriate for such varied neurologic disorders as cerebrovascular accident, Alzheimer's disease, and Parkinson's disease. The Physical Self-Maintenance Scale is often used in conjunction with the Instrumental Activities of Daily Living Scale devised by Lawton and Brody (113), which assesses more cognitively mediated activities critical to independent living. Items address activities such as shopping, use of transportation and telephone, and handling finances. Used in conjunction, the Physical Self-Maintenance Scale and Instrumental Activities of Daily Living Scale are unique and provide comprehensive psychometrically sound measurements of two specific subdomains of activities of daily living. The scale developed by Katz et al. (114) is an ordinal measure of six activities of daily living functions that are presumed lost and regained sequentially. The Barthel Index (115) is the most widely used activities of daily living scale. The 11 items are rationally weighted such that mobility and continence contribute disproportionately to the total score. Scales developed by Nagi (116) and by Rosow and Breslau (117) have proved helpful in community studies. A useful supplement to other report measures of the physical capacity to carry out daily living activities is provided by direct measurement of physical functioning. Such an approach is especially helpful when a reliable informant is unavailable. A carefully specified and well-validated set of direct physical performance measures was developed by Guralnik and colleagues for use with the elderly (118,119). These measures focus heavily on lower extremity function. A range of approaches to measuring manual dexterity, speed, and strength are described by Lezak (120).

Psychological Function

The most disabling aspect of neurologic illness is cognitive dysfunction, often resulting in various forms of amnesia, aphasia, and cognitive disorganization. Diffuse encephalopathies seen with degenerative disorders such as Alzheimer's disease or Huntington's disease may produce global cognitive deterioration, generally referred to as dementia. Specific measures are detailed by Lezak (120), as well as the Folstein Mini Mental State exam (121). Rating scales are an alternative or supplement to direct measurement of cognitive functioning, using the patient, a significant other, a trained clinician, or some combination of these raters (122). For example, the Brief Cognitive Rating Scale (123) and the Global Deterioration Scale (124) require the clinician to rate either a single or multiple dimensions of cognition. The Katz Adjustment Scale (125) and the Sickness Impact Profile (126) allow for rating by either the patient or significant other. In assessing cognitive decline, ratings by a significant other or clinician, or both, are preferable to the patient's rating. Affective changes also are part of a psychological investigation, including a range of disordered emotional behavior, including disinhibition, depression or hypomanic episodes, or hallucinations, may result and affect quality of life. Depressive reactions frequently develop as a secondary result of new disability or chronic illness.

Economic Function

The financial impact of neurological disease can be measured with objective measures including days of work missed, hospital days or outpatient visits to health care professionals, and medication. These direct costs can be supplemented by indirect costs such as residential alterations necessitated by the disease and days of work missed by family members providing care to the patient. The Multidimensional Functional Assessment Questionnaire (127) rates medical costs and the subjective impact on finances of the illness. The Work and Home Management scales of the Sickness Impact Profile (126) measure the extent to which the patient is able to perform occupational and household duties.

Social Function

The usual approach to assessing social networks begins with the patient or an informant identifying a set of key individuals in the patient's life. Each is rated along several dimensions. Thus, in the Philadelphia Geriatric Scale (128), the extent to which each individual provides emotional support, encouragement, companionship, and advice is rated. In other inventories, the focus is on more objective variables, such as the proximity of these key individuals and their frequency of contact with the patient. In either case, the intent is to determine whether the patient's social world has contracted as a result of illness. On the Social Interaction subscale of the Sickness Impact Profile, the same construct is assessed less tediously through a series of questions requiring only a yes/no response.

Epilepsy

Epilepsy is "both a medical diagnosis and a social label" with stigma and underlying worry about recurrence even in people with few or no recent seizures. Requirements for special driver's license approval and reporting of epilepsy on job and insurance applications may encumber patients forever, making epilepsy different from almost all other medical disorders because of these legal restrictions and requirements. One of the earliest approaches to HRQOL was the Washington Psycho-Social Inventory (WPSI), a self-report profile measure largely assessing psychological and social constructs (129). In the 1990s, several groups developed assessments that covered all the relevant aspects of HRQOL. The initial version of the Liverpool Battery (130) included a series of five standard questionnaires [Nottingham Health Profile (131), Scale of Positive Affect (132), Self-esteem Scale (133), Mastery Scale (134), Stigma Scale (135)] and a seizure severity scale with perception/control and ictal/postictal components (136). Kendrick and Trimble hypothesized that quality of life could be improved either by increasing actual abilities or decreasing expectations, and that people judge their current quality of life in relation to past experiences and other people. The Quality of Life Assessment Schedule (QOLAS) (137), based on a repertory grid technique, was used in extensive interviews. This labor-intensive interview method for assessment of quality of life is not feasible for large populations, but works well for hospital settings where extended time periods for interviews are available, such as during evaluation for epilepsy surgery.

The Epilepsy Surgery Inventory (ESI-55) was developed to assess the health-related quality of life outcomes of patients who undergo surgical treatment of intractable epilepsy (138). Development of this measure used the method of combining a generic core measure, the RAND 36-Item Health Survey 1.0 (SF-36) (139,140), with a 19-item supplement. Supplemental items tapped into areas of particular importance to individuals who undergo epilepsy surgery, such as cognitive function, role limitations due to memory problems, and epilepsy-specific health perceptions. The method used to develop the ESI-55 was replicated in the development of an expanded quality of life measure for the large proportion of patients with epilepsy whose seizures are controlled or for those who have low-to-moderate seizure frequency (not severe epilepsy that might be treated with surgery). The Quality of Life in Epilepsy (QOLIE-89) Inventory, contains 86 items grouped into 17 multi-item scales and three single items (141), with four dimensions: epilepsy-targeted, cognitive, mental health, and physical health. Two shorter instruments also have been developed, containing subsets of items in the QOLIE-89. The QOLIE-31 (142) has 31 items grouped into seven multi-item scales and the QOLIE-10 (143) contains ten single items. Each instrument has a summary score. The QOLIE-31 has been translated into a number of languages using a rigorous forward-backward-forward translation process.

Adolescents and children require specialized approaches. One approach to assessment of children is to interview the parent/caregiver, albeit recognizing that the responses might not reflect what is important to the child. Another issue of concern in families is the impact of a sibling's epilepsy on the other children. Austin et al. (144) have described correlates of behavior problems in children. Measures included the Child Behavior Checklist (145), the Family Inventory of Life Events (146), and the Family Inventory of Resources for Management

(146), in addition to demographic and seizure variables. A version of the QOLIE for adolescents (aged 11–17 years) is in development.

SEVERE MENTAL ILLNESS

The pervasive effects that severe, chronic psychiatric disorders can have on individuals' lives, limiting their range of life experiences, renders general population measures of quality of life insensitive to the issues faced by people with schizophrenia, chronic depression, and severe personality disorders. Conversely, for persons with nondisabling mental health problems, such as short-term depression and anxiety reactions, instruments available to assess quality of life in the general population are probably adequate. A major problem with using normative quality of life measures in this population is that floor effects are frequently encountered in social and economic functioning. Such floor effects are not typically a problem with the severely mentally ill in the quality of life areas of physical functioning and psychological functioning (life satisfaction). Significant numbers of these patients have problems with task perseverance and comprehension. Therefore, pencil-and-paper questionnaires are generally not advised. All of the instruments use face-to-face interviews. Psychopathology affects patients' ratings of their quality of life. Therefore, quality of life assessments of these patients should be accompanied by a concomitant assessment of psychopathologic symptoms to reduce the confounding effects of psychiatric syndromes on quality of life assessments. The most important point about interpretation is the need to distinguish psychological quality of life, e.g., life satisfaction or morale, from clinical symptomatology, particularly depression. Measures of psychological quality of life functioning are clearly affected by clinical symptomatology (147). However, at least conceptually, life satisfaction and its quality of life equivalents are to be distinguished from clinical syndromes. This distinction has particular relevance with regard to implications for interventions. That is, one might attempt to effect various changes in a patient's environment to improve housing, financial, or work dissatisfaction, whereas one might prescribe a clinical intervention, such as an antidepressant, to alleviate symptoms of depression.

The Satisfaction with Life Domains Scale (148) has been used for chronically mentally ill patients. It is a self-report scale of 15 items administered by interview (10 minutes). It covers psychological functioning, satisfaction with housing, neighborhood, food to eat, clothing, health, people lived with, friends, family, relations with other people, work/day programming, spare time, fun, services and facilities in area, economic situation, place lived in now compared to state hospital, and has a total life satisfaction score.

The Oregon Quality of Life Questionnaire (149,150) has been used to assess the chronically mentally ill, drug abusers, alcoholics, and general psychiatric patients. The questionnaire includes 263 items in a self-report version (45 minutes), or 146 items in a semistructured interview version. The topics covered include: physical functioning as meaningful use of leisure time, economic functioning as work at home, employability, work on the job, school, social functioning as Independence, friend role, close friend role, spouse role, parent role, social support, psychological functioning as psychological distress, well-being, tolerance of stress, and other negative consequences (e.g., alcohol, drugs).

The Standardized Social Schedule (151) is designed to assess the nature and extent of social maladjustment and dysfunction in chronic neurotic patients attending their family doctors. It is a semistructured interview with patient (and key informant, if available) by a trained interviewer, with ratings by interviewer and subject. There are from 17 to 48 items, depending on version. The scales include material conditions, social management, satisfaction and housing, occupation/social role, economical, leisure/social activities, family and domestic relations, marital; extent of leisure activities; housing conditions, occupational stability, family income; household care; housekeeping, quality of relations with workmates, neighbors and family; marital relationship quality; extent of social activities; satisfaction with housing, work, income, leisure, social relationships, family relationships, parental role, marriage; residential stability; opportunities for leisure and social activities, interaction with neighbors, interactions with relatives.

The Quality of Life Scale developed by Heinrichs et al. (152) is widely used to assess deficits in patients with schizophrenia. It is a semistructured interview by a trained clinician, covering 21 items (45 minutes) as intrapsychic foundations, interpersonal relations, and instrumental role function. The areas are: commonplace activities, occupational role, work functioning, work level, possession of commonplace objects; interpersonal relations (household, friends, acquaintances, social activity, social network, social initiative, social withdrawal, sociosexual functioning); sense of purpose, motivation, curiosity, anhedonia, aimless inactivity, empathy, emotional interaction, and work satisfaction.

The Quality of Life Interview developed by Lehman et al. (153–155) is widely used to assess HRQOL of persons with severe mental illness living in board-and-care homes, hospital, and other supervised settings. It is a structured interview by trained lay interviewers, containing 143 items (45 minutes). The areas covered are: physical functioning (number of leisure activities); economic functioning (current employment status, total monthly financial support, monthly spending money); social functioning (frequency of family contacts, frequency of social contacts, frequency of religious activities, legal problems and victimization); psychological functioning (general perceived health status), general life satisfaction (satisfaction with living situation, family relations, social relation), leisure, work, religious activities, finances, safety, and health; and medical and psychiatric care during the past year.

The Quality of Life Self-Assessment Inventory (156) provides information about which aspects of quality of life are particularly important to patients and natural raters to assist in therapeutic planning. It is a self-report inventory (100 items, 10 minutes) completed by patient, followed by a semistructured interview with a clinician (45 minutes) to confirm patient's ratings of satisfaction and dissatisfaction and to discuss implications for treatment planning. Ratings are "satisfactory" or "unsatisfactory." The topics are: physical health, finances , household and self-care, contacts, dependence, work, and leisure, knowledge and education, inner experiences, mental health, housing, housing environment, community services, and religion.

The Community Adjustment Form (157) assesses life satisfaction and other quality of life outcomes in a randomized study of an experimental system of community-based care for the severely mentally ill versus standard care. It is a semistructured self-report interview with 140 items (45 minutes). The areas are: Leisure activity scale (same as Lehman Quality of Life Interview); Quality of living situation; employment history and status; income sources and amounts; free lodging and/or meals; Contact with friends, family contact, legal problems; a 21-item life satisfaction scale, self-esteem scale; and medical care, and agency utilization.

The Lancaster Quality of Life Profile (158) assesses the impact of community care programs serving persons with severe mental illnesses. It is a structured interview by trained lay interviewer, with 100 items (1 hour). Topics include: health, finances, work/education, leisure/participation, social relations, family relations; satisfaction with work/education, leisure/participation, religion, finances, living situation, legal and safety, family relations, social relations, and health; as well as living situation, legal and safety, religion.

RENAL REPLACEMENT THERAPIES

Little is known about comparative HRQOL in the two major methods of dialysis: center hemodialysis and continuous ambulatory peritoneal dialysis. Comorbidity and biochemistry have a great influence on HRQOL in terms of physical and psychosocial well-being. However, other factors are as important in emotional well-being, and to a lesser extent physical well-being. Therefore, we should not expect major improvement in HRQOL by improving only the medical aspects of renal replacement therapy. Because of the high costs, HRQOL measures need to reflect utility and quality-adjusted life-years of the various renal replacement therapies.

Many generic measures have been used, including the Karnofsky performance scale (159) of physical activity. Although some regard the scale as a drawback when administered to the medical staff, others regard it as an "objective" measure of physical condition. Activities in daily living is another measure regarded as an "objective" measure. However, different researchers have used different activities of daily living scales, such as the scale developed by Spitzer et al. (160), the Barthel Index (161), the Katz Index (162). Deniston et al. (163) developed an Activities of Daily Living (ADL) Index for this population. The Medical Outcomes Study 36-Item Short Form Health Survey (SF-36) has been used in dialysis patients (164). One advantage of this measure is that there are norms for the American healthy population as well as the American general population. The questionnaire covers both physical and mental dimensions. The Sickness Impact Profile has been used quite often as either the whole questionnaire or as only the physical subscale. It has the advantage of having been used in many diseases, as well as in the general population.

A number of specific measures have been developed for renal replacement patients. The most commonly used general measure is that of Campbell et al. (165) for evaluation of emotional well-being, well-being (nine items), general affect (eight items), and overall life satisfaction. Using these measures, great differences were found in the emotional well-being of end-stage renal disease patients by modality of renal replacement therapy with center hemodialysis doing worst and transplanted patients doing best. Transplanted patients had higher emotional well-being than the well American population. Parfrey (166) developed and validated a health questionnaire specific for end-stage renal disease which examines physical as well as psychosocial well-being. The Kidney Disease Questionnaire (KDQ) (167) has not been widely used. Some measures were developed because of cultural reasons, i.e., feeling that translation of measures into another language and into another culture could be inappropriate (168). Unfortunately, many questionnaires are not well developed and tested measures but a collection of items that seem to have face validity (169).

ASTHMA AND ALLERGY

HRQOL research in asthma and rhinoconjunctivitis has highlighted the areas of impairment that patients experience. Adults with asthma are not only troubled by the symptoms themselves, such as shortness of breath, wheeze, and cough, they also are troubled by limitation of daily activities (occupational, social, and physical), sleep impairment, emotional problems such as anxiety and frustration, and problems associated with exposure to atmospheric stimuli such as cigarette smoke (170–173). The burden of illness for children with asthma is similar. However, children also experience important HRQOL impairments because of their inability to integrate fully with their peers (174–177). The impact of rhinoconjunctivitis (hayfever) is frequently underestimated by clinicians (178). However, a survey using a generic HRQOL instrument, the SF-36, showed that the actual degree of HRQOL impairment in these patients can be quite severe (179). Not only are the patients troubled by their nasal and eye symptoms, they are also bothered by fatigue, headaches, lack of sleep, poor concentration, impairment and limitation in their normal daily activities and emotional problems such as frustration and embarrassment (180).

Asthma Quality of Life Questionnaire (Jumiper) (170,181) is a 32-item questionnaire for adults with asthma. The items, identified by asthma patients as being important, are in four domains: symptoms, emotions, exposure to environmental stimuli, and activity limitation. Patients respond to each item on a seven-point scale. Five of the 11 items in the activity limitation domain are self-identified by patients. The instrument is in both interviewer and self-administered format and takes approximately 10 minutes to complete at the first visit and 5 minutes at follow-up.

Using global rating of change questionnaires (182), the clinical interpretability of the Asthma Quality of Life Questionnaire was determined. Studies showed that a change in score of 0.5, both for overall quality of life and for the individual domains, represents a minimal important difference. The minimal important difference is defined as the smallest difference in score in the domain of interest that patients perceive as beneficial and would mandate, in the absence of troublesome side effects or excessive cost, a change in the patient's management (183). It was also shown that a change in quality of life score of approximately 1.0 represents a moderate change and a change in score greater than 2.0 represents a large change in HRQOL. Using the responsiveness index derived from the minimal important difference and the pooled within-subject standard deviation, clinical study sample sizes have been calculated for various alpha and beta error rates (181). For example, a parallel group design clinical trial with the alpha error rate (two-sided) set at 0.05 and the beta error rate at 0.1, requires a sample size of 35 patients per group.

Asthma Quality of Life Questionnaire (Marks) (AQLQ) (171,184) is designed for adults with asthma, is a self-administered questionnaire containing 20 items in four domains: breathlessness and physical restrictions, mood disturbance, social disruption, and concerns for health. Patients rate each item on a five-point scale. The investigators selected items using both importance as rated by patients and psychometric techniques. The questionnaire takes approximately 5 minutes to complete.

Living with Asthma Questionnaire (Hyland) (172,185) is a 68-item instrument with 11 domains: social/leisure, sport, holidays, sleep, work, colds, morbidity, effects on others, medication use, sex, and dysphoric states and attitudes. Items, identified from patient focus group discussions, were selected for the questionnaire using psychometric techniques and factor analysis. Unlike the instruments of Juniper (181) and Marks et al. (171), impairments experienced as a direct result of asthma symptoms are not included. Responses are given using a three-point scale, suggesting that it may have acceptable discriminative properties but be less responsive to within-patient changes.

St. George's Respiratory Questionnaire (Jones et al.) (186) is self-administered and is applicable to adult patients with both reversible and fixed airway obstruction. It contains 76 items in three domains: symptoms, activity, and impacts (on daily life).

Life Activities Questionnaire for Adult Asthma (Creer et al.) for adults (173) with asthma has 70 items in seven domains (physical activities, work activities, outdoor activities, emotions and emotional behavior, home care, eating and drinking activities, and miscellaneous). Items were selected on the basis of frequency of experience by patients. Responses are given on a five-point scale and the questionnaire is self-administered.

Respiratory Illness Quality of Life Questionnaire (Maille et al.) (187) has 55 items in seven domains (breathing problems, physical problems, emotions, situations triggering or enhancing breathing problems, daily and domestic activities, social activities, relationships and sexuality, general activities) and is applicable to patients with COPD or asthma.

Asthma Bother Profile (Hyland et al.) (188) has 22 self-administered items selected from five earlier asthma and COPD quality of life instruments (181, 184–186) to measure the psychological impact of asthma.

Pediatric Asthma Quality of Life Questionnaire (189) has been designed for children with asthma, aged 7–17 years. It has 23 items in three domains: symptoms, activity limitation, and emotional function; three of the activity items are self-identified by the patient. Items were selected on the basis of their importance to the children themselves. It is both self- and interviewer-administered with seven-point response options and takes approximately 10 minutes to complete. Patients experience no difficulty understanding the questions or the response options.

Life Activities Questionnaire for Childhood Asthma (Creer et al.) (190) is a 71-item questionnaire focused on activity limitations.

Childhood Asthma Questionnaires (French et al.) (191) includes three separate questionnaires developed for children aged 4–7 years (CAQA), 8–11 years (CAQB), and 12–16 years (CAQC). Lack of ability to differentiate between these children suggests that the instrument may have poor discriminative properties.

Rhinoconjunctivitis Quality of Life Questionnaire (180) has been designed for use in adult patients with both seasonal and perennial atopic and also nonatopic rhinoconjunctivitis. There are 28 items, selected on the basis of their importance to patients, in seven domains: sleep, nonrhinoconjunctivitis symptoms, activity limitations, nasal symptoms, eye symptoms, practical problems, and emotional function. Seven-point response options are used and the instrument may be interviewer or self-administered.

Adolescent Rhinoconjunctivitis Quality of Life Questionnaire is similar to the adult questionnaire, but the 25 items in this instrument (192) were selected because they are important to adolescents (aged 12–17 years). These younger patients do not experience so much trouble with sleeping as adults but the rhinoconjunctivitis has a much larger impact on ability to function in role activities (school). There are six domains—practical problems, nonhayfever symptoms, nasal symptoms, eye symptoms, activity limitations, and emotional problems—and seven-point response options are used. The instrument showed good responsiveness in being able to detect significant differences between two treatments for all domains except activity limitations and eye symptoms. The Rhinitis Quality of Life Questionnaire (193) was derived from the adult Rhinoconjunctivitis Quality of Life Questionnaire by removing all items that relate specifically to eye symptoms.

CHRONIC OBSTRUCTIVE PULMONARY DISEASE

Chronic obstructive pulmonary disease (COPD) is a debilitating disease characterized by the presence of chronic bronchitis or emphysema that may lead to the development of airways obstruction. COPD affects physical activity, and may also affect cerebral function. The Sickness Impact Profile (SIP) (194) and the Quality of Well-Being Scale (QWB) (195) have been used in several studies of COPD and have established validity for this population (196–198).

A few COPD-specific quality of life measures are available. The best known and most completely described is the Chronic Respiratory Disease Questionnaire (CRDQ) developed by Guyatt and colleagues (199). The CRDQ contains 20 questions and covers four dimensions of functioning: dyspnea (shortness of breath), fatigue, emotional function, and mastery or "a feeling of control over the disease" (200). The CRDQ is administered to the patient by a trained interviewer and requires approximately 20 minutes to complete.

The St. George's Respiratory Questionnaire (201–203) is a 76-item questionnaire that measures three dimensions: (a) symptoms (associated with pulmonary disease), (b) activities (which are likely to be limited by dyspnea), and (c) impacts (social and psychological functioning). The test correlates well with the SIP and the QWB, while being more sensitive to changes in the level of disease severity, especially in cases of mild to moderately severe respiratory disease (201).

Maille and colleagues have developed the Quality of Life Questionnaire for Respiratory Illness, which is intended for use with asthma as well as with COPD (204,205). Fifty-five items were chosen for the questionnaire from a pool of 221 accordingly to whether COPD or asthma patients indicated that an item applied to their recent experience. The items are grouped into seven subscales: (a) breathing problems; (b) physical problems; (c) emotions; (d) situations triggering or enhancing breathing problems; (e) daily and domestic activities; (f) social activities, relationships, and sexuality; and (g) general activities. The scales demonstrated moderate and significant correlations with several measures of severity of illness, including degree of dyspnea. A major limitation of the instrument is that it is only available in Dutch and French versions. Other COPD-specific instruments, which are documented to varying degrees, include a longer questionnaire by Guyatt and colleagues (206), as well as questionnaires by Cox et al. (207), Dardes et al. (208), Hanson (209), Kinsman et al. (210), and Moody et al. (211,212).

A survey of COPD patients by Hanson (209) included 40 items assessing 11 areas, including several aspects of social role functioning and activities of daily living, such as employment, self-care, home/personal business, marriage, care of grandchildren, and dependency on others. Sexton and Monro (213) studied women with COPD and 40 demographically similar women who had no chronic illness were compared on their perceived health status, problems of daily living, amount of subjective stress, and life satisfaction. The questionnaire used for this study included demographic and illness-related questions as well as adapted versions of the Subjective Stress Scale (214) and the Life Satisfaction Index (215), which had been tested in an earlier study of COPD spouses' quality of life (216).

DIABETES MELLITUS

The psychological impact of diabetes reflects the condition's potential for disability on the one hand, and the complexity of the therapeutic regimen on the other. Health-related quality of life perceptions for people with diabetes cannot be separated from the complex diabetes treatment regimen that includes dietary behavior, exercise, medication, glucose monitoring, and safety and preventive measures.

Jacobson et al. (217) compared a generic measure, the Medical Outcome Study Health Survey—SF-36—and a disease-specific measure, the Diabetes Quality of Life Measure (DQOL). The authors concluded that although the DQOL was more sensitive to life style issues and concerns of younger patients and the SF-36 provided more information on functional health status, the measures could be useful in combination in quality of life studies in patients with type I and type II diabetes. Parkerson et al. (218) compared the health-related quality of life of adult IDDM patients using a disease-specific instrument, the DQOL, and two generic instruments, the Duke Health Profile (DUKE) and the General Health Perceptions Questionnaire. They reported that the generic measures provided as much or more information on these patients.

Nerenz et al. (219) established an Outcomes Management data base to provide an ongoing assessment of health status in patients with type I and type II diabetes to obtain information on quality of life from the patient's perspective, as well as from clinical predictor variables. A combination of instruments provided information for the data base: the patient self-reported health status using the SF-36; physician ratings of patients' health status along the major dimensions of the SF-36; a set of diabetes-specific health status items, demographic information, and a set of clinical variables known collectively as the Diabetes Technology of Patient Experience (TyPE) scale Form 2.2. Information was obtained either by mail or in person in a clinic setting and used for assessment and intervention of clinical outcomes.

In a study comparing three measures of health status, Bardsley et al. (220) used the Nottingham Health Profile (NHP), four categories of an anglicized version of the Sickness Impact Profile (the Functional Limitations Profile (FLP), and a scale of Positive Well-Being (PWB). The PWB scale was independent of physical disability, but the NHP and the FLP provided a useful assessment of general health in diabetes with a bias in identifying the minority of patients with more severe health problems. The NHP and FLP, and possibly the PWB, were insensitive to the subtle changes in well-being associated with managing metabolic disturbances and did not appropriately assess the impact of diabetes on the disruption of life style.

The Diabetes Quality of Life instrument (DQOL) (221) is a diabetes-specific quality of life measure originally constructed for the DCCT (222), a clinical trial that evaluated the effects of standard diabetes treatment or an insulin pump. The DQOL is an easily administered multiple-choice assessment instrument, applicable to patients using different methods of diabetes management. It has four primary scales with 46 core items designed to measure the patient's personal perceptions of diabetes care and treatment: satisfaction with treatment, impact of treatment, worry about the future effects of diabetes, and worry about social/vocational issues. There is also a single overall well-being scale derived from national surveys of quality of well-being. A 16-item scale that assesses schooling, experience, and family relationships for patients living with their parents can provide relevant information in adolescent populations. Responses to questions are made with a five-point Likert scale.

Anderson et al. (223) revised a Diabetes Attitude Scale, originally designed to measure the attitudes of health care professionals, to also include the perceptions of people with diabetes. Using a generic model, Hanestad et al. (224) surveyed persons with IDDM to determine to what degree metabolic control was associated with self-assessed quality of life. They found that well-regulated persons felt less sociable and more lonely than poorly regulated persons.

CHRONIC RHEUMATIC DISORDERS

Rheumatic disorders (225) are characterized by musculoskeletal complaints that result in disability, and reduce quality of life, but do not shorten life span. There are five common patterns of rheumatic disability: rheumatoid, osteoarthritis, spondylitis, and systemic rheumatic disease and soft tissue disease disabilities.

The McMaster Toronto Arthritis Patient Preference Disability Questionnaire (MACTAR) was developed for use in clinical trials in rheumatoid arthritis (226). Using a semi-structured interview, patients are asked to designate key functional activities based on their own preferences, and the five activities that rank highest are evaluated. At the end of a study period, patients are asked if their ability to perform the ranked activities has improved, worsened, or stayed the same. This technique may be more sensitive to small changes when compared with conventional standardized questionnaires. The problems in evaluating each patient in a different way are formidable, and this approach requires further investigation.

The Toronto Functional Capacity Questionnaire assesses function in personal care, upper extremity activities, mobility, work, and leisure activities (227). The instrument is administered by an interviewer and requires approximately 10 minutes to complete. Weighting of responses is based on preferences derived from panels of occupational and physical therapists and rheumatologists. Reliability and validity have been demonstrated. The instrument has been shown to be sensitive to change in clinical trials (226).

The Modified Health Assessment Questionnaire (MHAQ) is an arthritis-specific short form of proven reliability, validity, sensitivity to clinical change and prognostic utility (228). The MHAQ evaluates physical function through questions derived from the HAQ and adds new scales for change in function, satisfaction, and pain in the performance of each of these activities. It can be completed in less than 5 minutes. Although the MHAQ was not responsive to the beneficial effect of methotrexate in RA in one large study (229), it has been demonstrated to predict important outcomes such as morbidity, mortality, and costs (230,231).

The Arthritis Impact Measurement Scale (AIMS-2) was developed to "evaluate health status in patients with rheumatoid disease" (232,233). The AIMS-2 evaluated patients both with rheumatoid and osteoarthritis. The 78-item questionnaire is divided into 12 subscales: mobility level, walking and bending, hand and finger function, arm function, self-care, household tasks, social activities, support from family and friends, arthritis pain, work, level of tension, and mood. Validity was determined by correlation of the AIMS-2 with patients' overall ratings of health status and was able to discriminate between different disease groups, sex, age, and subjects' educational level. The scale, which is self-administered, is reported to take approximately 20 minutes to complete. The 48-item AIMS has been reduced to a short form with 18 items by selecting two items with highest internal consistency and correlation with the total scale score from each of the nine AIMS subscales (234).

The Western Ontario and McMaster University Osteoarthritis (WOMAC) index is a scale based on interviews with patients with lower extremity arthritis. Although it was not developed specifically to measure the outcome after surgical procedures, such as joint arthroplasty, the scale was derived from out-patients with osteoarthritis of the hip and/or knee (235,236), a group similar to patients receiving hip and knee arthroplasty. The final scale, based on a consensus of the 100 patients, includes 5 pain items, 2 stiffness items, and 17 physical function items, which all receive equal weighting and are summed together as three subscales to obtain the final scores (236). Responsiveness was demonstrated in a randomized controlled trial of nonsteroidal anti-inflammatory drugs (NSAIDs) in the treatment of osteoarthritis (237).

The Patient-Specific Index (PASI), evaluates all important symptoms mentioned by patients and uses patient's individual ratings of importance to generate weights for the complaints (238). Patients rate separately the severity and importance of their individual complaints which are combined together to generate a patient-specific score. The disadvantage of a patient-specific scale is the requirement for interviewer administration.

The North American Spine Society Scale evaluates "patient-centered" pain and functional outcome of patients with spinal disorders (239). The self-administered questionnaire requires approximately 20 minutes to complete and focuses on pain and functional limitations, such as dressing, walking, sitting, recreation, work, and sex life. The St. Thomas Disability Questionnaire (or Roland and Morris scale) is a modification of the Sickness Impact Profile (240). The scale focuses on those issues from the SIP relevant to the spine, and the symptoms and disabilities are attributed to the spine. The instrument is self-administered with

24 yes/no questions focusing on symptoms and functional disabilities, such as walking, climbing stairs, sitting, dressing, standing, and work. A second part of the questionnaire requires patients to rate their pain using a "thermometer" (modified) visual–analog scale.

The Pediatric Evaluation of Disability Inventory (PEDI) focuses on children with chronic illnesses 6 months to 7 years of age (241). The scale requires a structured parent interview or clinician observation focused on domains of self-care, mobility, and social function. The Juvenile Arthritis Functional Assessment Form (JAFAR) was developed to evaluate children aged 7–18 years with rheumatoid arthritis. This 23-item scale, which is self-administered, can be completed by parents or children and evaluates both upper and lower extremity function (242,243). The scale was also able to discriminate between normal and control patients and correlated with the Steinbrook classification and the number of involved joints.

A number of instruments have been compared in a variety of descriptive and evaluative studies: Sickness Impact Profile, Index of Well-Being, Functional Status Index, Arthritis Impact Measurement Scale, and Modified Health Assessment Questionnaire (244). All the instruments correlated highly with one another and demonstrated change. The Arthritis Impact Measurement Scale, Functional Status Index, and Sickness Impact Profile were equally efficient in detecting improvement in mobility, but the Health Assessment Questionnaire and Index of Well-Being were about a half as efficient as the other three instruments. For pain evaluation, the Arthritis Impact Measurement Scale was more sensitive than the Health Assessment Questionnaire. The Index of Well-Being and Sickness Impact Profile do not have a pain subscale. With regard to social function, the Sickness Impact Profile, Index of Well-Being, and Health Assessment Questionnaire were more sensitive than the Arthritis Impact Measurement Scale. For global function the Sickness Impact Profile, Arthritis Impact Measurement Scale, and Index of Well-Being were more efficient than the Functional Status Index or Health Assessment Questionnaire. Studies of the relative sensitivity to change, or responsiveness of the AIMS and four short health status measures, the SF-36, FSQ, MHAQ and shortened AIMS, showed that the short measures were as sensitive to change in the global dimension as the SIP and all but the shortened AIMS were sensitive to change in the physical dimension (245).

REFERENCES

1. Cadman D, Goldsmith C, Torrance GW. *A methodology for a utility-based health status index for Ontario children.* Final report to the Ontario Ministry of Health. Hamilton, Ont.: McMaster University, 1986.
2. Boyle M, Offord D, Hoffman H, et al. Ontario child health study: methodology. *Arch Gen Psychiatry* 1987;44:826–831.
3. Torrance GW. Social preferences for health states: an empirical evaluation of three measurement techniques. *Socio-econ Plan Sci* 1976;10:129–136.
4. Feeny D, Furlong W, Barr RD, Torrance GW, Rosenbaum P, Weitzman S. A comprehensive multi-

attribute system for classifying the health status of survivors of childhood cancer. *J Clin Oncol* 1992; 10:923–928.

5. Barr RD, Pai MKR, Weitzman S, et al. A multi-attribute approach to health status measurement and clinical management—illustrated by an application to brain tumors in childhood. *Int J Oncol* 1994; 4:639–648.

6. Churchill DN, Torrance GW, Taylor DW, et al. Measurement of quality of life in end-stage renal disease: the time trade-off approach. *Clin Invest Med* 1987;10:14–20.

7. Achenbach TM, McConaughy SH, Howell CT. Child/adolescent behavioral and emotional problems: implications of cross-informant correlations for situational specificity. *Psychol Bull* 1987;101: 213–232.

8. Saigal S, Rosenbaum PL, Feeny DH, Furlong WJ. Comparison of the perception of health status within premature and control teen/parent dyads. *Pediatr Res* 1995;37(4):271A.

9. Barr RD, Feeny D, Furlong W, Weitzman S, Torrance GW. A preference-based approach to health-related quality of life for children with cancer. *Int J Pediatr Hematol Oncol* 1995.

10. Saigal S, Furlong WJ, Rosenbaum PL, Feeny DH. Do teens differ from parents in rating health-related quality of life?: a study of premature and control teen/parent dyads. *Pediatr Res* 1995;37: 271A.

11. Bibace R, Walsh ME. Development of children's concepts of illness. *Pediatrics* 1980;66:912–917.

12. Maddux JE, Roberts MC, Sledden EA, Wright L. Developmental issues in child health psychology. *Am Psychol* 1986;41:25–34.

13. Perrin EC, Gerrity PS. There's a demon in your belly: children's understanding of illness. *Pediatrics* 1981;67:841–849.

14. Tyler DC, Ahn Tu JD, Chapman CR. Toward validation of pain measurement tools for children: a pilot study. *Pain* 1993;52:301–309.

15. Adesman AR, Walco GA. Validation of the Charleston Pediatric Pain Pictures in school-age children. *J Clin Child Psychol* 1993;21:10–13.

16. Achenbach TM, Edelbrock CS. The child behavior profile. I. Boys aged 6–11. *J Consult Clin Psychol* 1978;46:478–488.

17. Achenbach TM, Edelbrock CS. The child behavior profile. II. Boys aged 12–16 and girls aged 6–11 and 12–16. *J Consult Clin Psychol* 1979;47:223–233.

18. Piers EV. *Revised manual Piers–Harris children's self–concepts scale.* Los Angeles: Western Psychological Services, 1985.

19. Weissman MM, Wickramaratre P, Warner V, et al. Assessing psychiatric disorders in children. *Arch Gen Psychiatry* 1987;44:747–753.

20. Fry E. Fry's readability graph: clarifications, validation, and extension to level 17. *J Reading* 1977; Dec:242–252.

21. Privette G, David S. Reliability and readability of a questionnaire: peak performance and peak experience. *Psychol Rep* 1986;58:491–494.

22. Starfield B, Reiley A, Green B, Ensminger M, Ryan S, et al. The adolescent child health and illness profile: a population-based measure of health. *Med Care* 1995;33(5):553–566.

23. Baribeau P, Berger D, Jette A, Kairys S, Keller A, Landgraf J, Wasson G, Wasson J. Coop functional health status charts for children and adults: a system to measure functional health status in physicians' offices. Final Report to the Henry J. Kaiser Family and the W.T. Grant Foundations. Dartmouth Medical School. Hanover, NH: Dartmouth COOP Project, Department of Community and Family Medicine, Dartmouth Medical School, 1991.

24. Wasson JH, Kairys SW, Nelson EC, Kalishman N, Baribeau P. A short survey for assessing health and social problems of adolescents. *Fam Pract* 1994;38:489–494.

25. Stein REK, Jessop DJ. Functional status II(R): a measure of child health status. *Med Care* 1990;28: 1041–1055.

26. Lewis CC, Pantell RH, Keickhefer GM. Assessment of children's health status. Field test of new approaches. *Med Care* 1989;27:S54–S65.

27. Kurtin PS, Landgraf JL, Abetz L. Patient-based health status measurements in pediatric dialysis: expanding the assessment of outcome. *Am J Kidney Dis* 1994;24:376–382.

28. Landgraf JM, Ware JE Jr, Schor E, Davies AR, Roh K. Health profiles in children with psychiatric and other medical conditions. Paper presented at Ninth World Congress of Psychiatry, Rio de Janiero, Brasil, June 6–12, 1993.

29. Landgraf JM, Ware JE Jr, Schor E, Davies AR, R-Roh K. Comparison of health status profiles for children with medical conditions: preliminary psychometric and clinical results from the Children's

Health and Quality of Life Project. Paper presented at the Tenth Annual Meeting of the Association for Health Services Research, Washington, DC, June 27–29, 1993.

30. Eisen M, Donald C, Ware JE, Brook R. *Conceptualization and measurement of health for children in the health insurance study. Publication R-2313-HEW.* Santa Monica, CA: RAND, 1980.

31. Eisen M, Ware JE, Donald C. Measuring components of children's health status. *Med Care* 1979;17: 902–921.

32. Newacheck PW, Taylor WR. Childhood chronic illness: prevalence, severity, and impact. *Am J Public Health* 1992;82:364–371.

33. National Health Interview Survey. Current Estimates from the National Health Interview Survey. NHIS Child Health Supplement 1988.

34. Boyle MH, Offord DR, Hofmann HG, et al. Ontario child health study. I. Methodology. *Arch Gen Psychiatry* 1987;44:826–831.

35. Mulhern RK, Horowitz ME, Ochs J, Friedman AG, Armstrong FD, Copeland D, Kun LE. Assessment of quality of life among pediatric patients with cancer, psychological assessment. *J Consult Clin Psychol* 1989;1:130–138.

36. Williams TF. Current status of biomedical and behavioral research in aging. In: Andreopoulos S, Hogness JR, eds. *Health care for an aging society.* New York: Churchill Livingstone, 1989:123–137.

37. National Center for Health Statistics. Data on older Americans: United States, 1992. Centers for Disease Control and Prevention/National Center for Health Statistics, Series 3, Number 27.

38. Fretwell MD, Raymond PM, McGarvey S, Owens N, Silliman RA, Mor V. The Senior Care Study: a controlled trial of a consultant/unit based geriatric assessment program in acute care. *J Am Geriatr Soc* 1990;38:1073–1081.

39. Katz S, Vignos PJ, Moskowitz RJ, Thompson HM, Suec KH. Comprehensive outpatient care in rheumatoid arthritis. *JAMA* 1968;206:1249–1254.

40. Mahoney FI, Barthel DW. Functional evaluation: the Barthel Index. *Md S Med J* 1965;14:61–65.

41. Fillenbaum GG. *Multidimensional Functional Assessment: the Oars Methodology,* 2nd ed. Durham, NC: Duke University, The Center for the Study of Aging and Human Development, 1978.

42. Spitzer WO, Dobson AH, Hall J, et al. Measuring quality of life in cancer patients: a concise QL-index for use by physicians. *J Chronic Dis* 1981;34:585–597.

43. Carp FM. Maximizing data quality in community studies of older people. In: Lawton MP, Herzog AR, eds. *Special research methods for gerontology.* Amityville, NY: Baywood, 1989:93.

44. Guyatt GH, Deyo RA, Charlson M, et al. Responsiveness and validity in health status measurement: a clarification. *J Clin Epidemiol* 1989;42:403–408.

45. Deyo RA, Diehr P, Patrick DL. Reproducibility and responsiveness of health status measures. *Controlled Clin Trials* 1991;12(suppl):142S–158S.

46. Tugwell P, Bombardier C, Bell M, et al. Current quality-of-life research challenges in arthritis relevant to the issue of clinical significance. *Controlled Clin Trials* 1991;12:217S–225S.

47. McHorney CA, Kosinski M, Ware JE. Comparisons of the costs and quality of norms for the SF-36 health survey collected by mail versus telephone interview: results from a national survey. *Med Care* 1994;32:551–567.

48. Leinbach RM. Alternatives to the face-to-face interview for collecting gerontological needs assessment data. *Gerontologist* 1982;22:78–82.

49. Dawson D, Hendershot G, Fulton J. NCHS Advance Data, Vital and Health Statistics of the NCHS, No. 133, June 10.

50. Herzog AR, Rodgers WL, Kulka RA. Interviewing older adults: a comparison of telephone and face-to-face modalities. *Public Opin Q* 1983;47:405–418.

51. Kutner NG, Ory MG, Baker DI, et al. Measuring the quality of life of the elderly in health promotion intervention clinical trials. *Public Health Rep* 1992;107:530–539.

52. Zimmerman SI, Magaziner J. Methodological issues in measuring the functional status of cognitively impaired nursing home residents: the use of proxies and performance-based measures. *Alzheimer Dis Assoc Disord* 1994;8(suppl):S281–S290.

53. Guralnik JM, Branch LG, Cummings SR, et al. Physical performance measures in aging research. *J Gerontol* 1989;44:M141–M146.

54. Guralnik JM, LaCroix AZ. Assessing physical function in older populations. In: Wallace RB, Woolson RF, eds. *The epidemiologic study of the elderly.* New York: Oxford University Press, 1992:159.

55. Rodgers WL, Herzog AR. Collecting data about the oldest old: problems and procedures. In: Suzman RM, Willis DP, Manton KG, eds. *The oldest old.* New York: Oxford University Press, 1992:135.

56. Teresi J, Lawton P, Ory M, et al. Measurement issues in chronic care populations: dementia special care. *Alzheimer Dis Assoc Disord* 1994;8(suppl):S144–S183.

57. Grut M, Jorm AF, Fratiglioni L, et al. Memory complaints of elderly people in a population survey: variation according to dementia stage and depression. *J Am Gerontol Soc* 1993;41:1295–1300.

58. DeJong R, Osterlund OW, Roy GW. Measurement of quality-of-life changes in patients with Alzheimer's disease. *Clin Ther* 1989;11:545–554.

59. David P. Effectiveness of group work with the cognitively impaired older adult. *Am J Alzheimers Care Relat Disord Res* 1991:10–16, volume 6.

60. Yale R. *A guide to facilitating support groups for newly diagnosed Alzheimer's patients.* Palo Alto, CA: Alzheimer's Association, Greater San Francisco Bay Area, 1991.

61. Foley JM. The experience of being demented. In: Binstock RH, Post SG, Whitehouse PJ, eds. *Dementia and aging.* Baltimore, MD: Johns Hopkins University Press, 1992:30.

62. McGowin DF. *Living in the labyrinth: a personal journey through the maze of Alzheimer's.* San Francisco: Elder Books, 1993.

63. Kiyak HA, Teri L, Borson S. Physical and functional health assessment in normal aging and in Alzheimer's disease: self-reports vs family reports. *Gerontologist* 1994;34:324–330.

64. Magaziner J, Simonsick EM, Kashner TM, et al. Patient-proxy response comparability on measures of patient health and functional status. *J Clin Epidemiol* 1988;41:1065–1074.

65. Winogrond IR, Fisk AA. Alzheimer's disease: assessment of functional status. *J Am Gerontol Soc* 1983;31:780–785.

66. Stewart AL, Sherbourne CD, Hays RD, et al. Summary and discussion of MOS measures. In: Stewart AL, Ware JE Jr, eds. *Measuring functioning and well-being: the Medical Outcomes Study approach.* Durham, NC: Duke University Press, 1992:345.

67. Jette AM, Davies AR, Cleary PD, et al. The Functional Status Questionnaire. *J Gen Intern Med* 1986;1:143–149.

68. Parkerson GR, Gehlbach SH, Wagner EH, et al. The Duke-UNC Health Profile: an adult health status instrument for primary care. *Med Care* 1981;19:806–828.

69. George LK, Fillenbaum GG. OARS methodology: a decade of experience in geriatric assessment. *J Am Gerontol Soc* 1985;33:607–615.

70. Lawton MP, Moss M, Fulcomer M, et al. A research and service oriented Multilevel Assessment Instrument. *J Gerontol* 1982;37:91–99.

71. Brook RH, Ware JE, Davies–Avery A, et al. Overview of adult health status measures fielded in Rand's Health Insurance Study. *Med Care* 1979;17(suppl).

72. Neugarten BL, Havighurst RJ, Tobin SS. The measurement of life satisfaction. *J Gerontol* 1961;16:134–143.

73. Lawton MP. The Philadelphia Geriatric Center Morale Scale: a revision. *J Gerontol* 1975;30:85–89.

74. Liang J, Bollen KA. The structure of the Philadelphia Geriatric Center Morale Scale: a reinterpretation. *J Gerontol* 1983;30:77–84.

75. Kessler RC, Foster C, Webster PS, et al. The relationship between age and depressive symptoms in two national surveys. *Psychol Aging* 1992;7:119–126.

76. Yesavage JA, Brink TL, Rose TL, et al. Development and validation of a geriatric depression screening scale: a preliminary report. *J Psychiatr Res* 1983;17:37–49.

77. Krenz C, Larson EB, Buchner DM, et al. Characterizing patient dysfunction in Alzheimer's-type dementia. *Med Care* 1988;26:453–461.

78. Wallace RB, Kohout FJ, Colsher PL. Observations on interview surveys of the oldest old. In: Suzman RM, Willis DP, Manton KG, eds. *The oldest old.* New York: Oxford University Press, 1992:123.

79. Kohout FJ. The pragmatics of survey field work among the elderly. In: Wallace RB, Woolson RF, eds. *The epidemiologic study of the elderly.* New York: Oxford University Press, 1992:91.

80. Aday LA. *Designing and conducting health surveys: a comprehensive guide.* San Francisco: Jossey-Bass, 1991.

81. Nelson EC, Landgraf JM, Hays RD, et al. The functional status of patients: how can it be measured in physicians' offices? *Med Care* 1990;28:1111–1126.

82. Nelson EC, Landgraf JM, Hays RD, et al. The COOP Function Charts: a system to measure patient function in physicians' offices. In: WONCA Classification Committee, ed. *Functional status measurement in primary care.* New York: Springer-Verlag, 1990:97.

83. Andrews FM, Withey SB. *Social Indicators of Well-Being.* New York: Plenum Press, 1976.

84. Cella DF, Tulsky DS, Gray G, et al. The Functional Assessment of Cancer Therapy Scale: development and validation of the general measure. *J Clin Oncol* 1993;11(3):570–579.

85. Cella DF. *Manual for the Functional Assessment of Cancer Therapy (FACT) and Functional Assessment of HIV Infection (FAHI) quality of life scales,* 3rd ed. Chicago: Rush-Presbyterian-St. Luke's Medical Center, 1994.

86. Cella DF, Tulsky DS, Bonomi A, Lee-Riordan D, Silberman M, Purl S. The Functional Assessment of Cancer Therapy (FACT) scales: incorporating disease-specificity and subjectivity into quality of life (QL) assessment. *Proc Am Soc Clin Oncol* 1990;9:307 (#1190).
87. Tulsky DS, Cella DF, Bonomi A, Lee-Riordan D, Silberman M. Development and validation of new quality of life measures for patients with cancer. *Proc Soc Beh Med 11th Ann Meeting* 1990;11: 45–46.
88. Tulsky DS, Cella DF, Sarafian B. The Functional Assessment of Cancer Treatment: three new site-specific measures. *J Cancer Res Clin Oncol* 1990;116(suppl):54–241.
89. Schipper H, Clinch JJ, McMurray A, Levitt M. Measuring the quality of life of cancer patients: The Functional Living Index-Cancer: development and validation. *J Clin Oncol* 1984;2:472–483.
90. Harvey RM, Doyle EF, Ellis K, et al. Major changes made by the Criteria Committee of the New York Heart Association. *Circulation* 1974;49:390.
91. Goldman L, Hashimoto B, Cook EF, et al. Comparative reproducibility and validity of systems for assessing cardiovascular functional class: advantages of a new Specific Activity Scale. *Circulation* 1981;64:1227–1234.
92. Rose GA, Blackburn H. *Cardiovascular survey methods.* Geneva: World Health Organization 1986; 56:1–188.
93. CASS Principal Investigators and their Associates. Coronary artery surgery study (CASS). A randomized trial of coronary artery bypass surgery. Quality of life in patients randomly assigned to treatment groups. *Circulation* 1983;68:951–960.
94. Visser MC, Fletcher AE, Parr G, Simpson A, Bulpitt CJ. A comparison of three quality of life instruments in subjects with angina pectoris: the Sickness Impact Profile, the Nottingham Health Profile, and the Quality of Well-Being Scale. *J Clin Epidemiol* 1994;47:157–163.
95. Wiklund I, Comerford MB, Dimenas E. The relationship between exercise tolerance and quality of life in angina pectoris. *Clin Cardiol* 1991;14:204–208.
96. Wiklund I, Herlitz J, Johansson S, Bengtson A, Karlson BW, Persson NG. Subjective symptoms and well-being differ in women and men after myocardial infarction. *Eur Heart J* 1993;14:1315–1319.
97. Bulpitt CJ, Dollery CT, Carne S. A symptom questionnaire for hypertensive patients. *J Chronic Dis* 1974;27:309–323.
98. Bulpitt CJ, Fletcher AE. Measurement of quality of life in hypertension: a practical approach. *Br J Clin Pharmacol* 1990;30:353–364.
99. Dahlof C, Dimenas E, Olofsson B. Documentation of an instrument for assessment of subjective CNS-related symptoms during cardiovascular pharmachotherapy. *Cardiovasc Drug Ther* 1989;3:919–927.
100. Dimenas E, Dahlof C, Olofsson B, Wiklund I. An instrument for quantifying subjective symptoms among untreated and treated hypertensives: development and documentation. *J Clin Res Pharmacoepidemiol* 1990;4:205–217.
101. Jern S. Questionnaire for the assessment of symptoms and psychological effects in cardiovascular therapy (the ASPECT scale). *Scand J Prim Health Care* 1990;1:(suppl) 31–32.
102. Bar-On D, Amir M. Reexamining the quality of life of hypertensive patient. A new self-structured measure. *Am J Hypertens* 1993;6:62S–66S.
103. Weir MR, Josselson J, Ekelund L-G, et al. Nicardipine as antihypertensive monotherapy: positive effects on quality of life. *J Hum Hypertens* 1991;5:205–213.
104. McNair DM, Lorr M, Doppleman LF. *Manual of the profile of mood states.* San Diego, CA: San Diego Educational and Industrial Testing Service, 1971.
105. Goldberg D. *The detection of psychiatric illness by questionnaire.* Oxford: Oxford University Press, 1972.
106. Kellner R, Sheffield BF. A self-rating scale of distress. *Psychol Med* 1973;3:88–100.
107. Fanshel S, Bush JW. A health status index and its application to health service outcomes. *Oper Res* 1970;18:1021–1066.
108. Fahn S, Elton RL. Unified Parkinson's Disease Rating Scale. In: Fahn S, et al., eds. *Recent developments in Parkinson's disease,* vol. II. Florham Park, NJ: Macmillan Healthcare, 1987:153–163.
109. Hoehn MM, Yahr MD. Parkinsonism: onset, progression, and mortality. *Neurology* 1967;17:427–442.
110. Schwab RS, England AC. Projection technique for evaluating surgery in Parkinson's disease. In: Gillingham FJ, Donaldson MC, eds. *Third symposium on Parkinson's disease.* Edinburgh: Churchill Livingstone, 1969:152–157.
111. Shoulson I, Fahn S. Huntington's disease: clinical care and evaluation. *Neurology* 1979;29:1–3.
112. Koller WC. *Handbook of Parkinson's disease.* New York: Dekker, 1987:482–488.
113. Lawton MP, Brody EM. Assessment of older people: self-maintaining and instrumental activities of daily living. *Gerontologist* 1969;9:179–186.

114. Katz S, Ford AB, Moskowitz RW. Studies of illness in the aged: the index of ADL, a standardized measure of biological and psychosocial function. *JAMA* 1963;185:914–919.

115. Mahoney FJ, Barthel DW. Functional evaluation: the Barthel Index. *Md Med J* 1965;14:61–65.

116. Nagi SZ. An epidemiology of disability among adults in the United States. *Millbank Mem Fund Q* 1976;54:439–468.

117. Rosow I, Breslau N. A Guttman health scale for the aged. *J Gerontol* 1966;21:556–559.

118. Guralnik JM, Branch LG, Cummings SR, Curbe JD. Physical performance measures in aging research. *J Gerontol Med Sci* 1989;44:M141–M146.

119. Guralnik JM, Simonsick EM, Ferrucci L, Glynn RJ, Berkman LF, Blazer DG, Scherr PA, Wallace RB. A short physical performance battery assessing lower extremity function: association with self-reported disability and prediction of mortality and nursing home admission. *J Gerontol Med Sci* 1994;49:M85–M94.

120. Lezak M. *Neurological assessment.* New York: Oxford University Press, 1983.

121. Folstein MF, Folstein SE, McHugh PR. Mini-Mental State. A practical guide for grading the cognitive state of patients for the clinician. *J Psychiatr Res* 1975;12:189–198.

122. Mackenzie TB, Robiner WN, Knopman BS. Differences between patient and family assessments of depression in Alzheimer's disease. *Am J Psychiatry* 1989;146:1174–1178.

123. Reisberg B, Schneck MK, Ferris SH, Schwartz GE, de Leon MJ. The Brief Cognitive Rating Scale (BCRS): findings in primary degenerative dementia (PDD). *Psychopharmacol Bull* 1983;19:47–50.

124. Reisberg B, Ferris SH, de Leon MJ, Crook T. The Global Deterioration Scale (GDS): an instrument for the assessment of primary degenerative dementia (PDD). *Am J Psychiatry* 1982;139:1136–1139.

125. Katz MM, Lyerly SB. Methods for measuring adjustment and social behavior in the community. 1. Rationale, description, discriminative validity and scale development. *Psychol Rep* 1963(suppl 4-V13);13:503–535.

126. Bergner M, Bobbitt RA, Carter WB, Gilson BS. The Sickness Impact Profile: development and final revision of a health status measure. *Med Care* 1981;19:787–805.

127. Duke University Center for the Study of Aging. *Multidimensional functional assessment. The OARS methodology,* 2nd ed. Durham, NC: Duke University Press, 1978.

128. Lawton MP, Moss M, Fulcomer M, Kleban MH. A research and service oriented multilevel assessment instrument. *J Gerontol* 1982;37:91–99.

129. Dodrill CB, Batzel LW, Queisser HR, Temkin NR. An objective method for the assessment of psychological and social problems among epileptics. *Epilepsia* 1980;21:123–135.

130. Baker GA, Smith DF, Dewey M, Jacoby A, Chadwick DW. The initial development of a health-related quality of life model as an outcome measure in epilepsy. *Epilepsy Res* 1993;16:65–81.

131. Hunt S, McKewan J, McKenna SP. *The Nottingham Health Profile: user's manual.* 1981.

132. Bradburn NM. *The structure of psychological well-being.* Chicago: Aldine, 1969.

133. Rosenberg M. *Society and the adolescent self-image.* Princeton, NJ: Princeton University Press, 1965.

134. Pearlin L, Schooler C. The structure of coping. *J Health Soc Behav* 1978;19:2–21.

135. Hyman MD. The stigma of stroke. *Geriatrics* 1971;5:132–141.

136. Baker GA, Smith DF, Dewey M, Morrow J, Crawford PM, Chadwick DW. The development of a seizure severity scale as an outcome measure in epilepsy. *Epilepsy Res* 1991;8:245–251.

137. Kendrick AM, Trimble MR. Patient-perceived quality of life: what is important to the patients with epilepsy? *Seizure* 1992;1(suppl A):1–10.

138. Vickrey BG, Hays RD, Graber J, Rausch R, Engel J, Brook RH. A health-related quality of life instrument for patients evaluated for epilepsy surgery. *Med Care* 1992;30:299–319.

139. Hays RD, Sherbourne C, Mazel E,. The RAND 36-item health survey 1.0. *Health Econ* 1993;2: 217–227.

140. Ware JE, Sherbourne CD. A 36-item Short Form Health Survey (SF-36). I. Conceptual framework and item selection. *Med Care* 1992;30:473–483.

141. Devinsky O, Vickrey BG, Cramer JA, Perrine K, Hermann B, Meador K, Hays RD. Development of the quality of life in epilepsy (QOLIE) inventory. *Epilepsia* 1995;36:1089–1104.

142. Cramer JA, Perrrine K, Devinsky O, Bryant-Comstock LB, Meador K, Hermann, BP. Development of the Quality of Life in Epilepsy (QOLIE-31) and cross-cultural translation. *Epilepsia* 1997;38:

143. Cramer JA, Perrine K, Devinsky O, Meador K. A brief questionnaire to screen for quality of life in epilepsy: The QOLIE-10. *Epilepsia* 1996;37:577–582.

144. Austin JK, Risinger MW, Beckett LA. Correlates of behavior problems in children with epilepsy. *Epilepsia* 1992;33:1115–1122.

145. Aschenbach TM, Edelbrock C. *Manual for the child behavior checklist and revised child behavior profile.* Burlington, VT: University of Vermont Department of Psychiatry, 1983.

146. McCubben HI, Thompson AI, eds. Family assessment inventories for research and practice. *Family stress coping and health project.* Madison: University of Wisconsin, 1987.
147. Lehman AF. The effects of psychiatric symptoms on quality of life assessments among the chronic mentally ill. *Eval Program Plann* 1983;6:143–151.
148. Baker F, Intagliata J. Quality of life in the evaluation of community support systems. *Eval Program Plann* 1982;5:69–79.
149. Bigelow DA, Brodsky G, Steward L, Olson M. The concept and measurement of quality of life as a dependent variable in evaluation of mental health services. In: Stahler GJ, Tash WR, eds. *Innovative approaches to mental health evaluation.* San Diego: Academic Press, 1982:345–366.
150. Bigelow DA, McFarland BH, Olson MM. Quality of life of community mental health clients: validating a measure. *Community Mental Health J* 1991;27:125–133.
151. Clare AW, Cairns VE. Design, development and use of a standardized interview to assess social maladjustment and dysfunction in community samples. *Psychol Med* 1978;8:589–604.
152. Heinrichs DW, Hanlon TE, Carpenter WT. The quality of life scale: an instrument for rating the schizophrenic deficit syndrome. *Schizophren Bull* 1984;10:388–398.
153. Lehman AF, Ward NC, Linn LS. Chronic mental patients: the quality of life issue. *Am J Psychiatry* 1982;10:1271–1276.
154. Lehman AF, Possidente S, Hawker F. The quality of life of chronic mental patients in a state hospital and community residences. *Hosp Community Psychiatry* 1986;37:901–907.
155. Lehman AF. A quality of life interview for the chronically mentally ill. *Eval Program Plann* 1988; 11:51–62.
156. Skantze K. *Defining subjective quality of life goals in schizophrenia: the Quality of Life Self-Assessment Inventory, QLS-100, a new approach to successful alliance and service development.* Goteborg, Sweden: Department of Psychiatry, Sahlgrenska Hospital, University of Gothenburg, 1993.
157. Stein LI, Test MA. Alternative to mental hospital treatment. I. Conceptual model, treatment program and clinical evaluation. *Arch Gen Psychiatry* 1980;37:392–397.
158. Oliver JPJ. The social aftercare directive: development of a quality of life profile for use in community services for the mentally ill. *Social Work Social Sci Rev* 1991–1992;3:4–45.
159. Karnofsky DA, Burchenal JH. In: McLeod CM, ed. *Evaluation of chemotherapeutic agents.* New York: Columbia University Press, 1949:191.
160. Spitzer WO, Dobson AJ, Hall J, et al. Measuring the quality of life of cancer patients: a concise quality of life for use by physicians. *J Chron Dis* 1981;34:585–597.
161. Mahoney FI, Barthel DW. Functional evaluation: the Barthel index. *Md Med J* 1965;14:61–65.
162. Katz S. Assessing self-maintenance activities of daily living, mobility and instrumental activities of daily living. *J Am Geriatr Soc* 1983;37:721–727.
163. Deniston OL, Carpentier-Alting P, Kneisley J, Hawthorne VM, Port FK. Assessment of quality of life in end-stage renal disease. *Health Serv Res* 1989;24:555–578.
164. Levin NW, Lazarus JM, Nissenson AR. Maximizing patient benefits with erythropoietin in alfa therapy. National cooperative rHu erythropoietin study in patients with chronic renal failure—an interim report. *Am J Kidney Dis* 1993;22(suppl 1):3S–12S.
165. Campbell A, Converse PE, Rodger WL. *The quality of American life.* New York: Russell Sage Foundation, 1976.
166. Parfrey PS, Vavasour H, Bullock M, Harnett JD, Gault MH. Development of a health questionnaire specific for end-stage renal disease. *Nephron* 1989;52:20–28.
167. Laupacis A, Wong C, Churchill D, and the Canadian erythropoietin study group. The use of generic and specific quality–of–life measures in hemodialysis patients treated with erythropoietin. *Controlled Clin Trials* 1991;12:168S–179S.
168. Park H, Bang WR, Kim SJ, Kim ST, Lee JS, Kim S, Han JS. Quality of life of ESRD patients: development of tool and comparison between transplant and dialysis patients. *Transplant Proc* 1992;24 (4):1435–1437.
169. Gorlen T, Ekeberg O, Abdelnoor M, Enger E, Aarseth HP. Quality of life after kidney transplantation. A 10–22 years follow-up. *Scand J Urol Nephrol* 1993;27:89–92.
170. Juniper EF, Guyatt GH, Epstein RS, Ferrie PJ, Jaeschke R, Hiller TK. Evaluation of impairment of health-related quality of life in asthma: development of a questionnaire for use in clinical trials. *Thorax* 1992;47:76–83.
171. Marks GB, Dunn SM, Woolcock AJ. A scale for the measurement of quality of life in adults with asthma. *J Clin Epidemiol* 1992;45:461–472.
172. Hyland ME, Finnis S, Irvine SH. A scale for assessing quality of life in adult asthma sufferers. *J Psychomat Res* 1991;35:99–110.

173. Creer TL, Wigal JK, Kotses H, McConnaughy K, Winder JA. A life activities questionnaire for adult asthma. *J Asthma* 1992;29:393–399.
174. Townsend M, Feeny DH, Guyatt GH, Seip AE, Dolovich J. Evaluation of the burden of illness for pediatric asthmatic patients and their parents. *Ann Allergy* 1991;67:403–408.
175. Christie MJ, French D, Sowden A, West A. Development of child-centred disease-specific questionnaires for living with asthma. *Psychosomat Med* 1993;55:541–548.
176. Nocon A. Social and emotional impact of childhood asthma. *Arch Dis Child* 1991;66:458–460.
177. Usherwood TP, Scrimgeour A, Barber JH. Questionnaire to measure perceived symptoms and disability in asthma. *Arch Dis Child* 1990;65:779–781.
178. International Rhinitis Management Working Group. International consensus report on the diagnosis and management of rhinitis. *Allergy* 1994;19(suppl):1–34.
179. Bousquet J, Bullinger M, Fayol C, Marquis P, Valentin B, Burtin B. Assessment of quality of life in chronic allergic rhinitis using the SF-36 questionnaire. *J Allergy Clin Immunol* 1994;94:182–188.
180. Juniper EF, Guyatt GH. Development and testing of a new measure of health status for clinical trials in rhinoconjunctivitis. *Clin Exp Allergy* 1991;21:77–83.
181. Juniper EF, Guyatt GH, Ferrie PJ, Griffith LE. Measuring quality of life in asthma. *Am Rev Respir Dis* 1993;147:832–838.
182. Juniper EF, Guyatt GH, Willan A, Griffith LE. Determining a minimal important change in a disease-specific quality of life questionnaire. *J Clin Epidemiol* 1994;47:81–87.
183. Jaeschke R, Singer J, Guyatt GH. Measurement of health status: ascertaining the minimal clinically important difference. *Controlled Clin Trials* 1989;10:407–415.
184. Marks GB, Dunn SM, Woolcock AJ. An evaluation of an asthma quality of life questionnaire as a measure of change in adults with asthma. *J Clin Epidemiol* 1993;46:1103–1111.
185. Hyland ME. The living with asthma questionnaire. *Respir Med* 1991;85:13–16.
186. Jones PW, Quirk FH, Baveystock CM, Littlejohns P. A self-complete measure of health status for chronic airflow limitation. *Am Rev Respir Dis* 1992;145:1321–1327.
187. Maille AR, Kaptein AA, Konig CJM, Zwinderman AH. Developing a quality of life questionnaire for patients with respiratory illness. *Monaldi Arch Chest Dis* 1994;49:76–78.
188. Hyland ME, Ley A, Fisher DW, Woodward V. Measurement of psychological distress in asthma and asthma management programs. *Br J Clin Psychol* 1995;34:601–611.
189. Juniper EF, Guyatt GH, Feeny DH, Ferrie PJ, Griffith LE, Townsend M. Measuring quality of life in children with asthma. *J Allergy Clin Immunol* 1995;95:226.
190. Creer TL, Wigal JK, Kotses H, Hatala JC, McConnaughty K, Winder JA. A life activities questionnaire for childhood asthma. *J Asthma* 1993;30:467–473.
191. French DJ, Christie MJ, Sowden AJ. The reproducibility of the childhood asthma questionnaires: measures of quality of life for children with asthma aged 4–16 years. *Qual Life Res* 1994;3:213–224.
192. Juniper EF, Guyatt GH, Dolovich J. Assessment of quality of life in adolescents with allergic rhinoconjunctivitis: development and testing of a questionnaire for clinical trials. *J Allergy Clin Immunol* 1994;93:413–423.
193. Juniper EF, Guyatt GH, Andersson B, Ferrie PJ. Comparison of powder and aerosolized budesonide in perennial rhinitis: validation of rhinitis quality of life questionnaire. *Ann Allergy* 1993;70:225–230.
194. Bergner M, Bobbitt RA, Carter W, et al. The Sickness Impact Profile: development and final revision of a health status measure. *Med Care* 1981;12:787–805.
195. Kaplan RM, Bush JW, Berry CC. Health status. Types of validity and the index of well-being. *Health Serv Res* 1976;11:478–507.
196. McSweeny AJ, Creer TL. Health-related quality of life assessment in medical care. In: Bone RC, ed. *Disease-a-Month.* St. Louis: CV Mosby, 1995;16:1–72.
197. McSweeny AJ, Grant I, Heaton RK, et al. Life quality of patients with chronic obstructive pulmonary disease. *Arch Intern Med* 1982;142:473–478.
198. Kaplan RM, Atkins CJ, Timms R. Validity of a quality of well-being scale as an outcome measure in chronic obstructive pulmonary disease. *J Chron Dis* 1984;37:85–95.
199. Guyatt GH, Berman LB, Townsend M, et al: A measure of quality of life for clinical trials in chronic lung disease. *Thorax* 1987;42:773–778.
200. Cottrell JJ, Paul C, Ferson S. Quality of life measures in COPD patients: how do they compare? *Am Rev Respir Dis* 1992;145(suppl):A767.
201. Jones PW, Baveystock CM, Littlejohns P. Relationships between general health measured with the Sickness Impact Profile and respiratory symptoms, physiological measures, and mood in patients with chronic airflow limitation. *Am Rev Respir Dis* 1989;140:1538–1543.

202. Jones PW, Quirk FH, Baveystock CM. The St. George's Respiratory Questionnaire. *Respir Med* 1991;85(suppl B):25–31.
203. Jones PW, Quirk FH, Baveystock CM, et al. A self-completed measure of health status for chronic airflow limitation. *Am Rev Respir Dis* 1992;145:1321–1327.
204. Maille AR, Koning CJM, Kaptein AA. Developing a quality of life questionnaire for patients with respiratory illness. *Qual Life Newslet* 1993;6:5.
205. Maille AR, Kaptein AA, Koning CJM, et al. Developing a quality of life questionnaire for patients with respiratory illness. *Monaldi Arch Chest Dis* 1994;49:76–78.
206. Guyatt GH, Townsend M, Berman LB, et al. Quality of life in patients with chronic airflow obstruction. *Br J Dis Chest* 1987;81:45–54.
207. Cox NJM, Hendricks JCM, Dijkhuizen R, et al. Usefulness of a medicopsychological questionnaire for lung patients. *Int J Rehabil Res* 1991;14:267–272.
208. Dardes N, Chiappini MG, Moscatelli B, et al. Quality of life of COPD patients treated by long-term oxygen. *Lung* 1990;168(suppl):789–793.
209. Hanson EI. Effects of chronic lung disease on life in general and sexuality: perceptions of adult patients. *Heart Lung* 1982;11:435–441.
210. Kinsman RA, Yaroush RA, Fernandez E, et al. Symptoms and experiences in chronic bronchitis and emphysema. *Chest* 1983;83:755–761.
211. Moody L, McCormick K, Williams A. Disease and symptom severity, functional status, and quality of life in chronic bronchitis and emphysema. *J Behav Med* 1990;13:297–306.
212. Moody L, McCormick K, Williams A. Psychophysiologic correlates of quality of life in chronic bronchitis and emphysema. *West J Nurs Res* 1991;13:337–352.
213. Sexton DL, Monro BH. Living with a chronic illness: the experience of women with chronic obstructive pulmonary disease (COPD). *West J Nurs Res* 1988;10:26–44.
214. Chapman JM, Reeder LG, Massey FJ. The relationship of stress, tranquilizers and serum cholesterol levels in a sample population under study for coronary heart disease. *Am J Epidemiol* 1966;83: 537–547.
215. Neugarten B, Havinghurst R, Tobin S. The measurement of life satisfaction. *J Gerontol* 1961;16: 134–143.
216. Sexton DL, Monro BH. Impact of a husband's chronic illness (COPD) on the spouse's life. *Res Nurs Health* 1985;8:83–90.
217. Jacobson AM, de Groot M, Samson JA. The evaluation of two measures of quality of life in patients with type I and type II diabetes. *Diabetes Care* 1994;17:267–274.
218. Parkerson GR, Connis RT, Broadhead WE, et al. Disease-specific versus generic measurement of health-related quality of life in insulin-dependent diabetic patients. *Med Care* 1993;31:629–639.
219. Nerenz DR, Repasky DP, Whitehouse FW, Kahkonen DM. Ongoing assessment of health status in patients with diabetes mellitus. *Med Care* 1992;30(5 suppl):MS112–MS123.
220. Bardsley MJ, Astell S, McCallum A, Home PD. The performance of three measures of health status in an outpatient diabetic population. *Diabetic Med* 1993;10:619–626.
221. The DCCT Research Group. Reliability and validity of a Diabetes Quality of Life Measure (DHRQOL) for the Diabetes Control and Complications Trial (DCCT). *Diabetes Care* 1988;11(9): 725–732.
222. The Diabetes Control and Complications Trial Research Group. The effect of intensive treatment of diabetes on the development and progression of long-term complications in insulin-dependent diabetes mellitus. *N Engl J Med* 1993;329:977–986.
223. Anderson RM, Donnelly MB, Dedrick RF. Measuring the attitudes of patients towards diabetes and its treatment. *Patient Educ Counsel* 1990;16:231–245.
224. Hanestad BR, Hornquist JO, Albrektsen G. Self-assessed quality of life and metabolic control in persons with insulin-dependent diabetes mellitus (IDDM). *Scand J Soc Med* 1991;19(1):57–65.
225. Classification of the rheumatic diseases. In: Schumacher HR, ed. *Primer on the rheumatic diseases.* Atlanta, GA: Arthritis Foundation, 1993:81–83.
226. Tugwell P, Bombardier C, Buchanon WW, Goldsmith CH, Grace E. The MACTAR Questionnaire— an individualized functional priority approach for assessing improvement in physical disability in clinical trials in rheumatoid arthritis. *J Rheumatol* 1987;14:446–451.
227. Helewa A, Goldsmith CH, Smyth HA. Independent measurement of functional capacity in rheumatoid arthritis. *J Rheumatol* 1982;9:794–797.
228. Pincus T, Summey JA, Soraci SA Jr, Wallston KA, Hummon NP. Assessment of patient satisfaction in activities of daily living using a modified Stanford Health Assessment Questionnaire. *Arthritis Rheum* 1983;26:1346–1353.

229. Weinblatt ME, Kaplan H, Germain BF, Merriman RC, Solomon SD, Wall B, Anderson L, Block S, Irby R, Wolfe F, et al. Low dose methotrexate compared with auranofin in adult rheumatoid arthritis. A thirty-six week, double-blind trial. *Arthritis Rheum* 1990;33:330–338.

230. Pincus T, Callahan LF, Sale WG, Brooks AL, Payne LE, Vaughn WK. Severe functional declines, work disability, and increased mortality in seventy-five rheumatoid arthritis patients studied over nine years. *Arthritis Rheum* 1984;27:864–872.

231. Pincus T, Brooks RH, Callahan LF. Prediction of long-term mortality in patients with rheumatoid arthritis according to simple questionnaire and joint count measures. *Ann Intern Med* 1994;120:26–34.

232. Meenan RF, Mason JH, Anderson JJ, Guccione AA, Kazis LE. AIMS2: the content and properties of a revised and expanded arthritis impact measurement scales health status questionnaire. *Arthritis Rheum* 1992;35(1):1–10.

233. Potts MK, Brandt KD. Evidence of the validity of the arthritis impact measurement scales. *Arthritis Rheum* 1987;30(1):93–96.

234. Wallston KA, Brown GK, Stein MJ, Dobbins CJ. Comparing the short and long versions of the Arthritis Impact Measurement Scales. *J Rheumatol* 1989;16:1105–1109.

235. Bellamy N. Pain assessment in osteoarthritis: experience with the WOMAC osteoarthritis index. *Semin Arthritis Rheumatol* 1989;18:14–17.

236. Bellamy N, Buchanan W. A preliminary evaluation of the dimensionality and clinical importance of pain and disability in osteoarthritis of the hip and knee. *Clin Rheumatol* 1986;5:231–241.

237. Bellamy N, Buchanan W, Goldsmith C, Campbell J, Stitt L. Validation Study of WOMAC: a health status instrument for measuring clinically important patient relevant outcomes to anti-rheumatic drug therapy in patients with osteoarthritis of the hip or knee. *J Rheumatol* 1988;15:1833–1840.

238. Wright J, Rudicel S, Feinstein A. Asking patients what they want. *J Bone Joint Surg* 1994;76B:229–230.

239. Daltroy LH, Cats-Baril WL, Katz JN, Fossel AH, Liang MH. North American Spine Society back pain questionnaire reliability and validity study. *Spine* 1996;21:741–745.

240. Roland M, Morris R. 1982 Volvo Award in Clinical Science. A study of the natural history of back pain. Part I. Development of a reliable and sensitive measure of disability in low-back pain. *Spine* 1983;8:141–144.

241. Feldman AB, Haley SM, Coryell J. Concurrent and construct validity of the pediatric evaluation of disability inventory. *Phys Ther* 1990;70:602–610.

242. Lovell DJ, Howe S, Shear E, Hartner S, McGirr G, Schulte M, Levinson J. Development of a disability measurement tool for juvenile rheumatoid arthritis. The Juvenile Arthritis Functional Assessment Scale. *Arthritis Rheum* 1989;32:1390–1395.

243. Howe S, Levinson J, Shear E, Hartner S, McGirr G, Schulte M, Lovell D. Development of a disability measurement tool for juvenile rheumatoid arthritis. The juvenile arthritis functional assessment report for children and their parents. *Arthritis Rheum* 1991;34:873–879.

244. Liang MH, Larson MG, Cullen KE, Schwartz JA. Comparative measurement efficiency and sensitivity of five health status instruments for arthritis research. *Arthritis Rheum* 1985;28:542–547.

245. Katz JN, Larson MG, Phillips CB, Fossel AH, Liang MH. Comparative measurement sensitivity of short and longer health status measures. *Med Care* 1992;30:917–925.

6 / Utilities and Outcomes

INCORPORATING TRADE-OFFS
IN QUALITY OF LIFE ASSESSMENT

Quality of life is an important factor in the evaluation of many medical therapies and treatment decisions, as is information on survival benefits (or risks) and economic costs. These data may be difficult to interpret when trade-offs arise between aspects of quality of life, or between overall quality of life and other outcomes. In such cases, the relative value of treatment benefits versus costs (both economic and otherwise) are important in decision making. Some of the approaches to understanding the relative value of treatments employ formal methodologies, such as decision analysis (1), to systematically incorporate large amounts of information into the trade-off assessment. In cases where a formal analysis is conducted, information from clinical trials may assist in providing more accurate estimates of risks or probabilities for different health outcomes. Decision analysis methods may be used to evaluate the specific information obtained. Alternatively, the components of quality of life domains may be combined within the trial itself and assessed as global quality of life scores or other combined measures (e.g., subscales). The utility of different outcomes is implicit in these combined scores. Approaches that allow the use of individual preferences to be applied to data from clinical trials are also presented.

Trade-offs Between Aspects of Quality of Life

Quality of life outcomes may be critical in many treatment choices, dominating survival or financial issues. For some situations, the impact of treatment on quality of life may be clear-cut with a benefit of one treatment over another in terms of each aspect of quality of life measured. More often, however, each therapy will be associated with some advantages and some disadvantages. How the components of quality of life are then combined is very important in determining which approach appears to be preferred. Although it is often desirable to collapse these data into a single summary measure to facilitate treatment comparisons, it can be difficult or even inappropriate to do so without additional information on the subjective importance that patients place on the various components. Figure 6.1 presents a framework for the development and validation of utility measures.

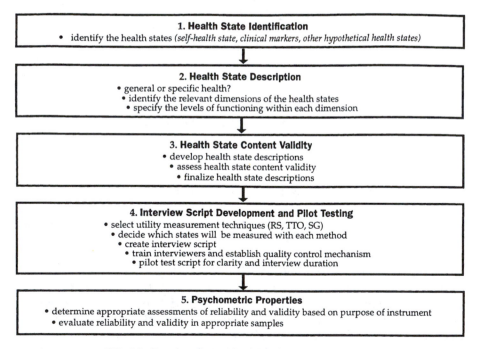

FIG. 6.1. Development and validation of utility measures.

Trade-offs Between Quality of Life and Quantity of Life

Quality and quantity of life are clearly both important treatment outcomes, and ideally a treatment should enhance the two. Sometimes treatment may provide gains in survival at the expense of worse quality of life due to side effects or as a consequence of major surgery. For example, adjuvant chemotherapy can result in modest survival gains (e.g., 10% increase in the 5-year survival rate for pre-menopausal patients with node positive breast cancer) (2) while inducing a number of unpleasant side effects such as nausea, vomiting, and hair loss. Here, patients opting to have chemotherapy should feel that the increased chance for longer survival justifies the toxicity of treatment. In contrast, some treatment decisions may be dominated by concerns to improve quality of life rather than survival.

Early Versus Later Treatment Benefits and Costs

In addition to weighing up the relative importance of different outcomes, the timing of benefits and costs may also be critical in treatment choice. A therapy that improves life expectancy or 5-year survival rates will not necessarily be preferred if the immediate mortality risk is too high, such as with some radical surgery with intraoperative risk. A smoking cessation intervention may ultimately lead to substantial improvements in future quality of life and survival but at the expense of more immediate unpleasant withdrawal symptoms. The poor compliance rates in some programs are consistent with people placing more value on their immediate well-being relative to future health benefits. People tend to discount the value of future outcomes, in part because preferences for treatment outcomes may be affected by the timing of benefits and costs including the concepts of risk-aversion, time preference, and decreasing marginal value (3). Therefore, it may be important that future health benefits are discounted at an appropriate rate or, even better, that utilities on treatment outcomes incorporate patient preferences based on the timing of those outcomes.

Trade-offs Between Treatment Benefits and Their Financial Costs

For many treatment decisions, after consideration of the above trade-offs, there may be a clear net clinical benefit for one treatment over the other for the individual patient. Yet difficult decisions may still need to be made from the community perspective as to which health care programs to finance in order to best use limited health care resources. If the health gain for individual patients is small and at considerable expense to health care resources, then alternative uses of the funds may provide greater health benefit to the community. Health care policy makers must therefore weigh up the therapeutic benefits of a treatment against its economic cost to ensure that health care resources are used efficiently. Trade-offs between treatment efficacy and their financial cost are unavoidable and must be assessed.

General Approaches in Assessing Trade-offs

Three general steps are suggested to optimally assess trade-offs involving quality of life outcomes in clinical trials. First, accurate and detailed information on quality of life and other treatment outcomes should be collected. Second, the relative importance of these outcomes, from the patient's perspective, must be assessed so that a treatment recommendation can be made. Third, the robustness of such recommendations to individual patient preferences or values should be subjected to a sensitivity or threshold analysis.

Evaluating the Importance of Benefits and Costs

In weighing up the relative benefits and costs of each treatment, a value judgment is needed on the importance of each outcome. This may be undertaken *implicitly* by the decision maker by considering all relevant information simultaneously and subconsciously applying value judgments to trade-offs in the different outcomes. However, trade-off evaluations quickly become an overwhelming task to handle implicitly when the volume of information that needs to be considered is large, when there are uncertainties relating to benefits, costs or their relative importance, and/or when the evaluation incorporates the preferences of more than one individual. In these situations it is often desirable to estimate the relative importance of the separate components of an assessment along a value or utility scale and combine these data more *explicitly* using methods such as decision analysis.

Value and Utility Scales

The distinction between value and utility scales is subtle, though important. *Value* scales can be thought of as reflecting preference for certain or sure outcomes, whereas *utility* scales reflect strength of preference of uncertain outcomes. The utility of 5 years' symptom-free survival may differ, for example, from the utility of an uncertain outcome that on average results in the same 5 years symptom-free survival, but with some probability of a longer or shorter time. Utility assessments provide a means of comparing the importance of a therapy that offers a good chance of a mediocre outcome and a therapy that offers a slim chance of an especially valued outcome.

Combining Outcome Data

Two broad strategies can be adopted when combining outcomes and incorporating trade-offs in quality of life assessment. The first involves asking individuals themselves to make a trade-off evaluation based on the information for the separate component outcomes. The second involves combining data on quality of life and/or other outcomes from a clinical trial to form a summary measure that reflects averaged or group preferences.

SPECIFIC APPROACHES TO TRADE-OFF EVALUATIONS

Single Direct Measures

The simplest way of assessing trade-offs between aspects of quality of life is to ask individuals to rate the value or utility of their overall quality of life as a single measure. Here patients implicitly weigh up the relative importance of different aspects of quality of life. The average quality of life score for the trial will then reflect averaged individual, or group, preferences. An example of a value-based global quality of life measure is the GLQ-Uniscale (4), on which the patients rate their quality of life on a single linear analog scale. An example of a utility-based global quality of life measure is the standard gamble (5), where the patients rate their current quality of life against taking a gamble with a chance of full health and a risk of death. The utility assigned to their overall quality of life is obtained by varying the probabilities of the gamble until it is considered of equivalent value to present quality of life. The time trade-off method, devised by Torrance et al. (6), is a simpler alternative to the standard gamble and produces scores that are similar to, but usually lower than, those elicited using standard gambles (7,8). These questions ask for the shorter time period in full health considered equivalent to a longer period of survival with current quality of life. Time trade-off questions are a theoretically less attractive means of assessing utility than standard gamble questions, but in practice are generally easier to administer. Standard gamble questions are more complicated and need to be administered in a face-to-face interview. In contrast, even self-administered time trade-off questions are feasible. However, irrespective of whether these three methods provide a true utility measure or not, they each enable any trade-offs between different components of quality of life to be reflected in the summary measure.

Combined Measures

A disadvantage of single-item quality of life assessments, be they value- or utility-based, is that they provide no descriptive information on the components comprising quality of life. This makes it more difficult to explicitly state what trade-offs are involved (if any) in the summary measure and whether there is a need to tailor treatment choice to individual preferences. A number of multidimensional instruments with value-based (9,10) and (quasi) utility-based scoring systems (11–13) exist. One problem common to several of these instruments is that their scoring systems are based on the preferences of population samples, and so do not necessarily reflect the preferences of the patient.

If both a multidimensional instrument and a simple overall quality of life measure are administered to the same group of subjects, it is possible to produce a self-calibrating measure of overall quality of life, where the relationship between the dimensions of quality of life is estimated by linear regression and the resulting weights are applied to calculate an overall score. The effect of this is to produce a single score that measures the same overall quality of life as the original unidimensional measure but has substantially less test–retest variability due to the incorporation of information from the multidimensional questionnaire. The weights derived by this procedure also indicate the relative importance of quality of life dimensions and it is possible to calculate the extent to which the unidimensional measure contains information from unmeasured dimensions of quality of life.

SENSITIVITY AND THRESHOLD ANALYSIS

Many of the methods discussed so far for evaluating trade-offs between treatment benefits and costs are based upon the preferences of groups of individuals, that is, on averaged data from clinical trials. This sort of information is important in terms of providing overall treatment recommendations and for making policy decisions. Nevertheless, it is important to realize that group-based preferences do not necessarily reflect the opinions of individual patients faced with a treatment decision. Sensitivity and threshold analyses provide a means of exploring the impact of a range of different perspectives on treatment decisions or evaluations (14). If conclusions are especially sensitive to differences in individual patient preferences then the universal adoption of a therapy cannot be recommended. Consequently, the threshold analysis can help identify and simplify what information on patient preferences is needed for treatment recommendations.

UTILITY MEASUREMENT OF HRQOL

Utility, a concept used in economics and decision analysis, refers to the level of satisfaction or enjoyment experienced by the consumer of the good or service. Because many investigators are unfamiliar with the utility approach to assessing HRQOL, a brief review is provided. In general, economists do not attempt to measure utility (the preferences of consumers for various consumption alternatives) directly.

The measurement of cardinal scores for the utility of health states is performed using one of two techniques: standard gamble or time trade-off. In the standard gamble approach (Fig. 6.2), the subject is offered a choice between two alternatives: living in the health state in choice B with certainty or taking a gamble on treatment, choice A, with an uncertain outcome. The most straightforward approach to measurement is to suggest that treatment A leads to perfect health for a defined remaining lifetime with probability p and immediate death with probability $(1 - p)$, and that the health state in choice B also lasts for the same

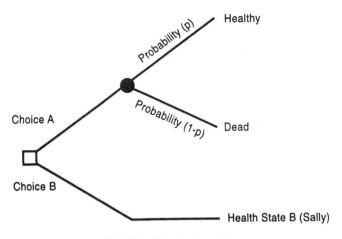

FIG. 6.2. Standard gamble.

defined lifetime. The probability p is then varied until the subject is indifferent between choices A and B. The lower the indifference probability, the greater the risk of death the subject is willing to consider and, thus, the lower the utility of the health state described under choice B. The utility scale is defined with 1.0 as perfect health and 0.0 as death.

Because some respondents have experienced difficulty in understanding probabilities, an alternative technique, time trade-off, has been developed (Fig. 6.3). In this technique the subject is first offered a choice of living for t years in perfect health or t years in some alternative health state that is less desirable (and the one for which the analyst wants the utility score). Obviously the subject will choose perfect health. The interviewer then reduces the period of perfect health, x, in a systematic fashion designed to minimize measurement biases, until the subject is indifferent between the shorter period in perfect health and the longer period in the less desirable state. The time trade-off preference score for the state then equals x/t.

Using current preference-elicitation technology, the cognitive burden of the standard gamble only marginally exceeds that of the time trade-off technique. Although most respondents can readily handle the feeling thermometer, a few (adult) respondents will not be able to handle the standard gamble, because of the need for short-term memory, concentration, and focus. Of those who cannot handle the standard gamble, only a small minority will in fact be able to handle the time trade-off, which requires the same basic cognitive skills.

Standard gamble, time trade-off, and variations on these techniques provide reliable and valid methods for eliciting scores for health-state utilities. The prior use of the feeling thermometer appears to assist respondents in their introspection concerning their preferences for the health states being evaluated. The preference measurement interview assists respondents in their efforts to discover and construct their preferences for health states. The health states to be evaluated may

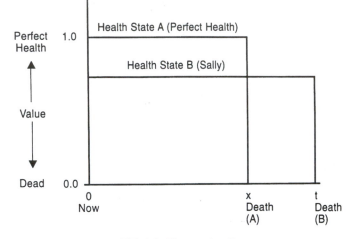

FIG. 6.3. Time trade-off.

include states the respondent has experienced or is now experiencing or has never experienced (hypothetical states). In this regard, the utility approach differs from the other high-related quality of life measures. The utility approach, when it includes hypothetical states, allows the investigator to obtain important information from all patients on how they think they would feel if they experienced some of the infrequent outcomes. Evidence to date shows that evaluations by persons experiencing the state and by others for whom the state is hypothetical usually do not differ substantially (15). If there is a systematic difference it is that persons experiencing the state rate it marginally higher than those who have not experienced it, but this is not as yet conclusive. Thus, the HRQOL of rare or infrequent outcomes may be assessed along with that of the frequent outcomes by combining actual and hypothetical states in the set of outcomes for evaluation.

Given that specific HRQOL instruments have been developed only recently, it is not surprising that few, if any, studies combining dollar cost with these HRQOL measures have appeared in the literature. One can speculate, however, that given the increasing popularity of the specific measures, such studies will be forthcoming. On the other hand, recent pharmacoeconomic guidelines (16–18) stress the usefulness of cost/utility analyses for making broad comparisons and thus may have reduced enthusiasm for using HRQOL as an outcome measure in cost-effectiveness analysis. The advantage in generalizability may, however, come at a cost in clinical sensibility. Clinicians may not readily understand changes in HRQOL as measured on such scales. Thus, while the results of such a cost-effectiveness evaluation may be useful for clinical managers, hospital administrators, and third-party payers, they may not be especially meaningful to health care providers. Furthermore, the approach can provide useful information only if there are no differences in mortality among the relevant treatment alternatives. If there are differences in mortality, then a framework capable of combining mortality and morbidity (such as quality adjusted life-years) is required.

The use of specific and health-profile measures in cost-effectiveness analysis will, however, not always be appropriate. The meaningfulness of cost-effectiveness analysis depends on comparing costs to a relevant and comprehensive measure of outcome or consequences (19). For specific health-profile instruments that do not provide a single score, the meaningfulness of cost-effectiveness analyses that utilize them is dubious. For instruments for which single summary cardinal (interval scale) scores are available, the cost-effectiveness analysis is much more meaningful, but will still fall short of the potential available in cost/utility analysis in which mortality and morbidity effects may be combined.

Combining utility measures of HRQOL with pecuniary measures of cost converts cost-effectiveness analysis into cost/utility analysis. The outcome is a comparison of the cost to the gain in utility expressed as quality-adjusted life-years. At the pragmatic level the approach shares the advantages and disadvantages of combining pecuniary and health-profile measures; the procedure facilitates broad comparisons but comes at the expense of attenuated clinical sensibility.

At a more fundamental methodological level, however, cost/utility analysis has an important advantage with respect to cost-effectiveness studies that employ health-profile or specific HRQOL measures. Both the family of economic evaluation approaches and the utility approach to the measurement of HRQOL are based on the same underlying economic theory The assumptions made in both approaches are consistent. Furthermore, the assumptions are explicit. Thus, the analyst knows precisely what is being assumed about the structure of human preferences. In general, the same cannot be said for psychometrically based measures.

In summary, it makes sense to combine economic evaluations and HRQOL measures in cost-effectiveness and cost/utility studies. Cost estimates summarize important, but incomplete, information on treatment alternatives. HRQOL is frequently the most important outcome. Thus, cost-effectiveness ratios that reflect both sets of information provide a more complete assessment of the implications of treatment options. Specific, health-profile, and utility measures of HRQOL can all be appropriate for use in such cost-effectiveness studies. The utility approach has the advantages of generalizability, its ability to combine mortality and morbidity effects, and its inherent compatibility with pecuniary evaluations.

Pecuniary and HRQOL evaluations complement each other by adding important information about the consequences of various health care interventions. Economic evaluation provides a framework for comparing the costs of care to its effects measured in both pecuniary and nonpecuniary terms. HRQOL measures provide crucial information on the outcomes of the clinical intervention. In this way, the use of HRQOL assessment conforms to an underlying premise in the health and social sciences that health care is provided to improve the welfare of patients and, indirectly, their families. More traditional pecuniary measures, and the more recently developed HRQOL measures, provide a means for quantification of these goals. Such studies provide clinicians with information that is useful in their decisions concerning patient management. The studies also provide third-party payers, regulatory authorities, and others with important information on the costs and consequences, now measured in a more comprehensive fashion by including HRQOL measurement, of various uses of scarce health care resources. The combination of pecuniary and specific and health-profile HRQOL measurement is still in its infancy. Although more fully developed, cost/utility analysis is less than three decades old. HRQOL measurement is rapidly evolving at the conceptual, methodological, and pragmatic levels. It is, however, very likely that the incorporation of pecuniary measures, HRQOL measures, and combinations of the two approaches will become increasingly common. Cost/utility analysis is well suited for these purposes.

HEALTH UTILITIES INDEX

The Health Utilities Index (HUI) is a generic approach to the measurement of health status and assessment of HRQOL. The HUI provides a comprehensive framework within which to measure health status and calculate HRQOL scores. The HUI is comprised of two complementary components. The first component is a multiattribute health status classification system that is used to describe health status. The second component is a multiattribute utility function that is used to value health status as measured within the corresponding multiattribute health status classification system.

In the context of assessing health status, the HUI is conceptually similar to a number of traditional multidimensional systems. In the context of the valuation of health status, however, the HUI, by exploiting multiattribute utility theory, differs importantly from traditional multidimensional systems. In the HUI, the health status of a person at a point in time is assessed in terms of his/her ability to function on each attribute of health status. The ability to function on each attribute is described by levels that vary from severely impaired to normal. The HUI is an example of the generic approach to the assessment of HRQOL (20,21).

Measures of health status are often used for one of three major purposes: discrimination, evaluation, or prediction (20,22). Discriminative measures are used to distinguish differences in health status within and among populations. Evaluative measures focus on the assessment of changes in health status within an individual over time. Predictive measures are used for prognostic purposes. It is not uncommon for an investigator to be interested in more than one of these purposes. Nonetheless, in the context of clinical trials and pharmacoeconomics, evaluative and discriminative applications are usually the most relevant.

Theoretical Foundations of Multiattribute Utility Theory

An important advantage of the multiattribute approach utilized in the HUI is its complementarity with multiattribute utility theory. Multiattribute utility theory provides the intellectual foundation for estimating a scoring function that is used to value health status as described in the multiattribute system. Thus, the basis for the valuation of health status—the source for HRQOL scores—is both explicit and based on a rigorous normative theory. Von Neumann-Morgenstern utility theory (23), first postulated in the 1940s, continues to be the dominant normative paradigm for decision making under uncertainty. In the 1970s, the theory was extended to the class of problems in which the outcomes are described by multiple attributes (24–29). The extension is known as *multiattribute utility theory*. Multiattribute utility theory is the basis for scoring the HUI Mark II and Mark III classification systems.

TYPES OF PREFERENCES

The fundamental underlying principle for the HUI is that individuals have preferences for alternative health outcomes, they can express them, and their preferences should count. Preferences may be ordinal or cardinal. Ordinal preferences are simply a rank order of alternative health outcomes from most preferred to least preferred. Cardinal preferences are interval scale measurements such that the numbers associated with the health outcomes represent the strength of preference for the outcome. More precisely, because an interval scale is unique up to a positive linear transformation (e.g., temperature in degrees Celsius), ratios have no meaning whereas intervals do. For example, if on an interval scale of preference A = 0.60, B = 0.30, and C = 0.15, it is inappropriate to state that A is twice as preferred as B, but it is appropriate to state that the difference in preference between A and B is twice as much as the difference between B and C.

There are two types of cardinal preferences: values and utilities. Values are cardinal preferences measured under certainty and for use in situations of certainty. That is, there are no probabilities involved in performing the measurement and there are no probabilities in the problem to which the resulting scores are applied. Value measurements are based on value theory (30,31). In contrast, utilities are preferences measured under uncertainty, and for use in problems with uncertainty. Utility measurements are founded on von Neumann-Morgenstern (23) utility theory. Values and utilities for health states differ empirically. Because risk (uncertainty) is a factor in the measurement of utilities but not values, the difference can be attributed to the risk attitudes of the respondents. In general, the utility score for a health state exceeds the value score for the same health state (32–35).

APPLICATIONS OF PREFERENCE SCORES

Preference scores are widely used as quality weights for quality adjusting life-years in undertaking cost-effectiveness analyses or cost/utility analyses. There are a number of reasons why utilities are appropriate scores for use as quality weights in these applications. The weights should be based on individuals' preferences and utilities measure preferences. Future health is uncertain and utilities are preferences measured under conditions of uncertainty. Utility measurements are based on an explicit, well-established theory and measurement methodology, so the resulting utility scores have a clear unambiguous interpretation.

Utility scores can also be used as quality weights for calculating health expectancy in population health studies. Health expectancy represents a relatively new concept for measuring, monitoring, and comparing the health of populations (32). An age- and sex-adjusted health expectancy table captures, in an integrated way, both the quantity of life (life expectancy) and the quality of life of the population. Unfortunately, terminology in this field has not yet been standardized. Health expectancy is also called quality-adjusted life expectancy, health-adjusted life expectancy (36), disability-adjusted life expectancy, and years of healthy life. All of these concepts are identical; all use quality weights to adjust life-years in calculating life expectancy results.

The HUI provides a comprehensive but compact method for describing health status in both clinical studies and population health surveys. Thus, the HUI allows for comparison of clinical populations and population norms. The HUI provides detail on an attribute-by-attribute basis and the ability to represent combinations of problems with varying levels of severity. The HUI health status classification approach can be used serially in the context of clinical trials as a method for assessing health status at points in time and changes in health status over time. It is a generic approach to assessing health status. In general, its use should be supplemented with specific measures (20). The HUI system is also an efficient method of determining a general public-based utility score for a health outcome or for the health status of an individual. The utility score is based on von Neumann-Morgenstern utility theory, and in particular, on the extension into multiattribute utility theory. The HUI utility scores have three related uses: in clinical populations to provide a single summary measure of HRQOL, in cost/utility analyses as quality weights in calculating quality-adjusted life-years, and in population health studies as quality weights for calculating quality-adjusted life expectancy and a population health index.

MEASURING HEALTH STATE PREFERENCES AND UTILITIES

HRQOL, Health State Preferences and Utility Measurement

HRQOL measures are self- or interviewer-administered questionnaires about health, functional status, and quality of life. This type of measure is complementary to physician and laboratory assessments of health status, disease activity, and improvement following a clinical or health care intervention. A taxonomy has been derived that identifies three classes of HRQOL measures, namely generic health indices and profiles, specific measures (disease, condition, population), and preference-based measures (37,38). Utility measurement is a preference-based approach.

Health state preferences and utility measures differ from generic and specific measures in important ways. First, preference-based measures assess the preferences of individuals for alternative health states or outcomes, whereas generic and disease-specific HRQOL approaches concentrate on identifying the presence, absence, severity, frequency, and/or duration of specific symptoms, impairments, or disabilities. Second, preference-based measures provide a comprehensive measure of HRQOL in which the respondent combines the positive and negative dimensions of a particular health state into a single number. This number reflects the trade-off, that is, it represents the net effect of the positive and negative aspects of the health state as seen by the respondent. Third, in contrast to specific HRQOL measures, preference-based measures provide a common unit of analysis and thereby allow the outcomes of different types of programs to be compared on the same scale.

Measurement of Health State Preferences and Utilities

Preference and utility measurement is concerned with quantifying preferences for health states or outcomes. As will be described in the next section, the measurement process consists of a set of health state descriptions that are usually presented to respondents by a trained interviewer in a structured interview. The interview questions are constructed using specialized preference measurement techniques that include the standard gamble, time trade-off, and rating scale. Respondents can be asked about their own self-health state and about other hypothetical health states that they may or may not have experienced in the past. The feasibility, reliability, and validity of preference and utility measurement has been shown in a range of chronic diseases (39). Most recently, we have applied utility measures to assess mental health states.

Traditionally, the preference or utility scale in health extends from 1, perfect health, to 0, death, and possibly beyond. The objective of the measurement process is to determine the score (desirability or preference) for specific health states (or outcomes) on this scale. Several investigators have reported health states that are considered to be worse than death. However, the appropriate method of scaling for these states is not yet established (40–42).

Preference and utility measures are not "off the shelf" HRQOL instruments like generic and specific measures. Rather, the approach consists of a set of measurement techniques that can be applied by the researcher to develop a preference or utility questionnaire. The use of utility measures has increased steadily over the past two decades. Utility measures have been developed to assess acute and chronic physical health states and mental health states. However, despite the growing use only a few researchers will be fortunate enough to find a preexisting utility instrument that is appropriate for their research purposes. Instead they will need to develop their own instrument using the measurement techniques available. This chapter should assist those who wish to embark on this task.

Uses of Utility Measures

Utility measures can be used in at least four types of evaluations. First, they can be used in studies of clinical and health care interventions to determine the incremental gain in utility due to the experimental treatment compared with no treatment or the standard treatment. These results can be used to draw conclusions about the gain in HRQOL associated with the intervention under study. Second, utility measures can be applied in economic evaluations to analyze the cost/utility of alternative programs and to make recommendations regarding the allocation of resources. In these types of studies, utility weights are applied to calculate the quality-adjusted life-years gained as a result of the intervention or program under study. Third, utility measures are needed for medical decision-making models that explore possible courses of action and express the associated outcomes in terms of probability of occurrence and utility. Finally, utility measures can be used as a method of combining morbidity and mortality in the measurement and monitoring of population health (43).

Substantial experience with the use of rating scale, time trade-off, and standard gamble preference measurement techniques has been gained in a wide variety of disease populations and types of evaluations. The techniques are acceptable to respondents and comprehension appears to be good. Although most investigators will need to develop their own instrument, many will find an application in the literature relevant to their research question and patient population. Clinical marker health states should aid in interpreting the clinical importance of instrument scores.

CHOOSING A HEALTH PROFILE (DESCRIPTIVE) AND/OR A PATIENT-PREFERENCE (UTILITY) MEASURE FOR A CLINICAL TRIAL

The selection of either a health profile or a patient-preference questionnaire for a clinical trial depends upon the information needs of the particular audience(s) to whom the research is directed. In addition, selection and use of an instrument depends on the focus of the research, specifically on whether the focus is on the individual patient or on society as a whole. Table 6.1 summarizes the main concepts in nine standard generic approaches for collecting information to estimate years of healthy life.

Health profile measures group questions reflective of *individual* patient and provider disease concerns and/or intervention effects into separate domains or

TABLE 6.1 *Principal concepts of health-related quality of life contained in existent instruments for assessing years of healthy life*

Concept	Disability distress ratio	EuroQol	15D	Health Utility Index Mark I	Health Utility Index Mark II	Health Utility Index Mark III	Index of Health-Related QOL	HP2000 Years of Healthy Life	Quality of Well-Being Scale
Health perceptions			**					**	
Social function									
Social relations		**		**			**		**
Usual social role		**		**			**		
Intimacy/sexual							**		
Function									
Communication/speech			**		**				
Mental function			**		**	**	**		
Cognitive function						**			
Emotional function		**		**			**		
Mood/feelings									
Physical function						**			**
Mobility	**	**	**	**	**	**	**		**
Physical activity	**			**		**	**		
Self-care		**	**						
Impairment									
Sensory function/loss			**		**	**	**	**	
Symptoms/impairments	**	**		**	**	**	**		

dimensions of patient function and satisfaction. These descriptive questionnaires provide disaggregated measures of changes in patient functional status and satisfaction attributable to the intervention—throughout this chapter, a pharmacologic drug(s)—being assessed. In contrast, where decisions for groups of patients are required for program administrators, health policy makers, and regulators, the focus is on *society* as a whole and the societal allocation of health care resources. In this case, preference-weighted measures, which assign a single aggregated score for changes in health status based on patient relative preferences, allow comparison of the impact of the drug on HRQOL to other treatments for the same condition and/or to other treatments for different conditions.

Health Profile Measures for Physicians and Patients

A new pharmacologic treatment will be evaluated within a clinical trial, and results from the trial will determine whether a physician recommends its use to a patient to control or eliminate the particular medical condition. Because information about the intervention's impact upon the individual patient will be used by both clinicians and patients to make a decision regarding its use, there is nothing more relevant to making the decision than the patient's own quality of life assessment (44). Circumstances such as these, involving physician and patient decision making, favor use of health profile measures because they reflect the individual patient's multidimensional, disaggregated concerns exclusively, that is, without consideration of the preferences of others. This situation permits each individual patient to weight each dimension separately.

Preference-Weighted Measures for Program Administrators and Health Policy Makers

Patient-preference (utility-weighted) measures differ from health profile measures in their intended approach and utilization. Health profile measures are, for the most part, developed by psychometricians to measure areas of behavior, function, or experience; neither the individual questions nor the domains are weighted. The importance that a patient may attach to a specific dimension(s) is considered relevant only insofar as its impact upon that desired construct. The result is that each domain's score must be interpreted individually; a five-point change in one domain does not necessarily mean the same thing in another domain. Decision makers who require a single summary score of the net change in HRQOL—e.g., HRQOL treatment gains minus HRQOL side-effect burdens—would find interpreting health profiles difficult.

Utility measures of quality of life are derived from economic and decision theory and reflect the preferences of groups of persons for particular treatment outcomes and disease states (45,46). These types of questionnaires incorporate preference measurements where HRQOL is summarized as a single number along a continuum that extends from death (0.0) to optimal health (1.0). The preference values for states of health (often called "utilities") reflect both the health status and the value of that status to the patient. Since changes in health status are captured in a single number, the effect is unambiguous and more easily interpretable to program administrators, health policy makers, and others whose primary focus is society as a whole.

Although preference-weighted measures are useful for determining if patients improve overall, they do not reveal in which domains the improvement or deterioration occurs. Essentially, the measures lack the ability to distinguish specific effects upon quality of life and may have limited use in the evaluation of specific treatment effects over time. Another reason to consider a preference-weighted measure for a clinical study is that the preference values derived can be combined with survival data to estimate the quality-adjusted life-years (QALYs) gained by treatment. Once determined, an economic evaluation comparing treatments in terms of their cost per QALY gained is one form of cost/utility analysis that will be useful to conduct for the societal decision-making audience (47).

An example of this type of health policy initiative occurred recently in the state of Oregon, where, in an attempt to ensure access to basic health care, the state's government adopted a priority-setting process based upon cost and outcome of all health services delivered by the state under its Medicaid health insurance program. Outcomes were evaluated using a set of health and functional states described by the Quality of Well-Being Scale. Panels of physicians were consulted to establish norms from the literature and clinical experience (48). Although this initial experiment was generally considered a failure—for technical rather than conceptual reasons—further attempts by policy makers to employ patient-weighted measures within the public policy process are likely once methods by which utilities are determined are improved.

League tables have been created to rank interventions in terms of their cost per quality-adjusted life-year. Dissimilar interventions can thus be compared using a common framework, e.g., value for money. Gudex (49), for example, estimated that given a life expectancy of 10 years and a 4% discount rate, the cost per QALY for a kidney transplant would be £1,342 ($2,300) but only £599 ($950) for a shoulder joint replacement. Using league tables, administrators are thus able to select between programs competing for resources on the basis of a synthesis of cost and health benefit. The attractiveness of league tables notwithstanding, however, a lack of data on many interventions, ethical objections to the use of QALYs, and unresolved methodological controversies with respect to cost-effectiveness analysis has checked their widespread acceptance by societal decision makers.

APPLICATIONS OF HEALTH STATUS ASSESSMENT TO HEALTH POLICY

Most people look to health policy decision makers at the national level to help decide how to make health expenditures reap more benefits. Increasingly, decision makers, providers, patients, and the public ask that every additional expenditure be justified according to expected outcomes. Health decision making has never been more important, whether to reduce inefficiency, eliminate ineffective medical procedures, increase competition, improve quality, change reimbursement formulas, or ration services.

Health policy is largely shaped by the way in which resources are distributed to competing programs based on anticipated benefits, even though most health policy decisions have not been made using an explicit set of economic and sociopolitical criteria (50). The measurement of anticipated benefits associated with health care is the logic for using estimates of costs and benefits of different health care interventions in deciding which alternatives to fund. Sometimes this information is derived from clinical trials, and hence, the importance of including this issue.

Health Status as the Outcome

Health and quality of life outcomes can be used to measure the benefits of health expenditures and to assess the structure and process of health care delivery, as the most relevant and comprehensive outcome measure for comparing costs. HRQOL, in this discussion, is defined as the *value assigned to duration of life* as modified by impairments, functional states, perceptions, and social opportunities that are influenced by disease, injury, treatment, or policy (50). Because HRQOL incorporates social values, life expectancy, and a comprehensive description of health, it addresses the trade-off between how *long* people live and how *well* they live. HRQOL can be used as an indicator of both the process of care and the structure of health.

Health Resource Allocation Strategy

Quantity of health is the expected duration of survival or life expectancy of a population, as influenced by mortality and health status. Expected duration of life depends on prognosis or course of illness and wellness across time. Assigning preferences to health states permits different domains of HRQOL to be combined with prognosis into a single index called *years of healthy life*. Years of healthy life can be calculated by adjusting the expected duration of survival by the point-in-time estimate of HRQOL (51).

Ranking Costs and Outcomes

The ranking of costs and outcomes ratios should be done using marginal estimates of both costs and health outcomes to permit policy makers to deal with allocation decisions that address not only whether an intervention should be funded but also those decisions that consider the extent, intensity, or how much of a particular intervention should be funded. In practice, marginal data are rarely available and analysts make do with information about average costs and outcomes. Care must be exercised in interpreting the information in composite league tables that rank interventions using different methods for estimating costs and outcomes. These differences may mean that the ratios are not comparable even though they all reflect the cost per year of healthy life gained (52).

USING DECISION-ANALYSIS APPROACHES TO INTEGRATE QOL AND COST DATA IN DRUG THERAPY SELECTION

Weinstein and Fineberg (53) define decision analysis as "a systematic approach to decision making under conditions of uncertainty." Decision analysis is an approach that is explicit, quantitative, and prescriptive. It is explicit in that it forces the decision maker to separate the logical structure into its component parts so they can be analyzed individually then recombined systematically to suggest a decision. It is quantitative in that the decision maker is compelled to be precise about values placed on outcomes. Finally, it is prescriptive in that it aids in deciding what a person should do under a given set of circumstances. The basic steps in decision analysis include identifying and bounding the decision problem, structuring the decision problem over time, characterizing the information needed to fill in the structure, and then choosing the preferred course of action (54).

Mechanisms that are being utilized and published in the health care literature include decision analysis and multiattribute utility theory. Decision trees (as described in Chapter 7) may be considered to be the most familiar framework for decision analyses. The mathematics along a "branch" in decision trees can be converted to rows in a spreadsheet (55–57). Multiattribute utility theory is a procedure for identifying, characterizing, and comparing the variables that may affect a decision. Multiattribute utility theory has been used for years to analyze managerial and policy decisions and it is now being seen in health care publications. In his paper on decision making for selecting calcium-channel blockers, Schumacher (58) elaborates on a ten-step process:

1. Determine the viewpoint of the decision makers.
2. Identify the decision alternative.
3. Identify the attributes to be evaluated.
4. Identify the factors used to evaluate the attributes.
5. Establish a utility scale to evaluate each attribute (e.g., 0–100).
6. Transform the values from each factor to scores on the utility scale.
7. Determine the relative weight of each attribute and factor.
8. Calculate the total utility score for each decision alternative.
9. Determine which alternative has the greatest utility score.
10. Perform a sensitivity analysis.

Using decision analysis for formulary evaluation of third-generation cephalo-sporins, Cano and Fujita (59) have warned that drug class reviews without the benefit of the systematization of decision support are at greater risk for subjec-tivity, hastiness, and emotional and often ill-advised decision making (even in the face of well-established pharmacy and therapeutics committees). Their pre-sentation of a multitiered decision-analysis approach includes the following:

1. Identify and establish boundaries of the decision problem
   a. Select drugs for formulary review
   b. Establish evaluation criteria
   c. Collect data (clinical and financial)
2. Structure the decision problem
   a. Assign weights to the evaluation criteria
   b. Agree to select the two top-ranking agents
3. Characterize the information needed to fill in the cells
   a. Record drug-specific data necessary for evaluation
   b. Quantitate each drug's ranking score per criterion and in total
4. Choose the preferred course of action
   a. Apply sensitivity analysis to the data
   b. Recommend formulary inclusion based on total evaluation scores

COMBINING COSTS AND QUALITY OF LIFE

An important part of model building is the listing of key attributes or factors to be compared in the model. The following factors are generally recognized as important in drug therapy evaluations (1):

1. Costs
   A. Direct costs
      a. Acquisition cost of drug
      b. Administration cost
      c. Monitoring cost
      d. Laboratory cost
   B. Indirect costs
      a. Days lost from work for patient
      b. Productivity lost due to premature death
2. Outcomes
   A. Drug cure rate (efficacy rate at controlling symptoms)
   B. Compliance
   C. Adverse reaction rates
   D. Quality of life scores
   E. Years of life gained

The effort required of formulary committees or group purchasing committees to engage in formal decision analysis can often be quite daunting. With the advent of the computer and its ability to help organize information, however, well-documented computer programs are beginning to facilitate these important decisions.

No matter how powerful a computer and its program might be, it is obvious that the emphasis must be on effective decisions that generate good patient outcomes. These decision support systems should help to add more rational decision tools for decision makers or prescribers who in the past may have made their determinations impulsively and irrationally and clouded with personal biases and personal heuristics that often lead to inappropriate patient care.

OUTCOMES RESEARCH AND QUALITY OF CARE

The role and likely contribution of health status information in health policy that should be considered include:

1. Policy-relevant information on the effectiveness of medical care and methods to improve it,
2. Information to inform consumers (patients) regarding choices and their likely impact on outcomes, and
3. Information relevant for policy makers facing issues involving insurance coverage, benefit design, provider organization, and payment reform.

It is clear that no single source of information alone will shape the future of health care. However, shifts in perspectives and values can significantly refocus policy objectives. Giving greater weight to the patient's perspective and values may lead us toward a system that puts increased emphasis on treatments and technologies that improve people's lives, with less emphasis on extending life that lacks substantial quality for the individual.

Definitions

Outcomes research is a comprehensive approach to determining the effects of medical care using a variety of data sources and measurement methods. Outcomes research includes the rigorous determination of what works in medical care and what does not, and how different providers compare with regard to their results on patient outcomes. In outcomes research, a distinction is made between efficacy and effectiveness. *Efficacy* refers to how a treatment works in ideal circumstances, when delivered to selected patients by providers most skilled at providing it. *Effectiveness* refers to how a treatment works under ordinary conditions by the average practitioner for the typical patient.

Quality of care can be defined as the difference between efficacy and effectiveness that can be attributed to care providers. It is necessary to assess the "structure, process, and outcomes" of care.

Structure refers to stable elements that form the basis of the health system, such as the type of facility, administrative organization, and provider qualifications.

Process refers to what happens in the medical interaction and includes the technical and interpersonal skills of the physician and other providers. Process measures compare care delivered with relevant standards.

Outcomes are the measurable events and observations that are presumed to occur, in part, due to the structure and process of medical care.

Health status as defined by Bergner (60) includes at least five dimensions: (a) genetic and inherited characteristics; (b) biochemical, physiologic, and anatomic condition, including impairment of these systems, disease, signs, and symptoms; (c) functional status, which includes performance of the usual activities of life, such as self-care, physical activities, and work; (d) mental condition, which includes positive and negative feelings; and (e) health potential, including longevity and prognosis.

Quality of life encompasses a person's assessment of all aspects of their experience. Some important dimensions are distant from medical concern (e.g., achievement and spiritual fulfillment).

Appropriateness studies establish standard indications against which the use of a particular medical intervention is judged. Methods to produce indications involve careful analysis of what is known and the use of expert physicians to fill in gaps in knowledge and come to consensus about indications. Appropriateness studies can inform guidelines to help the practicing physician decide under what circumstances a procedure should or should not be done.

CONCEPTUAL MODEL:
LINKING HEALTH STATUS AND HEALTH CARE SERVICES

Health status incorporates measures of the physical, mental, and social functioning of individuals. The determinants of health status are broadly conceived to include environmental, genetic, behavioral, and biological influences. To the extent these factors lead to decrements in health status, they may translate into needs for care. Health services are designed to meet needs for care and to contribute toward improvements in health status and/or the prevention of future decrements. It is notable that not all health services are directed at needs for care that result from changes in health status. Preventive services are prescribed to prevent risks to future health. Table 6.2 lists the eight steps of a health resource allocation strategy.

Health status can be conceptualized as a starting point for defining health care needs. These needs are translated by health professionals into specific disease and syndrome categories that may be expected to benefit from treatment and preventive services. Ultimately, changes in health status become a measure of the patient's outcomes and a metric against which to assess effectiveness of treatment.

TABLE 6.2 *Eight steps in the health resource allocation strategy*

1. Specify the health decision by
   Describing the sociocultural and health services context of the decision
   Identifying alternative courses of action under consideration
   Identifying stakeholders
   Defining stakeholder values for outcomes of alternatives
   Recognizing the assumptions used in the socioeconomic evaluation
   Specifying the budgetary constraints to be considered
2. Classify health outcomes as health states by
   Identifying relevant concepts, domains, and indicators of health-related quality of life
   Listing the hypothesized relationships among concepts, domains, and indicators
   Selecting combination of domains to be included in the health state classification
3. Assign values to health states by
   Identifying population of judges to assign preferences
   Sampling health states to be assigned preference weights
   Selecting a method of preference measurement
   Collecting preference judgments and assigning preference weights to health states
4. Measure health-related quality of life of target population using primary data collection or
   secondary analysis to
   Classify individuals in target population into health states
   Assign a preference weight to the health state of each individual
   Average scores of all individuals to obtain a point-in-time estimate of the target population's
   health-related quality of life
5. Estimate prognosis and years of healthy life by
   Calculating expected duration of survival (life expectancy) of target population
   Calculating years of healthy life by adjusting duration of survival by the point-in-time estimate or observed differences in health-related quality of life
6. Estimate direct and indirect health care costs by
   Identifying all organizing and operational costs attributed to each of the alternative courses
   of action
   Specifying out-of-pocket expenses and productivity losses incurred by the recipients of
   each alternative
7. Rank costs and outcomes of health care alternatives by
   Calculating the ratio of costs per year of healthy life gained for each alternative course of
   action
   Ranking the ratios from low to high with the budget constraint including in this ranking
   Identifying ratios that are less than the budget constraint as cost effective
8. Revise rankings of costs and outcomes by
   Reviewing rank order of each alternative course of action with stakeholders in the decision
   Adjusting the rank order based on stakeholder challenges and community consensus on
   the values and goals of health care
   Recommending the revised rank order to political decision makers

Adapted from ref. 50.

EFFECTIVENESS: MEASURING AND IMPROVING HEALTH CARE

Medical effectiveness researchers strive to explain how well diagnostic, treatment, and preventive services work in day-to-day practice. Sometimes effectiveness research is confused with efficacy studies in which the impact of services
(e.g., new drug) is tested under ideal conditions. Ideal conditions may differ
from actual practice in many ways. Under ideal conditions, highly motivated and
compliant patients are chosen for the study, patients get the treatment for free,
and patients with complicating conditions are excluded.

Insurance Coverage Decisions: Oregon's Experience

In 1990, the state of Oregon attempted to use outcome measures as a tool for prioritizing conditions and treatments to be covered under Medicaid. By applying a cost/utility formula to a list of 2,000 medical conditions, it was hoped that the Medicaid program could eliminate coverage of nonbeneficial treatments and expand its base, thereby offering the greatest benefit to the greatest number of people.

Oregon approached this decision-making process with the use of the General Health Policy Model (61). This model expressed benefits and side effects of any health care service in terms of equivalent values of completely well-years of life. By dividing the cost of the program by the well-years added, an estimate of the cost/utility of the program could be calculated. This cost/utility ratio could then be used to compare the relative value of different services, since all treatment–condition pairs had a common metric. The focus of this model departed from those with a traditional emphasis on the progression of a single disease, since these have often neglected the side effects introduced by treatment. Hence, by incorporating benefits, side effects, and the relative importance of each, a comprehensive view of net treatment benefits could be obtained (62).

When the ranking from the above formula was completed, however, many felt uncomfortable with the result. The ranking of several condition-treatment pairs seemed counterintuitive (that treatments for thumb-sucking and acute headaches ranked higher than treatments for AIDS is an often cited example). Subjective reordering of the list by Oregon Health Services Commissioners was then

TABLE 6.3 *Health-related quality of life measures by type and appropriate policy context*

Policy context	Appropriate type of measure
Clinical	
Perfect agency	Disease-specific descriptive profile with no scoring system
Imperfect agency	Disease-specific descriptive profile with weights reflecting clinician's opinions
Practice	
Narrowly restricted budget	Disease-specific profile or index with weights reflecting values of specific clientele
Broadly restricted budget	Generic profile or index with weights reflecting values of patients and potential patients
Provider	
With a specific clientele	Generic profile or index with weights reflecting values of the population served
With a variety of clienteles	Generic profile or index capable of incorporating a variety of values
Purchaser	
Serving and financed by same population	Generic index with weights reflecting the values of the population served
Serving one population but financed by a different one	Generic index capable of incorporating a variety of values

employed, along with the three other levels of human judgment used in the model (community values assessed in town meetings, medical judgment of treatment efficacy, and ratings of the desirability of health states) to determine the final ranking. When the application was submitted to the Department of Health and Human Services (DHHS) in 1992, it was rejected based on distrust of the health state ratings. They believed that the Oregon preference survey on quality of life "quantified stereotypic assumptions about persons with disability" (62). A revised application that eliminated the quality of life component was approved by DHHS in 1993. However, Kaplan (63) has demonstrated that of the four levels of judgment used, the health state ratings had the greatest evidence of reliability and validity. Kaplan points out that the most replicable part of the model was omitted from the proposal since the health state ratings were the only component that was obtained using a systematic methodology. Public policy is made at many levels in the health care system, by many different people, each providing a role for a variety of HRQOL measures. Table 6.3 outlines the context in which measures may be useful.

REFERENCES

1. Weinstein MC, Fineberg HV, Elstein AS, Frazier HS, Neuhauser D, Neutra RR, McNeil BJ. *Clinical decision analysis*. Philadelphia: WB Saunders, 1980.
2. Early Breast Cancer Trialist's Collaborative Group. Effects of adjuvant tamoxifen and of cytotoxic therapy on mortality in early breast cancer. An overview of 61 randomized trials among 28,896 women. *N Engl J Med* 1988;319:1681–1692.
3. Gafni A, Torrance GW. Risk attitude and time preference in health. *Manage Sci* 1984;30:440–451.
4. Coates A, Glasziou P, McNeil D. On the receiving end: measurement of quality of life during cancer chemotherapy. *Ann Oncol* 1990;1:213–217.
5. Torrance GW, Feeny D. Utilities and quality-adjusted life years. *Int J Technol Assess Health Care* 1989;5:559–575.
6. Torrance GW, Thomas WH, Sackett DL. A utility maximization model for evaluation of health care programs. *Health Serv Res* 1972;7:118–133.
7. Read JL, Quinn RJ, Berwick DM, Fineberg HV, Weinstein MC. Preferences for health outcomes: comparison of assessment methods. *Med Decis Making* 1984;4:315–329.
8. Stiggelbout AM, Kiebert GM, Kievit J, Leer JWH, Stoter G, de Haes JCJM. Utility assessment in cancer patients: adjustment of time tradeoff scores for the utility of life years and comparison with standard gamble scores. *Med Decis Making* 1994;14:82–90.
9. Bergner M, Bobbitt RA, Carter WB, Gilson BS. The Sickness Impact Profile: development and final 10 revision of a health status measure. *Med Care* 1981;19:787–805.
10. Chambers LW. The McMaster Health Index Questionnaire: an update. In: Walker SR, Rosser RM, eds. *Quality of life assessment: key issues in the 1990s*. Dordrecht, Boston, London: Kluwer Academic, 1993:131–150.
11. Kaplan RM, Anderson JP, Wu AW, Mathews C, Kozin F, Orernstein D. The Quality of Well-Being Scale: applications in AIDS, cystic fibrosis, and arthritis. *Med Care* 1989;27:S27–S43.
12. Torrance GW, Boyle MH, Horwood SP. Application of multi-attribute utility theory to measure social preferences for health-states. *Operations Res* 1982;30:1043–1069.
13. Gudex C, Kind P. *The QALY toolkit*. Discussion paper number 38. York, UK: University of York, Centre for Health Economics, 1988.
14. Simes RJ. Application of statistical decision theory to treatment choices: implications for design and analysis of clinical trials. *Stat Med* 1986;5:411–420.
15. Torrance GW. Measurement of health state utilities for economic appraisal: a review article. *J Health Econ* 1986;5:1–30.
16. Canadian Coordinating Office for Health Technology Assessment. *Guidelines for economic evalua-*

tion of pharmaceuticals: Canada, 1st ed. Ottawa: Canadian Coordinating Office for Health Technology Assessment, 1994.

17. Henry D. Economic analysis as an aid to subsidisation decisions: the development of Australian guidelines for pharmaceuticals. Review article. *Pharmacoeconomics* 1992;1(1):54–67.

18. Detsky AS. Guidelines for economic analysis of pharmaceutical products: a draft document for Ontario and Canada. *Pharmacoeconomics* 1993;3(5):354–361.

19. Kamlet MS. *The comparative benefits modeling project. A framework for cost-utility analysis of government health care programs.* Public Health Service, U.S. Department of Health and Human Services, 1992.

20. Guyatt GH, Feeny DH, Patrick DL. Measuring HRQOL. *Ann Intern Med* 1993;118:622–629.

21. Torrance GW, Furlong W, Feeny D, et al. Multi-attribute preference functions: Health Utilities Index. *Pharmacoeconomics* 1995;7:503–520.

22. Kirshner B, Guyatt G. A methodological framework for assessing health indices. *J Chronic Dis* 1985; 38:27–36.

23. Von Neumann J, Morgenstern O. Theory of games and economic behaviour. Princeton, NJ: Princeton University Press, 1944.

24. Keeney RL. Utility functions for multiattributed consequences. *Mgmt Sci* 1972;18(5):276–287.

25. Keeney RL. Building models of values. *Eur J Operational Res* 1988;37:149–157.

26. Farquhar PH. A fractional hypercube decomposition theorem for multiattribute utility functions. *Oper Res* 1975;23:941–967.

27. Farquhar PH. Pyramid and semicube decompositions of multiattribute utility functions. *Oper Res* 1976;24:256–271.

28. Farquhar PH. A survey of multiattribute utility theory and applications. *TIMS Studies Mgmt Sci* 1977; 6:59–89.

29. Keeney RL, Raiffa H. *Decisions with multiple objectives: preferences and value tradeoffs.* New York: John Wiley, 1976.

30. Von Winterfeldt D, Edwards W. Value and utility measurement. In: *Decision analysis and behavioral research.* Cambridge: Cambridge University Press, 1986:205–241.

31. Krantz DH, Luce RD, Suppes P, Tversky A. Difference measurement. In: *Foundations of measurement.* New York and London: Academic Press, 1971:136–198.

32. Torrance GW, Boyle MH, Horwood SP. Application of multi-attribute utility theory to measure social preferences for health states. *Operations Res* 1982;30:1043–1069.

33. Read JL, Quinn RJ, Berwick DM, Fineberg HV, Weinstein MC. Preferences for health outcomes: comparisons of assessment methods. *Med Decis Making* 1984;4(3):315–329.

34. Elstein AS, Holzman GB, Ravitch MM, et al. Comparison of physicians' decisions regarding estrogen replacement therapy for menopausal women and decisions derived from a decision analytic model. *Am J Med* 1986;80:246–258.

35. Patrick DL, Starks HE, Cain KC, Uhlmann RF, Pearlman RA. Measuring preferences for health states worse than death. *Med Decis Making* 1994;14:9–18.

36. Berthelot JM, Roberge R, Wolfson MC. The calculation of health-adjusted life expectancy for a Canadian province using a multi-attribute utility function: a first attempt. In: Robine JM, Mathers CD, Bone MR, Romieu I, eds. *Calculation of health expectancies: harmonization, consensus and future perspectives,* vol. 226. Montrouge, France: John Libbey Eurotext, 1993:161–172.

37. Guyatt GH, Patrick DH, Patrick DL. Measuring HRQOL. *Ann Intern Med* 1993;118:622–629.

38. Canadian Coordinating Office for Health Technology Assessment. *Guidelines for economic evaluation of pharmaceuticals: Canada,* 1st ed. Ottawa: CCOHTA, 1994.

39. Torrance GW. Measurement of health state utilities for economic appraisal. A review. *J Health Econ* 1986;5:1–30.

40. Torrance GW, Boyle MH, Horwood SP. Application of multi-attribute utility theory to measure social preferences for health states. *Oper Res* 1982;30:1043–1069.

41. Torrance GW. Health states worse than death. In: van Eimeren W, Engelbert R, Flagle CD, eds. *Third International Conference on System Science in Health Care.* Berlin: Springer, 1984:1085–1089.

42. Patrick DL, Starks HE, Cain KC, Ullmann RF, Pearlman RA. Measuring preferences for health states worse than death. *Med Decis Making* 1994;14(1):9–18.

43. Berthelot JM, Roberge R, Wolfson MC. The calculation of health-adjusted life expectancy for a Canadian province using a multi-attribute utility function: a first attempt. In: Robine JM, Mathers CD, Bone MR, Romieu I, eds. *Calculation of health expectancies: harmonization, consensus and future perspectives,* vol 226. Montrouge, France: John Libbey Eurotext, 1993:161–172.

44. Ganz PA. Quality of life measures in cancer chemotherapy. *Pharmacoeconomics* 1994;5(5):376–388.
45. Jaeschke R, Guyatt GH, Cook D. Quality of life instruments in the evaluation of new drugs. *Pharmacoeconomics* 1992;1(2):84–94.
46. Guyatt GH, Feeny DH, Patrick DL. Measuring HRQOL. *Ann Intern Med* 1993;118(8):622–629.
47. Drummond M. Quality of life measurement within economic evaluations. Paper presented at the ESRC/SHHD workshop on Quality of Life, Edinburgh, April 27–28, 1993.
48. Eddy DM. Oregon's methods: did cost-effectiveness fail? *JAMA* 1991;166(15).
49. Gudex C. QALYs and their use by health service. Discussion Paper 20. York, UK: University of York, Centre for Health Economics, 1986.
50. Patrick DL, Erickson P. *Health status and health policy: allocating resources to health care.* New York: Oxford University Press, 1993.
51. Erickson P, Wilson RW, Shannon I. *Years of healthy life. Statistical note.* Hyattsville, MD: National Center for Health Statistics, 1995.
52. Gerard K, Mooney G. QALY league tables: handle with care. *J Health Econ* 1993;2:59–64.
53. Weinstein MC, Fineberg HV. Clinical decision analysis. Philadelphia: WB Saunders, 1980.
54. Bootman JL, Townsend R, McGhan WF. *Principles of pharmacoeconomics.* Cincinnati: Harvey Whitney, 1991.
55. Barr JT, Schumacher GE. *Decision analysis.* In: Bootman JL, Townsend R, McGhan WF, eds. *Principles of pharmacoeconomics.* Cincinnati: Harvey Whitney, 1991.
56. Schumacher GE, Barr JT. Applying decision analysis in therapeutic drug monitoring: using decision trees to interpret serum theophylline levels. *Clin Pharm* 1986;5:325–333.
57. Barr JT, Schumacher GE. Applying decision analysis in therapeutic drug monitoring: using receiver-operating characteristic curves in comparative evaluations. *Clin Pharm* 1986;5:239–246.
58. Schumacher GE. Multiattribute evaluation in formulary decision making as applied to calcium-channel blocker. *Am J Hosp Pharm* 1991;48:301–308.
59. Cano SB, Fujita NK. Formulary evaluation of third-generation cephalosporins using decision analysis. *Am J Hosp Pharm* 1988;45:566–569.
60. Bergner M. Measurements of health status. *Med Care* 1985;23:696–704.
61. Kaplan RM, Anderson JP. A general health policy model: update and applications. *Health Serv Res* 1988;23:203–235.
62. Kaplan RM. Value judgment in the Oregon Medicaid Experiment. *Med Care* 1994;32(10):975–988.
63. Kaplan RM, ed. *The Hippocratic predicament: affordability, access, and accountability in American medicine.* San Diego, CA: Academic Press, 1993.

7 / Pharmacoeconomics

OVERVIEW

Changing health care systems, as well as increasing expenditures for health care services, have placed an emphasis on performing economic evaluations of new medicines. These studies are directed at demonstrating value in terms of health outcomes of the expenditures associated with adopting the new medical treatment into the health care system. The medical outcomes (effectiveness) movement has further encouraged the assessment of new and existing medical treatments (1). Types of outcomes commonly examined in medical effectiveness research include, among others, mortality, morbidity, costs, length of stay, quality of care, and patient satisfaction. Measures of HRQOL are increasingly viewed as important outcomes of medical and surgical interventions (2,3). The primary pharmacoeconomic problem results from the tension between providing all medical services that are technically feasible or that patients desire and somehow financing these services with limited resources (4). Without information on patient outcomes, decisions about new medical treatments may be made based only on economic considerations. Cost and effectiveness were brought together by using incremental cost-effectiveness methods. Although initially applied to costly medical technologies, pharmacoeconomic evaluations are now applied to assess the value of medications and treatments, e.g., to compare the medical costs and health outcomes associated with a new medical therapy to the costs and outcomes of the existing alternative medical treatment or health care intervention (5,6). To complete a pharmacoeconomic study, both the medical costs and health outcomes need to be specified and collected, and then analyzed to determine the cost effectiveness of the new drug treatment compared to the alternative treatment.

Many costs are increased with the introduction of new drugs and treatments, but some redistribution is possible if an expensive alternative or negative health consequence is avoided. If a new drug or treatment provides an equal or better health outcome than existing modalities, it will be an advantage for healthcare resource utilization (e.g., renal transplantation over hemodialysis (7). Pharmacoeconomics has become increasingly important in response to the need for data on costs relative to effectiveness or benefit. Cost-effectiveness analyses are widely used to determine resource allocation and to assist policy formation. Outcomes research in the health care field can be defined as analysis that attempts to explain or describe the results of any type of medical treatment or intervention.

CONCEPTUAL FRAMEWORK TO ASSESS
THE VALUE OF A TREATMENT

What one would really like to know has not changed; however, what one considers measuring has shifted. Early discussion of the acquisition cost of pharmaceuticals was quickly replaced by conjectures (based on somewhat casual support from data) regarding possible downstream cost savings consequent to product use. The core element for pharmacoeconomic analysis is cost. The next most important issue is determination of effectiveness versus other treatments. If the new treatment is equal in effectiveness, then cost is the determinant. Finding differences in both cost and effectiveness leads to evaluation of cost effectiveness. However, before proceeding, definition of effectiveness and selection of an effectiveness endpoint for the treatment must be determined. Adjustments might be necessary for HRQOL or utility.

COSTS

It is useful to think of costing as consisting of three steps: identification, measurement, and valuation. Identification is the task of identifying in advance all the types of costs that will need to be gathered for the analysis. Measurement consists of capturing data on quantities of resources used. Valuation places a price, actually a cost, on them.

Direct costs are linked to the production of goods and services (e.g., pharmaceutical products, disposable surgical devices, personnel salaries), whereas *indirect costs* are those not directly related to the treatment (e.g., office rent, electricity, administrative support, as well as lost wages, transportation, and other nonmedical expenses). In most nonmedical areas, the price of a product or service is equal to the cost of production plus a profit. In medical areas, there is little relationship between *costs* and *charges,* and many health care providers do not compete with each other on price. The concept of not-for-profit enterprise in medicine does not exclude the likelihood of charges disproportionate to cost. Patients (consumers) rarely have sufficient information to make decisions based on price, although the trend toward selection of generic medications is based on informing patients about equivalence among branded and generic products. Many hospitals convert charges to costs using Medicare cost/charge ratios (RCC). In "top-down" cost estimates, this ratio is used to determine the cost of each resource used, including the general hospital overhead costs. In a "bottom-up" approach, the resources consumed are summed.

Cost-effectiveness analyses measure the difference in life expectancy between the strategies under evaluation. Results are expressed as a ratio of incremental costs (numerator) to health care benefits and outcomes (denominator). Cost/utility analyses assess survival adjusted for less than full quality (quality-adjusted life-year, or QALY). The advantage of the QALY as a measure of health output is that it can simultaneously capture gains from reduced morbidity (quality gains) and reduced mortality (quantity gains), and integrate these into a single measure. Without the intervention, the individual's HRQOL would deteriorate according to the lower path and they would die at time Death 1. With the intervention, they would deteriorate more slowly, would live longer, and would die at time Death 2. The area between the two paths is the QALY gained by the intervention. For instruction purposes, the area can be divided into two parts, A and

3. Then, part A is the amount of QALY gained due to quality improvements (i.e., the quality gain during time that the person would have otherwise been alive anyhow), and part B is the amount of QALY gained due to quantity improvements (i.e., the amount of life extension, but factored by the quality of that life extension). QALY weights should be preferences, preferably von Neumann-Morgenstern utilities, measured on an interval scale anchored with a score of 0.0 for death and 1.0 for perfect health.

Von Neumann-Morgenstern utility theory is the dominant normative paradigm for decision making under uncertainty. That is, it is considered the best theory for how decisions under uncertainty ought to be made, in order to be both consistent with the fundamental axioms of the theory and internally coherent. The strength of the system comes from the fact that the fundamental axioms are compellingly simple and logical, and appear to represent desirable properties of good decision making under conditions of uncertainty. The paradigm has survived decades of attack, and still remains the leading paradigm for decision making under uncertainty (8).

Quality weights for QALY calculations can be based on values (measured with visual–analog scaling or time trade-off) or on von Neumann-Morgenstern utilities (measured with standard gamble). However, von Neumann-Morgenstern utilities are more attractive as quality weights for QALY calculations for a number of reasons. First, von Neumann-Morgenstern is the appropriate paradigm for decision making under uncertainty, that is, decisions that involve uncertainties and risk, and this clearly applies to decisions regarding health care interventions. Second, von Neumann-Morgenstern utilities are based on a sound theoretical foundation, and this, in turn, provides three advantages. The utilities are precisely interpretable. The utilities are also useful for clinical decision analysis at the patient level, and the development of clinical guidelines and, thus, their use can help integrate the two levels of decision making: bedside and policy. Finally, with additional assumptions, the QALY model using von Neumann Morgenstern utilities can be linked to welfare economics, which is considered by most economists to be the proper basis for societal resource allocation decisions (9).

Cost/utility analyses are an appropriate and highly desirable form of economic evaluation for use with clinical trials. In the trial design, consideration must be given to the comparator treatment or treatments, the length of follow-up, the outcomes measured, and the sample size in order to accommodate a cost/utility analysis. The analysis should use an intent to treat strategy, and the primary viewpoint of the analysis should be societal. Relevant resource utilization should be gathered prospectively during the trial, and costed later based on appropriate standard costs if available, or on special costing studies. Incremental outcomes should be converted into QALYs gained using preference-based quality weights that are measured on an interval scale anchored on perfect health and death. Von Neumann-Morgenstern utilities are the most appropriate type of preferences for use as quality weights; these may be measured directly using the standard gamble instrument or determined indirectly using the health utility index system.

PRODUCTIVITY OR HUMAN CAPITAL MODELS

The two major financial costs of disease are (a) treatment costs and (b) the loss in productivity during the course of the disease or subsequent disability. The productivity effects of death and disability have been incorporated in cost/benefit studies of health programs and in a variety of projects affecting public safety, such as highway improvements and flood control projects. One way of viewing this approach is to consider it as valuing individuals only for their productivity, much as one might value investment in industrial equipment. Loss of human capital, whether in the form of death or diminished capacity, reduces the ability of the economy to produce much like the destruction or impairment of capital equipment. Although "quality of life" certainly implies more than lost workplace activity, work remains one of the major human activities and the impact of disease on work will be reflected in other aspects of an individual's life condition. Loss of income may have serious impact on the other dimensions of the life, including effects on one's family.

THE WILLINGNESS-TO-PAY CONCEPT

In assessing the value of goods and services to individuals, economists often employ the concept of willingness to pay. The act of market exchange is an expression of the willingness of individuals to give up some goods or services in exchange for other goods and services. In most instances, money acts as a medium of exchange, breaking the direct link between items sold and items purchased in exchange.

To assess the value of different health states or quality of life, it is natural to determine the values in the manner in which the marketplace determines other values, i.e., by the willingness to pay for improved health or quality of life. As noted earlier there are no explicit markets for health, so one must uncover ways to calculate willingness to pay. The approaches taken can be divided into questionnaire-based and revealed preference-based methods.

Questionnaire-Based Models

Questionnaire-based willingness-to-pay approaches basically attempt to have the respondent estimate the value placed on different health states or quality of life. Designing a willingness-to-pay survey demands considerations similar to those for other survey research including the quality of life measures discussed in greater detail in other chapters. One must be concerned with validity and reliability as well as ease of administration (10–12). The questions may ask for direct responses for the items to be valued, use some forms of paired comparisons, or seek to value the specific attributes of the item or state, and aggregate to produce a value for the total. Specific issues arising when dollar values are involved in a health survey should be addressed.

In most instances the survey questions elicit a response for willingness to pay for an improvement or to prevent a worsening of health status. In such instances the respondents' evaluation will be affected by their income or assets, i.e., we should expect on average that wealthy individuals will be willing to pay a larger dollar amount for a given improvement than will a poor individual (although the percentage of income or wealth may be similar). Thus, the willingness-to-pay approach, like the human capital productivity approach, is also influenced by an individual's income.

An alternative formulation reverses the question to ask how large a payment would be required for the individual to willingly accept a reduction in health state or to forgo an improvement. Since the response is not bounded by the individual's current assets, the values are likely to be larger and there is a presumption that there would be less of an income bias, although it is probably not eliminated.

A general criticism of questionnaire-based estimates is that they are not validated. Opinions are being solicited about hypothetical situations that may be far removed from the experience of the respondent. Healthy individuals may have great difficulty imagining how their lives would change were they were partially paralyzed and, hence, have a hard time assessing their willingness to pay to avoid this condition. If the payment is hypothetical, i.e., they will not be charged based on their answers, their answers may be quite different than in situations in which they actually have to pay. There is also the problem of the respondents giving answers that they think the interviewer wants, particularly in personal interview situations using hypothetical payments.

The standard gamble approach has been employed to construct health indices (13). This approach confronts the respondent with a choice between a certain event and a gamble that will result in either a better or worse state than the certain event. By determining the probability level at which individuals are indifferent about the gamble and the certain state, the relative value assigned to each state can be estimated. By including a dollar value as part of one of these states it is possible to translate this model into one that estimates dollar values for death or disease risks, e.g., if the choice is between perfect health or a gamble that, if won, results in less than $10,000 plus retaining perfect health and, if lost, results in partial paralysis. The probability of winning, which makes the respondent indifferent between accepting the gamble or the certainty of perfect health, can be used to construct the respondent's assessment of the cost of paralysis. The rationale for this opinion-based method is similar to the revealed preference-based model discussed below.

Revealed Preference-Based Models

One of the difficulties with opinion-based willingness-to-pay models is that they usually measure what individuals state they would be willing to pay rather than measure what individuals do in fact pay. Several attempts have been made to develop willingness-to-pay measures based on actual behavior affecting health or quality of life. However, since there is not a direct market for health, this must be inferred from other actions.

Individuals make many decisions that involve risks of death/disability. These decisions include job choice, purchase of safety equipment, recreational activities, and diet. In these decisions they trade off potential changes in health states for other attributes such as income or pleasure. By observing the choices people make that involve risk of death or disability, one may be able to calculate the value individuals place on their health. The basic premise behind revealed preference-based models is that the observed choices reflect the individual's relative valuation of health and other attributes given the expected outcome probabilities.

There are many variations of revealed preference-based models, but most are based on the following. An individual chooses between two activities, A and B, that differ in two dimensions: income (or some surrogate) and risk of death or disability. Individuals who accept the higher-risk activity have revealed a willingness to face a higher probability of death/disability in return for an increase in income. For example, these individuals may choose an activity that exposes them to a 1 in 1,000 higher probability of death but offers a less than $2,000 higher income. These individuals value the 1 in 1,000 risk of death at a maximum value of less than $2,000. In some studies, linearity is assumed such that the implied "value of life" is $2 million.

Even among individuals who are willing to accept the basic design of these studies there are questions about the validity of the results. One source of concern is the extent to which the choices are being made by fully informed individuals. Are the probabilities of death or disabilities known to the individuals making the choice? To the extent that individuals act on incorrect estimates but the researcher uses true probabilities, the empirical estimates will be in error. For many occupations this difference may be substantial; however, for others the risks may be well known. Those who accept risky jobs (e.g., coal mining) may also have a constrained choice set due to limited mobility as well as information.

There is some evidence that individuals have difficulty dealing with low probability, high value events (14). The difference between a 1 in a million and a 1 in 10 million chance is a 10 to 1 ratio but may both be essentially zero to the average individual. Decisions also are made on absolute rather than relative risk increases. Yet the risk faced in some occupations on a weekly or monthly basis are of this order of magnitude. Individuals, particularly healthy persons, may be myopic in dealing with questions concerning their own death. The "it won't happen to me" phenomenon calls into question the rational choice-making assumptions of these revealed-preference models.

Evaluation of Costs

The techniques used to evaluate costs in pharmacoeconomic trials are usually the same for cost/benefit, cost-effectiveness, cost/utility, and cost-minimization

TABLE 7.1 *Selected direct costs that may be measured in pharmacoeconomic trials*[a]

1. Cost of the medicine (whether based on wholesale prices to the pharmacy or retail prices to the patient must be specified)[b]
2. Cost of the pharmacy and nurses' time to prepare the medicine
3. Cost of any equipment and supplies (e.g., syringes, tubing, vials) needed to administer the medicine
4. Cost of actually administering the medicine (e.g., nurses' time)
5. Cost of monitoring the patient on the day the medicine is given, as well as prior to that day (e.g., laboratory costs, professional charges)
6. Cost of monitoring the patient after the medicine is given
7. Cost of concomitant medicines or other treatments that must be given with the medicine (e.g., potassium supplements for a diuretic)
8. Cost of the clinic visit(s) for the occasion(s) when the medicine is given; costs may be calculated for one visit, one episode, or a fixed time, such as one year
9. Cost of hospitalization stays (e.g., room and board) per year or on another basis
10. Cost of all health professionals, support personnel, administrators, and any volunteers
11. Cost of continuing on a chronic medicine for the patient's lifetime
12. Cost of switching a patient from their existing treatment to a new treatment
13. Costs of diagnosing and treating anticipated adverse events

[a]Other items to add to this list could be chosen for relevant situations (e.g., cost to diagnose a patient). Not all items on this list will be relevant for a specific product or trial.
[b]The complexities of measuring this apparently straightforward cost are discussed in the text. Consistency must be used in comparing different treatments in terms of assessing actual costs to a group (e.g., hospital) versus charges (i.e., to the patient or their insurance company).

methods. Bias may be readily introduced in the evaluation of costs if only some of the direct or indirect costs are measured (Tables 7.1 and 7.2). If an investigator measures all direct and indirect costs, the results could be presented in a straightforward table. Alternatively, a list of all direct and indirect costs could be explained in the discussion of methods, with a summary of the totals included under results. If the reader does not know what specific categories of costs were measured, and only totals are given, the implication could be drawn that the missing values would have influenced the data and were intentionally omitted.

TABLE 7.2 *Selected indirect costs that may be measured in pharmacoeconomic trials*

1. Transportation to and from the clinic, hospital, or other place relating to the treatment
2. Food, hotel, parking costs, and other necessary expenses for patients and those who accompany them
3. Babysitting, child care costs, or costs for care of a parent
4. Other ancillary medical treatments and medicines recommended as a result of taking the primary medicine (e.g., the need for follow-up care, which may involve rehabilitation, physical, or mental therapies)[a]
5. Wages lost because of the disease or treatment, including adverse reactions
6. Costs of retreating patients who fail to respond to treatment
7. Costs of treating unexpected complications
8. Counseling required because of psychosocial problems, the inability to work, or for other reasons
9. Other consequences of treating patients
10. Overhead for the facilities used

[a]This category is often viewed as a direct cost of the therapy. Whichever classification is used, it must be considered.

TABLE 7.3 *Six alternatives for comparing costs[a]*

Cost	Medicine A	Medicine B	Medicine C
Per tablet[c]	*$1.00[b]*	$1.50	$2.00
Per dose	2 tablets make up one dose and cost $2.00	1 tablet costs *$1.50*	1 tablet costs $2.00
Per day	Medicine taken twice a day and costs $4.00	Medicine taken three times a day and costs $4.50	Medicine taken once a day and costs *$2.00*
Per course of therapy	Duration of 10 days costs $40	Duration of 10 days costs $45	Duration of 7 days costs *$14*
Per package	20 tablets per box costs *$20*	30 tablets per box costs $4	12 tablets per box costs *$14*
Per milligram	50 mg—$.02 per mg	150 mg—*$.01 per mg*	5 mg—$.40 per mg

Modified with permission of Raven Press from Spiker (51).

[a]Other ways to express the costs of the medicine include monitoring cost, cost of professional visits and services, and costs of hospitalization. Alternative or additional ways to express costs relate to costs saved or a comparison of costs with other treatments for the same problem.

[b]The least expensive medicine for each description is underlined, illustrating that each medicine *could* be described as the least expensive, depending on how the data are presented.

[c]Cost could be expressed per milliliter or solution or per unit of therapy (e.g., capsule, suppository, patch).

This is not solely a theoretical issue. In reading reports of many pharmacoeconomic trials, it is often impossible to determine which specific costs were measured. Table 7.3 describes six alternatives for cost comparisons.

Evaluation of Efficacy or Effectiveness

Measures of effectiveness can be readily tailored to achieve a desired result by carefully selecting (a) the time period for evaluation (e.g., only the first week, month, or year after treatment is started), (b) the health care providers whose time involved in the treatment is assessed (e.g., physicians, nurses, physical therapists), (c) the location and type of service (e.g., clinic, hospital), and (d) the test instruments, laboratories, and procedures used. There are cases when numerous tests and scales are used to measure quality of life, but only those that yield positive results are reported. Data from tests that show no difference or a beneficial effect for the alternative treatment are sometimes not reported. Similar situations could occur in clinical trials where only results of selective tests are reported.

It is generally easier to evaluate whether a pharmacoeconomic trial has introduced bias in the measurement of costs than in the measurement of efficacy or effectiveness. Several of the basic categories of efficacy in a clinical trial or effectiveness in clinical practice conditions that are vulnerable to manipulation in a pharmacoeconomic study are listed in Table 7.4. Some of the parameters measured in trials assessing a medicine's efficacy do not directly relate to an observable clinical benefit (e.g., apparent pharmacokinetic advantages in metabolism or elimination that are clinically nonapparent). The measure of effective-

TABLE 7.4 *Efficacy categories that may be manipulated in a pharmacoeconomic trial*

1. Parameters chosen to measure a disease, symptom, or clinical sign (e.g., swelling of legs or shortness of breath to assess patients with congestive heart failure)
2. Methods used to measure the parameter (e.g., assessing leg swelling by using a tape measure, a scale of 1 to 4, or pain on walking)
3. Instruments used and how they are applied (e.g., just before medicine is taken, at bedtime, 20 minutes after medicine, one hour after medicine)
4. Analysis of the data
5. Interpretation of the data
6. Extrapolation of the data
7. Other categories (e.g., patient compliance, comfort, and convenience of treatment)

ness or utility (Table 7.5) is subject to an even greater degree of bias. An experienced pharmacoeconomist can (if desired) almost always show any medicine to be more cost effective than any other.

THREATS TO THE VALIDITY OF PHARMACOECONOMIC ANALYSES BASED ON CLINICAL TRIAL DATA

Pharmacoeconomic methods continue to evolve because of pressures from various sources to scrutinize both costs and consequences of providing medical care. A debate has recently been sparked between those who engage in "outcomes research," using predominantly observational and other nonexperimental methods, and the traditional "hard core" medical researchers, who have a predilection for experimental design in the form of the randomized, controlled trial. Some of the latter group have assailed "outcomes research" as lacking in "scientific validity" (15). Although "outcomes research" methods are imperfect,

TABLE 7.5 *Selected efficacy categories usually measured in a pharmacoeconomic trial*

1. Time spent in hospital per year or other time period
2. Cost of hospitalizations per year or other time period
3. Number of physician, emergency room, or clinic visits per year or other time period
4. Number or times per year that ancillary treatment is required
5. Improvements of one or more clinical symptoms in severity, duration, or qualitative nature
6. Improvements of one or more clinical signs in intensity, duration, frequency, or qualitative nature
7. Improvements of one or more laboratory measures of a biological sample (e.g., blood, urine)
8. Improvement of one or more physical laboratory parameters (e.g., EEG, EKG, pulmonary function tests)
9. Improvement of a patient's quality of life
10. Subjective improvement reported by the patient, family, or others
11. Number of episodes or exacerbations per year
12. Changes in the natural history of the disease
13. Survival
14. Time spent by the physician and other health professionals per year
15. Number of days of work lost per year due to the disease

a critique of randomized, controlled trial-derived data in their use in economic evaluations (particularly in premarketing pharmaceutical trials) is needed. Specifically, the validity of inferences based on such data to the world of clinical practice may be questioned. It is this practice-based world that is of primary interest to those engaged in pharmacoeconomics. To date, the literature has been relatively silent on this topic (16).

SEVEN THREATS TO THE VALIDITY OF RANDOMIZED, CONTROLLED TRIAL-BASED PHARMACOECONOMICS

Although the high degree of internal validity associated with the randomized, controlled trial design is desirable for making causal treatment-outcome inferences about efficacy, the randomized, controlled trial design often suffers from poor external validity (i.e., generalizability to real-world clinical practice). This weakens its basis for estimating parameters on effectiveness and cost that are relevant to policy discussions on resource allocation. In this section, seven general threats to the validity of pharmacoeconomic studies are discussed that are based, retrospectively or prospectively, on randomized, controlled trial data.

1. Choice of Comparison Therapy

A fundamental threat to the validity of any pharmacoeconomic study exists when the comparison therapy is not the most relevant for the policy question being addressed. A comparison that may be relevant for testing safety and efficacy, such as placebo, is unlikely to be the most relevant comparison for an economic study of the new drug. If the relevant economic question is to assess whether the added population health benefits are worth the added cost, a relevant comparison is the most widely used current therapy for the disease in question. For example, in assessing the cost effectiveness of the new antiemetic drug, ondansetron, Buxton and O'Brien (16) made comparison (using published trials) against a widely used and effective existing therapy—metroclopromide (17). Earlier trials (18,19) comparing against placebo (i.e., proxy for no therapy) were not a relevant comparison for the incremental economic question. Even if no treatment is the relevant alternative, placebo controls are unlikely to represent a no-treatment alternative adequately. This follows from the very arguments that support their inclusion in trials. If there is a placebo effect, the no-treatment alternative will not be adequately proxied by placebo. Despite potential ethical (20) and economic arguments against the use of placebo, the U.S. Food and Drug Administration (FDA) regulatory rules encourage a continued use of such comparisons.

2. Gold Standard Measurement of Outcomes

A common problem facing the economist wishing to use clinical trial data for making inferences about cost effectiveness is that trials often employ measurements for outcomes that are more detailed, invasive or frequent than is custom-ary in usual care. For example, in comparing alternative acid suppressant drugs, the outcome of duodenal ulcer recurrence is usually determined in clinical trials by endoscopy of all patients at fixed follow-up times (21). Outside of a trial, the management of such patients would be based largely on symptoms. Therefore, for the economic analysis to be externally valid, it must reflect the fact that some persons without symptoms will have ulcer recurrence—although silent—and some persons with symptoms may not have ulcer recurrence. The use of rates of recurrence based on endoscopy will misrepresent the reality of clinical practice and bias the pharmacoeconomic results.

3. Intermediate Versus Final Health Outcomes

In clinical trials of diseases where event rates are small, such as reduction of cardiovascular risk factors or cases of DVT, it has become customary to study and report intermediate biomedical markers as outcomes because sample sizes to test differences in final outcome such as mortality are often prohibitive (22). Trials of cholesterol-lowering drugs are a good example in which the outcome is the measured change in total blood cholesterol or some subfraction (23). For economic analysis to inform resource allocation, the impact such changes will have on final health outcomes, such as mortality and morbidity, is important to evaluate. This often results in attempts to use existing epidemiologic data (e.g., cohort studies such as Framingham) to construct models that can predict changes in final outcomes (e.g., deaths and myocardial infarctions) from changes in risk factors (24). Canadian guidelines on pharmacoeconomic study design are clear that intermediate outcomes must, by some means, be translated into final health outcomes (25). The overall validity of the economic study, therefore, depends crucially upon the way in which the relationship between intermediate and final outcomes has been quantified. For example, the early cost-effectiveness model of tissue plasminogen activator (TPA) in acute myocar-dial infarction by Laffel et al. (26) was based on mortality projections of early trial data on the intermediate outcome of arterial patency by angiography. Sub-sequent trials with mortality as the measured outcome have yielded far more conservative estimates of the mortality benefits of this drug.

4. Inadequate Patient Follow-up

A particular problem with the retrospective use of clinical trial data is where patient follow-up and data collection terminate abruptly when the patient experi-ences one of the outcome "events" of interest. From the perspective of the eco-nomic analyst, this can be frustrating because much of the cost associated with the new therapy may be incurred in the treatment of such events. Many examples can be found in cardiovascular drug therapy where events such as stroke or myocardial infarction are recorded but with no indication of the health care resources used to manage the cases. This is familiar terrain for the health economist who must now devise some method (e.g., expert panel, practice audit, insurance claims database) to estimate what resources are typically used in such circumstances.

5. Protocol-Driven Costs and Outcomes

A problem with basing cost estimates on data gathered as part of a trial is the extent to which one is capturing resource use associated with the trial per se (i.e., costs of doing research) rather than the costs of providing the therapy. These so-called protocol-driven costs can arise in a number of different ways.

6. Geographical Transferability of Trial Evidence

Pharmacoeconomic evidence gathered in one country does not always extrapolate well to other countries. As demonstrated by Drummond et al. (27), using the example of misoprostol in reducing NSAID-induced gastrointestinal problems, this portability issue owes much to differences in practice patterns and resource prices between different health care systems. In the Drummond study, even though the price of misoprostol was higher in the United States (compared to the United Kingdom, France, and Belgium), the cost effectiveness was best in the United States because the cost of managing gastrointestinal problems was higher in the United States due mainly to higher surgeon fees.

7. Selected Patient and Provider Populations

To increase the ratio of statistical signal to noise when estimating a treatment effect, it makes sense to restrict the population for study to those individuals most likely to respond to the new drug. The price of increasing this aspect of internal validity is reduced external validity in that the generalizability of results to populations not studied comes into question. For example, how reasonable is it to presume that the results of cholesterol-lowering trials done predominantly in middle-aged men can be used to justify cholesterol-lowering therapy in the elderly and children (28)? Economics can offer no solution to this problem, but it brings it into sharp focus because cost-effectiveness inferences about a new drug should not be universal—"this drug is cost effective"—but conditional on factors such as age, sex, and disease risk status of the defined patient group.

EVALUATION OF HRQOL OUTCOMES

Two main approaches have been used to evaluate health-related outcomes in pharmacoeconomic studies, psychometric health status and utility/preference measures. The health status measures can be further subdivided into generic and specific measures (2,3,29,30). Both approaches have advantages and disadvantages, and their proponents have not demonstrated any clear superiority for the evaluation of medicines (3).

Psychometric Health Status Measures

The psychometric health status measures provide comprehensive, multidimensional assessment of relevant HRQOL dimensions and the generic measures can be used across populations, diseases, and medical treatments to measure HRQOL.

Utility/Preference Measures

The utility measures represent the strength of a person's preference for different health outcomes or conditions under conditions of uncertainty (30,31). Preferences are the values persons assign to health states when uncertainty is not a condition of measurement. Utilities, or preferences, are quantified on a scale from 1 (anchored as perfect health or the best possible health state) to 0 (anchored as death or the worst possible health state). A number of techniques have been used to assign preferences directly or indirectly, including categorical rating scales, standard gamble, time trade-off, and multiattribute indexes.

Utility scores can be combined with survival data to calculate quality-adjusted life-years (QALYs), which are useful indicators of outcome for cost-effectiveness analysis (or cost/utility analysis). Although utilities have clear advantages for pharmacoeconomic evaluations, especially those based on clinical decision analysis and modeling, there are some concerns. Utility scores vary by the structure and content of health state descriptions, how outcomes are framed, and different scaling methods (32,33).

Multiattribute Utility Measures

Multiattribute utility measures have been developed that represent hybrids of the psychometric and utility-based measures. The Quality of Well-Being Scale (QWB) (34–36) and the Health Utility Index (HUI) (37,38) use multidimensional health indexes and different scaling methods to calculate preference scores. However, there are differences in the way utility/preference scores are obtained by the QWB and HUI. The QWB obtains information about multidimensional health states and then use separate utility weights from population surveys to combine them. The HUI requires subjects to rate their own health state on a series of questions and then uses a multiattribute status classification to assign utility scores. The multiattribute approach may be easier to incorporate into clinical studies, although to date the QWB has been included in several clinical trials (35,36), and the HUI has also been used in clinical trials (38).

Relationship between Health Status and Utility/Preference Measures

Research has demonstrated that psychometric health status and utility/preference scores are at best only moderately correlated (32,39–41). Health status and utility/preferences scales measure different components of health outcomes. A person's current HRQOL may only partially account for his/her preferences for their current health state.

INTEGRATING HRQOL IN PHARMACOECONOMIC STUDIES

Utility-based HRQOL outcomes are an integral part of pharmacoeconomic evaluations (3,42). Quality-adjusted life-years represent years of life weighted in some way for the effects of treatment and disease progression on HRQOL. Most often, utility or preference scores supply the weights for this adjustment. Utility-based and psychometrically based HRQOL outcomes represent suitable measures for evaluating the positive and negative impact of both illness and treatment in pharmacoeconomic studies. In general, psychometrically based HRQOL measures assess the outcomes of medications more comprehensively, although utility-based measures are more easily integrated into cost-effectiveness analyses.

In cost/utility analysis, the outcomes of medical treatment are expressed as QALYs (43–45). QALYs integrate mortality and morbidity to express health status in terms of equivalents of well-years of life. Although QALYs are useful denominators for cost-effectiveness ratios, QALYs differ depending on the methods used to develop weights (or utilities/preferences) for adjusting years of life for impact on HRQOL (31).

ISSUES RELATED TO HRQOL IN PHARMACOECONOMIC EVALUATIONS

The world is a multivariate place. The outcomes of pharmaceutical interventions are multiple and it is most informative to provide information on the profile of HRQOL and other outcomes of medical treatment. Multiple outcomes give comprehensive and complete information on the impact of new treatments on patient functioning and well-being. Although it is sometimes difficult for clinicians and health policy makers to integrate multivariate outcomes, global summary scores fail to disclose the exact differences between treatment alternatives. Summary indicators, such as utility scores and QALYs, can easily be incorporated into cost-effectiveness analyses. These indicators may hide outcomes that may be important to patients or to clinicians.

Utilities are used increasingly to generate QALYs as measures of effectiveness in economic evaluations. The use of potentially insensitive measures in cost-effectiveness analysis may lead to inaccurate decisions about the impact of new medicines on health-related outcomes. The health status measures do have substantial evidence for responsiveness to clinically meaningful changes in patient outcomes so there remains the possibility of conflicting findings.

HRQOL outcomes are important and necessary components to defining "effectiveness" in cost-effectiveness analyses. More widespread requirements to demonstrate effectiveness of new medicines and cost effectiveness will necessitate integrating HRQOL into pharmacoeconomic evaluations. Pharmacoeconomic studies need to include measures of clinical outcomes and generic and specific health status, and collect data on the use and costs of health care services. When the new pharmaceutical therapy is expected to result in improved health benefits and somewhat higher medical costs, one of the utility/preference measures should be included to construct summary indicators of health outcome, such as the QALY. Given the current state of health status measurement technology, no single instrument or measurement approach can be used for every pharmacoeconomic evaluation. Selection of HRQOL measures depend on the objectives of the evaluation, the targeted disease and population, psychometric characteristics, practical issues, such as respondent burden, and available resources (2,3,46).

ECONOMIC TESTS AND SCALES

To place the economic measures of quality of life assessments in perspective, one should consider the types of issues that are of concern to economists. Generally economists are concerned with the allocation of resources to alternative ends or objectives. Resources are broadly defined to include not only natural resources but also a wide variety of factors involved in the production of goods and services such as labor, capital equipment, knowledge, skills, and location. The objectives may be stated in terms of the production of goods and services but ultimately involve the satisfaction of individual wants and desires.

Although economists frequently use the terms *utility, individual well-being,* and *satisfaction,* there is no consensus on how to measure these domains. We can often identify changes that increase or decrease individual satisfaction, but attempts to quantify the level of satisfaction are fraught with many problems. Moreover, even if one were satisfied with a scale for a particular individual, it is impossible to make interpersonal comparisons of utility. The question "Has John reached a higher level of utility or satisfaction than Harry?" is not answerable.

COST-EFFECTIVENESS METHODS

Designing and Conducting Cost/Benefit Analyses

In cost/benefit analyses both costs and benefits are measured in monetary terms. Unlike cost-effectiveness analysis, in which the ratio of costs to effects must be compared with an external standard to judge the desirability of a health program, cost/benefit analysis permits a direct comparison of benefits and costs in the same units (47). The challenge, however, is to measure health benefits in monetary units.

CONTINGENT VALUATION AND CLINICAL RESEARCH

If a clinical trial is used as a basis for a cost/benefit analysis, there are two different ways to use the contingent valuation method. The contingent valuation method could be incorporated directly in a clinical trial that compares two or more alternative treatments to investigate the willingness to pay for the treatments in the different groups. One test of validity could then be carried out by testing if the willingness to pay increases with the size of the health effects (although this exercise is rarely used in actual practice). This assumes that the size of the health effects can somehow be measured. If, for example, an experimental treatment reduces the risk of some event, one could measure the perceived risk reduction of the patients and test whether the willingness to pay increases with the perceived risk reduction. For treatments that improve quality of life, it may be possible to correlate improvements in quality of life with willingness to pay. If the number of QALYs gained are estimated in the trial for the different treatments, it could also be tested whether willingness to pay increases with the number of QALYs gained. An advantage of using the contingent valuation method within a clinical trial is that it should be possible to achieve a high response rate.

Alternatively, the results of the clinical trial could be used to describe the health consequences of different treatments, and then these health improvements could be valued using the contingent valuation method in either a general population sample or a sample of patients with the disease under study. By valuing the size of the health improvement in different subsamples, it can be tested if willingness to pay increases with the size of the health improvement. It should be noted that cost/benefit analysis and cost-effectiveness analysis should not necessarily be viewed as mutually exclusive approaches to economic evaluation. To use cost-effectiveness analysis for decision making, the willingness to pay per effectiveness unit (e.g., life-years or QALYs gained) has to be determined. The contingent valuation method (or revealed preference studies) could then be used to estimate the willingness to pay per unit of effectiveness in order to provide an external standard for cost-effectiveness ratios. The usefulness of this system is questionable.

DESIGNING AND CONDUCTING COST-MINIMIZATION AND COST-EFFECTIVENESS ANALYSES

Basing decisions solely on daily treatment cost may lead one to the false economizing. Downstream events, not the least of which is some measure of out-

TABLE 7.6 *Major study designs for economic evaluations*

Type of analysis	Compares	To
Cost effectiveness	$ Value of resources used up	Clinical effects
Cost/utility	$ Value of resources used up	Quality of life produced by the clinical effects
Cost/benefit	$ Value of resources used up	$ Value of resources saved or created

come, must be considered if economic analysis is to be honestly brought to bear on an issue. Other downstream issues relating to costs must also be considered, for example, the use of concomitant medications, monitoring of blood levels, hospitalizations, physician visits, etc. A simple look at daily treatment cost will lead to proper economic decisions only fortuitously. Table 7.6 summarizes three major forms of economic evaluation.

Defining CMA and CEA

Cost-effectiveness analyses (CEA) is the major analytical method in the pharmacoeconomic armamentarium, accompanied by cost-minimization analyses (CMA), cost/utility analysis (CUA) and cost/benefit analysis (CBA) in being designed to pronounce on the optimality of various types of interventions in an economic context. Often the list of analytical methods also includes quality of life (QOL) analysis and cost-of-illness (COI) studies. These latter methods do not explicitly consider the optimality of an intervention, but serve to measure its impact on either outcome or cost alone. The primary differentiating factor between the two methods addressed in this section and CBA and CUA (as alternative methods) lies in the way intervention effects are treated. In CUA and CBA effects are explicitly valued in either "utility" or monetary terms. In CMA and CEA, effects are not valued (48).

CEA can only indicate relative superiority to answer questions such as "Which is better?" or "What does it cost to bring about a certain effect?" from an economic point of view. CEA does not claim that what is better is necessarily worth doing. Thus, treatment A may be economically superior in producing an outcome compared to treatment B, but it may still cost so much to produce such a marginally valuable effect that its use remains unappealing. CBA is the only method that is generally suited to pronouncements on anything but relative worth in that it explicitly states whether benefits exceed costs. If so, the project is worth pursuing (although others may be even more worthwhile).

In CMA, effects are placed in a completely subordinate position and more or less wholly ignored except to assume equivalence in effect between interventions. The CMA task then is limited to assessing costs of the alternatives. Since effects are the same, the decision as to optimal intervention is based on cost alone. The cheapest intervention is deemed (relatively) optimal, barring any other relevant noneconomic considerations (e.g., ethical arguments). This is the simplest of all methods of economic evaluation, though its simple definition belies the potential for error. To the extent that the assumption of equal effect is flawed, the analysis makes an incorrect cost comparison of two different things. Furthermore, costing issues are not always clear, leading to oversimplification.

CEA requires not that effects be identical, but that they be comparable in terms of some "natural unit" of effect, such as cases detected, number of lives saved, or years of life saved. Once effects are reduced to these common natural units, the cost of achieving them can be compared. This method shares the costing difficulties of CMA and introduces the added dimension of differential effect, making it at the same time both more useful and more difficult to implement. Clearly this is a much more useful method as it permits comparisons among highly diverse interventions. Thus, two treatments might save lives with different probabilities and costs; however, both treatments can be described by their cost per (statistical) life-year saved, making them comparable in terms of the costs of achieving that outcome. Figure 7.1 illustrates CEA ratios of a treatment. A drawback of CEA is that all effects are assumed to be valued identically. This is a potential problem for two reasons. First, some effects that may be equal in terms of effects expressed in "natural units," may differ markedly in quality associated with the effect (hence the development of CUA from CEA). Second, natural units are assumed to be all equivalent in another sense. One year of life saved for each of 20 people is assumed to be equivalent to 20 (discounted) years

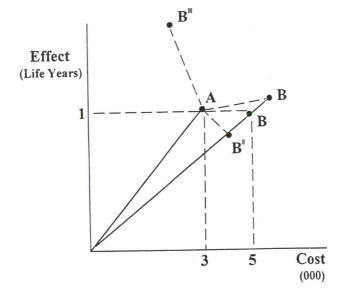

FIG. 7.1. Illustration of effectiveness cost ratios of a new treatment B (various versions) versus that of an established treatment A.

of life for one person. This issue leads to the question of whether to use a utilitarian or a pragmatic approach to resource allocation.

A further drawback of CEA is that health care interventions are rarely so similar so as to be measurable in terms of a single effect. For example, Edelson et al. (49) found captopril to rank poorly as compared to other angiotensin-converting enzyme (ACE) inhibitors from a cost-effectiveness standpoint when the effect measure was projected mortality. However, Croog et al. (50) found captopril to be superior in terms of blood pressure control and HRQOL. Multiple effects cannot typically be incorporated in CEA. Drummond et al. (48) suggested using CEA when one of the following conditions apply: "(a) that there is one, unambiguous objective of the intervention(s) and therefore a clear dimension along which effectiveness can be assessed; or (b) that there are many objectives, but that the alternative interventions are thought to achieve these to the same extent."

COMMON ISSUES

Elusive Effects

Measuring effects is crucial for CEA (and CBA and CUA). The typical effect measure in pharmacoeconomics is taken from a randomized, controlled trial of one or more pharmaceuticals. The choice of a comparator is primarily a clinical issue, so that all the clinical limitations in a randomized controlled trial are carried forward into the pharmacoeconomic analyses. Marketing factors should also be considered. In the case where placebo is the comparison in the trial, an economic evaluator is faced with a difficult problem, in that placebos are not in fact given in practice and the data from such a comparison will not (unless there is a complete absence of a placebo effect) reflect the effects to be expected under "no treatment." Clearly, if "no treatment" is not a relevant alternative, the placebo comparison helps even less. For a CEA that relies on data solely from a trial, the placebo comparison is of little value. More reasonable is an active comparator—not just any active comparator, but a market-relevant one. This too may mean many things to many people. In short, the comparator should be that which is most relevant to whomever the study is being used to influence. Based on formal economic evaluation guidelines for the Australian government reimbursement authority, the relevant comparator is the most widely used alternative in Australia (51). In the latest version of the Canadian guidelines, the relevant comparator is "both existing practice and minimal practice," each of which is defined in the guidelines. It is therein further emphasized that "all other reasonable alternative therapies should be at least discussed" (52). That decided, there remains a crucial issue that is very difficult to overcome—the randomized, controlled trial framework is generally a biased study design for making economic (or other) inferences about the population of most relevance—those who will in practice be given the drug. The randomized, controlled trial recruitment patterns, and protocol-driven treatment, among other influences, will tend to lessen the real world relevance of randomized, controlled trial-based studies. This precaution should always be kept in mind when basing effect measures on randomized, controlled trial results (53,54).

Incremental CEA results are presented in ratio form: the cost per additional unit of effect. Thus, a cost of $100,000 to save 20 (discounted) years of life implies a $5,000 cost per life-year saved. Sometimes results are presented in units of effect per dollar cost, driving home the opportunity cost in effects of dollars spent (55). The relevant issue is what the new treatment provides in addition to the old treatment (and what additional costs it imposes). This is not meant to imply that it is used with the old treatment.

DESIGNING AND CONDUCTING COST/UTILITY ANALYSES

Cost/utility analyses are a particular form of economic evaluation in which the outcomes are expressed in QALYs gained, and the quality-adjustment weights come from utilities (56). In this definition, the term *utility* is used in its broad sense referring to any cardinal measure of preference. Cost/utility analyses are in fact just a special form of cost-effectiveness analysis, and all the requirements and considerations for cost-effectiveness analysis apply equally to cost/utility analysis. Figure 7.2 illustrates the use of QALY as a measure of health (morbidity and mortality).

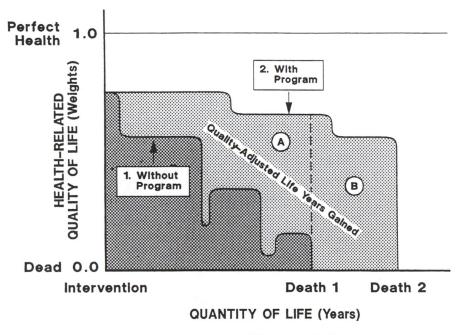

FIG. 7.2. Quality-adjusted life-years gained.

The potential advantage of cost/utility analysis is threefold. First, the QALY is an absolutely general measure of health outcome that simultaneously captures changes in both mortality and morbidity, and is applicable to all diseases and conditions. Thus, it provides a common metric for comparing programs of all types. Second, cost/utility analysis incorporates the preferences of individuals for the outcomes. Clearly, any approach that wishes to be responsive to individuals must incorporate their preferences. Third, when the preferences are measured using von Neumann-Morgenstern utilities (57), cost/utility analysis has the added advantage that the measured preferences are precisely interpretable. They are cardinal measures of preference by individuals, on an interval scale with two predefined anchor points, based on the dominant normative paradigm of decision making under uncertainty, von Neumann-Morgenstern utility theory (57). Because it enables comparability across studies of all diseases and conditions, cost/utility analysis is an important analytic technique for economic evaluation in general, and for clinical trials in particular.

STATISTICAL ISSUES AND CEA

Those in the business of efficacy determination are sometimes confused by the apparent lack of statistical hypothesis testing or confidence interval estimation in pharmacoeconomic studies. In pharmacoeconomics, the potential variation in results of studies is typically captured in sensitivity analyses where parameters (e.g., efficacy rates) are varied to determine the sensitivity of the results to such variation (58). However, sensitivity analysis leaves much to be desired in terms of its being arbitrary in scope and interpretation and practically limited in its ability to indicate effects of simultaneous variation in more than a few underlying parameters (59). Next to the apparently more highly developed statistical methods used in comparing clinical endpoints, economic analysts of CEA data appear to be somewhat lacking in statistical sophistication.

Economic evaluations should estimate an incremental cost-effectiveness ratio and judge the treatment to be "worth it" by comparing it to other interventions that cost more in bringing about a similar incremental effect. Economic analysis still frequently uses average cost-effectiveness ratios (though calling them simply, "cost-effectiveness ratios"), ignoring the necessity of using incremental analysis in defiance of all methodological discussions in the literature. Formal considerations of whether interventions are worthwhile are often done with so-called league tables, which rank interventions by cost per life-year saved. Implicitly such league tables assume that all analyses they include are done (a) correctly, and (b) with comparable methods (since method variability can lead to variability in results).

In cost/utility analysis (CUA), the measure of clinical effects is adjusted to reflect the HRQOL of the outcome. In this approach life-years are converted into quality-adjusted life-years (methods for estimating the quality adjustments are

TABLE 7.7 *Example of cost/utility analysis*

	Total cost ($)	Expected utility	Cost/utility ratio (dollars per utile)	Rank
Drug A	$40	20.8	1.92	Third
Drug B	$50	27.5	1.82	Second
Drug C	$75	52	1.44	First

Note: The drug with the lowest cost per utile would be the preferred therapy.

discussed below). Table 7.7 gives an example of CUA. As in CEA, the analyst is not required to place a dollar value on the outcome. Unlike the CEA approach, however, the approach does explicitly incorporate HRQOL information in the results. Utility measures share some characteristics with health profiles and specific instruments. Like health profiles, utility measures are widely applicable. Utility instruments give scores on a very generalizable 0 (death) to 1 (perfect health) scale, thus facilitating broad comparisons of the effects of alternative health care programs. The design of utility measures for specific applications, however, allows the analyst to incorporate, as with specific instruments, items of particular importance or relevance in that setting. Health-state descriptions used with utility instruments typically include physical mobility, vision, hearing, speech, emotion, cognition, dexterity, and pain. The utility approach has an advantage relative to the specific approach in that the patient globally assesses the net effect of the treatment on his/her HRQOL. Thus, the patient's response summarizes his/her evaluation both of the positive treatment effects and the negative side effects. With specific instruments, these are measured separately and, therefore, the analyst has little or no information on the patient's trade-offs among the therapeutic improvements and treatment side effects. The same point applies to health-profile instruments for which no single summary score is available. Table 7.8 lists the many different items for inclusion in calculations of direct and indirect costs.

In cost/benefit analysis (CBA) costs and consequences are all expressed in pecuniary terms. This technique was first applied to the evaluation of public expenditures in water resource development. In the context of health care, however, most analysts have found CBA to be less satisfactory than CEA or CUA for several reasons. In particular, many analysts are uncomfortable with the ethical

TABLE 7.8 *Example of cost considerations in economic study*

Alternatives	Direct costs ($)	Indirect costs ($)	Total costs ($)
Drug V	20	90	110
Drug W	30	75	105
Drug X	25	80	105
Drug Y	45	70	115
Drug Z	40	85	125

TABLE 7.9 *Example of quality of life scores and (ADR) considerations combined through a multiattribute approach*

Alternatives	QOL score[a] (%)	Absence of ADR[b] (%)	Success index (%)
Drug V	84	91	75
Drug W	84	70	59
Drug X	95	89	84
Drug Y	95	78	73
Drug Z	95	89	84

[a]QOL Score as a percent of maximum possible score.
[b]In this example, the absence of ADR is calculated as 100% minus the total percent of ADRs.
Note: These numbers are generally developed through review of the literature and input of expert panel. In this example, success index is calculated by multiplying QOL percent score by absence of ADR score. ADR, adverse drug reactions.

judgments that appear to accompany assigning dollar values to peoples' lives and their suffering. The result has been that CEA studies have become the dominant study design in health care evaluation. In recent years, however, there has been a resurgence in interest in cost/benefit analyses, relying on elicitations from patients of willingness to pay as the source for the estimation of benefits expressed in pecuniary terms.

The focus in the health care evaluation literature on cost-effectiveness analysis has, in concert with the growth in the breadth of outcome measures for clinical studies, shifted toward comparing pecuniary and HRQOL outcome measures. The trend reflects two factors. First, as health care interventions are increasingly focused less on reducing mortality, and more on reducing morbidity and improving HRQOL, it has become more important to measure these outcomes directly and accurately. Second, clinical managers and third-party payers have become increasingly interested in the evaluation of new and existing treatment alternatives and have demanded evidence on costs and effects both in pecuniary and nonpecuniary terms. Table 7.9 is an example of how to use a multiattribute approach and expert opinion to generate total scores based on HRQOL and adverse drug reactions (ADR).

CONDUCT OF STUDIES

As pharmacoeconomics has grown in importance, much more attention has been focused on the credibility of studies in the public domain. The use of acceptable methods is one component of this, but a growing emphasis has been placed on issues of conduct, including the declaration of financial interests and the nature of the contractual relationship between the researcher and the sponsoring company (60). The issues of credibility need to be addressed if pharmacoeconomics is to have any future, and it is therefore likely that both researchers and the sponsors of studies will ultimately realize that some regulation of the process is beneficial to both parties, as well as to the users of studies.

STUDY DESIGN

Sample Size

At the moment there are no well-established procedures for determining the appropriate sample size for an economic evaluation. Two different approaches are possible: hypothesis testing and estimation. In the hypothesis testing approach, the sample size would be determined for the economic question in the same way that it is handled for the clinical question. This would require the researcher to specify policy significant differences in the costs and QALYs, to estimate variances for costs and QALYs, and to select acceptable error rates for type I and type II errors—and there is no reason that the conventional rates of 5% and 10%, respectively, should apply. Although research is underway, procedures to implement the hypothesis testing approach have not yet been developed (61,62).

In the estimation approach, the cost/utility ratio is treated as the variable of interest, and methods are developed to estimate the confidence interval around this ratio, given a particular sample size. Then, depending upon the magnitude of the ratio and the confidence interval, statements can be made about the probability that the true ratio lies above or below certain policy significant threshold levels (63). The problem with this approach is that it requires one to know the final cost/utility ratio in order to determine an appropriate sample size.

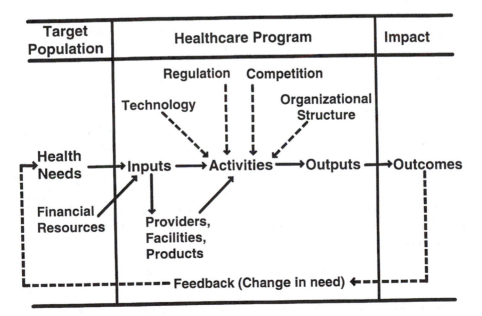

FIG. 7.3. Framework for examining health care programs' expenditures.

DEVELOPING GUIDELINES FOR PHARMACOECONOMIC TRIALS

Pharmacoeconomic trials provide extremely important data that assist formulary committees, physicians and other health care professionals, regulatory authorities, health policy experts, and pharmaceutical companies in decision making. Data are obtained through prospective trials or by retrospective analyses, although it is generally accepted that prospective trials provide more accurate and reliable data than retrospective studies (64–66). Figure 7.3 provides a framework for examining health care expenditures.

HOW BIASES ARE INTRODUCED
INTO PHARMACOECONOMIC TRIALS

It is remarkably easy for the author of a pharmacoeconomic protocol to abuse the scientific process. The most egregious example is where the author starts with the answer he/she wants and then works backward to determine the trial design, parameters, methods, and measures needed to demonstrate that effect. The protocol is then written to accomplish that purpose. For example, the group involved in creating the protocol asks themselves how their product can be shown to be more cost effective than another. Even if a clinical trial design is already written—as it often is for trials where pharmacoeconomic evaluations are intended to be superimposed on an existing protocol—authors also may work backward. In that situation, however, there are usually more constraints on the trial designs and parameters than if the pharmacoeconomic trial is designed de novo (i.e., from the beginning). The process for designing clinical trials differs substantially from pharmacoeconomic trials. In Phase II clinical trials, the test drug is usually compared to a placebo, to an active control, or with itself by using two or more doses. Standard designs and procedures are used that do not allow significant bias to be purposely included. In Phase III trials, after the drug's efficacy and initial safety have been established and the parameters (endpoints) of greatest interest are chosen, these must make the most medical and scientific sense or else the medical community will question and reject the results. For example, the parameters for both safety and efficacy used to evaluate patients in any clinical trial with hypertension, heart failure, or other diseases must be those accepted by medical scientists and practitioners. Moreover, the ability to manipulate the standard procedures for measuring parameters or dosing patients is limited. Thus, standards of clinical trials are generally well established and make the introduction of intentional bias more difficult than in the case of pharmacoeconomic studies.

THE DEBATE ON METHODS

Recent criticisms of "outcomes research," generally defined so as to exclude the randomized, controlled trial, have emphasized the inferential problems associated with methods in observational epidemiology. These problems have been acknowledged by experts in epidemiology for years (71), although their conclusions are somewhat less pessimistic than those of some recent critics. Perhaps chief among the problems is the possibility of selection bias—that allocation of patients to treatments is influenced by patient or disease attributes (e.g., severity). Such selection can obviously interfere with the assignment of responsibility for outcome to the treatments. Randomization, at least in theory, solves this problem.

USE AND OPPORTUNITIES FOR ADMINISTRATIVE DATABASES IN PHARMACOECONOMIC RESEARCH

The use of administrative databases in health services research received a tremendous boost through the establishment of the medical effectiveness/patient outcomes research team (PORT) program supported by the Agency for Health Care Policy and Research (AHCPR) (68,69). Outcomes research in the health care field can be defined as analysis that attempts to explain or describe the results of any type of medical treatment or intervention. Types of outcomes commonly examined in medical effectiveness research include, among others, mortality, morbidity, costs, length of stay, quality of care, and patient satisfaction. Many of these outcomes can be elucidated by retrospective examination of administrative data, i.e., data collected and archived primarily for management, versus research, purposes. All the AHCPR-funded PORTs have included components that use administrative data to examine outcomes. Important applications have included (a) natural history of disease and impact of illness studies, including assessments of rates and trends over large and small geographic areas; (b) examination of costs, access, treatment, and utilization issues relating to procedures and medical regimens, including pharmaceuticals; (c) study of adverse events requiring large populations (i.e., for rare but important reactions), and long-term follow-up (i.e., for late side effects); (d) as an adjunct to clinical trials and to study effectiveness of therapies under "real-world" situations; and (e) as potential sampling frames for subsequent primary data collection (70). Applications in pharmacoeconomic research for administrative data analyses range across the spectrum, from preclinical drug development, where natural history/impact of illness studies are needed, through postmarketing support, where comparative "real-world" effectiveness/outcome/safety studies and modeling of different therapies are possible. Administrative databases can also be used to determine transition probabilities costs of health states for decision models (i.e., natural history).

TYPES OF ADMINISTRATIVE DATABASES

In general, an administrative database is any collection of information recorded in a uniform manner and used for ongoing program operation or assess-

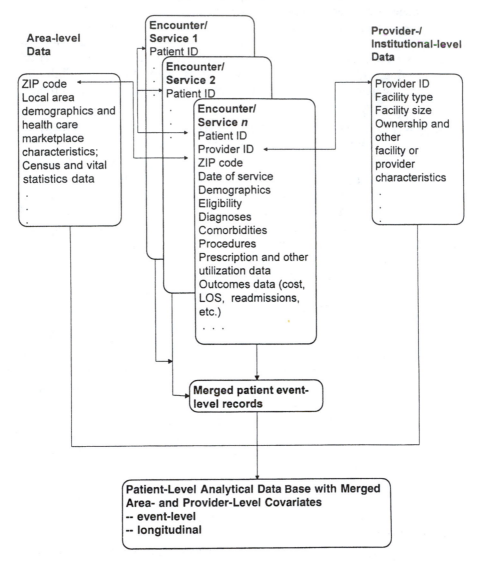

FIG. 7.4. Relationships and linkages among three main types of administrative databases.

ment. Within administrative databases, a "record" or "observation" may refer to the demographics of a particular patient, or may refer to a hospitalization or other health care encounter, such as an office visit, laboratory test, or a prescription. Different administrative databases also focus on health care providers, the health care "marketplace," or any of several other units of interest. Usually, information for these databases is collected over a span of time and is regularly updated. Data are gathered for a variety of purposes, commonly related to health care resource use, and submitted for the purpose of reimbursement, such as in fee-for-service Medicaid, or used for business management, such as in managed-care situations. Administrative databases can focus on specific patient populations, such as enrollees in a health management organization (HMO), or on more general populations, such as aged Medicare Part A recipients, which can in turn serve as proxies (e.g., for all U.S. residents or for those over the age of 65) (70).

Large administrative databases useful for pharmacoeconomic research can be broadly grouped into three types: (a) service/utilization data; (b) provider/institutional data; and (c) area-level socioeconomic/health care marketplace data. Although these databases may have different units of analysis, they can often be linked by a common variable in order to create an analytical database focused on the particular research question, and gathering necessary analytical covariates from several sources that might be missing from a single source. The power of administrative database research is fully realized only when such linkages are accomplished (69). Figure 7.4 provides a schematic view of the interrelationship of the three types of administrative databases. Note that the primary administrative data of interest are usually the patient service-level data, linked within and across episodes by a unique patient identifier, and with provider data and area-level data by provider identifiers and patient postal code of residence. The goal is

TABLE 7.10 *Examples of administrative data bases, by category*

I. Service/Utilization Data
  A. Federal-level data
    1. HCFA Medicare Statistical System
    2. Medicaid data (federal-level)
    3. Department of Veterans Affairs Data
    4. Department of Defense data (including CHAMPUS)
  B. State-/provincial-level data
    1. Medicaid Management Information System data
    2. State hospital discharge data systems
    3. Provincial health plans/prescription drug plans (e.g., Saskatchewan, Manitoba)
  C. Private/proprietary data bases
    1. Blue Cross-Blue Shield data; databases from other insurers
    2. Hospital system and HMO databases
    3. Pharmacy Benefit Manager (PBM) databases
    4. Hospital discharge databases and proprietary data (e.g., CPHA)
    5. Automated medical record datasets (e.g., Regenstrief, GPRD)
II. Provider/Institutional Data
  A. Medicare provider of service data
  B. American Hospital Association Annual Survey data
  C. American Medical Association Master File data
III. Area-level Sociodemographic Data
  A. Health resource and human resources data (e.g., area resource file)
  B. Vital and health statistics databases (e.g., census; National Death Index)
IV. Clinical/epidemiologic/health survey databases
  A. Disease registries (e.g., cancer, end-stage renal disease)
  B. Epidemiologic data bases (e.g., Framingham Study, Manitoba Provincial Health Database)
  C. Health survey data (e.g., National Health Interview Survey)

to produce a patient-level analytical database that builds health care events out of discrete service-level data and merges in useful data from other sources. Furthermore, longitudinal patient-level databases can be built from events linked over time for systems, such as Medicare, in which patient enrollment is consistent. Longitudinal databases, such as those possible with some of the Canadian provincial systems, provide some of the best opportunities for outcomes research.

In addition to population-based administrative data, there are many specialized large databases which are of potential use in pharmacoeconomics. These other databases include disease registries, epidemiologic cohort databases, health survey data, and some large clinical trial databases. Linkage of these databases with administrative databases, although often desirable and potentially informative, can be highly problematic as a result of logistical and confidentiality considerations; moreover, the populations represented by these specialized databases are usually highly selected and nonrepresentative of populations as a whole. It is important initially to establish the expected role and value of each database proposed for linkage and avoid unnecessary work and possibly misleading information. Table 7.10 provides examples of administrative and other large databases within this classification system.

Advantages, Disadvantages, Applications and Caveats of Administrative Databases

There are several immediate and obvious advantages to the use of administrative databases in health services and pharmacoeconomic research. First, because they are already in place, administrative databases offer the ability to address matters of policy concern in a timely and cost-effective manner. Although interim conclusions may have to be validated with longer-term studies (e.g., clinical trials or more traditional epidemiologic studies), the short-term responsiveness of these data sources is a major strength. Administrative databases also provide large numbers of records and broad patient coverage, including both standard and nonstandard treatment. The sizes and coverage offered through administrative databases are often much greater than could be realized in a much more costly primary data collection effort. Administrative databases can have good external validity, although it is critical to understand fully the population represented by the database (71,72). Fundamental to large database research is an understanding of the realities behind the database, often possible only by rigorous investigation and validation, including consulting sources and medical record abstraction.

Even though many potential opportunities have been shown, researchers must also address potential problems. Principal among the problems is that which is inherent in all population-based, nonexperimental approaches: nonrandom selection of patients, with resulting unknown potential biases. This problem may be addressed through careful and cautious use of the database and presentation of results. It is also possible to validate conclusions reached through large database analyses by using more robust experimental approaches. Hlatky et al. (73) showed that clinical trial data can be processed through models built with administrative data. The extent to which predicted values from the resultant models correspond to actual clinical trial outcomes becomes the basis for assessing the validity of the administrative data model.

Within pharmacoeconomic research, problems can occur in establishing the indication for the use of a particular drug, since both on- and off-label use is frequent within a population, and use for multiple indications is also possible. Careful examination of diagnoses and comorbidities on the current record (and previous as well as subsequent records, if possible) can often provide confidence in including or excluding the case from consideration.

There are also important analytical and statistical issues to consider when using administrative databases. Among the most important is an understanding of the coverage of the database, i.e., inclusion or exclusion criteria for cases, events, or variables (74), and the completeness of the database for the population, both within a record and across an individual's records. Lack of familiarity with the database can easily lead to improper generalization if it turns out that the coverage and completeness are not fully understood (71).

The fact that many of the administrative databases have to do with reimbursement is a potential strength for pharmacoeconomic research. These databases, however, are generally organized around payment line items (e.g., physician, pharmacy, hospital charges) that require construction of "episodes of care" by linkage of service-level records. Mitchell et al. (75) describe critical analytical issues faced by the PORTs in administrative database analysis, and approaches related to (a) identification of index cases or patient cohorts; (b) defining the length of the episode; (c) measuring outcomes; and (d) identifying adverse events and associated sequelae. Most importantly, administrative databases should not be used for comparisons among treatments because the data are confounded by indication (e.g., patient selection by diagnosis).

Because of the large number of records in administrative databases, caution must be used in interpreting and reporting statistical results. As the number of records used in an analysis increases, the standard errors of estimates will diminish. This leads to a higher likelihood of statistical significance (i.e., smaller p values). In other words, a small difference between two values is likely to be a statistically significant difference. It is up to clinicians and other experts associated with the study, however, to determine whether the difference is "clinically significant." Furthermore, large administrative databases provide the opportunity for large numbers of multiple comparisons. The risk of meaningless chance association is substantial if "data dredging" or "fishing expeditions" are undertaken. It is therefore essential for the validity and credibility of the research that the research questions and the methodologic and statistical approach be established a priori.

It is also important to get current clinical input with regard to codes, since conventions for coding may vary from one database to another, based on function, and reimbursement incentives related to coding may change over time. Coding of comorbid conditions, functional status, and severity of illness also represent potentially critical information gaps in the use of administrative databases. For pharmacoeconomic research, inadequate linkages may exist between pharmacy and patient medical data, or services and episodes may be defined differently, requiring great care in producing the merged analytical file.

Finally, there may be subtle and/or complex characteristics of the databases, and unwritten or non-updated documentation. Lack of familiarity with file designs and/or survey sampling designs can lead to erroneous conclusions. It is important to have an early working relationship with people who are familiar with the structure of the database, so that the "oral" as well as written documentation may be accessed, and not-so-obvious as well as obvious pitfalls avoided. All of these analytical and statistical issues are made more complex when multiple administrative databases are combined or linked.

Administrative database analysis is becoming a vital component of pharmacoeconomic research. There is currently little standardization in the approaches researchers have taken with administrative databases. "Validation protocols," defined as careful documentation of all steps in constructing analysis files from the source databases, would allow both replication of results as well as research audits. Furthermore, the validation of a statistically representative sample of records against primary sources may be necessary. Although administrative databases allow great opportunity for data exploration and hypothesis generation, research protocols need to be explicit about the questions the administrative database research is expected to address. Administrative data should be seen as only one of several important sources of information for outcomes research. The use of pre-existing administrative databases in the assessment of health care technologies, resource use, and patient outcomes will probably become increasingly prevalent due to favorable cost, timeliness, and ease-of-access issues. Uses in the area of pharmacoeconomic research are just developing but have great promise with the increasing sophistication and coverage/linkage potential of databases at all levels—provider, insurer, and government. The increasingly greater use of computer support for health care administration under managed care also makes it highly likely that these databases will be harnessed. The potentially great influence this research may have, however, and the wide-ranging nature of conclusions make it critical that the use of this methodology be done carefully and that analyses be subject to strict research designs.

USING DECISION ANALYSIS TO CONDUCT PHARMACOECONOMIC STUDIES

Decision analysis provides an orderly, analytical approach to assist the decision maker in identifying the preferred course of action from among competing alternatives. It is *explicit*—it forces you to structure the decision you face as well as identify the consequences of the possible decision outcomes; it is *quantita-tive*—it forces you to assign numbers to probability estimates and outcome valuations; and it is *prescriptive*—the analysis identifies the route to take to maximize the expected value of the decision as you have specified the structure of the decision, its probabilities, and its outcome values.

RESPONSES BY PHARMACEUTICAL AND OTHER HEALTH-RELATED COMPANIES

Adequate standards are needed for designing, conducting, and interpreting pharmacoeconomic trials. Pharmaceutical and other health-related companies should strive to raise the rigor of current practices. Trials should be approached in a logical, objective, and scientifically disinterested way. This reduces the risks to both the investigator and the medicine developer. A company cannot afford to develop medicines based on false data, misleading interpretations, inappropriate analyses, or the subjective desires of senior managers for a medicine "to work." This is one reason that more economic models are being used to decide whether to stop a drug development or other project. The same thinking, attitudes, and also the same consequences do not currently exist for pharmacoeconomic trials. It is often the clinical group or their managers in a pharmaceutical company that has the most difficulty stopping a program they have fostered from preclinical testing. The pharmacoeconomic team may reveal the low likelihood of product success in the marketplace based on pharmacoeconomic studies.

ESTABLISHING STANDARDS FOR PHARMACOECONOMIC TRIALS

It is clear that no single pharmacoeconomic methodology (cost effectiveness, cost/utility, cost/benefit) will be suitable for evaluating new medicines or treatments in all situations. Appropriate parameters for each pharmacoeconomic trial must be identified on a case-by-case basis. Nonetheless, there are a number of principles that should be discussed to establish practice standards (76). A consensus document would be a valuable first step. Among the guidelines to be discussed are the following:

1. All direct and indirect costs of a treatment must be measured in a pharmacoeconomic trial, unless there are specific reasons not to do so and these are clearly stated. Evaluating only certain costs is unacceptable because bias can result. All costs should be explicitly stated in publications and reports or by reference to an accepted list.
2. Intangible costs such as grief, pain, anxiety, depression, loss of companionship, are not to be measured directly in pharmacoeconomic trials, even though these costs are often quite important in legal cases and from other perspectives (e.g., ethical). These emotions are often experienced by the

family, friends, and coworkers of the patient in addition to the patient himself/herself. Circumstances may be established when it is relevant to measure these costs in pharmacoeconomic trials. These factors are often either directly or indirectly included in most evaluations of quality of life, which in itself is an important efficacy measure. Intangible costs are not generally assigned a financial value in an analysis of costs.

3. Cost/benefit methods are rarely, if ever, relevant for pharmaceutical companies to use when evaluating the pharmacoeconomics of a single medicine or treatment. This method, however, is valid and has other important uses (e.g., for academic studies, for allocating national resources among various diseases for treatment or research).

4. There is no single method (e.g., cost/utility or cost effectiveness) that is preferable to use in all pharmacoeconomic studies.

5. If data are obtained in an artificial environment as is true for most clinical trials, then their relevance for actual clinical practice environments should be discussed in detail when interpreting results.

6. Wherever relevant, every effort should be made to conduct randomized, controlled, prospective studies and all studies should be as rigorously controlled as is possible.

7. Pharmacoeconomic trial protocols, either add-ons to clinical trials or as independent trials should be reviewed prior to conduct, whenever possible, by at least one experienced economist, an experienced clinical trialist, and by a statistician. It may also be relevant to discuss the trial protocol with one or more members of the target group that will eventually review the results.

8. It is not always mandatory to measure the most important efficacy parameters when designing a cost-effectiveness assessment. The most important parameter could be too difficult to measure, take too much time to evaluate, or be too expensive to evaluate. In addition, an adequate surrogate marker may be readily available. For example, in most diseases, efficacy or effectiveness can be measured with a number of parameters including clinical symptoms, clinical signs, laboratory parameters, laboratory tests, physician or other health professional assessments (including subjective evaluations), and patient-based measures (including subjective evaluations), not to mention economic assessments of efficacy (e.g., days at work). The basis on which the choice is made is critical. This issue requires further discussion to determine what standards are appropriate.

9. It is often counterproductive to conduct pharmacoeconomic trials early in a medicine's development when the most appropriate dosages and means of using the medicine are incompletely known. This practice can lead to the collection of incorrect data that may lead to inappropriate conclusions. An early trial on erythropoietin reported that it cost £126,290 to achieve a QOL-adjusted year, whereas a later trial found the value was £20,022 (77).

10. A logical series of steps to design and conduct a pharmacoeconomic trial should be discussed and recommended.

Other principles and standards will undoubtedly emerge from discussions among the participants who create these guidelines. Given the great number of reasons to reduce biases in the design and conduct of pharmacoeconomic trials, it is concluded that establishing guidelines for pharmacoeconomic trials will provide a major benefit to all people who use these data and ultimately to all patients. Fortunately, this goal can be achieved through national and international cooperation among academic, regulatory authority, and industry personnel.

STEPS AND METHODOLOGIC CONSIDERATIONS IN THE DECISION ANALYTIC PROCESS

Decision analysis involves six major steps.

1. Identify the decision, including the selection of the decision options to be studied. Bound the time frame of the decision and determine from which perspective the decision is to be made.
2. Structure the decision and the consequences of each decision option over time.
3. Assess the probability that each consequence will occur.
4. Determine the value of each outcome (e.g., in dollars, quality-adjusted life-years saved, utilities).
5. Select the option with the highest expected outcome.
6. Determine the robustness of the decision by conducting a sensitivity analysis and varying the values of probabilities and outcomes over a range of likely values.

Without such a structured process, decisions involving multiple factors are often flawed when the decision maker implicitly attempts to juggle and combine important elements (78). Errors occur because it is difficult to intuitively combine complex information, generate revised probabilities, and give proportional weight to events of differing importance which occur at differing times (79,80). Decision analysis provides the structure to identify these factors explicitly and to combine the various sources of information quantitatively to identify the decision option that offers the best chance for the desired outcome.

But decision analysis is more than a systematic approach to solving problems under conditions of uncertainty. It creates a fundamental change in the way in which one approaches a decision. The use of decision analysis engenders an attitude toward the problem or decision—to think more analytically; to force the consideration of consequences of actions; to recognize explicitly that uncertainty is present, to estimate the degree of uncertainty, and to assess your attitude toward risk; and to determine which are the relevant outcome measures and to value your preferences for the alternative outcomes.

The decision tree model graphically structures and follows the progress of a patient or patient population from the choice of decisions through a defined period of time. It is best used to structure decisions when any event subsequent to the decision usually happens only once and at some prespecified time, and the patient is not at continuous risk for the condition or sequelae to reoccur. If an event does recur, it must be inserted as a branch within the decision tree. The decision tree model is limited if the event of interest does not always happen at the same time, and different values or preferences are associated with the event occurring at different times (e.g., death in 1 year versus 10 years). The differential timing of the event cannot be built into the model but must be reflected in the utility of the outcome. Currently, most decision analyses involving pharmaceutical products use the decision tree model (often for lack of actual patient data).

A Markov model should be considered when patients fluctuate among a finite number of clinical states over time, when events can reoccur because patients remain exposed to risk, and when the timing of the transition between health states is uncertain but affects the utility of the state. In this model, the prognosis of a disease is viewed as a set of transitions between a set of health states during the time horizon of the decision. The period of time is divided into equal increments of time or cycles. During each cycle, the patient may make a transition from one clinical state of a given utility to another state with a different utility. Although the transitions cannot be predicted definitely, their probabilities can be estimated. The length of time spent in each state and the associated utility of the state are combined to determine the expected value for each decision option (81,82).

Structure the Decision and Its Consequences Over Time

This is one of the most powerful features of decision analysis. Using the decision tree model, the decision maker is forced to explicitly structure the situation, thus changing the unexamined, intuitive process into one in which the thought process is clearly articulated. Laying out the tree prods the decision maker to identify the relationships that exist between the decision options and the consequences of selecting each of the alternative options. The tree becomes a tool to assist in thinking through a decision, as well as to assist in communications among individuals and departments working on the same analysis. With a decision tree, coworkers can identify where they agree or disagree in the considered alternatives and consequences, suggest additional consequences that must be included in the tree, or recommend that a branch be trimmed.

A decision tree begins with a choice node (a small square) with branches indicating the considered options originating from the choice node and structured to the right. The choice node indicates that the decision maker has the ability to choose among the options or branches originating from that node. The structure of the tree continues to the right as the consequences of each action are identified and added. These consequences are structured chronologically over time by asking a series of "if/then" questions. For example, if the decision maker chooses Option A, what will happen? If the decision maker cannot control the occurrence of the next event, and a possibility exists that any one of several things will hap-

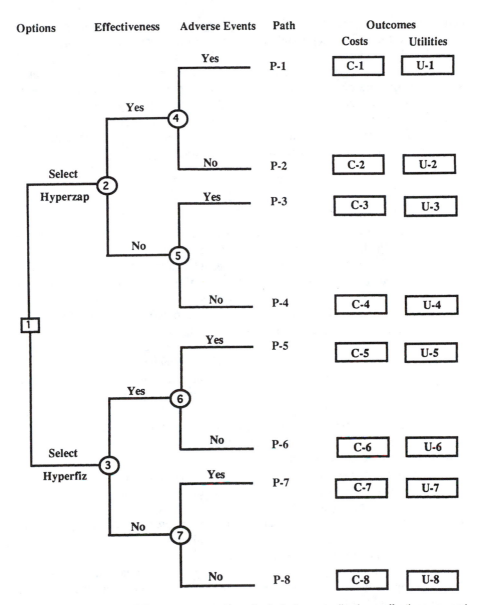

FIG. 7.5. Decision tree of Hyperzap versus Hyperfiz, including complications, effectiveness, and outcomes of decision options.

pen if Option A is chosen, a choice node (a small circle) is inserted in the Option A branch followed by the possible events which may occur. A choice node indicates that there is uncertainty about what will happen next.

To conduct a comprehensive pharmacoeconomic study, the decision maker must structure the decision tree to include both the effectiveness and adverse events of the medication. At a minimum, this ensures that both the cost of the medication, as well as the induced costs associated with adverse events, are included in the analysis. Figure 7.5 presents a simplified tree of a decision between two fictional antihypertensive medications.

Assess Probabilities

The decision maker must estimate the probability that each of the consequences at each chance node will occur. That means that in the simplified decision tree in Fig. 7.5, probabilities must be determined for each consequence originating from chance nodes 2 to 7. The sum of the probabilities of all consequences originating from each chance node must sum to 1.0; therefore, it is essential that all possible consequences be identified at each chance node. Because there is a 100% certainty that something will happen at each chance node, nodes with probabilities totaling less than 1.0 have not identified all possibilities, or probabilities have been estimated incorrectly.

A large, randomized control trial providing information on the options being considered would provide an ideal database to determine probabilities. However, those are rarely found in the clinical literature. Instead the investigator must obtain probability estimates from limited clinical trial information, meta-analyses, expert opinion, or other clinicians. These sources are flawed. Clinical trials may be of insufficient size to detect rare events. This leads to distortions in the model, especially when a rare event occurs and is associated with great cost. Expert or peer estimates could be considered, but psychologists say that we are poor estimators of probabilities (82). Overestimates of the occurrence of rare events and underestimate the frequency with which common events happen. And experts, basing their estimates on their atypical and more seriously ill patient population, also overestimate the frequency of the uncommon. Using data from pivotal clinical trials helps overcome concerns about external validity (i.e., the trial data represent only a select population). Transition probabilities and costs can be varied within the model, within reasonable limits.

Value Outcomes

Just like any other type of pharmacoeconomic analysis, decision analysis requires that the economic costs and other outcome valuations be determined for the different treatment options. However, what makes decision analysis different from the other approaches is that decision analysis provides a clear, explicit structure that outlines discrete paths of events—a decision path—which needs to be valued. A decision path originates from the initial choice nodes on the left and proceeds to the right as the consequences of the initial decision are detailed and the tree is developed. For our simplified case, eight decision paths are identified and are labeled P-1, P-2, P-3, and so on.

Choose the Preferred Course of Action—
Calculate the Expected Value for the Economic and Noneconomic
Outcome of Each Decision Option or Strategy?

How does one combine the various decision options, probability estimates, and outcome valuations to choose the preferred course of action? How does one "solve" a decision tree? First, it is necessary to break the decision tree into its component parts and analyze smaller sections. This is done in reverse order of the tree's development by starting from the right and working back to the initial decision or choice node on the left. The process is called "averaging out and folding back," since each path's outcome value weighted by its probability of occurrence (averaging out) working from right to left, from outcomes to options (folding back). The weighted value at the chance node is called an "expected value" because it is the expected, but not certain, value based on probabilistic estimates that events of different valuations will occur.

At each chance node, outcome values are combined with, and weighted by, their respective probability of occurring. This yields an expected value at each chance node. If the decision analysis has only one choice node, the averaging out and folding back process continues until the expected values are determined for the options originating from the original choice node. If there are one or other choice nodes embedded in the analysis, at each embedded choice node, the option with the highest expected value is selected, and this value is carried to the left to the next chance node.

From the identification of the decision options, the time frame, the decision criteria, and the objectives of the decision maker—through the structuring of the decision and the identification of all consequences—to probability estimation and outcome valuation; the clinical question now has had an explicit, structured, analytic, and quantitative assessment with a preferred action course identified.

Pharmacoeconomic evaluations would be strengthened by the use of fully developed and specified decision analytic models. The explicit processes of decision analysis provides the template upon which all forms of pharmacoeconomic evaluations—cost/efficiency, cost-effectiveness, cost/utility, and cost/benefit studies—can be more carefully and comprehensively organized and conducted. From the framing of the question, to identifying the options, perspective, and time frame for the analysis; identifying and structuring the sequence of events and consequences that may follow when an option is chosen;

estimating the probabilities that these events and consequences will occur; valuing the outcomes for each chosen option in both economic and noneconomic units; and finally determining the option with the highest expected value or outcome for the decision maker—all are explicit steps that assist the decision maker to incorporate all factors affecting the decision, its consequences, and outcomes. Given that institutional constraints and limited financial resources will continue to influence health care allocations, decision analysis provides a method by which we can improve our position within this new health care market.

CURRENT DIRECTIONS

Early experience with pharmacoeconomics relied on retrospective looks at trial data which were never intended to be used for economic purposes. Unavoidably, these pharmacoeconomic analyses relied on modeling techniques to speculate on the economic implications of certain efficacy or safety endpoints. Databases were examined, expert opinion solicited or literature surveyed (informally or formally via meta-analytic methods). This information was combined with retrospective analyses of trial data, typically in a decision analytic model. More recently, we have seen the development of prospective trial designs that explicitly incorporate economic data collection. Reliance on randomized, controlled trials, even those prospectively designed to include economic variables, will not provide all necessary information for pharmacoeconomics.

Applications and Uses of Pharmacoeconomics

1. *The main trend in the development of methods:* This trend is likely to be toward the measurement of economic parameters alongside clinical trials and to lead to more naturalistic trials and to developments in the statistical analysis of economic data.
2. *The main trend in the conduct of studies:* This trend will be toward the development of ethical codes that will have, as their main purpose, maintenance or improvement of the credibility of pharmacoeconomic studies. Such a trend is inevitable because, in the long run, it is in the interests not only of the users of studies but also researchers and sponsors.
3. *The main trend in the application and use of studies:* This trend will not be toward the growth of formal requirements, such as in Australia, but toward a more widespread interest in economic data at all levels in the health care system. Therefore, there will be a number of potential audiences for pharmacoeconomic data. The main role for guidelines for the provision of data will be in the establishment of standards for the methodology and conduct of studies. There will also be a move toward greater harmonization in the standards of analysis required by different jurisdictions.

THE FUTURE OF PHARMACOECONOMICS

The distinction between modeling studies and trial-based studies is a little artificial. Some modeling studies draw heavily on data from randomized controlled trials. Some trial-based studies incorporate an element of modeling, either to adapt what was found in the trial to other settings or to project costs and outcomes beyond the period observed in the trial. However, even where modeling is used as an adjunct, the study user is likely to expect the "within-trial" result to be reported and increased emphasis is likely to be placed on what was found, rather than what was assumed.

The demand for trial-based pharmacoeconomic studies is likely to become most apparent in situations in which measurement is considered feasible, that is, where the clinical effect of the medicine concerned can be observed within a reasonable amount of time, or where the impact on resource use of superior efficacy or a better side effect profile can be assessed during a clinical trial. The estimation of these parameters through physician Delphi panels is likely to be regarded as less convincing in the future.

This leaves those problematic situations where the true clinical effect of a medicine can only be observed as the result of a large, long-term, clinical trial, e.g., the impact of lowering cholesterol on overall mortality, or the impact of hormone replacement therapy on fractures in postmenopausal women. Here, one still expects a resistance from some quarters to modeling studies, and there are no obvious solutions for the analyst, other than to keep refining the models as new data become available. Also, it seems somewhat unfair to take economists to task for modeling in these situations, since they are usually only trying to predict the likely outcome of the use of drugs that have already been licensed for the indications concerned.

Another likely trend is that the clinical trials themselves will become more naturalistic; that is, they will be undertaken in settings that more closely reflect regular clinical practice. This change would probably have come about in any case, but it has certainly also been driven by the increased interest in pharmacoeconomics, where data closely reflecting the real world are required for the assessment of cost effectiveness.

REFERENCES

1. Ellwood P. Outcomes management: a technology of patient experience. *N Engl J Med* 1988;318: 1549–1556.
2. Patrick DL, Erickson P. *Health status and health policy: allocating resources to health care.* New York: Oxford University Press, 1992:1–478.
3. Revicki DA. Health care technology assessment and HRQOL. In: Banta HD, Luce BR, eds. *Health care technology and its assessment: an international perspective.* New York: Oxford University Press, 1993:114–131.
4. Eisenberg JM. Clinical economics: a guide to economic analysis of clinical practices. *JAMA* 1989; 262:2879–2886.

5. Drummond MF, Stoddart GL, Torrance GW. *Methods for the economic evaluation of health care programmes.* New York: Oxford University Press, 1987:1–182.
6. Banta HD, Luce BR. *Health care technology and its assessment: an international perspective.* New York: Oxford University Press, 1993:1–352.
7. Eggers P. Comparison of treatments costs between dialysis and transplantation. *Sem Nephrol* 1992; 12:284–289.
8. Edwards W. Toward the demise of economic man and woman: bottom lines from Santa Cruz. In: Edwards W, ed. *Utility theories: measurements and applications.* Boston: Kluwer Academic Publishers, 1992:253–267.
9. Garber AM, Phelps CE. Economic foundations of cost-effective analysis. NBER Working Paper No. 4164. Cambridge, MA: National Bureau of Economic Research, 1992.
10. Brooks RG. *The development and construction of health status measures: an overview of the literature.* Lund: The Swedish Institute for Health Economics, 1986.
11. Kaplan RM, Bush JW, Berry C. Health status: types of validity and the index of well-being. *Health Serv Res* 1976;11:478–507.
12. Read JL, Quinn RJ, Hoefer MA. Measuring overall health: an evaluation of three important approaches. In: Lohr KN, Ware JE Jr, eds. *Advances in health assessment conference proceedings. J Chronic Dis* 1987;40(suppl 1):7S–21S.
13. Torrance GW. Measurement of health state utilities for economic appraisal: a review. *J Health Econom* 1986;5:1–30.
14. Kunreuther H. Limited knowledge and insurance protection. *Public Policy* 1976;24:229–261.
15. Sheldon TA. Please bypass the PORT. *BMJ* 1994;309:142–143.
16. Buxton MJ, O'Brien BJ. Economic evaluation of ondansetron: preliminary analysis using trial data prior to price setting. *Br J Cancer* 1992;66(suppl XIX):564–567.
17. Rusthoven J, O'Brien BJ, Rocchi A. Ondansetron versus metoclopramide in the prevention of chemotherapy-induced emesis and nausea: a meta-analysis. *Int J Oncol* 1992;1:443–450.
18. Beck TM, Ciociola AA, Jones SE, et al. Efficacy of oral ondansetron in the prevention of emesis in outpatients receiving cyclophosphamide-based chemotherapy. *Annals Intern Med* 1993;118:407–413.
19. Cubeddu LX, Hoffmann IS, Fuenmayor NT, Finn AL. Efficacy of ondansetron (GR 38032F) and the role of serotonin in cisplatin-induced nausea and vomiting. *N Engl J Med* 1990;332:810–816.
20. Rothman KJ, Michels KB. The continuing unethical use of placebo controls. *N Engl J Med* 1994;331: 394–398.
21. Walt RP, Hunt RH, Misiewicz JJ, et al. Comparison of ranitidine and cimetidine maintenance treatment of duodenal ulcer. *Scand J Gastro-enterol* 1984;19:1045–1047.
22. Rittenhouse BE. Is there a need for standardization of methods in economic evaluations of medicine? Med Care 1996; 34 (12 Suppl): DS13–22
23. O'Brien BJ. *Cholesterol and coronary heart disease: consensus or controversy?* London: Office of Health Economics, 1991.
24. Edelson JT, Weinstein MC, Tosteson ANA, et al. Long-term cost-effectiveness of various initial monotherapies for mild to moderate hypertension. *JAMA* 1990;263:407–413.
25. CCOHTA (1994) Canadian Coordinating Office for Health Technology Assessment. *Guidelines for the Economic Evaluation of Pharmaceuticals: Canada,* 1st ed. Ottawa: CCOHTA, November 1994.
26. Laffel GL, Fineberg HV, Braunwald E. A cost-effectiveness model for thrombosis/reperfusion therapy. *J Am Coll Cardiol* 1987;10(suppl B):79B–90B.
27. Drummond MF, Bloom BS, Carrin G, et al. Issues in the cross-national assessment of health technology. *Int J Technol Assess Health Care* 1992;8:671–682.
28. Patrick DL, Deyo R. Generic and disease-specific measures in assessing health status and quality of life. *Med Care* 1989;27:S217–S232.
29. Guyatt GH, Feeny DH, Patrick DL. Measuring HRQOL. *Ann Intern Med* 1993;118:622–629.
30. Keeney RL, Raiffa H. *Decisions with multiple objectives: preferences and value trade-offs.* New York: John Wiley, 1976.
31. Kaplan RM, Feeny DH, Revicki DA. Methods for assessing relative importance in preference based outcome measures. *Qual Life Res* 1993;2:467–475.
32. Revicki DA. Relationship between health utility and psychometric health status measures. *Med Care* 1992;30:MS274–MS282.
33. Mulley A. Assessing patient's utilities: can the ends justify the means? *Med Care* 1989;27:S269–S281.
34. Kaplan RM, Bush J. HRQOL measurement for evaluation research and policy. *Health Psychol* 1982; 1:61–80.

35. Kaplan RM, Anderson J, Wu AW, et al. The quality of well-being scale: applications in AIDS, cystic fibrosis, and arthritis. *Med Care* 1989;27:S27–S43.
36. Kaplan RM, Anderson JP. The general health policy model: an integrated perspective. In: Spilker B, ed. *Quality of life and pharmacoeconomics in clinical trials.* New York: Raven Press 1995;32:309–322.
37. Torrance GW, Zhang Y, Feeny D, et al. *Multi-attribute preference functions for a comprehensive health status classification system.* Paper 92–18. Hamilton, Ontario: McMaster University, 1992.
38. Feeny DH, Torrance GW, Furlong WJ. Health utilities index (HUI). In: Spilker B, ed. *Quality of life and pharmacoeconomics in clinical trials.* New York: Raven Press, 1995;26:239–252.
39. Revicki DA, Kaplan RM. Relationship between psychometric and utility-based approaches to the measurement of HRQOL. *Qual Life Res* 1993;2:477–487.
40. Tsevat J, Goldman L, Lamas GA, et al. Functional status versus utilities in survivors of myocardial infarction. *Med Care* 1991;29:1153–1159.
41. Fryback DG, Dasbach EJ, Klein R, et al. Health assessments by SF-36, quality of well-being index and time-tradeoffs: predicting one measure from another. *Med Decision Making* 1992;12:348.
42. Revicki DA, Rothman M, Luce BR. HRQOLassessment and the pharmaceutical industry. *Pharmacoeconomics* 1992;1:394–408
43. Torrance GW, Feeny DH. Utilities and quality-adjusted life years. *Int J Tech Assess Health Care* 1989; 5:559–575.
44. Kamlet M. *The comparative benefits modeling project. A framework for cost-utility analysis of government health care programs.* Washington, DC: US Department of Health and Human Services, Public Health Service, 1992.
45. Kaplan RM. Utility assessment for estimating quality-adjusted life years. In: Sloan F, ed. *Cost-effectiveness of pharmaceuticals.* New York: Cambridge University Press, 1994.
46. Bergner M, Rothman M. Health status measures: an overview and guide for selection. *Annu Rev Public Health* 1987;8:191–210.
47. Boadway RW, Bruce N. *Welfare economics.* Oxford: Blackwell, 1984.
48. Drummond MF, Stoddart GL, Torrance GW. *Methods for the economic evaluation of health care programmes.* New York: Oxford University Press, 1987.
49. Edelson JT, Tosteson AN, Sax P. Cost-effectiveness of misoprostol for prophylaxis against non-steroidal anti-inflammatory drug-induced gastrointestinal tract bleeding (see comments). *JAMA* 1990;264:41–47.
50. Croog SH, Levine S, Testa MA, et al. The effects of antihypertensive therapy on the quality of life. *N Engl J Med* 1986;314:1657–1664.
51. Drummond MF. Basing prescription drug payment on economic analysis: the case of Australia. *Health Affairs* 1992;11:191–196.
52. Canadian Coordinating Office for Health Technology Assessment. Guidelines for economic evaluation of pharmaceuticals, 1st ed. Ottawa: CCOHTA, 1994.
53. Gafni A, Birch S. Equity considerations in utility-based measures of health outcomes in economic appraisal: an adjustment algorithm. *J Health Econ* 1991;10:329–342.
54. Rittenhouse B. Another deficit problem: the deficit of relevant information when clinical trials are the basis for pharmacoeconomic research. *J Res Pharm Econ* 1996;7: 3.
55. Russell L. Opportunity costs in modern medicine. *Health Affairs* 1992;11:167–169.
56. Drummond MF, Stoddart GL, Torrance GW. *Methods for the economic evaluation of health care programmes.* Oxford: Oxford University Press, 1987.
57. von Neumann J, Morgenstern O. *Theory of games and economic behaviour.* Princeton, NJ: Princeton University Press, 1944.
58. Weinstein MC, Stason WB. Foundations of cost-effectiveness analysis for health and medical practices. *N Engl J Med* 1977;296:716–721.
59. O'Brien BJ, Drummond MF, Labele RJ, Willan A. In search of power and significance: issues in the design and analysis of stochastic cost-effectiveness studies in health care. *Med Care* 1994;32:150–163.
60. Hillman AL, Eisenberg JM, Pauly MV, et al. Avoiding bias in the conduct and reporting of cost-effectiveness research sponsored by pharmaceutical companies. *N Engl J Med* 1991;324:1362–1365.
61. Drummond MF, O'Brien BJ. Clinical importance, statistical significance and the assessment of economic and quality-of-life outcomes. *Health Econ* 1993;2:205–212.
62. O'Brien BJ, Drummond MF, Labelle RJ, et al. In search of power and significance: issues in the design and analysis of stochastic cost-effectiveness studies in health care. *Med Care* 1994;2:150–163.
63. Willan AR, O'Brien BJ. Cost-effectiveness ratios in clinical trials: from deterministic to stochastic

models. *1994 Proceedings of the Biopharmaceutical Section.* Alexandria, VA: The American Statistical Association, *American Statistical Association,* 1994:19–28.

64. Spilker B. *Guide to clinical trials.* New York: Raven Press, 1991

65. Spilker B. *Multinational pharmaceutical companies: principles and practices.* 2nd ed. New York: Raven Press, 1994.

66. Drummond MF, Stoddart GL, Torrance GW. *Methods for economic evaluation of health care programmes.* Oxford: Oxford University Press, 1987.

67. Hennekens CH, Buring JE. *Epidemiology in medicine.* Boston: Little, Brown, 1987.

68. Roper WL, Winkenwerder W, Hackbarth CM, Krakauer H. Effectiveness in health care: an initiative to evaluate and improve medical practice. *N Engl J Med* 1988;319:1197–1202.

69. Agency for Health Care Policy and Research (AHCPR). Report to Congress: the feasibility of linking research-related data bases to federal and non-federal medical administrative data bases. Publ. no. 91–0003. Rockville, MD: Agency for Health Care Policy and Research, 1991.

70. Paul JE, Melfi CA, Smith TK, Freund DA, Katz BP, Coyte PC, Hawker GA. Linking primary and secondary data for outcomes research: methodology of the Total Knee Replacement Patient Outcomes Research Team. 1994 in "Proceedings of the Sixth Conference on Health Survey Methods." Rockville, MD: National Center for Health Statistics, 1995.

71. Fisher ES, Baron JA, Malenka DJ, Barrett J, Bubolz TA. Overcoming potential pitfalls in the use of Medicare data for epidemiologic research. *Am J Public Health* 1990;80:1487–1490.

72. Paul JE, Weis KA, Epstein RA. Databases for variations research. *Med Care* 1993;31(suppl): YS96–YS102.

73. Hlatky MA, Califf RM, Harrell FE, Lee KL, Mark DB, Pryor DB. Comparison of predictions based on observational data with the results of randomized controlled clinical trials of coronary artery bypass surgery. *J Am Coll Cardiol* 1988;11:237–245.

74. Cherkin DC, Deyo RA, Volinn E, Loeser JD. Use of the international classification of diseases (ICD-9-CM) to identify hospitalizations for mechanical low back problems in administrative data bases. *Spine* 1992;17:817–825.

75. Mitchell JB, Bubolz T, Paul JE, Pashos CL, Escarce JJ, Muhlbaier LH, et al. Using Medicare claims for outcomes research. *Med Care* 1994;32(suppl):7.

76. Kassirer JP, Angell M. The "journal's" policy on cost-effectiveness analyses. *N Engl J Med* 1994;331: 669–670.

77. Risks of Early Cost-benefit Conclusions. *SCRIP* No. 1876, November 26, 1993, p. 27.

78. Kassier JP, Kopelman RI. Cognitive errors in diagnosis: instantiation, classification, and consequences. *Am J Med* 1989;86:433–441.

79. Berwick DM, Fineberg HV, Weinstein MC. When physicians meet numbers. *Am J Med* 1981;71: 991–998.

80. Moskowitz AJ, Kuipers BJ, Kassirer JP. Dealing with uncertainty, risks, and tradeoffs in clinical decision: a cognitive science approach. *Ann Intern Med* 1988;108:435–449.

81. Beck JR, Pauker SG. The Markov process in medical prognosis. *Med Decis Making* 1983;3:419.

82. Sonnenberg FA, Beck JR. Markov models in medical decision making: a practical guide. *Med Decis Making* 1993;13:322–338.

83. Tversky A, Kahneman D. Judgment under uncertainty; heuristics and biases. *Science* 1974;185: 1124–1131.

Subject Index